Return to Sri Lanka

27th Feby 2020

To

With compliments,

[signature]

A Note on the Author

Razeen Sally was born to a Sri Lankan Muslim father and a Welsh mother. He grew up in Colombo and completed his later schooling and university studies in the UK. He taught for many years at the London School of Economics, and then at the Lee Kuan Yew School of Public Policy, National University of Singapore, where he still teaches. His academic and advisory work has taken him around the world, but, in his early forties, he felt Sri Lanka calling him back for the first time since childhood. He has spent the last decade travelling all over the island.

Return to Sri Lanka

Travels in a Paradoxical Island

Razeen Sally

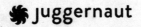

JUGGERNAUT BOOKS
KS House, 118 Shahpur Jat, New Delhi 110049, India

First published by Juggernaut Books 2019

10 9 8 7 6 5 4 3 2 1

P-ISBN: 9789353450601
E-ISBN: 9789353450618

Typeset in Adobe Caslon Pro by R. Ajith Kumar, Noida

Printed at Thomson Press India Ltd

To Mummy

The bravest battle that ever was fought!
Shall I tell you where and when?
On the maps of the world you will find it not;
'Twas fought by the mothers of men.
Nay not with the cannon of battle-shot,
With a sword or noble pen;
Nay, not with eloquent words or thought
From the mouths of wonderful men!
But deep in a walled-up woman's heart –
Of a woman that would not yield,
But bravely, silently bore her part –
Lo, there is the battlefield!

– Joaquin Miller, 'Motherhood'

In the 1960s, you came to a seemingly peaceful Ceylon, married a Muslim, changed your religion and started a family. In the turbulent Sri Lanka of the 1970s, when our world shattered, you managed, single-handed, to keep home and hearth together. Almost sixty years since you stepped ashore at Colombo harbour, our relatives still marvel at how you blended in, despite internecine extended-family wars; not one has a bad word to say about you, only words of praise and affection. You dealt with problems not of your making with the old-fashioned British virtue of stoicism, overcoming daily crises and getting things done, always understated, never complaining, never taking credit. Against the odds, you gave three boys a stable childhood and equipped them for adulthood.

I owe you everything. Without you this book, and much else besides, would not have been possible. This is my first 'non-academic' book. It is for you.

Contents

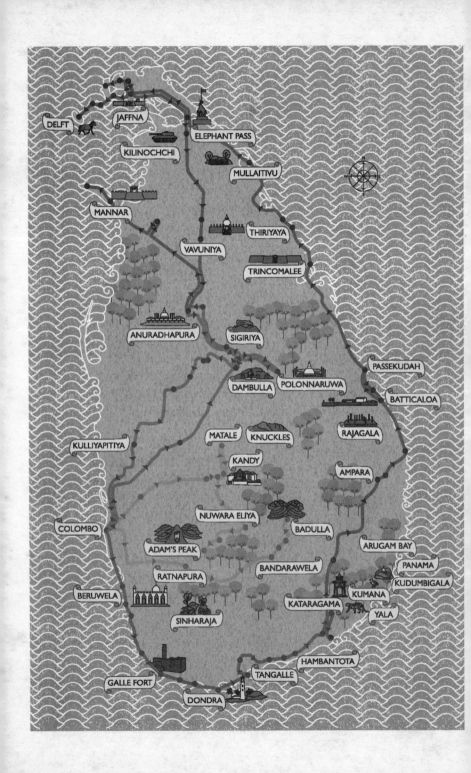

Introduction

I was born 'half-half' in a Colombo suburb, the first issue of an Anglo-Welsh mother and a Ceylonese-Muslim father. So I was sown in Ceylon, and I grew in Sri Lanka (as the country was renamed in 1972). But not for long: I left for England just before my teens. I hardly went back in my twenties and thirties. But in my forties, I returned.

I have spent most of my life, indeed all my adult life, in universities. First came seven years as a student at the London School of Economics, and then eighteen years teaching in the Department of International Relations there. In 2012 I moved to the Lee Kuan Yew School of Public Policy at the National University of Singapore, where I still teach. I have written some books, many journal articles, policy papers and whatnot. My readers think of me as a wonk specializing in international trade policy, opining on free trade and protectionism, the World Trade Organization and free trade agreements, and other matters of 'globalization'. An even smaller readership remembers my writing on the history of economic ideas – or, as I prefer to label it, the sometimes wrong, sometimes right ideas of dead white men. For the past decade, Sri Lankans, at least in English-speaking circles, have known me as a commentator on economic affairs. From 2015, when the government changed, to 2018, some also knew me as a policy adviser to the prime minister and minister of finance.

So, when friends and acquaintances heard I was writing a book on Sri Lanka, they said: 'Ah, a book on the Sri Lankan economy,' or 'Your take on Sri Lanka after the war.' 'No,' I replied. 'It's a memoir, a travel book.' Eyes squinted, brows furrowed, foreheads contracted into widening wrinkles. Puzzlement all round.

~

I saw little of Sri Lanka between the ages of twelve and forty-two. We left as a family in January 1978; I returned solo in December 2006. In between I cast my childhood world out of my mind. Sri Lanka dimmed in my memory as other geographies – schooling in North Wales, London as a student and professor, continental Europe and the USA – took hold. In these three decades I saw Sri Lanka through my father's looking glass; he continued to live there while my mother, my two younger brothers and I settled in the UK. But this was through a glass darkly. I did not grasp it fully then, and Daddy certainly did not think of it that way, but he was my mental and physical block on Sri Lanka. On my four visits home in the 1980s and 1990s, I always felt myself in his shadow, restricted and uncomfortable. He never forbade me anything, but I never felt a free agent in what was once 'home'. Sri Lanka, at the time, felt limited and distant – 'foreign'. So I looked the other way.

Daddy died suddenly in 2002. Gradually, imperceptibly, my mental block lifted: Sri Lanka revived in my imagination, as did memories of childhood. It took a few years, but I started going back, no longer in Daddy's shadow but as a free agent.

First I returned on holiday with Western and Indian friends, all seeing Sri Lanka for the first time. I recall my first morning in Colombo, after a gap of almost a decade, looking out of my room window at Galle Face Hotel. It was just before Christmas 2006.

The hotel – Colombo's oldest colonial hostelry, receiving guests since 1864 – was quiet, almost sepulchral. The ceasefire had unravelled, civil war had resumed and tourists were steering clear of Sri Lanka. It was rainy and gusty outside, my ocean view crowded in with low, dark clouds, turbulent waves and navy gunboats patrolling the horizon. To one side, perched in a watchtower high above the hotel's side wall, soldiers manned a gunpost – to protect Colombo from the Tamil Tigers.

I had mixed emotions that morning, and it took a while to make sense of them. I still felt a stranger in what used to be home; I hadn't even informed Colombo relations of my visit. But I sensed dawning exhilaration too. There was a presentiment, a glimpse, of something surprising and wondrous around the corner.

As the days unfolded I noticed things – people, buildings, landscapes, flora – I had hardly noticed before. I kept comparing familiar people and landmarks to what they had looked like in my childhood. I had almost forgotten my Sinhala, the second language of my childhood, but now words and phrases popped back into my brain and, occasionally, on to my tongue, slowly, in uglified pidgin.

I became curious about Sri Lanka's history for the first time. What were the years, decades, centuries and millennia leading up to my childhood like? How did they shape my parents' Ceylon, my childhood Sri Lanka, and Sri Lanka in the years of my absence?

Ethnic and religious tensions had swirled and gurgled and bubbled up in my childhood years, and indeed a good decade before I was born, rather like an East Asian volcano slowly working itself to a climax. Sri Lanka's Krakatoa erupted with race riots in July 1983, and the molten lava of civil war flowed for a quarter century. By the time I returned to Colombo, in the war's final years, Sinhala Buddhists and Hindu Tamils had retreated into rival solitudes. Was it so different in previous ages? My elderly relatives and family friends from my parents' generation thought so. They gazed back wistfully to peaceful times – of harmony and easy mixing among the races and creeds. Were they seeing the past through old rose-tinted spectacles?

Then the biggest question: How can such a blessed island, bursting with nature's bounty, with such easygoing, pleasure-loving people, be cursed with such violence? What had this violence done to the flesh and blood and consciousness of relatives and friends from my childhood, and the people I would encounter were I to rediscover Sri Lanka?

These questions churned in my mind on those first two visits back, between Christmas and New Year in 2006–07, and again exactly a year later. It surprised me that I had not – or hardly – had such thoughts before. Why now?

On these trips I spent just a couple of days in Colombo. What I really wanted was to travel 'outstation' – out of Colombo – to revisit childhood haunts. I had in mind the coastal beaches, interior lowlands and uplands, towns and villages and open spaces of short weekends and school holidays from long ago. So we drove down the south coast to Galle on these vacations, just as I did on weekend family trips in the 1970s. We went to Kandy, the hill capital; Nuwara Eliya, the main hill station, Sri Lanka's answer to Shimla; and the Uva hills, close to Daddy's ancestral town of Badulla. But these were short excursions, truncated into a rushed tourist schedule. Time was too short for other childhood way stations – the glittering beaches of Trincomalee on the north-east coast, which I had last seen in the mid-1970s, before war put them out of bounds; and the ruins of ancient capitals in north-central Sri Lanka I had first seen as a tot with Mummy and my grandmother visiting from Wales.

Two brief forays back to Sri Lanka convinced me to get properly reacquainted. So I resolved to go back 'properly' next time, not as a fleeting, distracted tourist. In 2009, I returned, this time with Mummy. We saw relations and old friends and relived old times, happy and sad. Travelling around Sri Lanka in the last months of the war, we saw people and places we had not seen in decades.

By the time I could return, in 2011, the war had ended. On the surface, much had changed. With six months to spend in the country, I rented a flat in Colombo and criss-crossed the island, south to north and east to west. I moved to Singapore at the start of 2012, but for the next four years went back to Sri Lanka at least three or four times a year.

Then, in January 2015, the government changed. The new prime minister asked me to advise the government on economic policy, and chair the board of Sri Lanka's main economic think tank. A cabinet reshuffle in mid-2017 triggered a closer engagement: I accepted a position as adviser to the new finance minister. My life as a part-time policy adviser lasted until late 2018. This took me back to Colombo once every month or two – a four-hour flight from and to Singapore, which was to become very familiar.

I tried to wrangle as many weekends as I could to travel around Sri Lanka. Early on, I found myself shedding many opinions disparaging Sri Lanka and Sri Lankans that I had held during my years in the West. I still found fault in much I saw. But a new tolerance, a new sympathy, sneaked inside me, and with it the young blossom of empathy. There was much I did not know and did not understand – things the sheltered world of a child and the shuttered mind of a distant adult had kept out of view.

I wanted to probe, learn, understand. But Sri Lanka pulled me back emotionally too, not just intellectually. That emotional tug was my Sri Lankan childhood: I yearned for reconnection, especially to my world of the 1970s, and to use it as a lens, a point of comparison, to discover Sri Lanka today, the Sri Lanka

I so belatedly started to experience as an adult. And ultimately, I suppose, to discover myself.

~

Why a book on Sri Lanka? Why *not* a book on Sri Lanka? There are shelf-loads of recent books about bigger and better-known countries, not least on Sri Lanka's giant northern neighbour. But little Sri Lanka hardly pops up on the world's radar screen. When it does, it presents a fractional, distorted view – bombs going off one day, ethnic riots another day, alleged war crimes. On more peaceful days, it yields tourist images of 'Paradise'. One has to go back several decades for synthetic accounts of the country, mostly penned by the odd visiting journalist and British colonial for foreign readers. With few exceptions, these were superficial or impossibly exotic. The British colonial typically specialized in purple prose set among palm-fringed beaches, spice gardens and tea estate bungalows, not forgetting sleek, beaming, white-toothed, dark-skinned natives. Sir Ivor Jennings, writing in the 1950s (more on him later), remarked that 'most of the better books on Ceylon have been written by Englishmen, and most of them are not very good'.

Specialists have written about this or that slice of the country – its history, political systems, economy, rural development, social structure, religion, ethnic conflict, civil war, and so on. But mine is a personal journey. It is a half-outsider's voyage of rediscovery. That is my way of making sense of Sri Lanka as a whole: its history before and after independence, its current affairs, its land and people. That I never wanted to do, and could not do, as an academic. I take to heart the travel writer's Hippocratic Oath, immortalized by Robert Byron in his 'Traveller's Confession':

Then travel must rank with the more serious forms of endeavour. Admittedly there are other ways of making the world's acquaintance. But the traveller is a slave to his senses; his grasp of a fact can only be complete when reinforced by sensory evidence; he can know the world, in fact, only when he sees, hears, and smells it.

A last word of self-justification. Never before have I done this kind of writing – much more free-ranging and eclectic than anything else I have written. It is my attempt to burst out of the academic or policy-wonk straitjacket – and take the open road. Here goes.

Part One

A Sri Lankan Childhood

1

My Parents' Ceylon

Paradise island with its fern trees and palm-lined shores and . . . gentle doe-eyed Sinhalese.

– Hermann Hesse

They met on a ship.

Pat Kneen was barely eighteen, bored with life in drab post-war Britain. She was an only child, raised in Rhyl, North Wales, by her widowed mother. Her father was killed in the Second World War when she was three. She was a grammar school girl who loved to read and did well in her O-levels: she should have gone on to A-levels and university. But it was the early 1950s, and Granny said she should leave school and find work. So she did, working as a telephone exchange operator. But she couldn't wait to get away and see the world. She had an elderly relative in Sydney, Australia, who was willing to sponsor her.

In those days, the Australian government paid 'Poms', as Aussies call the British, and other Europeans to populate the land 'down under'. 'Populate or Perish' was their slogan – but 'whites only'.

'Darkies' were not welcome then. Mummy became a 'five-pound Pom': her passage cost her five pounds, not the standard ten, for she was under nineteen. The rest was paid for by the Australian government. It was a cheap way to see the world, and jobs were available aplenty on the new continent.

This migration to Australia as a young, single woman was an early sign of her courage and independence of mind. Once every ten or fifteen years, back at the family home in North Wales, I pore over family photo albums – mostly Mummy's 'snaps' of distant and more recent yesteryears. Her neatly labelled black-and-white snaps from the 1950s show her in full English bloom: tallish, slim and vigorous, with short, curly hair and a broad smile, demurely attired in sweaters, long skirts and short socks.

The photos she took on her first trip abroad, on board the *Orion* in May 1955, irradiate her interest in a new world with new sensations and new adventures to come. The journey took six weeks, with halts at Gibraltar, Naples and Port Said, going down the Suez Canal, and on to Aden, Colombo, Fremantle, Adelaide, Melbourne and finally Sydney. On board, she mingled eagerly with a European cocktail of Italians, Maltese, Greeks and Balts, all, like her, emigrating to Australia.

On the *Orion* she met a group of Ceylonese air force cadets, only slightly older than her, returning home after training in Britain. Among them was one named Farouk Sally. Mummy's snaps, taken during the passage, show a bony, wiry, sharp-featured, confident young man, slightly shorter than her, always with a cigarette between his fingertips. His smile and gaze are open, fresh, guileless; he brims with hope and good cheer and sociability, just as she does. Somehow he exudes decency and wholesomeness – the qualities that drew Mummy to him. He was just nineteen. I tear up with sadness whenever I look at these photos of Daddy, who did not fulfil youthful promise. I will write about that one day, but not here.

Daddy was born and grew up in Badulla, a hill station nestled in a valley bowl surrounded by the tea-clad Uva hills. It lies in Sri Lanka's central highlands, south-east of Kandy, the hill capital, and beyond Nuwara Eliya, Sri Lanka's main hill station. Daddy was number four of three boys and three girls; his mother was one of thirteen. When Daddy was alive, at the last count, he had nearly seventy first cousins. Like Mummy, he yearned to break out of a sheltered backwater and discover the world. Her ticket was a subsidized sea passage to Australia; his was the Royal Ceylon Air Force (RCAF). He joined up at sixteen, without asking his parents' permission. In that year, 1952, the RCAF sent him for training in radio and radar to RAF Locking, near Weston-super-Mare in England's West Country.

Daddy's fondest memories were of his three years at RAF Locking. Its discipline and training 'set me up for life', he said. There he bonded with his Ceylonese batchmates. They were part of the national mosaic: many Sinhalese, a few Tamils, and many mixed-race Burghers with their traces of European blood and names like Paget Jackson, Shelley Bousted, Ralph Nadorf and Mike Harvey. Most emigrated to the UK, Australia and Canada by the mid-1960s; many remained friends for life. Getting together, however small or large the group, was an excuse for long smoking, drinking, joshing and reminiscing sessions.

At home in 1970s' Colombo, I recall lying on my parents' bed on long post-prandial weekend afternoons. Daddy occupied the middle capaciously, with his sons and a couple of nephews – sometimes more – squeezed in on his flanks. We took turns to massage his legs, feet and toes. That put him in the mood for storytelling, often a medley of ripping yarns from his Badulla boyhood and RAF Locking. How he and his batchmates painted the camp commander's herd of pigs blue one night. How he shinnied up the camp flagpole and made away with the British flag the night before Princess Margaret's visit.

How they appropriated a supercilious batchmate's clothes and forced him to march naked up and down the barracks, with a tin of baked beans tied to his penis with a piece of string.

Something clicked on the *Orion* – a 'shipboard romance'. Daddy got off the boat in Colombo, to spend the next six years in the RCAF; Mummy sailed on as she had planned. For three happy, peripatetic years, she travelled around Australia and New Zealand. She got temporary jobs in Sydney (in an insurance office), Goulburn (as an untrained psychiatric nurse in an asylum – a mistake), Melbourne (at a telephone exchange) and Wellington (again at a telephone exchange). Her happiest year was on a farm in southern Queensland, an expanse of 23,000 acres of scrub with 4000 sheep. There, she was governess to the resident farming family, taking two boys, aged barely five, through their primary school correspondence courses before they left for boarding school in faraway Brisbane.

Mummy always intended to return to the UK after her Antipodean sojourn, but her romance with Daddy blossomed over correspondence. He proposed by letter; she accepted by return post. At that time Daddy, like most of his air force mates, intended to emigrate to the UK. And so, in May 1958, Mummy took the ship back to the UK. The boat stopped in Colombo, but she could not go on land because a Sinhala–Tamil race riot was raging. Daddy came on board instead, just for a few hours. He had to return to active duty: the governor general had declared an emergency and ordered the armed forces out of their barracks and on to the streets to restore order.

Back in England, Mummy got her old job back; she did relief work at telephone exchanges all over North Wales, often riding her bicycle long distances from home in Rhyl. Daddy returned to the UK for another bout of air force training in 1959–60, this time conveniently close to the North Wales coast at RAF Broughton, near the north-western English city of Chester. Soon after, they decided it was time to tie the knot – in Ceylon, for the RCAF would not release Daddy from his contract to emigrate to the UK.

Their wedding day was 11 July 1961. It was the day Mummy stepped onshore in Ceylon for the first time; the day that ended a six-year, long-distance letter-writing courtship. It was also the day she converted from the Church of England to Islam, and the day she acquired two Muslim names, Jamaliathuma and Jameela, though 'Pat' was what she remained. Not religious to begin with, marrying into a conventional South Asian family to whom a marriage outside the faith would have been unthinkable, hers was a pragmatic conversion.

When Daddy came to meet Mummy on the boat in Colombo harbour, he surprised her with the news that they were going to get married that very day. It was a modest ceremony at the Sea View Club in central Colombo. A priest officiated; the guests were Daddy's parents and siblings, and a handful of his friends. Mummy met Daddy's family for the first time. They sat around a small table. The priest recited something in Arabic, which he asked Mummy to repeat – she didn't understand a word, of course. He asked her to choose a Muslim name. She chose 'Jameela', the name of a Muslim friend in Sydney; Daddy chose 'Jamaliathuma' for her – his mother's name. It was all over in under ten minutes.

That evening, the newlyweds had dinner with Daddy's friends at Mount Lavinia Hotel. Then they went upcountry on honeymoon. After a fortnight in Ceylon, Mummy sailed alone to Australia for a two-month holiday before returning to a new married life in Ceylon. She thought it would be a brief interlude – a matter of months – before emigrating to the UK. But Ceylon became her home for the next sixteen years.

～

At the time, Mummy had only the faintest notion that marrying into a Ceylonese Muslim family meant she was also marrying into a distinctive religious and cultural community. Everything was so new to her. But she was open, adaptable and eager to blend in.

There are about two million Muslims on the island – just under 10 per cent of the population. Well over 90 per cent are Sunni 'Moors'; they trace their descent to Arab and Persian traders from the Gulf and Yemen, who rode the monsoon winds to dominate Indian Ocean trade.

In the southern coastal town of Beruwela there is the small Kechimalai mosque, believed to be one of the oldest on the island. Beruwela was the first major Arab Muslim settlement in Sri Lanka, going back to the ninth century CE. Its location is perfect, roughly halfway on the ancient trade route between the Middle East and the Southeast Asian archipelagos. The mosque stands bleach-white on a promontory. From afar, approaching Beruwela on the coast road from Colombo, it gleams with purity, and seems to float ethereally, suspended between land and sea. Round the back, once through its simple fanlighted doors and unadorned interior, is a dargah, the shrine, it is said, of a Yemeni trader who died in 1024 CE. Sri Lanka's oldest recorded stele with a Koranic inscription, a tombstone found on a little island off the north-east coast, dates back much earlier, to the eighth century CE.

Muslims knitted the island together through trade, both before and after Portuguese conquistadors muscled in in the early 1500s. Sri Lanka's Arab trading heritage, however, predates Islam itself. The Chinese pilgrim-monk Faxian, who sojourned in the Sinhala Buddhist kingdom of Anuradhapura in the fifth century CE, noted that the king conceded a section of his capital to Arab traders. They exported local produce from big warehouses in Mantota and Mannar on the north-east coast, and were favoured at court. The Alexandrite Claudius Ptolemy created his second-century CE map of the island from information he gleaned from Arab traders.

The Greek merchant Cosmas Indicopleustes described the island as the hub of Indian Ocean trade in the sixth century CE. By the eighth century, the Arab Muslims who now dominated this trade probably converted locals of pre-Muslim Arab descent to the new faith. Sri Lanka became famous in the Arab world for its cinnamon and rubies. Hindu rulers in Kerala and Buddhist rulers in Sri Lanka, eager for revenue, continued to welcome Arab traders. These men took local wives; Muslim settlements fanned out on the Malabar and Coromandel coasts, and in coastal south-west Sri Lanka. Muslims became commercially dominant in ports such as Calicut and Colombo. In Sri Lanka, by the twelfth and thirteenth centuries, they had established island-wide networks of agents and sub-agents to procure and sell goods for trade. Strong commercial, cultural and migrational ties developed between Muslims in Sri Lanka and South India. Tamil became their common mother tongue.

Their fortunes reversed with the Portuguese encounter. When Lourenço de Almeida's expedition sailed from Goa into Colombo harbour in 1505, the Portuguese found a small Muslim trading town with two mosques, surrounded by white parapet walls. Almeida concluded a treaty with the local Sinhala Buddhist king, which gave the Portuguese trading rights, but local Muslim traders resisted. Only after the Portuguese built a fort in Colombo, in 1519, did the tide really turn. Under Portuguese pressure, the king expelled Muslim traders from his territory in 1526.

By the end of the century, the Portuguese had expelled Muslims from coastal territory they controlled. Oppression, though less brutal, continued under Dutch occupation in the following two centuries. Still, Muslims found refuge, and prospered, in the interior Sinhala Buddhist Kandyan kingdom, which rebuffed European colonists before finally succumbing to the British in 1815.

Muslims did well during the century and a half of British

rule. They were free to practise their faith. As small shopkeepers and big businessmen, they took full advantage of expanding commercial opportunities. However, unlike Tamils, Christians and elite Sinhalese, they did not take advantage of English-language education, preferring to stick to trade rather than go into government service or the professions. 'Ceylon Moors' – Sunnis claiming Arab Muslim descent – remained the majority. But now there were also 'Coast Moors', Tamil Muslim traders from coastal South India who came over during British rule. Sri Lanka also became home to a small community of Malays, the descendants of Javanese soldiers and exiled nobles brought over by the Dutch, and even smaller communities of Indian Muslim trading castes of Bohras and Khojas, offshoots of Shia Islam, and Memons, a Sunni offshoot. Sufism, the mystical devotional branch of Islam, also flourished.

In July 1961, Mummy encountered not just a new Muslim family, consisting of Daddy's parents, siblings, young nephews and nieces, and a vast extended family of uncles, aunts and first, second and third cousins. She also began her encounter with Muslim communities dotted all over the island, along the coast and in the interior, in towns large and small. The mosque, the shops; the men in prayer caps, long, flapping white shirts and sarongs, sporting goatees or wispy beards; the women wrapped in saris, which cover their heads as well as their bodies – these are tell-tale signs of a Muslim trading neighbourhood. Mummy saw these scenes first in Colombo, then in Daddy's home town of Badulla, and afterwards, over the next decade and a half, on countless trips around the country.

Trading, as Mummy soon discovered, is in the family blood. Now, when I take her back for her annual December–January visit, we meet innumerable male in-laws, cousins, nephews and distant relatives who trade in one form or another. A plurality are in 'gems': Muslims still dominate the gems and jewellery trade.

Some of my forefathers probably came as traders from the Gulf and Yemen, Lord knows how many centuries ago. My grandmother harboured the conceit that we descend from Moroccan princes. But, cleaving to an Arab race myth, Sri Lankan Muslims conveniently forget they have South Indian blood coursing through their veins – the product of Arab settlement and miscegenation on the Malabar and Coromandel coasts, and subsequent intercourse with Muslim trading communities in Sri Lanka.

Tamil became the lingua franca of South Indian and Sri Lankan Muslims, not only because it prevailed in South India, but also because it was, for more than a millennium, the region's main language of commerce. Then, from the late nineteenth century, English insinuated itself into the lives and homes of a select minority of educated and prosperous Muslims. Daddy's mother and her siblings went to English-medium schools run by European nuns and priests, and sent their children to such schools, too. Daddy and his siblings were probably the first generation to speak English as their preferred language. But the sounds of Tamil still rang constantly at home.

Nevertheless, Sri Lankan Muslims, insisting they are 'Moors' or 'Malays', never call themselves 'Tamils', unlike Muslims in Tamil Nadu, who have no problem calling themselves 'Tamilian Muslims'. Nowadays, when I visit Aunty Iyna, Daddy's youngest sister, in her Colombo home, I tell her that we – our family, and the Muslims of Sri Lanka – are more Tamil than anything else, knowing exactly the reaction I will provoke. 'No,' she expostulates. 'We are Moors, descended from Arabs. We are *not* Tamils.' She will turn, the next moment, to chatter away in Tamil to a relative or servant.

The tiny Malay Muslim minority numbers no more than 40,000, or 0.2 per cent of the Sri Lankan population. Family lore has it that my grandfather's ancestors were aristocrats at the court of the sultan of Mataram in Java. They were Javanese, but also of Arab descent. My grandfather's great-grandfather married another aristocrat, but against the wishes of the court. He had to flee Java and fetched up in Ceylon, when both Ceylon and the East Indies were Dutch colonies.

My grandfather – 'Appa' to his grandchildren – was exceptionally fair, with blue eyes. He was born rich; his father was a wealthy trader in pepper and other spices. Appa, a whimsical man, never did a serious day's work in his life, and frittered his inheritance away. When the urge took hold, he absented himself from wife and children in Badulla and wandered off for months at a time. The rest of the family is called 'Salih', which is a Middle Eastern name. 'Sally', a variant of 'Salleh' or 'Salie', has a Malay provenance, though still pronounced SAR-LI. Appa registered Daddy as 'Sally' because he thought it more fashionable to be Malay than Moor in the 1930s. Daddy remained 'Sally' while his siblings were 'Salih'; only in his fifties did he change it to 'Salih'. My younger brothers started calling themselves 'Salih' at school. Today, I remain the only 'Sally' in the family.

Daddy's maternal grandfather was a wealthy tea transporter who sired thirteen children. From his Badulla headquarters, his lorries serviced surrounding tea estates in Uva, and he enjoyed privileged relations with the British planters who ran them. Daddy's mother – 'Mummy-umma', sometimes abbreviated to 'Mummyma', to her grandchildren – was spoilt like a princess, waited on by an army of servants and dressed in imported European finery. Her father, too, left a fortune when he died. And his sons, part of Ceylon's interwar playboy generation, also spent it all extravagantly and speedily. One of them inherited one of the largest tea estates in Ceylon, complete with two factories; he gambled the lot away over a game of billiards in the late 1920s.

Mummyma did whatever her brothers asked. That included dutifully signing her share of her father's inheritance to them, asking no questions. She bore six children to a husband who was busy squandering his own inheritance. Daddy, my uncles and aunts, recalled growing up poor in Badulla, knowing that Mummyma often sacrificed a daily meal in order to keep them from hunger. As 'poor relations', they depended on handouts from richer relatives, and were humiliated accordingly.

All the Salihs made their way to Colombo by the late 1950s and early 1960s. My aunts escaped relative poverty in Badulla through arranged marriages to richer men in Colombo. Daddy escaped to the air force at sixteen. My uncle Razeen, the Benjamin of the family, after whom I am named, was a late starter. He took extra time to pass his A-levels. But soon after, he met a Thai Sinhala heiress to a jewellery business while doing an internship in Hong Kong. They married, and he converted her from Buddhism to Islam; Sita Sena became Saida Salih.

She and he ran the business in Bangkok; and by the late 1960s Uncle Razeen, barely thirty, was one of Ceylon's richest expatriates. That enabled him to buy lots of property in Colombo and elsewhere. His jewel in the crown was the Mount Lavinia Hotel, just outside Colombo – one of Asia's legendary colonial hotels, and the venue of Mummy and Daddy's wedding celebrations on her very first evening in Ceylon. Little did they know then that Daddy would return eight years later to run it when Uncle Razeen bought it.

~

What was going through Mummy's mind on that ship to Ceylon in July 1961? She was thinking of Daddy, of course, of their wedding, of meeting her new in-laws and Daddy's circle of friends. But what did she expect of Ceylon? She hardly knew anything about it. What she knew came from Daddy's mouth and his letters during their courtship. But that would have been all about his air force life, family and friends – not about Ceylon's history, its ethnicities and religions, its landscapes and flora and fauna. That was not Daddy's thing.

All she had was a vague notion of arriving somewhere tropical and exotic, this time not for a one-day boat stopover between England and Australia, but to live in. It was almost a decade before the jet age, when mass travel and tourism made Ceylon, and almost everywhere else, less unfamiliar to the outside world. Ceylon had relatively few tourists in the early 1960s, and even fewer expats. That must have heightened her anticipation of a totally new world as Colombo harbour drew nearer.

Foreign visitors rhapsodized about Ceylon (or Sri Lanka) long before Mummy arrived – its seashores and landscapes, its governing religion, Buddhism, and its majority ethnicity, the Sinhalese. Hermann Hesse, coming in search of Oriental spirituality in 1911, did so. Two decades later, George Bernard Shaw thought Ceylon 'India without the hassle.' In India he saw parched-brown landscapes, dust, dirt, and teeming, importuning, generally ill-mannered millions. In Ceylon he delighted upon deep-green vistas, ample spaces and warm, gracious Sinhalese.

Ibn Batuta, arriving in the first half of the fourteenth century, described the whole coast covered with cinnamon trees 'heaped up like hills on the shore.' Inland he came across a lake of rubies and other gems galore – topazes, sapphires, amethysts and garnets. Arab traders called the island *Sarandib* or *Serendib*, possibly a corruption of *Sinhadipa* ('land of the Sinhalese'). Horace Walpole found the word in a Persian fairy tale, *The Three Princes of Serendip*; from this he coined 'serendipity'. Writing in 1754, Walpole described the heroes of this tale 'always making discoveries, by accident and sagacity, of things they were not in quest of'. The Oxford English Dictionary defines serendipity as 'the occurrence and development of events by chance in a happy or beneficial way.' Such is the tourist encounter with Sri Lanka, and why so many *suddha*s ('white foreigners' in Sinhala) have fallen hopelessly in love with it.

Many Europeans, both resident colonials and visitors, were drawn to the sensuality of the tropics. What was 'forbidden fruit' in the prudish West became fair game here. Alec Waugh, older brother of Evelyn, wrote openly in *Hot Countries,* his 1920s travel book, of going in search of prostitutes in Colombo. Pablo Neruda was the Chilean consul to Ceylon in the late 1920s and early 1930s. In his memoirs he spoke of 'girls of various colourings (visiting) my campaign cot, leaving no trace but the lightning spasm of the flesh ... They went to bed sportingly, asking nothing in return.' He even described his rape of a dazzling Tamil girl of untouchable caste who emptied his toilet every morning. Apart from 'lightning spasms of the flesh', Neruda had a lonely time in Ceylon, but there he wrote *Residencia en la Tierra* – some of his most luminous poetry.

Ceylonese sensuality beckoned literary and artistic homosexuals too. Lithe, sleek, gregarious and poor Sinhalese boys and young men were irresistible magnets. Ceylon never quite acquired Bali's reputation as the expat gay aesthete's choicest tropical honeypot, but the reality came close. The self-styled Count de Mauny, owner of Taprobane island (which we will come across later), Sir Arthur C. Clarke, the sci-fi writer, Donald Friend, the Australian artist, Lord Robin Maugham, Somerset's nephew, Major Roland Raven-Hart, war veteran, globetrotting canoeist, hiker and writer, were among a colourful galaxy of gay foreigners who succumbed. They also loved Ceylon for other reasons, and sometimes painted and wrote about it beautifully. Perhaps Arthur C. Clarke, Sri Lanka's most celebrated expat for forty years until he breathed his last in 2008, expressed it best:

> The island of Ceylon is a small universe; it contains as many variations of culture, scenery and climate as some countries a dozen times its size. What you get from it depends on what you bring; if you never stray from your hotel bar or the dusty streets of Westernized Colombo, you could perish of fulminating boredom

in a week, and it would serve you right. But if you are interested in people, history, nature and art – all the things that *really* matter – you may find, as I have, that a lifetime is not enough . . . . There are islands in the Pacific perhaps more lovely and more temperate than Ceylon, but they have no culture, no sense of the past – nothing to engage the intellect. Ceylon offers far more than the empty, mindless beauty that lured Gauguin to his destruction; it has 2500 years of *written* history, and the ruins of cities that were once among the greatest in the world.

During British rule, a few colonial officials stood out with precisely this fascination for local culture, which they combined with a strong sense of public service – the 'white man's burden' of making public administration efficient, ensuring the rule of law and good order, building schools and hospitals. Leonard Woolf, husband of the novelist Virginia, was one. Another was John D'Oyly, whose ambivalent role was critical to Britain's conquest of the Sinhala Buddhist Kandyan kingdom in 1815. D'Oyly drafted the subsequent treaty between the British Crown and Kandyan chiefs that sealed British rule over the whole island. (He was also a founding member of my London club, The Travellers.)

D'Oyly went thoroughly native. He spoke fluent Sinhala, dressed like the locals and preferred their company to that of fellow colonials. Then there was George Turnour, Government Agent in Ratnapura, who learned Pali and Sinhala from Buddhist monks. Serendipitously, he discovered the *tika*, the code to deciphering the Pali of the *Mahavamsa* ('Great Chronicle'), the Sinhala Buddhist national epic, at the Mulkirigala rock temple in the deep south. His subsequent translation of thirty volumes of the *Mahavamsa* unlocked over 2000 years of Lankan history.

But these were exceptions. At the other extreme, and much more numerous, were snobs and racists who lorded it over the natives.

Alec Waugh, visiting in the 1920s, wrote, 'Here, it seemed to me, were a number of undistinguished people of no account in their own country, who possessed no qualities that would entitle them in their own country to recognition and esteem, behaving as if they were feudal chieftains for no better reason than that they happened to be whites.' Viscount Torrington, a mid-nineteenth-century governor, wrote of the sordid ways of coffee planters: 'The mass of (them), many of them the very worst class of Englishmen has very much tended to lower and degrade our caste and character in the eyes of the natives.' Leonard Woolf was put off by the philistinism, self-isolation and snobbery of his own kind in Ceylon; it was one reason that turned him from an unquestioning servant of Empire to a committed anti-imperialist.

For all those colonials and visitors who, like Hermann Hesse, were bewitched by Ceylon, there were a handful who were not. Edward Lear was in a bilious mood: 'The brown people of this island seem to me odiously inquisitive and bothering . . . All the while the savages go on grinning and chattering to each other.' He thought Colombo's Galle Face Hotel 'a nasty, second-rate place'. D.H. Lawrence rated Ceylon 'an experience, but heavens, not a permanence'. And he could not abide 'paw-paw stinking Buddhists'.

Mummy anticipated serendipity before she arrived. Unlike Lear and Lawrence, she certainly found it when she got there. There were also other, less happy and beneficial experiences, but that will come later in the story.

~

For their honeymoon, Mummy and Daddy drove from Colombo to Ella, 3000 feet up in the Uva hills. It would have taken nearly all day then, along what was a fairly narrow road which curled up from the lowlands to tea plantation country. Now Ella is a humming, expanding little tourist town, crammed with backpacker guest houses, cafes and bars, little hotels for mid-budget tourists, and even one or two pricier hotels. In 1961, all it had was a small railway station and a lovely rest house. It was surrounded by tea estates with British planters and Tamil labourers. Scattered in the hills were Sinhala villagers in their hamlets, tending paddy terraces and orchards of fruit and vegetables.

Before the 1970s – that is, before mass tourism and proliferating tourist hotels – rest houses were the only comfortable hostelries for middle- and upper-class visitors to stay out of Colombo. Ella was no exception. When Mummy and Daddy honeymooned at the rest house there, it had a front porch leading to a small reception area, a few guest rooms, and a dining room backing on to a veranda. It is a little bigger and certainly busier more than half a century on, but it hasn't changed overmuch. Beyond the back veranda is a broad stretch of lawn bordered by red cannas and a white railing. And, from the lawn, one takes in the stunning Ella panorama.

Its supreme attraction is Ella Rock, to one's right facing forward from the rest house lawn: a massive crag, 3500 feet high, which towers over a precipitous forested gorge. This is Ella Gap, sandwiched tightly between the Uva hills and the flattish southern plain. Sheer up the other side of the gorge is a ridge of smaller peaks, topped by Little Adam's Peak. They seem to bow in obeisance to the dominating presence of Ella Rock opposite, which sprinkles tufts and slivers of mist over them at daybreak and spreads its commanding shadow across their faces during the day. In 1961, the tarmac road ended abruptly halfway down Ella Gap, at Ravanella Falls that spill down from Ella Rock. Here the Uva hills were cut off from the south. Now the road continues, descending sharply to the junction town of Wellawaya, the gateway to points east, south and the coast. In twenty minutes' drive, and a descent (or ascent) of 3000 feet, the Uva hills and the south are connected.

Tucked under Ella Rock, out of sight from the road through Ella Gap, is 'Sita's cave'. Mummy and Daddy clambered up there on their honeymoon; so did I as an adolescent fifteen years later. It is a major tourist attraction now, for that is where the conventional story of Lanka begins, wrapped in primeval legend and myth. There are several versions of the Ramayana, the great Hindu epic, but Valmiki's is the most popular – the standard version. In it Ravana, the demon king of Lanka, abducted Sita from India, brought her to Lanka and kept her captive in this very cave (though there are rival claimants to the honour elsewhere on the island). Sita was an avatar of the goddess Lakshmi and wife of Prince Rama, an avatar of the god Vishnu. Rama, aided by his monkey general Hanuman, came to Lanka, slayed Ravana, rescued Sita and took her back to India.

So Lanka enters history in the ancient Indian epics, centrally in the Ramayana and more tangentially in the Mahabharata. But it is in a much later indigenous epic, the *Mahavamsa*, that the story of Lanka takes flight. Its supposed author, Mahanama Thera, was the abbot of the Mahavihara, one of the three great monasteries in the capital city of Anuradhapura, sometime in the fifth century CE. The script is Pali, the language of Theravada Buddhism's sacred texts. The *Mahavamsa* covers almost a thousand years of Lankan history through the rule of fifty-four kings. A sequel, the *Culavamsa* ('Lesser Chronicle'), was also written by Buddhist monks; it covers the rule of 111 kings from the fourth to the eighteenth centuries.

Early passages in the *Mahavamsa* recount the Buddha's three flying visits to Lanka (yes, he 'flew' there and back to north India). In Lanka he subdued *yakkas*, a demon race; preached to and converted *devas*, a race of gods; settled a dispute between two *naga* kings, of a race of half-human, half-cobra, semi-divine beings; and left his footprint on a holy mountain. As he lay dying, never to be reborn, for he had already achieved *nibbana*, or eternal release from the cycle of rebirths and suffering, he told his followers that Lanka would be the home and refuge of his teaching, long after Buddhism disappeared from India.

In parallel, the *Mahavamsa* recounts the origins of the Sinhala race and Sinhala kingship. The founding father was Prince Vijaya, whose parents, a brother and sister, were the issue of a lion and an Aryan princess. Hence *Sinhala* – the 'lion race'. Their kingdom lay in what is now Bengal. Vijaya was errant, so his father the king put him and 700 followers on ships and cast them off. This was around 540 BCE. They landed about halfway up the west coast of Lanka, according to the *Mahavamsa*, on the very day the Buddha died in northern India. Thus was made the first implicit link between Buddhism and the Sinhala race. Soon after he arrived, Vijaya united with Kuveni, a yakka princess, and fathered two children. Later he abandoned wife and children to marry a South Indian princess and found a dynasty. His fellow Aryan castaways followed by marrying maidens from the same South Indian court. Vijaya, childless from his second bride, bequeathed his throne to a nephew, whose descendants ruled from Anuradhapura in the north-central plain.

This short summary gives a flavour of the *Mahavamsa*'s tone. It mixes history with mythical stories, magical deeds and morality plays, or so it would appear to dispassionate modern readers. But not in Sri Lanka, and not to the vast majority of Sinhala Buddhist laity, the *sangha* or Buddhist priesthood, and Sinhala politicians. They treat the *Mahavamsa* as gospel truth.

There is no evidence, archaeological or otherwise, to prove many shibboleths of the *Mahavamsa*. Indo-Aryan migration from north-west and north-east India to Sri Lanka probably did occur around the time of Vijaya. But genetic studies also show that Sri Lankan Sinhalese and Tamils, who claim South Indian Dravidian descent, share a large gene pool. Given how close Sri Lanka is to the Coromandel coast – less than twenty miles at its shortest point – and waves of migration from South India to Sri Lanka, there was likely extensive racial mixing over more than two millennia. But none of this diminishes the hegemony of a Sinhala race myth.

The *Mahavamsa* fuses this race myth with a blatant politico-religious agenda. Mahanama Thera, its author, was both a leading monk from the state-backed Theravada school of Buddhism and the uncle of a Sinhala king. His leitmotif was the symbiotic alliance of Sinhala kingship and Theravada Buddhism. In the *Mahavamsa*, this started with Mahinda, the son of the Indian emperor Ashoka, who came to Lanka in 246 BCE, over two centuries after the Buddha's death. Ashoka famously converted to Buddhism and, through his Mauryan empire, spread it across India. Mahinda, already a Buddhist monk, was his emissary, charged with introducing the faith to Lanka. He encountered King Devanampiya Tissa at Mihintale Rock, not far from Anuradhapura; there he preached to the king and his followers and converted them on the spot. The king subsequently built temples and monasteries to house *bhikkus* (Buddhist monks). Later, Princess Sanghamitta, Ashoka's daughter and Mahinda's sister, came to Lanka with a sapling from the bo (or bodhi) tree in Kushinara, under which Prince Siddhartha meditated, attained enlightenment and became the Buddha. The sapling was planted at a site in Anuradhapura, and the tree stands yet, as one of the major shrines and pilgrimage sites of Buddhism. Sanghamitta, like her elder brother Mahinda, had embraced monasticism: she founded the first order of Buddhist nuns in Sri Lanka.

~

With her marriage, Mummy immersed herself in the world of Ceylonese Islam. But she was starting a new life in a predominantly Buddhist country. Sinhala Buddhists account for over two-thirds of Sri Lanka's population. She had never encountered Buddhism, and even during her sixteen-year stay, her encounter with it was superficial. That was my childhood experience too. We had Buddhist servants at home. Daddy had Buddhist work colleagues and oversaw Buddhist workers; Mummy met Buddhist shopkeepers when she did the family 'marketing'; I had Buddhist teachers at school. On trips outstation we visited Buddhist ruins and witnessed colourful, exuberant festivals at Buddhist temples – as any tourist would. Daddy had many Buddhist friends. But with almost no exceptions, they were meat-eating, alcohol-swilling Colombo professionals who paid lip service to Buddhist social conventions and rituals: hardly devout.

None of this got beneath the epidermis of Sinhala Buddhism. Only by rediscovering Sri Lanka, as an adult over the past decade, have I begun to appreciate Buddhism, both in general and in its Sri Lankan incarnation. I always knew, instinctively, that I could not begin to understand Sri Lanka without a basic understanding of its majority religious culture, but I did not bother until fairly recently. Bothering about Sinhala Buddhism has been central to my rediscovery of Sri Lanka.

~

Sinhala Buddhist kings ruled from Anuradhapura for thirteen centuries, from Devanampiya Tissa, the first converted king, to the late eleventh century CE. They built great monasteries and *dagoba*s (circular monuments called stupas, pagodas, *chedi*s and *zedi*s elsewhere in the Buddhist world), reservoirs and canals. By the third century CE, Anuradhapura housed three of the largest man-made constructions in the world after the Egyptian pyramids – the Ruwanvelisaya, Abhayagiri and Jetavanarama dagobas. Faxian, the Chinese pilgrim-monk who visited Anuradhapura at its cultural zenith in the fifth century CE, spoke of 5000 monks in the Abhayagiri monastery, 3000 in the Mahavihara monastery and perhaps 60,000 throughout the kingdom. The sangha were the source of literary and artistic culture, had a powerful administrative system that extended to village temples, and were the largest landowners and repositories of wealth. Kings took great care to appease and cultivate the sangha; their protection of Buddhism was the rootstock of their legitimacy. The *Mahavamsa* and *Culavamsa* abound with passages of 'virtuous' kings who built temples and monasteries, and showered the sangha with food and lands.

But Sinhala kingship was blood-spattered. In the Anuradhapura kingdom, in the period covered by the *Mahavamsa* (from the third century BCE to the early fourth century CE), fifteen kings ruled for less than one year and thirty for fewer than four years. Twenty-two were murdered by their successors, six murdered by others, four were suicides, and thirteen slain in battle. Anula, one of only four queens to rule in her own right, murdered her husband and several lovers.

Sinhala–Tamil bloodletting perennially overlaid intra-Sinhala bloodletting. Successive South Indian invasions put at least nine Tamil kings on the throne in Anuradhapura during the *Mahavamsa* period. The most illustrious was Elara, in the late second century BCE. In the most celebrated tale of Sinhala supremacy, Dutugemunu, king of Ruhunu (the deep south of Sri Lanka), defeated Elara's army outside Anuradhapura. The two kings fought each other mounted on elephants; Dutugemunu slayed the old Tamil king and entered Anuradhapura triumphant. In the *Mahavamsa* version, Dutugemunu reunited Lanka under Sinhala rule and saved Buddhism from Tamil incursion. Naturally, he was very devout, always praying in temples and solicitous towards monks – building monasteries, feeding them lavishly and so on.

Early on, Sinhala kings allied with Theravada Buddhism and effectively made it the state religion. It became established in the Mahavihara monastery in Anuradhapura, which, over the centuries, was especially favoured by Sinhala kings. Theravada's self-image, then and now, is that it is purer, closer to the Buddha's original teaching in the Pali *Tipitaka*, than the ritual-laden Mahayana and Vajrayana schools with their pantheons of bodhisattvas (enlightened beings who delay their entry to nibbana to guide mortals on the right path) and lamas (reincarnated spiritual guides in Tibetan Buddhism). Theravada is a philosophy, not a religion, they say; it is all about rational self-inquiry for personal salvation. And, of course, it is non-violent. That is disingenuous, to put it mildly.

Theravada monopolizes Sri Lankan Buddhism today and has written its historiography. But this monopoly is about a millennium old; earlier, there were strong traces of Mahayana influence. This came through religious connection with north-east India, where Mahayana was a powerful force in the first millennium CE. It had an impact on two of Anuradhapura's great monasteries, Abhayagiri and Jetavanarama. And its influence was greatest between the eighth and tenth centuries CE, when several Sinhala kings fancied themselves as bodhisattvas. Its lasting legacy can be seen in devotional aspects of Theravada Buddhist practice today, such as the worship of the Buddha and other godlike images, and of holy relics.

A prize exhibit at the National Museum in Colombo is a gilded bronze of Avalokiteshvara, the bodhisattva of compassion. He sits languidly, one leg dangling, the other hoicked up to one side. A bewitching companion piece, another gilded bronze dating back to the eighth century CE, stands in the Asia Gallery of the British Museum in London. This is Tara, Avalokiteshvara's consort. She is bent gently, at the hip and the knee, but her torso is erect. A wrap-around cloth covers her below the tummy; the torso is bare. Her breasts are voluptuous. Her eyes are downcast, her expression one of serene meditation. Her headdress has an empty niche that would have contained a miniature Buddha. One hand is outstretched; the palm of the other faces outward in the mudra of charity or gift-giving. This Tara was discovered on Sri Lanka's east coast at the beginning of the nineteenth century and taken to Britain in the early years of British rule.

Hindu influence crept into Sinhala Buddhist practice through trade and war with South Indian Tamil kingdoms. Tamils came as traders, invaders and mercenaries hired by Sinhala kings. Pandyan and Chola invasions from South India became more frequent from the seventh century CE. Hindu deities – Shiva and Vishnu, in particular – were incorporated in the Buddhist pantheon.

Sinhala Buddhism enjoyed its last ancient golden age in the twelfth century CE, with Polonnaruwa, also in the north-central plain, as its capital. But this was fleeting. A thirteenth-century Tamil invasion dealt a death blow: the north-central plain emptied and the Sinhalese fled south. The following centuries saw political and economic enervation and decline. Weak kings established small, short-lived capitals as they drifted farther south into hilly 'wet zone' country. Today, these places – Dambadeniya, Yapahuwa, Kurunegala, Sitivaka, Gampola, Dedigama – are, at best, nondescript, small to middling towns. Ibn Batuta, visiting in 1344, found a highly fragmented polity: no one ruler controlled the whole island; Sinhala rulers were little more than warring chieftains.

But Buddhism survived, even flourished. There was much Sinhala–Tamil, Buddhist–Hindu mixing. Some Sinhala kings seemed to be of South Indian origin, but gained power by displaying Buddhist religiosity and courting the sangha. Many took wives from South Indian courts. They imported Brahmin advisers and ministers, had Brahmins recite Vedic texts at court, and practised Brahmin rituals. Tamil was widely spoken at court and as a trade language. A more ornate Dravidian influence crept into Sinhala art and architecture.

Religious syncretism, above all, characterized this ethnic overlap. *Devale*s, shrines for Hindu deities, became fixtures of Buddhist worship; many were housed in Buddhist temples. That remains a hallmark of Sri Lankan Buddhism. Harry Williams, a British colonial writing about Ceylon in the first half of the twentieth century, described local Buddhist practice as 'atheism qualified by idolatry'.

Sri Lanka experienced four and a half centuries of Western colonial rule, from the early 1500s to 1948 – longer than nearly all other colonies in Asia. Because of this, the influence of the West ran deeper, first in the coastal regions subject to Portuguese and then Dutch rule, and thereafter throughout the island under the British. Until the mid-nineteenth century, Western colonization accomplished what ancient Tamil invasions did not: a steep decline in Sinhala Buddhism.

The Portuguese, driven by religious fanaticism and commercial plunder – 'We come in search of Christians and spices,' as Vasco da Gama reputedly said on landing in Calicut – were particularly destructive. They unleashed religious terror, following their pattern in Goa and elsewhere. Many forced conversions followed. Buddhist and Hindu temples and Muslim mosques were desecrated and destroyed; Buddhist temple lands were confiscated. All this was exceedingly foreign to Sri Lanka. For all the blood and gore on their hands, Sinhala kings had a record of religious tolerance and even one of encouraging syncretism.

One thing saved Sinhala Buddhism: the emergence and survival of the interior Kandyan kingdom, which fended off Portuguese, Dutch and British attempts at conquest until 1815. For two centuries, kings ruling from the hill town of Kandy protected and renewed Sinhala Buddhist traditions. They deepened the syncretism of previous Sinhalese kingdoms. Royalty patronized temples and devales; they and their subjects worshipped Hindu deities alongside the Buddha. Religious festivals were prominent, featuring ceremonial processions of Hindu gods. Buddhist–Hindu syncretism naturally extended to tolerance of Sri Lanka's newer religions; the Kandyan kingdom was a haven for Muslims during Portuguese and Dutch rule of the maritime provinces, and for Roman Catholics fleeing Dutch persecution.

The Kandyan Sinhala line of kingship died out in 1739. In Sinhala Buddhist historiography, this ended Vijaya's line after 2200 years and 165 kings. Kandyan kings had continued the previous tradition of marrying princesses from South Indian courts. So a brother-in-law of the last, childless Sinhala king, from the Tamil Hindu Nayakkar dynasty (ruling from Madurai in what is now Tamil Nadu) ascended the throne. Three Nayakkar kings followed him before the British defeated the Kandyan kingdom in 1815. Irony of ironies, these four Tamil kings were among the most ardent nurturers of a 2000-year-old Sinhala Buddhist tradition.

The British defeat of the Kandyan kingdom ruptured what had held fast since the third century BCE: the umbilical link between Buddhism and the state. But it also brought relief to the rest of the island. The British relaxed and then abolished religious restrictions the Portuguese and Dutch had imposed. Still, Buddhism was beleaguered and declining. Over three centuries of Western colonialism had battered it; the fall of the Kandyan kingdom, the severance of the link between Buddhism and the state, the confiscation of temple lands, Christian missionaries and the conversion of elite families to Christianity had brought it to a new low.

This set the stage for a Sinhala backlash, cloaked in a Buddhist revival. Its opening act was a series of debates between Buddhist monks and Protestant missionaries in the 1860s and early 1870s, culminating in a 'great debate' in Panadura, a coastal town south of Colombo, in August 1873. Then came Colonel Henry Steele Olcott – the 'White Buddhist', fresh from the United States. Olcott, a veteran of the American Civil War, had founded the Theosophical Society with Madame Blavatsky; they converted to Buddhism and moved their headquarters to Madras in India.

Olcott and Blavatsky arrived in Ceylon in 1880. On this and

subsequent visits over the next two decades, Olcott lectured to huge crowds all over the island. His impact was enormous. Imagine the novelty of an educated white man preaching Buddhist renewal in a two-millennium-old Buddhist heartland. Then there was his message. He railed against Protestant missionaries – 'enemies and slanderers', and a 'pestilential lot', he wrote in his diaries. He disapproved strongly of local Buddhists eating fish and meat and drinking liquor, and of worshipping Hindu deities alongside the Buddha, often in the same temple compound – 'an excrescence on pure Buddhism', he said. And he excoriated Sinhala caste practices. Olcott, in effect, brought a 'Protestant' version of Buddhism to Ceylon, viewed through his Western lens of scientific rationalism. He emphasized the individual's interior spiritual experience based on rational self-examination. To him, Buddhism's core was the laity and personal introspection, not the sangha, ceremony and ritual.

Olcott's impact lasts to this day. He sparked a reorganization of Buddhist ritual, notably the celebration of full-moon *poya* days, especially Vesak, which celebrates the Buddha's birth, enlightenment and death. He established what are now leading schools, which combine Buddhism with Western-style secular education. His *Buddhist Catechism* became a bestseller. He even designed a Buddhist flag. An Olcott statue stands prominently outside Colombo's main railway station; Colombo and Kandy streets bear his name.

But Olcott failed to 'Protestantize' Ceylonese Buddhism, or, to put it differently, return it to the Buddha's original austere, stripped-down message. From its early days, Theravada Buddhism was clerico-centric. In a rather Brahminical way – precisely what the Buddha rebelled against – it elevated the sangha to an exalted pedestal. Monks became the sole, unquestioned guardians and purveyors of the *dhamma*, the Buddha's teaching. The laity's duty was to follow monks' teaching and look after them. Generosity to the sangha, more than anything else, became the benchmark for accumulating merit for a good rebirth.

Theravada in Sri Lanka became encrusted in a doctrinal conservatism, centred on the dos and don'ts of the *vinaya*, the monastic code, and the duties of the laity towards the sangha. Over the centuries it became increasingly ritualistic as it competed with and assimilated elements of Mahayana; indeed it became pantheistic, with its motley assembly of minor deities and spirits alongside the Buddha. None of this is unique to Theravada or Sri Lanka. Hierarchy and ritual – not forgetting political promotion – turn religions into mass phenomena everywhere: Buddhism would not have become a mass religion otherwise. Olcott's Protestant Buddhism did not stand a chance against 2200 years of Theravada Buddhist practice in Sri Lanka.

Initially, the Buddhist revival was apolitical and religiously tolerant. But it turned political and chauvinist with Olcott's chief local disciple, Anagarika Dharmapala. Born Don David Hewavitharane, he came from a rich Sinhala merchant family and was educated in English. But he renounced this gilded life to become a lay preacher, and took the name Anagarika (the honorific for a celibate Buddhist lay worker) Dharmapala. He travelled the world to propagate Theravada Buddhism, and spent most of his last three decades in India; there he devoted himself to restoring Buddhist control of ancient Buddhist shrines, especially the Mahabodhi temple in Bodh Gaya, where the Buddha attained enlightenment.

Dharmapala had a much more intolerant, exclusivist streak than Olcott. He hyper-mythologized the Sinhala Buddhist past. To him, the Sinhalese were a pure Aryan race who had once occupied an ideal Buddhist state. This state's foundation was a sacred alliance of kingship and religion. Life was ethical and altruistic in a prolonged golden age. But Western colonization and the Nayakkar kings in Kandy polluted and enervated the 'once virile' Sinhala race, and Buddhism with it. Purity gave way to unspeakable 'hybridity'. Predictably, Dharmapala called for the restoration of a glorious Buddhist past. Here he is in full flow:

This bright, beautiful island was made into a Paradise by the
Aryan Sinhalese before its destruction was brought about by
the barbaric vandals. Its people did not know irreligion . . .
Christianity and polytheism are responsible for the vulgar practices
of killing animals, stealing, prostitution, licentiousness, lying
and drunkenness . . . The ancient, historic, refined people, under
the diabolism of vicious paganism, introduced by the British
administrators, are now declining slowly away.

Dharmapala's worldview encompassed violent antipathy towards
other peoples and religions, often expressed in bald racist language.
Europeans were 'infidels of a degraded race'. Jews were the 'degraded
tribe of Israel'. Early Christians, led by a 'Nazarene Jew', were the
'riff-raff of Galilee'. Hindus were shocking idolaters. And on the
subject of Muslims:

The Muhammedans, an alien people . . . by Shylockian methods
become prosperous like Jews. The Sinhala sons of the soil, whose
ancestors for 2358 years had shed rivers of blood to keep the
country free of alien invaders . . . are in the eyes of the British
only vagabonds. The alien South Indian Muhammedan comes
to Ceylon, sees the neglected villager, without any experience in
trade . . . and the result is that the Muhammedan thrives and the
sons of the soil go to the wall.

One wonders what the Buddha would make of these diatribes.
In normal civilized society, they would be taken as the rants of a
deranged bigot. But Dharmapala is a central icon in modern Sinhala
Buddhism. His name is spoken reverentially in respectable company.
His statues are everywhere; streets bear his name in towns large
and small.

Dharmapala became the beacon for a more militant, chauvinistic

Buddhism in twentieth-century Ceylon. And he was the harbinger of a shrill, hardline, often violent Sinhala Buddhist nationalism that took hold after independence. Politicians and monks ape his rhetoric, packing every sentence with incendiary words and phrases.

~

Sinhala Buddhism had become more overtly political and chauvinistic by the early 1960s. By then Ceylon's ethnic and religious tensions, between Buddhists and Christians, and much more so between Sinhalese and Tamils, were on the boil. But Mummy had little inkling of that when she arrived, and hardly felt it for most of her years there. It was far away from her immediate world, which was Daddy's world – not just his family, but also his wide circle of multi-ethnic, multi-religious friends and colleagues.

In 1961, when Mummy came back to Colombo from her Australian holiday, the newlyweds moved into a small rented annex in a house in Wellawatte, the southernmost district within Colombo municipality. Daddy had just left the air force and joined the Ceylon subsidiary of Lever Brothers (now Unilever) as a foreman, earning 350 rupees a month. His air force buddies were emigrating to the UK, and he intended to do the same. But Mummy loved her new life and wanted to stay. Everything was new to her, and she embraced it joyfully. Even as a child I admired her for that – felt proud of my white British mother blending into Ceylon so well, without changing her character in any way.

It was a lucky career break for Daddy that changed their plans to emigrate. Mummy noticed a job advert in a newspaper for the manager of a new factory in Ratmalana, a suburb about ten kilometres south of Colombo's city limits. It was a joint venture between a multinational, Chesebrough-Ponds, and Maharajas, a local Tamil-owned business house. The factory would manufacture the Ponds Vaseline Petroleum Jelly that boys and men used to slather on their hair. Daddy applied for the job, with no expectations, for it was a huge leap from being a foreman at Lever Brothers. But he interviewed well and got it, with a salary of 750 rupees a month, plus a housing allowance and a car. Mummy and Daddy moved to the upstairs section of a house around the corner from the factory on Hindu College Square.

Mummy always smiles when she looks back to these early, happy years of marriage. Daddy's income was modest, especially before he got the Ponds factory job. They lived in modest housing, without servants, until I was born. Life was simple and carefree. Mummy quickly made friends with her new relatives, especially her three sisters-in-law. Mummy and Daddy went to the cinema once or twice a week – to the Savoy, close to their Wellawatte flat, Liberty, Majestic, Regal, Odeon and Empire, all art deco theatres that showed Western films, usually arriving in Ceylon about a year after their release in the West. From these cinema-going years she recalls Ingmar Bergman's suicidally depressing *Wild Strawberries*, and the more uplifting *Sound of Music* and *The Magnificent Seven*.

Once a week, after a film at the Savoy, they walked across Galle Road to the Golden Gate, a cheap and cheerful Chinese restaurant housed in an old family mansion. Dinner for two cost just ten rupees. Occasionally, they ate at Kinross, a swimming club on the beach in Wellawatte, cheek by jowl with the railway track, and had biriyani at Hotel de Buhari. They socialized a lot with Daddy's air force friends, most now accompanied by their own fiancées and wives. There was rugger and cricket on weekends, and the odd drinks and dinner dance. Daddy bought his first car, a Borgward Isabella, made in South America, then known as the 'poor man's Benz'. In it they took a big family trip to Kandy and thence to the remote east coast. There Mummy attended a *nikah*, the Muslim marriage ceremony. She remembers the tiny bride-to-be's dark face caked with talcum powder to make her look fair; she was only twelve. Another big family outstation trip, this time to the deep south, took them to Hambantota beach. Mummy raced her sisters-in-law and Daddy's younger brother Razeen; she won.

Mummy had no British or other foreign friends during these years. But she did not miss the UK at all. The Ceylonese were very nice to her, she recalls; they welcomed her with open arms.

~

Tamils, Dravidians who trace their ancestry to South India and speak Tamil, have probably inhabited parts of Sri Lanka, especially the north, as long as the Sinhalese. Racial mixing took place all over the island, but two distinct cultural identities emerged, one Shaivite Hindu and Tamil-speaking in the far north, the other Buddhist and Sinhala-speaking elsewhere. Faxian noted a community of vaishyas (Indian merchant castes) when he stayed in Anuradhapura in the fifth century CE. Well before and afterwards, South Indian merchant guilds, mainly of Tamils, controlled trade in the kingdom's ports on the north-eastern and north-western coasts. But their numbers were small: there is little evidence of a large, permanent Tamil presence before the tenth to thirteenth centuries CE. That changed with decisive Chola and Pandyan invasions. Tamil migration from South India accompanied Sinhala retreat and decline. A Pandyan general established a Tamil kingdom in the northern capital of Jaffna in the thirteenth century; it lasted four centuries before the Portuguese conquered it.

Jaffna Tamils, perhaps more than any other group, took advantage of British rule. Christian mission schools run by American Methodists came to the Jaffna peninsula early in the nineteenth century. Locals used English-language education as their passport to clerical jobs in government administration, and later to become teachers, professionals and indeed senior civil servants. From the late nineteenth century, educated Jaffna Tamils poured into Malaya and the Straits Settlements to take up jobs like these. Throughout British rule and to this day, Jaffna Tamils have a reputation for thrift, hard work and an education ethic; not for nothing are they called the 'Scots of Asia' and 'God's gift to the government official'.

Daddy's Colombo Tamil friends came from this background. Most of Daddy's Christian friends, on the other hand, were Burghers – Eurasians with a tropical cocktail of Sinhala, Tamil, Portuguese, Dutch and British ancestry. Nearly all were Anglican and a lighter shade of brown. All had English as their mother tongue. All had emigrated by the mid- to late 1960s.

Thanks to the Portuguese, Christianity came to Sri Lanka by the sword. The Portuguese occupied the maritime provinces of Sri Lanka from the early 1500s to the mid-1650s. Their settlers married local women, as they did in their other colonies. These *cassado*s were given land; they and their *mestizo* progeny had privileged status. Those who stayed on after Portuguese rule ended merged gradually into the local population. Their language was a Portuguese creole called Indo-Portuguese. Today, their descendants, a tiny number of 'Portuguese Burghers', live in the eastern coastal towns of Batticaloa and Trincomalee. Portuguese influence survives in food and the *kaffrinha* music and dance of the community. Portuguese loan-words survive in Sinhala and Sri Lankan English. In wider Sri Lankan culture, Portuguese influence comes alive in the popular musical genre of *baila;* its fast, catchy beat is made for a collective frenzy of gyrating heads, hips and shoulders. But, much more than anything else, Portugal's legacy to Sri Lanka is Roman Catholicism: today, 90 per cent or more of Sri Lankan Christians are Catholics.

The Dutch East India Company (*Vereenigde Oost-Indische Compagnie – VOC*) ruled the maritime provinces from the 1650s to the 1790s. It oppressed the established religions, which now included

Roman Catholicism, and privileged the Dutch Reformed Church. But it was mainly interested in commerce, especially a monopoly of the cinnamon trade, not religious conversion. There were conversions to the Dutch Reformed Church, but this was skin-deep. After the Dutch left, most converts reverted to their traditional religions.

The Dutch bequest to Sri Lanka includes impressive coastal forts, a network of canals, a distinctive tropical colonial architecture, household furniture and Roman Dutch law – the latter still in use today. They also left their progeny. Dutch male settlers (Burghers) and mixed-race descendants (Mixties), all members of the Dutch Reformed Church, had special status in law and society. The 'Dutch Burghers' of Ceylon did well out of subsequent British rule – out of all proportion to their tiny numbers. Like Jaffna Tamils, they took advantage of English-language education in mission schools. That was their ticket to clerical jobs in government administration and, later, to the professions; they became highly Anglicized and a mainstay of the emerging middle class. They were notoriously race-conscious, proud of their fair skin and supposed Dutch pedigree; they looked down on dark-skinned natives and even on Portuguese Burghers and 'Eurasians' (mixed-race descendants of the British). Like the Sinhalese and Moors, they clung to a race myth – that they had pure Dutch ancestry on the male side. In reality, VOC soldiers and officials included mercenaries and conscripts from all over Europe and indeed from Java.

Anglicans, predictably, did best under British rule. They were part of the political, business and cultural elite. Generally, both Anglicans and Catholics favoured British colonial rule, resisted social change and invariably opposed Ceylonese nationalist initiatives in the decades before independence. By independence, they had accumulated a rich fund of resentment, particularly among Sinhala Buddhists. Sinhalese had a pejorative term for Burghers – *sudu lansi karapotha* ('white cockroach'). The albino cockroach grows darker by degrees when exposed to sunlight – a reference to the gradual darkening of Burgher skin as they mixed with the natives over the generations.

Michael Ondaatje is Sri Lanka's most celebrated living writer, and an expat who has lived in the West all his adult life. He is also a Burgher. *Running in the Family* is his bittersweet yet hilarious ode to the land of his early childhood, and particularly to Burgher life in Ceylon between the wars. His parents' generation were the gilded youth of the 1920s and 1930s who never grew up – a tropical equivalent of the characters in Scott Fitzgerald's *The Great Gatsby* and *Tender Is the Night*. They came from landed families, partied constantly and squandered fortunes. They radiated exuberance and eccentricity. Ondaatje's maternal grandmother, Lalla, had a false breast that kept dropping out – what she called her Wandering Jew. Her brother Vere was a 'sweet drunk'. Their male relatives 'tormented the Church sexually'. 'Love affairs rainbowed over marriages and lasted forever . . .' Young Michael's father was another sweet partying drunk who descended into alcoholism. My favourite passage in the book is Ondaatje *père*'s drunken rendition of *My Bonnie Lies Over the Ocean*:

> My whiskey comes over the ocean
> My brandy comes over the sea
> But my beer comes from F.X. Perera
> So it's F.X. Perera for me.
> F.X. . . . F.X.
> F.X. Perera for me for me.

~

Daddy was born in 1936. His Badulla boyhood played out in the last decade of British rule, which ended in 1948, and in the first four years of independence. Then he spent three years of air force training in the UK. Back in Ceylon, in the second half of the 1950s, he was stationed at air force bases around the island – mainly at Katunayake, the main base north along the coast from Colombo (now next to the international airport), but also at Diyatalawa, in the Uva hills, not far from Badulla, and at China Bay near the north-eastern coastal town of Trincomalee.

His childhood and youth were a time of transformational change in Ceylon. In 1931, following the Donoughmore Commission, Ceylon acquired a new constitution with universal adult franchise – a first in the Empire outside the 'white Dominions' of Australia, New Zealand and Canada, and way beyond what the Crown was willing to concede to India.

After Ceylon evaded an expected Japanese invasion during the Second World War, it had a smooth passage to independence. Indian idealism and nationalist agitation had its admirers in Ceylon, but the Ceylonese nationalist elite, drawn from the thoroughly Anglicized upper class, stuck to pragmatic cooperation with their British rulers. That made Ceylonese nationalism seem dull and insipid. But it ensured successful negotiations between Ceylonese leaders and the Colonial Office in London that led to a new constitution. Elections were held in September 1947, the month after Indian and Pakistani independence, and independence came to Ceylon on 4 February 1948. The handover of power was seamless. The summer of 1947 was a bloodbath in India. The assassination of General Aung San led to civil war in Burma in 1947 and 1948. In Ceylon, not a drop of blood was shed.

The British had every reason to be satisfied with a favourite colony – a model colony. They had prepared it rather well for independence – better than nearly all their other colonies. They passed the baton of power, with consummate ease, to a local elite of 'brown sahibs' trained in self-government under the Donoughmore constitution. Ceylon was at peace. Leonard Woolf, writing about his experiences at the beginning of the century, noted that there was the 'extraordinary absence of the use of force in everyday life and government. Ceylon . . . was the exact opposite of a police state.' On the economic front, Ceylon, while poor by Western standards, was one of the richest countries in Asia. It had by far the highest standard of living in South Asia, and was richer than most East Asian countries. The two decades preceding independence had seen considerable public expenditure on food subsidies for the poor, health care and education. Ceylonese were better housed, clothed and fed than most Asians.

Most observers predicted a golden future for independent Ceylon. And, in retrospect, that first decade of independence seems like a golden age. Foreign visitors waxed lyrical about the country and its prospects. The young Lee Kuan Yew, on a stopover from Singapore to London, wished Singapore could be as advanced as Colombo. A British journalist, Harry Hopkins, came to Ceylon in 1952 as part of his research for a book on early post-war Asia. He was charmed and impressed. In Colombo he found an ease and urbanity that, as an Englishman, made him feel completely at home. He could walk into the prime minister's office without security checks. Ceylon had a working parliamentary democracy with a stable government, a lively opposition and a free press. Seven out of ten people were literate. There were trappings of twentieth-century Western social democracy: free education, arbitration boards, minimum wage legislation, welfare benefits and town planning. This was a world away from turbulence elsewhere in Asia, and from the 'mass of starving humanity' in neighbouring India. Ceylon, it seemed to Hopkins, had already achieved the ideal which eluded other Asian countries.

That sense of peace and well-being, which so impressed foreign visitors, had much to do with D.S. Senanayake, independent

Ceylon's founding father. 'DS' was leader of the State Council before independence, founder of the United National Party (UNP), one of the two parties that went on to dominate post-independence politics, and first prime minister of independent Ceylon. He came from a Sinhala high-caste landowning family, but, exceptionally, he had a common touch. As a child, he played with village boys; as an adult, he came across as a rugged farmer with a sense of humour; as a politician, he had the knack of getting on with different sides and brokering reasonable compromises. He understood people and had practical sense.

Above all, DS had a liberal and secular vision for independent Ceylon – a multi-ethnic state with strict separation of the state from religion. He had no time for drumbeating Sinhala Buddhist nationalism and was sensitive to minorities' anxieties. He founded the UNP as a Sinhala-based party that would be acceptable to minorities and around which a consensus of moderate opinion would form.

The one significant blemish in his vision was his treatment of 'Indian Tamils' on the tea estates, 10 per cent of the voting population. He disenfranchised them a year after independence, flagrantly violating the constitution's safeguards to protect minorities' rights. Indian Tamils generally voted for Marxist left-wing parties, then the main political opposition to the UNP. They were also isolated on their estates, not assimilated into the rest of Ceylonese society. That, to DS, made them expendable.

DS stamped his mark on Ceylon's early post-independence years as much as he did in the run-up to independence. His secular, liberal vision held as long as he was in power. He co-opted minorities – Christians, Muslims and Ceylon Tamils; all were represented in his cabinet. Only the tea estate Indian Tamils, excluded from the electoral register, were left outside his big tent. DS's foreign and economic policies also continued the pre-independence pattern.

Foreign policy was pragmatically pro-West; the British continued to have military bases on the island. The economy was open to trade and foreign investment; British trading companies controlled plantation exports. DS faced a Marxist opposition, but it was weak and riven with doctrinal and personality splits.

DS died in office in 1952; he fell off his horse while taking his habitual pre-breakfast ride on Galle Face Green, not unlike Sir Robert Peel a century earlier. His son Dudley succeeded him as prime minister. Bradman Weerakoon, who was secretary to seven prime ministers, described Dudley to me as a 'true liberal – a liberal in his bones'. His commitment to democracy and the rule of law was total. He inherited his father's sense of decency, tolerance, reasonableness, concern for the poor and lack of communalism. But he had also been to Cambridge, was at home in sophisticated company and had a wider worldview. But Dudley's first term as prime minister ended in 1953; he resigned after a hartal to oppose cuts in food subsidies led to a few deaths.

Sir John Kotelawala succeeded Dudley as prime minister. He came from the same class as his predecessors – indeed, he was related to the Senanayakes – but he was a different character. Famously colourful and high-living, he also had an arrogant, impetuous streak and a political tin ear. To borrow Harry Hopkins's terminology, he came from a handful of landed families who led the 'nation in trousers', but he could not relate to the 'nation in sarongs' far away from Colombo's tiny urban elite.

The shine began to come off this golden age. As Kingsley de Silva, the doyen of Sri Lankan historians, writes, the country at independence was an 'oasis of peace, stability and order'. But 'beneath the surface . . . religious, cultural and linguistic issues were gathering momentum and developing into a force too powerful for the existing social and political set-up to accommodate or absorb. They were to tear the country apart within a decade.'

Something was rumbling in the 'nation in sarongs'. A resurgent Sinhala Buddhist nationalism was the main signal. This was directed initially at Anglicized Christians, rather than Hindu Tamils. The majority of these Christians were ethnic Sinhalese educated at English-language schools. The Sinhala rural intelligentsia felt cut out of power and influence by this elite. Resentment seethed that independence had not led to the re-establishment of a formal, privileged link between Buddhism and the state. Monks, inspired by Anagarika Dharmapala, became more politically active.

It was only a matter of time before surging Sinhala Buddhist nationalism would break the dam of the governing elite's secular liberalism. As prime minister, Sir John Kotelawala totally misread these emerging flashpoints of language, religion and culture. But others in the political elite were ready to exploit Sinhala Buddhist resentment, and overturn DS's legacy.

~

Daddy returned to Ceylon from his UK air force training in May 1955 on the *Orion*, where he met Mummy. He thought he was returning to a familiar country: peaceful, stable, run by an Anglicized oligarchy, and still pervaded by a British presence. British planters ran the tea estates surrounding Badulla, and tea and rubber plantations elsewhere in the country. British-run trading houses, based in Colombo, owned most of the estates and controlled the plantation exports that earned Ceylon most of its foreign exchange; they also dominated imports of consumer goods. The British still had large military bases in the island and trained the military, Daddy included. Some of these fixtures would be gone within a few years; in another decade or two, the rest were to disappear. It would not have occurred to Daddy that, three years after his return, he would be on the streets of Colombo keeping the peace after race riots.

The political man of the hour was S.W.R.D. Bandaranaike. 'SWRD' was an establishment figure, both a privileged member of the Anglicized elite and a Sinhala aristocrat. His father, Sir Solomon, was a *maha mudaliyar*, a Sinhala 'chief of chiefs', the most prominent position a native could hold in the British colonial administration. His family had converted to Anglicanism. After schooling at St Thomas' College, where I schooled over half a century later, SWRD went up to Oxford. Back in pre-independence Ceylon, he became a Buddhist, entered politics and rose to the top of the nationalist elite. Then, in 1952, when he realized he would not become leader of the governing UNP, he left the government and set up his own opposition party, the Sri Lanka Freedom Party (SLFP).

SWRD had the same class background as the Senanayakes, but there were vital differences. He did not have DS's common touch; indeed he was typically 'coconut brown' – brown on the outside but white on the inside. He spoke English with a pukka accent, went to the races, and felt most comfortable in his club, enjoying the company of other men of similar background and tastes. And SWRD did not have DS's and Dudley's sense of principle and fair play.

Sinhala Buddhist nationalism became SWRD's vehicle to political triumph. He tapped into the discontent of the Sinhala heartland – among low castes who felt deprived of economic opportunities, and among the rural and small-town intelligentsia of Sinhala schoolteachers, ayurvedic doctors and monks.

For the fateful general election of 1956, SWRD introduced a campaign slogan, 'The age of the common man', telling voters they should be treated as first-class Asians rather than third-class Europeans. But his paramount campaign pledge was 'Sinhala Only'. Sinhala would be the sole official language of the country, central to a new – or resurgent – vision of a Sinhala Ceylon. 'Sinhala Only' drove SWRD to power with a crushing electoral victory, despite the UNP doing a complete about-turn and adopting 'Sinhala Only' on the eve of the election. SWRD formed a coalition with one of the Left parties; the UNP was reduced to a rump in Parliament.

Ceylon Tamils felt cheated and excluded by 'Sinhala Only'. They feared they would be shut out of public sector white-collar jobs, a vital source of employment for Jaffna Tamils in particular. There would be all sorts of government forms to fill in in Sinhala, which most Tamils neither spoke nor wrote. The new Tamil leader, S.J.V. Chelvanayakam, took up the cause, aligned with other grievances caused by Sinhala majoritarianism. His Federal Party campaigned for devolution within a new federal system of government, including a Tamil-language administrative unit in the north and east.

More generally, Ceylon Tamils felt no part of a 'Sinhala Ceylon'. Their self-image was that of a separate people with a distinctive civilization. Professor Kingsley de Silva calls their psychology a 'minority with a majority complex'. Ceylon Tamils are a minority in the island, but have hegemonic claims to the northern and eastern third of it. He contrasts this with the Sinhala psychology of a 'majority with a minority complex' – a majority on the island, but one that feels threatened by sixty million Tamil Hindus in South India.

SWRD might have been a cynical political opportunist, but, according to those who knew him, he was not an out-and-out chauvinist. He was perfectly comfortable in the company of Tamils and other non-Sinhalese from his own class background. He had supreme self-confidence. Once he had uncorked the bottle and let loose the genie of ethnic conflict, he thought he could restrain and control it. That was his staggering miscalculation.

To appease mounting Tamil concerns, SWRD negotiated a deal with Chelvanayakam. Tamil would become an official language for administrative purposes in the north and east, regional councils with devolved powers would be established, and state-aided Sinhala settlement in the north and east would be restricted. But this soon sparked furious opposition from the SLFP backbench and the Sinhala Buddhist intelligentsia. So SWRD did an about-turn and abrogated the pact.

Worse was to come. Sinhala–Tamil riots broke out in May 1958. It was the first major racial explosion since independence. Anywhere between 300 and 1500 people were killed, mostly Tamils. Sinhala mobs raped Tamil women, and turned on Tamil men, women and children with clubs, home-made swords, grass-cutting knives and machetes. Tamil mobs retaliated in the north and east, though on a much smaller scale. For five days, SWRD's government did nothing. It took the governor general, Sir Oliver Goonetilleke, to stop the madness. He declared a state of emergency and ordered the military to restore order, which they did swiftly. That was when Daddy found himself, in uniform, keeping order on Colombo's streets.

By 1959, SWRD's government was sundered by splits and about to fall apart. Then he was assassinated on the veranda of his Colombo mansion, Tintagel, by a militant monk who could not abide SWRD's appeasement of Tamils. The murder was ordered by a leading monk.

A short interregnum followed SWRD's death. In 1960 his widow, Sirimavo, led the SLFP back to power. She was feted as the first elected female head of government in the world. In widow's weeds, 'Mrs B' played up her husband's martyrdom maximally. From Kandyan aristocracy, she was previously nothing more than a housewife. As a Bandaranaike family friend put it, 'In Solla's (SWRD's) time, Sirima presided over nothing fiercer than the kitchen fire.' But thrust into the political limelight, she proved herself a master manipulator with an iron will to power. She had none of her husband's cosmopolitan sophistication. She was even more willing to pander to Sinhala Buddhist chauvinists than he was. And her chauvinism went deeper than surface political opportunism. Her attitude to Ceylon's minorities seemed to be that they were welcome guests of the Sinhalese as long as they obeyed house rules. If they got uppity, well, they could go back whence they came.

The first sign of Mrs B's chicanery came when she reneged on a pre-election deal with the Federal Party to implement the Bandaranaike–Chelvanayakam Pact. Then came the state takeover of Christian mission schools that received public funding. Economic policy turned more socialist, more so when Marxist parties entered her government in 1963. Banks, insurance and oil companies were nationalized, as was the distribution of petroleum and kerosene. Protectionism increased enormously, with new import controls on luxury goods and many ordinary consumer goods. Foreign policy went further in a 'Second World' and 'Third World' direction, and Mrs B became a darling of the Non-Aligned Movement.

~

Ceylonese then, like Sri Lankans today, lived and breathed politics. Daddy, his family and friends were no exceptions. In the UK, and during her three years in Australia and New Zealand, politics was far, far away from Mummy's mind. Now it became animated, often heated conversational fare, another novelty alongside her immersion into Ceylon's multiple, overlapping worlds of Muslims, Buddhists, Christians and Tamils.

But politics did not stir the depths of their daily lives. Yes, Daddy's air force friends were emigrating for lack of decent job opportunities at home. Burghers and educated, professional Tamils were emigrating to escape increasing discrimination from the Sinhala Buddhist majority, especially after the 1956 election and the 1958 race riots. Yes, there were periodic strikes in Colombo and shortages of foreign goods in the shops. But Mummy and Daddy's life was peaceful and predictable. That was the 1960s for my parents: a prolonged period of calm before the storm burst in the 1970s.

And all the while, in those early, serendipitous years in Ceylon, Mummy's relatives kept nagging her: 'When are you going to have a baby?'

2

Childhood Sri Lanka

Sowing and Growing

In my mid-thirties I realized I had slipped past a childhood I had ignored and not understood.

— Michael Ondaatje, *Running in the Family*

I was born on 27 January 1965 in a small nursing home in southern Colombo. I was taken straight from hospital to a new family home on Hindu College Square, Ratmalana, almost opposite the Ponds factory Daddy managed.

This was home for my first five years. It was a plain three-bedroom bungalow with a small patch of lawn in front, ringed by a low parapet wall, at the non-factory end of the square in what was then a quiet, leafy, spacious little town. Ratmalana is not far from Colombo as the crow flies, but back then it felt like a distant outpost. Before urban settlement, Ratmalana had been full of coconut estates. In my childhood it still had vast patches of green – paddy fields and fruit and vegetable orchards, punctuated by 'shanties' – wattle-and-daub huts – where the local poor lived. Not far away was Ratmalana airport, Ceylon's first airport, and its international airport until 1967. I cannot recall hearing any noise from that direction. All it had was a small, twee art deco terminal, a short, narrow runway, and a clubhouse behind the terminal where Daddy sometimes met his friends for evening drinks.

I have faint memories of my first home and those early years on Hindu College Square – dim etchings barely discernible in the thick fog of time's passage, and only a few clearer flashbacks. Photos in the family album, some in black-and-white, some in colour; Mummy's reminiscences; and those of relatives and old family friends, fill in some of the large gaps.

Photos: Mummy holding me delicately, just a few days old, at my naming ceremony, with Daddy and a Muslim priest standing next to her. A big party at home for my first birthday, with the birthday boy sitting proudly in his new toy pedal car. Me sitting on the swing in the lawn, neatly dressed in shirt, shorts, white socks and sandals, with Mummy standing behind me. Sitting with her on a large straw mat on the lawn, surrounded by my collection of dinky cars. Kamala, my first ayah, who must have been in her early thirties, and Niaz, my nine-year-old playmate, both full-time, live-in servants from far-off villages, at a time when servants were still plentiful and cheap.

And flashbacks: In my new cowboy outfit, complete with cowboy hat and toy gun in a holster, standing guard outside our front gate. Our lovely neighbours the Mohideens – Mr and Mrs Mohideen and their four teenage children – who doted on me. The Jim Reeves records their eldest son, Rifai, was crazy about. Daddy's proud possession of a bulky Grundig radio and record player; the Trini Lopez, Tom Jones and Engelbert Humperdinck records he used to play. As a three-year-old, seeing my new brother Reyaz for the first time. Watching Daddy batting at a local cricket match – and getting out for a duck. Mummy, her face flush and crying softly, telling me quietly one night her eighty-nine-year-old grandmother had died in Rhyl, North Wales. Daddy and male relatives in the back of a van, crowding around his father's body, wrapped in a white sheet, about to set off for the cemetery.

Mummy continued to bloom like an English rose. She stood out in group photos: tall even by Ceylonese male standards, still slim, with a milky-white complexion unaffected by the tropical sun. She was a homebody now, with me and then my brother Reyaz to mother. But she still socialized a fair bit – dinner parties, occasional dances, and lots of Muslim weddings. Granny (Mummy's mother) came to Ceylon twice in the late 1960s; we went on long outstation road trips both times. On the second trip I vomited in the grand dining room of the Grand Hotel in Nuwara Eliya, Ceylon's main hill station.

Granny, then in her early sixties, exuded vigorous health and energy – as she did well into her eighties and even nineties. She loved to ride a bicycle around Ratmalana, exploring its verdant nooks and crannies. One afternoon, Mummy and she happened to ride past Sir John Kotelawala's ancestral coconut estate, right opposite the airport. There Sir John lived in post-prime-ministerial retirement; and there he hosted legendary breakfasts of hoppers, fish curry, mangoes and curd. The two white ladies caught Sir John's eye as they cycled past. Ever the ladies' man, he invited them in for tea and got his pet elephant to bow to him when instructed. Granny had no idea she was in prime ministerial company. But, back in Rhyl, she dined off that story for years to come.

Daddy's career took off. His employer, the Maharaja Group, made him manager of their S-lon pipe factory right next to the Ponds factory he already managed. Then they made him a director, with a seat on the company board and a salary of 3000 rupees a month, all when he was barely thirty. I was too young to notice, but sudden success made Daddy giddy: it changed him. He was no longer the simple, fresh-faced youth Mummy had met on the *Orion* over a decade earlier. Now he had a growing sense of his own importance, and showed it. With it came spiralling ambition for more professional success and its material trappings. The photos hint at this mental transformation, for Daddy looked so different from his engagement and wedding photos, and from those snaps Mummy took on the *Orion*. No longer was he thin and wiry; the fast-rising executive's lifestyle had filled him out. He grew fonder of his evening tipple of whisky with water; he smoked more than ever. His face was now puffy, and he was developing a paunch.

~

In the late 1960s, no one – Daddy least of all – would have dreamt that political vicissitudes would turn us upside down just a few years later. Now, when I meet aged members of Colombo's shrunken liberal intelligentsia, they turn wistful and misty-eyed when they travel back to these years of their youth and early adulthood. It was a time, for them, of secular liberality, of easy mixing among Sinhala Buddhists, Tamil Hindus, Christians and Muslims; of (relative) political stability and social peace; of (relatively) well-functioning British-endowed institutions; of manners and cultivation among the English-speaking elite; of optimism for the future. Many hark back to halcyon student days at the University of Peradeniya, surrounded by the lovely Hantane hills near Kandy.

No one embodied such liberal sentiments better than Dudley Senanayake. In 1965, Dudley came back as prime minister for his last stint, heading a UNP-led coalition. His previous stints, in the early 1950s and in 1960, had been very short; this time he was in office for five years. He remained the consummate gentleman-patriarch, and an instinctive and principled liberal on the neuralgic issues of race and religion – such a contrast to Mrs Bandaranaike, who preceded and succeeded him as prime minister.

Yet under his watch, the peace was but a surface calm. Dudley tried to implement the essentials of the old Bandaranaike–Chelvanayakam Pact to make Tamil an official language alongside Sinhalese, and to devolve power to regional councils. Once again, it ran aground on Sinhala Buddhist opposition, inside and outside Parliament, dashing Tamil hopes.

Successive governments increased public spending on all sorts of social welfare programmes, but the economy was hardly growing. Budget deficits became the norm. Foreign debt increased. Meanwhile, the population was increasing rapidly. Ceylon impressed the world with its human welfare indicators on literacy, schooling and health care. New universities churned out more and more graduates, even if economic stagnation meant they had no jobs waiting for them. Unemployment increased, especially among the bulging bracket of educated youth. And Ceylon continued to suffer a brain drain as more middle-class professionals emigrated to the UK, USA, Canada and Australia.

The writer Jan Morris visited Ceylon in the mid-1960s and stayed at Galle Face Hotel. He (this was before his sex-change operation, when 'James' became 'Jan') succumbed to the island's surface charms, but it was not, or no longer, *Serendib*. Ceylon had 'addled politics' and 'false finance', he wrote. It had 'fierce emotions': the murder rate was among the highest in the world; and domestic violence was widespread. He concluded that 'the primitive streak is strong'.

Bevis Bawa, older brother to Sri Lanka's world-famous architect Geoffrey Bawa, captured these times and their characters vividly in a series of contemporary newspaper columns called 'Briefly by Bevis'. He celebrated the quiet, laid-back, rural backwater that was Ceylon before mass tourism arrived, and the colourful, eccentric personalities of the Colombo elite. But he saw degeneration setting in. He bemoaned the new breed of politician and government official, giving themselves terrific airs and with no manners – no 'pleases' or 'thank yous'. A new coarseness was creeping into public life. But I don't think even Bevis would have foreseen what was to come in the 1970s.

~

In 1970, we moved to a large, airy bungalow in Ratmalana, not far from our old house and the Ponds factory on Hindu College Square. Mummy designed it, despite no architectural training, helped by a family friend who was a civil engineer and chartered surveyor. At its centre was an open-air atrium with rockery, potted plants, and a white wrought-iron table with chairs covered by a sunshade. Much dinner party entertaining took place here: drinks and snacks were served under the stars late into the night, before guests came inside for dinner. Our bedrooms and a big open living and dining area surrounded the atrium. Reyaz and I shared a playroom full of toys. Behind the bungalow was a large vegetable garden, a swing and a well; and in front a decent stretch of lawn led to a high parapet wall, topped with shards of glass to ward off burglars. And in the driveway, under the porch, was Daddy's hulking grey Humber with plush red seats and a rigid steering wheel the five-year-old me found impossible to turn.

We had moved up in life due to Daddy's career change. In 1969, my uncle Razeen bought Mount Lavinia Hotel. It was not far from Ratmalana, on the beach side off Galle Road on the way to Colombo. It was what prompted Daddy to leave the Ponds factory and resign his directorship of Maharajas to run the hotel as managing director. He told Mummy he wanted to be his own boss rather than continue to make money for other bosses. Uncle Razeen, not Daddy, owned the hotel, but Daddy felt this was his opportunity to run his own show and make a much bigger mark. Not least, running one of Ceylon's leading hotels was a major social elevation: Daddy was now a figure in Colombo society.

I still delight in going back to Mount Lavinia Hotel and can hardly believe I once practically lived there. There it stands on headland, as it has stood since 1806 when Governor Sir Thomas Maitland built it as his out-of-town residence. The original edifice is all classical colonial, whitewashed, pillared and pedimented. To one side is a whitewashed art deco wing, built in the 1920s; to the other a jarring extension put up by an Italian architect in the late 1970s. The hotel has two beaches: one sweeps down the south coast; the other, next to occasionally rough sea, sweeps up past Colombo's suburbs to the city and the harbour. From the hotel's terrace, the dusk and night-time view up Colombo's shoreline is bewitching. In my mind's eye, that view is framed with my parents and their friends in planters' chairs on the terrace, facing the lawn and its white railing and the turn-of-the-century beach pavilion by the rocks below, with the sea and the Colombo shoreline beyond. There they are, just so, whiskies and baby shams at hand, attended by white-coated, white-saronged, barefoot waiters.

The hotel's governing legend is of the affair between Governor Maitland and a local dancing girl called Lovinia. The governor, it is said, had a secret tunnel built from the residence to her dwelling. In Daddy's day, one particular room of the hotel was never given out to guests unless the hotel was fully booked – the room haunted by Lovinia's ghost.

By the late 1800s the governor's residence had become a hotel, popular with British and other overseas visitors who alighted from their P&O steamers in the harbour and took the short train ride to Mount Lavinia. From then on it was a Colombo institution. Until the 1970s, when modern five-star hotels arrived and new restaurants popped up, Mount Lavinia Hotel was one of three colonial city hotels where foreign visitors of name and repute stayed, and where the local elite entertained guests. The hospital scenes in David Lean's *Bridge on the River Kwai* were filmed there; William Holden kissed his nurse on the adjoining beach where I used to play and swim.

Even in Daddy's day, the hotel was the sort of establishment where waiters, gardeners, cooks and room boys arrived from their villages in their teens and retired in their sixties. Sri Lanka's most celebrated chef, T. Publis Silva – Chef Publis to all Sri Lankans – followed this trajectory, though he has yet to retire. He started as a gardener in his late teens; Daddy promoted him to the kitchens; he rose to become head chef; and he is now a director of the hotel. He still oversees the kitchens, when he is not doing a local TV show or exhibition cooking abroad. In 2016, he celebrated his sixtieth anniversary at the hotel. When Mummy and I visit he gives us special attention, in memory of the *loku mahatheya* (big boss) who gave him his break.

It was also time for me to start school. First I went to a small nursery, then to a Montessori on Hotel Road, not far from Mount Lavinia Hotel, and then down the road to St Thomas' boys' junior school. The Anglican St Thomas', founded in 1851, was modelled on Eton and Rugby. It self-consciously schooled the local elite to be 'Macaulay's children', to adopt the mental habits and outward forms of the mother country, all the better to help run the colony and serve Monarch and Empire. Recall Lord Macaulay's famous words in his *Minute on Education*: 'We must at present do our best to form a class of persons, Indian in blood and colour, but English in taste, in opinions, in morals, and in intellect.' These words, in a school environment of muscular Christianity, were turned into generations of Ceylonese flesh and blood.

By the 1970s these days were long gone, but St Thomas' continued as one of the two schools of choice for the local moneyed, landed and political elites. It educated future presidents, prime ministers, cabinet ministers and corporate captains, and still does so. Its age-old rivalry with Royal College in downtown Colombo – the other boys' school at the apex of the school system – reaches its annual climax in the Royal–Thomian cricket match. I recall one match when Thomians poured out the contents of bottles of the cooldrink Elephant House Orange Barley deposited outside Royal's hospitality tents, urinated in them to the brim, and carefully replaced the bottle caps.

In the early and mid-1970s, on a typical weekday, our family driver drove me from Ratmalana to school in Mount Lavinia. I took my lunch next door at the Cabanas, a small beachfront hotel also acquired by Uncle Razeen and managed by Daddy. I spent my evenings and weekends there and at Mount Lavinia Hotel. There I celebrated one birthday to the tune of Rudolf the Red-Nosed Reindeer in the Little Hut, the hotel's nightclub. On other evenings I listened to hotel bands belting out the hits of the early 1970s. When I hear 'Ob-La-Di Ob-La-Da', 'Knock Three Times on the Ceiling if You Want Me' and 'Daniel My Brother' on the radio, it transports me back to those balmy seaside nights.

One scene frames my 'hotel years', between the ages of five and ten when I was the son of a leading hotelier. It is not set in Mount Lavinia Hotel, but at La Langousterie, a seafood restaurant on the beach, separated from the Cabanas by the railway track that runs between Colombo and the south coast. On the evening of 18 September 1972, the whole Sally/Salih extended family gathered there for Reyaz's fourth birthday, including twelve first cousins, assorted family friends and their children, a group of tall, big-boned German tour guides staying at Mount Lavinia Hotel, and the members of the band that played early 1970s hits for us. In the photo, we all stand on the beach just as night falls; little Reyaz stands in the centre, impatiently cross-legged, holding his birthday present, a cricket bat. That was forty-seven years ago as I write this. But the memory of that night, that scene, lingers, somehow capturing my life – our family life – at the time.

~

Politics changed dramatically when Mrs Bandaranaike returned to power in the 1970 general election. The United Front coalition, comprising her SLFP and two communist parties, romped home with a two-thirds majority in Parliament, capitalizing on economic stagnation and social discontent. Dudley Senanayake's UNP was reduced, once more, to a rump. But the new government had barely settled in before a major insurrection broke out, in April 1971. It seemed to come out of the blue.

The rebels belonged to the Janatha Vimukthi Perumana (JVP – People's Liberation Front). It was a movement that emerged from bewildering splits among ultra-left parties in the 1960s. It combined Marxism with Sinhala nationalism; violent revolution was its objective. The established communist parties, in contrast, had settled down to parliamentary life and, from 1970, were in government with all the trappings of office. JVP recruits, numbering about 15,000, were mostly in their late teens and early twenties, drawn from the swelling reserve army of unemployed educated youth. They were a world away from the gilded, upper-caste, English-educated leadership of the established communist parties. JVP leaders came from the *karava* caste of fisherfolk on the south-west coast, and the foot soldiers from two so-called inferior castes, mainly in the south of the island. They were from poor rural families, and were the first generation to have A-levels and a university education. They were nearly all Sinhala Buddhists.

There was a quixotic, dreamlike quality to this first JVP rebellion. The rebels wore homemade dark-blue uniforms. Their masterplan was a 'one-day revolution': they were to launch, on a single day, coordinated attacks on police stations around the island, whereupon the government would collapse and they would take over. The attacks took place on 5 April 1971. It took the police and armed forces three months to quash the rebellion, costing 1200 lives according to government estimates, and thousands more by unofficial counts.

After defeating the rebels, the government responded by centralizing power, taking economic policy in a more left-wing direction still, and becoming far more authoritarian than any of its post-independence predecessors.

With its two-thirds parliamentary majority, the government pushed through a new constitution in 1972. The Dominion of Ceylon, with the British queen as its titular head of state, became the Republic of Sri Lanka, with its own head of state. The name-change was long overdue. Sri Lanka is Sinhala for 'resplendent isle'; Lanka is the ancient term for the island in the Hindu epics and in Sinhala. Ceilão, Ceylan and Ceylon were what the Western colonial powers called the island.

Safeguards for ethnic minorities in the constitution of 1948, already weak, were thrown out of the window. Sri Lanka ceased to be a secular state. The new constitution accorded Buddhism 'foremost place', with the duty of the state to 'protect and foster' it. This went a long way to re-establishing the constitutional link between Buddhism and the state that the British had severed in the mid-nineteenth century. Judicial review was weakened and the role of the executive strengthened. The government took advantage of the new constitution to prolong its term by two years.

Economic policy careened towards collectivism; the state took control of the economy's commanding heights. There were ceilings on incomes, expropriation of large landholdings, limits on land-ownership and draconian foreign exchange controls. Plantations were nationalized. Blanket quotas throttled imports. A state monopoly was established for purchasing rice from paddy farmers.

The minister of finance, the Trotskyite Dr N.M. Perera (a student of Harold Laski at the London School of Economics), had to personally approve every application to import a motor car. Sri Lanka quickly became one of the most 'planned' economies outside the Soviet bloc and China, with its equivalent of India's 'licence raj'.

By the mid-1970s, the economy was close to collapse. Growth was at its lowest since independence, inflation was rampant, and unemployment reached a quarter of the workforce. The public sector expanded uncontrollably, welfare expenditure continued to increase and consumer goods were rationed. Rice was in short supply. Long queues for bread were seen in Colombo and other towns for the first time. I recall one year when there was a severe shortage of toilet rolls and sugar, and we had to take jaggery with our tea.

Mrs B showed a much stronger dictatorial streak than she did in her first term of office. Emergency powers used to crush the JVP rebellion were extended and used for all sorts of partisan purposes. The Criminal Justice Commission, a special tribunal set up to try JVP leaders, was also used to destroy mainstream political and business opponents. The main newspaper group was nationalized, and another, critical of the government, shut down for three years. The state broadcaster became a government mouthpiece. Opposition parties' public meetings were banned while those of government parties went ahead. The civil service and judiciary, previously proud of their independence, became increasingly politicized; so did the police, military and universities.

Nepotism and corruption flourished, and ethnic relations also deteriorated. Particularly galling for Tamils was Mrs B's 'standardization' policy: the pass mark for university entrance was set at 80 per cent for Jaffna Tamils, while lowered to 50 per cent for Sinhalese. It was another indication to Tamils that they were second-class citizens.

Two decades of frustration had taken their toll, with the Tamil leadership repeatedly hitting a brick wall on language rights and devolution. Now Tamil militancy reared its head. Educated but unemployed youth, analogous to the JVP rebels in the south, were in the vanguard. They clamoured for a full break – a separate state, Eelam, rather than devolution. To their sporadic bombings, shooting and robberies in the Jaffna peninsula, the Sinhala-dominated police responded roughly.

There was also a caste backstory, just as there was with the JVP rebellion. Most militant youth were lower caste, in contrast to the political leadership who came from the *vellala* caste of landowning cultivators (equivalent to the *govigama*s, the highest caste in the Sinhala hierarchy). These caste splits were displayed dramatically in the first emblematic act of modern Tamil political violence. In 1975, Velupillai Prabhakaran, the future leader of the Liberation Tigers of Tamil Eelam (LTTE – otherwise known as the Tamil Tigers), shot and killed Alfred Duraiappah, the SLFP mayor of Jaffna, as he came out of the temple. Duraiappah was vellala, Prabhakaran from a lower caste. And Prabhakaran, because of his caste, was not allowed to use the temple's front entrance.

Under pressure, the Tamil political leadership moved to appease the militants. Tamil political parties came together in the Tamil United Front, later renamed the Tamil United Liberation Front (TULF). In their Vaddukodai Declaration of 1976 they came out, for the first time, for Eelam. The stage was now set for a big escalation of ethnic conflict.

By 1977, Mrs B's government was falling apart. First one then another communist party quit the government. Industrial strikes were frequent. There was desperate talk of postponing elections. All this cast a pall over the prime minister's regal chairmanship of the Non-Aligned Summit, held in Colombo in late 1976. The city was spruced up, beggars dispatched to the suburbs, roads widened, and a fleet of Holden limousines imported from Australia. Never before had Sri Lanka played host to so many tinpot dictators in one go.

~

Our family life seemed dandy circa 1971, until, one night, our world crashed.

Police officers raided and ransacked the house. They came around dinnertime, soon after it got dark. I remember them spending hours combing every room. Then they took Daddy away to the headquarters of the Criminal Investigation Department (CID) in central Colombo. That night the CID also raided his office at the hotel. And that night, aged six, I acquired political consciousness. We could not have guessed this was the beginning of six years of family topsy-turvy, lurching from one crisis to the next, swinging wildly from moments of despair to glimmers of hope and back to despair again.

It all started with a Hollywood producer called John Shelton-Price who came to Sri Lanka with a movie in mind. He and his family stayed for over a month in one of the old penthouse suites at Mount Lavinia Hotel. Daddy and he became friendly. But the Shelton-Prices left one night, suddenly, without paying their bill. Daddy alerted the police. They caught the Shelton-Prices on the way to the airport. When they went through John Shelton-Price's bags, they found a letter from Daddy concerning a foreign exchange transaction – which prompted the raids on our house and Daddy's office. And during those raids they found further evidence of foreign exchange transactions, this time involving Uncle Razeen in Bangkok.

Sri Lanka's new exchange control laws had criminalized even tiny foreign currency transactions. It meant that every Sri Lankan who had to pay for a stay abroad, even for one night in a cheap hotel in Madras, an hour's flight away, had to break the law. So practically every Sri Lankan who travelled abroad broke the law. Mrs B's government applied the new laws very selectively to target political and business opponents. Big businessmen who supported the opposition UNP, for example, were prime targets. Many other businessmen had their homes and offices raided, were taken away for questioning, and eventually charged, sentenced and jailed. Daddy was not quite big enough to matter, but Uncle Razeen was. And so what began as a minor CID inquiry based on Daddy's incriminating letter to a Hollywood producer who did not pay his hotel bill snowballed into a major investigation.

Our travails unfolded in a terribly charged political climate. The house raid and Daddy's confinement happened a few months after the JVP's April 1971 insurrection, while the government, army and police were hunting down and jailing rebels. There were island-wide curfews, including strict night-time controls imposed on Colombo and its suburbs. Before his confinement, Daddy had a special curfew pass because he had to spend so much time at Mount Lavinia Hotel. Almost every evening, Daddy, Mummy and I drove from our Ratmalana home to the hotel. Daddy had to stop the car at a checkpoint on Galle Road next to Mount Lavinia police station. We had to get out of the car, put our hands up in the air ramrod-straight, and walk very slowly towards soldiers pointing their guns straight at us, including little six-year-old me. Initially it was scary, but I got used to it and treated it as a daily, manly adventure. The hotel was eerily quiet: that year tourists stayed clear of Sri Lanka. John Shelton-Price and his family had the hotel almost to themselves during their month-long stay.

The CID detained Daddy at their headquarters for a few weeks. Then they dispatched him, along with other businessmen-detainees, to an old colonial house on Paget Road, in a leafy part of Colombo full of huge posh houses with huge gardens. Before independence, senior British administrative and military officers lived in these houses, and government ministers took them over as their official residences after independence. Daddy was under house arrest at the Paget Road house for the next nine months. Emergency regulations applied because of the JVP rebellion, and habeas corpus had been suspended. In theory, the police could have held him as long as they liked.

We had no face-to-face contact with Daddy during these nine months. All I remember is going with Mummy to the front gate of the house every evening to deliver Daddy's food. He appeared at the appointed time, dressed in a white banian, at a second-floor window barred by an iron grille. He waved to us; we waved back from the road, on the other side of the house's high parapet wall.

He was released in early 1972, but not for long. Soon after, he was remanded for three months, this time in the remand wing of Welikada, Colombo's main prison. I don't recall visiting Daddy there, though we must have. But when he came out he was full of stories of this, his second confinement. He had to sleep on a mat on the hard floor, in a dorm with many other detainees, including fellow businessmen he knew from Colombo circles, and the JVP leadership, on trial for trying to overthrow the government. Gregarious even behind barbed wire, Daddy quickly made friends with his dormmates, including the JVP top brass. The only exception, he said, was Rohana Wijeweera, the JVP's Leader Number One and the rebellion's mastermind, who was haughtily antisocial, and reeked to the rafters of body odour because he hardly ever washed.

Daddy became so friendly with JVP-ers that he gave a few jobs at Mount Lavinia Hotel and the Cabanas when they were released. The JVP's deputy leader, Loku Athula (his nom de guerre), became food and beverages manager at the Cabanas. Then there was Ariyadasa, an immensely likeable Sinhala villager who did fifteen years for manslaughter. In his previous career, he had been the getaway driver for a team of bank robbers, and accidentally killed a man during a heist gone wrong. Having done his time, Ariyadasa became the family driver for a couple of years. He was wonderful with children; my brothers and I adored him.

Daddy and Uncle Razeen were formally charged with foreign exchange violations, and put on trial. Uncle Razeen, of course, stayed away safely in Bangkok. Soon after that Daddy and Mummy decided we should leave for the UK, while Daddy, stripped of his passport, stayed back to fight the case. The main reason was my schooling. Mrs B's government had upended the school system, along with so much else, and English was to be banned as a primary medium of instruction. Mummy was in no mind to pack me off to boarding school in the UK, so she had to go too. But first we had to wait for Roshan, my youngest brother, to be born. He came into the world in April 1973. Soon after, we left for England.

~

My first memory of England was of a cold, overcast, wet day as we stepped out of Heathrow airport, even though it was almost midsummer; then a Black Cab driver took us on a circuitous route to inflate the taxi fare. Aged eight, I had worried that the plane would crash on our way here, carrying Mummy, my brothers and our ayah Fareeda. But Mummy assured me it wouldn't.

We were in the UK almost a year that time. First we rented the upstairs of a semi-detached house in Heston, near Heathrow. I recall the constant deafening roar and swoosh of planes flying overhead. Then Mummy rented a tumbledown cottage with a large overgrown garden in the Essex countryside, near the village of Shalford. For me it was idyllic. I had the run of the house and garden and our neighbouring farmer's path down to a lovely bubbling stream. Mummy and I went on country walks and picked mushrooms. I

liked my little village school with its caring elderly headmistress.
The ever-cheerful, golden-hearted Fareeda, a Muslim village girl
from the Uva hills, had the time of her life. But it was a struggle
for Mummy, thinking of Daddy's predicament back in Sri Lanka,
and now having to sustain a family without a secure income. When
she grew unable to afford the cottage rent, we moved all the way
to Rhyl, North Wales, to live with Granny in the three-bedroom
semi-detached house where Mummy had grown up.

Granny welcomed us, no questions asked. Before, she'd had
a comfortable little house to herself; now she shared it with five
others, including three young children. The Sally family and Fareeda
had the small dining room as their living and dining room; in one
room upstairs I slept in a bed with Mummy while Reyaz slept on
a small makeshift bed on the floor; Fareeda and Roshan slept in
the small bedroom which Mummy had had as a girl. But Granny
never complained. I did not particularly like my new primary school,
Ysgol Llewellyn: it felt big and impersonal, and I did not fit in with
my classmates.

I pined for Sri Lanka. At first I could not understand the regional
accents, colloquialisms and slang of my schoolmates and other locals.
I found British weather awful. I was depressed by monotonous rows
of semi-detached houses and poky interiors. Why did the British
have such pasty faces? Why did they have such greasy hair and smell
so much? I could not get used to the idea of taking a bath – washing
in self-soiled water – instead of the daily one or two showers I was
used to in Sri Lanka. The concept of the shower seemed limited to
rubber tubes attached to bath taps that spouted either scorching or
freezing water. I recoiled at my first sighting of a British beach. I
missed the Sri Lankan sea and sun; I missed the extended family
and large circle of family friends; I missed the trappings of class
privilege – large house, servants, driver, private school, swimming
club and, not least, the life of a colonial hotel.

Imagine my relief when Mummy told us, in summer 1974, that we would be going back to Sri Lanka. It seemed Daddy's court case was coming to a close, with a good chance he would be fined for foreign exchange violations, but nothing worse. He could resume his old life – or so he thought.

But things had changed. Daddy first rented out our Ratmalana house, then sold it. Now we occupied the upstairs flat in a house Uncle Razeen owned in Colpetty, central Colombo; Mummyma and Daddy's youngest sister and family occupied the downstairs flat. I went to the Overseas School, not back to St Thomas', where I would have had to school in the Sinhala medium.

We reacquired some of the trappings of our old life, but the golden age had passed. Family life was a perpetual round of crises. Daddy and Mummy were busy with lawyers and the court case. Daddy's trial did not end; the government declared a mistrial, and appointed a new bench of judges to preside over a new trial. Uncle Razeen was forced to sell Mount Lavinia Hotel to a businessman close to the Bandaranaike family for a song. By mid-1975, Mummy, Reyaz, Roshan and I, with a new ayah (Fareeda had left us to get married), were back staying with Granny in Rhyl; I was back at Ysgol Llewellyn. A year later we were back again in Colombo. This time Daddy's trial was coming to a close, and we would be with him for the verdict.

~

For me childhood Colombo was the 1970s, between the ages of six and thirteen. Of the time before that, my memories are hazy and intermittent. But 1970s Colombo always comes back to me in sharper relief, framed by a cerulean sky and the Indian Ocean lapping the city shoreline. The memories are bittersweet: bitter with the taste of crises swirling around Daddy's court case, his house arrest and remand, money worries; the yearly displacements to and from the UK, changing schools each time, not knowing when and how these convulsions would end.

Still, my childhood Sri Lanka had its share of sweet and sometimes comical moments to lighten the angst of our existence. Those I missed sorely, desperately, when we were in the UK.

Mount Lavinia Hotel gave me a lifelong fondness for the 'grand hotel', especially colonial hotels in the tropics. And, specifically, hotels that were pitstops on the P&O steamship route between England and Australia: the Cecil in Alexandria and the Mena House in Cairo, the Mount Nelson in Cape Town, the Taj in Bombay, the Connemara in Madras, the Strand in Rangoon, the Oriental in Bangkok, the Eastern and Oriental in Penang, Raffles in Singapore, the Peninsula in Hong Kong, and three old Colombo hotels in particular.

Apart from Mount Lavinia Hotel, there were two other colonial hotels in town. The grand old lady of the trio was Galle Face Hotel. It opened its doors in 1865; in the purple prose of hotel literature, it is 'dedicated to yesterday's charm and tomorrow's comfort'. It commands one end of Galle Face Green, right next to the Indian Ocean. Swooping Kandyan-style roofs top its light-brown pillared facade. Until the 1980s, barefoot, white-shirted, white-saronged waiters ministered to one's needs here. Capacious verandas give out to an interior lawn – one of Colombo's most delightful spots to watch the sun set on the ocean horizon.

Bevis Bawa wrote in one of his 'Briefly by Bevis' columns that he used to while away hours on his veranda chair at Galle Face Hotel watching the 'peoples of the world' go by. Arthur C. Clarke did much of his writing on its veranda. VIP guests – royalty, heads of government, film stars, diplomats, foreign correspondents, even Yuri Gagarin, the first man in space – were immortalized on a plaque by the main entrance. The hotel is owned by the Tamil Christian

Gardiner family. The eccentric Cyril Gardiner ran it for decades; he gave a generous discount to non-smokers and put up edifying signs on the upper floor enjoining guests not to smoke in bed ('It might be your last smoke'), and to use the stairs instead of the lift. Service was slipshod for as long as I could remember, but I always enjoyed its unchanging old-world character – a world apart from bland international hotels.

The dear old GFH shut down for a thorough renovation after Sri Lanka's civil war ended in 2009. I was half-relieved, half-disappointed when it reopened in 2015: relieved it had not been completely Disneyfied, but disappointed with its now blander opulence. The plaque with VIP names has gone, as have Cyril Gardiner's moralizing signboards, all consigned to a dusty storeroom. Pity.

The last of the trio was the Grand Oriental Hotel, known as the Taprobane in the 1970s. In Colombo Fort, on a corner of York Street, it stands directly opposite the harbour entrance. We used to go to its restaurant, the Harbour Room, for spaghetti bolognese and the night-time panorama of the harbour. The GOH was run-down even then, but it got worse during the war when much of the Fort was cordoned off. Now it is a shabby shadow of its colonial glory.

For Daddy's set, much out-of-home socializing took place in a handful of Colombo clubs. These were alcohol-sodden sanctuaries for male badinage and bonding, occasionally with wives and children in tow. Daddy's main club was The Capri in Colpetty, which was once the Burmese high commissioner's residence. One night the high commissioner came home to find his wife in bed with her Ceylonese lover. He did the natural thing: he got his gun out and started shooting at them. The lover had a narrow escape, doing a high jump over the garden wall. But her husband's bullet felled Mrs Boonwaat in the middle of the lawn. Mr Boonwaat promptly claimed diplomatic immunity and went back to Burma. The residence was then repurposed.

I recall many evenings on The Capri's terrace, eating my spaghetti bolognese or chicken-in-the-basket, listening to Daddy and his buddies joshing each other over Scotch and arrack, looking for that imaginary spot of blood on the lawn where Mrs Boonwaat fell. The bar had its obligatory share of regulars. Like Michael Ondaatje's male relatives before independence, many were drunks, some funny, some sweet with children, some monsters when they got back home late at night, most busy frittering away their inherited wealth.

My extended family took up much of my Colombo childhood. My cousins and I were in and out of each other's houses every day; our house was certainly not our 'castle'. My brothers and I went to see Mummyma almost every day when we lived in Ratmalana, and several times every day when we lived in the Colpetty house, whose lower level she occupied. There were always Muslim 'functions' to attend – betrothals, weddings, assorted religious functions.

Sri Lankan Muslim weddings were massive affairs: a guest list of 500 was 'moderate'; 1000 upwards was 'acceptable' for a rich family. Religious rites are brief in a Muslim wedding ceremony, as Mummy discovered at her exceptionally modest wedding. Womenfolk are slathered in layers of make-up; gold jewellery and gemstones weigh down their earlobes, necks, forearms and hands. In those days it was obligatory for the bride to look glum and rigid; female relatives would fidget around her constantly, adjusting her headdress and gown. More than anything, I remember Muslim weddings as gigantic feeding fests: men, women and children devoured masses of rich, oily chicken, mutton and beef biriyani, followed by wattalapam, a dessert of jaggery, coconut milk, cardamom, cloves and a bucket-load of eggs. Men and women ate separately, on the floor. Six would sit around a large bowl piled high with biriyani, dig their fingers in and chomp intently. Mummy, who adapted in every other way, drew the line at this: she refused to eat her food off the same plate as others – not with all those fingers sticking balls of rice, beef, mutton, chicken and pickles into salivated mouths.

The climax of the extended family's year was festival day – two festival days, to be precise, Eid-ul-Fitr, at the end of the fasting month of Ramadan, and Hajj, or Eid-ul-Adha. For well-off Muslim families, Ramadan fasting meant getting up in the middle of the night to wolf down a full breakfast, going back to bed and sleeping as late as possible, lounging listlessly in the afternoon, having a full early-evening meal to break the fast, another full meal a couple of hours later, and going to bed on a full stomach. And the same routine for thirty days. It was definitely not what the Prophet Muhammad intended. Then came festival day: a non-stop round of eating and visiting relatives.

There was also my preternaturally early political awakening. Having acquired political consciousness when the CID raided our home and took Daddy away, I became a current-affairs junkie, not just for Sri Lankan politics but also happenings abroad. I read the local *Daily News* and *Sunday Observer* religiously, though they were state-owned and parroted the government line. Once a week, Mummy took me to the British Council, next to the British High Commission on Galle Road; there I devoured six-week-old copies of London's *Daily Telegraph,* and of *Time* and *Newsweek.* I listened to BBC World Service news bulletins, and memorized the names of American, British and Indian cabinet ministers. Aged eight or nine, I even became an ardent communist. Uncle Ranjith, a relative and tea planter, gave me books by Lenin and Mao. I was in thrall to Red China after reading Mao's *Little Red Book* and Edgar Snow's *Red Star Over China.*

Thankfully, this phase passed before I hit my teens. It must have seemed very strange to those around me. It reinforced my solitary streak. I was never a good mixer, except with my cousins. How weird I must have seemed, on the Ysgol Llewellyn playground, reading the *Little Red Book* while other kids played their games during break.

Other fragments from my sweet memories of 1970s Colombo: Sitting on the lawn of the one-storey art deco Fountain Café, near the fountain, eating an ice cream sundae. Kreme House on Galle Road, drinking a large glass of ice-cold chocolate milkshake in the parked car. Playing cricket, cards and table tennis with my cousins. Sunday sea baths with Daddy and my male cousins, followed by a slap-up feed at Nafeesha, a simple Muslim eating-house in a poor quarter of central Colombo, to which we took our own supplies of filtered water and newspapers to cover its bug-ridden chair seats. Then devouring mountains of rice with fiery, greasy curries. My favourite house dish of curried cow's brains. Black Morris Oxford taxis. Clapped-out red double-decker buses slanted precariously, some at almost 45-degree angles, retired from service in the UK only to reappear on Colombo's main roads. The occasional bullock cart and rickshaw, before they disappeared from the city forever. Streets full of men in sarongs. The same men with betel-stained teeth and gums, and hair sprouting jungle-like out of their ears. Pavements spattered with expectorated betel juice. Going to see the MCC, the Aussies and West Indians play Sri Lanka at cricket. Watching rugger at Colombo sports clubs. Salivating at the prospect of smuggled tins of Nescafé and bars of Cadbury's Milk Chocolate when relatives returned from trips abroad, at a time when 'luxury' imports were banned.

Not-so-sweet memories: Lunches and dinners in appallingly decorated Muslim houses. Men and women sitting separately, not mixing. Parochial, gossipy, backbiting talk; relatives jabbering loudly in harsh Tamil, as if swearing at their grandmothers. Bad-mouthing this person, praising another, blowing up petty family quarrels into globally significant affairs of state. Daily histrionics. Mummy's endless meetings with Daddy's lawyers when he was under house arrest and in remand. Having to change school almost every year. All this while Colombo was down at heel, ravaged by Mrs B's government, a city of strikes, rationing, bread queues and discontent.

~

We returned to Colombo in July 1976 for what turned out to be our annus horribilis. This time we stayed with Daddy's sister, my Aunty Zara, at her house on Bagatelle Road, Colpetty, just off Galle Road. Aunty Zara had married a rags-to-riches Muslim businessman who built the Bagatelle Road house in the early 1960s. It was more a mansion than a house, with large, high-ceilinged rooms, expensive furniture, a grand central staircase, and a fleet of squabbling servants. We occupied two bedrooms, sharing the upstairs living area with Aunty Zara and her two boisterous children, Rifky and his older sister Kyria. Hilali, the eldest son, was already at public school in England; and Uncle Idroos, Aunty Zara's husband, was in exile in Hong Kong, staying clear of Sri Lanka like Uncle Razeen, for fear of being locked up for exchange control violations. We thought we would be staying with Aunty Zara and family for a few months. We stayed a year and a half.

The day of Daddy's verdict was Friday, 13 September 1976. That morning Daddy dressed in a sober charcoal-grey suit and tie; Mummy in a white-cream dress. Reyaz, Roshan and I waved them off after breakfast. Would Daddy return with Mummy that afternoon? All the family waited in fear and expectation.

It was our unluckiest day – unlucky Friday the 13th. I waited upstairs for agonizing hours. Then I saw Mummy come up that long, wide central staircase, tears streaming down her reddened face. Instantly I knew that Daddy was already back at Welikada, this time in the jail proper, not in the remand wing. He had been sentenced to two years 'rigorous imprisonment' (jail sentences in

Sri Lanka are, or were, always 'rigorous'), with a hefty fine. Uncle
Razeen had been sentenced to seven years in absentia, with an even
heftier fine. That moment, and for days after, I felt old, much older
than my eleven years, burdened with life's sorrows.

Mummy now had to look after three children on her own, with
a husband in jail, without a home of our own, and with precarious
finances. She set about it with exemplary fortitude. She bore all the
burdens, dealt with almost daily crises stoically, and never succumbed
to the tantrums, histrionics and breakdowns to which other members
of the extended family were prone. She gave us as much stability
and strength as she could in extreme circumstances, and never
complained. It was her finest, though far from happiest, hour.

Her first major decision was not to put Reyaz and me back in
school, fearing we would be victimized for having our father in
jail. So, for the next fifteen months, we were homeschooled. With
no prior training, Mummy taught herself how to teach. Every
weekday morning, upstairs at Bagatelle, in one of our bedrooms,
Reyaz and I had 'school'. We had lessons with Mummy until noon,
and homework after lunch. First I had a lesson, then it was Reyaz's
turn, and then my turn again. Mummy taught me English, English
literature (we studied *Macbeth*), history, French and geography.
Her one bit of outsourcing was maths, which she did not feel
competent to teach. So I had an almost daily afternoon maths
lesson with Godfrey Senaratne, a thirty-something accountant
and former teacher at St Thomas' College, who also tutored many
of my cousins. Godfrey was probably the best teacher I had,
flavouring his maths instruction with tales from Lewis Carroll's
Alice in Wonderland. When he emigrated a year later, ending up as a
lecturer in Melbourne, he left behind a huge reservoir of gratitude
and affection among the many pupils he taught.

Afternoons, after homework, I played table tennis on the veranda
and cricket on the front lawn with Rifky and other male cousins.

There were still lots of visits to relatives' houses in Colombo. We went often to the Cabanas in Mount Lavinia, which Mummy had to oversee on Daddy's behalf until it closed in late 1977. Once a month, we went to Welikada to visit Daddy. We entered through the massive iron grille front gate, built into a high, fearfully thick yellow-cream wall with watchtowers; then we crossed a forecourt into a dingy waiting room. There we waited until we were led into the unadorned adjoining room, where prisoners met family visitors. I had a sense of foreboding every time I went into Welikada, with that same faster, thumping heartbeat I had whenever I went to visit someone in hospital.

Once we were seated, a prison guard would lead Daddy in, dressed in regulation white vest and shorts, and shod in slippers. He had lost a fair amount of weight. Gone was his mid-1970s silhouette, with a bulging neck, full of folds, and an expanding belly, supported precariously by trousers buttoned up too tightly under its wide bottom rim. At Welikada, Daddy would put me at ease straight away, or almost, presenting a cheerful facade, telling me how wonderful life was going to be once this was all over.

But he could not mask our loneliness in the world. Our large circle of friends had faded away. A few remained loyal, mostly Daddy's buddies from air force days. The extended family was disintegrating. Daddy and Uncle Razeen, once so close, had stopped talking to each other a few years earlier, each blaming the other for causing their common predicament. Aunty Zara was our saviour. She had problems galore: money worries, with Uncle Idroos in enforced exile; a large, expensive household to maintain; thankless, never-ending financial obligations to relatives and sundry others, expected of a 'rich' relative; and her own mental illness, prone to excesses of religious zeal that led to several nervous breakdowns. But her heart was golden. She had helped Mummy and Daddy financially in their early married years, before Daddy's professional success. And now she shared her house with us, rent-free, treating us as part of her family.

For me, what redeemed this otherwise black year of Daddy's incarceration was 'Razeena'. This was the little tea estate Uncle Razeen had bought, about an hour's drive on a narrow, winding, potholed country road from the ancestral town of Badulla. It was named after a grand-aunt, and had once belonged to my great-grandfather, the tea transporter. Uncle Razeen never meant it to be a viable commercial enterprise, rather a holiday retreat for Mummyma and the extended family. Mummyma and her siblings had holidayed there when they grew up in Badulla; so had Daddy, Uncle Razeen and their siblings and cousins.

I loved Razeena, and still do. It fills a valley, nestled in the Uva hills, about 4000 feet above sea level. Dark-green tea grew all around. Razeena had ninety-nine acres of tea, with a little paddy cultivation, and was run by a *kanakapullai* (supervisor) who oversaw about fifty Tamil tea pluckers and their families. In the bowl of the valley stood the little estate bungalow, a yellow-cream house with a green corrugated iron roof surrounded by lawn, shrubs and flower beds.

The superintendent of Queenstown, the neighbouring large estate, oversaw Razeena. Initially, this was a burly, ruddy, moustachioed Scotsman, always clad in khaki shirt and shorts, knee-length socks and garters, Ceylon born and bred, who had spent his entire career planting in the island. He was a *periya dorai* (big boss in Tamil) who ran his estate like a feudal lord. His workers were Tamils from marginal and 'untouchable' castes, descendants of indentured labour brought over by the British in the second half of the nineteenth century and early twentieth century. They lived in 'lines', essentially dark hovels without electricity and running water. Tea bushes served as their toilets. A crew of cooks, gardeners, ayahs and houseboys kept his bungalow, garden and family shipshape. His Alsatian got first use of the swimming pool. He had once shot and killed a striking labourer; other estate workers burned his bungalow to the ground in retaliation. Yes, this could be straight out of a Somerset Maugham short story. But with one twist: Roger Summerville was a card-carrying member of the Ceylon Communist Party.

When the Bandaranaike government nationalized the plantations in the 1970s (Razeena and other small estates were spared), Roger Summerville and his ilk left Ceylon. Some went to plant in the Cameron Highlands in Malaysia and in Kenya; the rest retreated to the anonymity of desk jobs and semi-detached houses in British suburbia – what must have been crushing despair after gilded estate life in Ceylon. That was Roger Summerville's fate.

I was entranced by the hill country – the landscapes, the cool climate and crisp air, the hearty appetite it induced, the capacious estate bungalows and their gardens perched on hilltops with wraparound panoramas and shaded by flame trees, the smell of toasted tea from tea factories – everything except the appalling conditions of estate labourers and their families.

Our family, friends, uncles, aunts, cousins and servants used to pile into cars and make the long drive from Colombo to Razeena during school holidays. But I got to know Razeena best in that last year of my Sri Lankan childhood. In 1976–77, almost every month, Mummy, my brothers and I spent an idyllic couple of weeks at Razeena. How eagerly I anticipated our journey there from Colombo in our Peugeot 504 stationwagon. And how deflated I felt every time we came back to Colombo. At Razeena I had morning class with Mummy on the lawn, next to the lemon tree, did my homework in the bungalow, and wandered round tea trails in the afternoons. Reyaz and I would collect coffee plants in the midst of tea bushes, and replant them in our back garden. We took bracing baths under waterfalls. We admired the dexterity and strength of the slight, wiry female tea pluckers, carrying groaning baskets of tea leaves on their backs all day. I would take my transistor radio to the telegraph pole in the garden to get audible reception – to savour the rolling Hampshire vowels of John Arlott's Test match commentary, and to take in All India Radio's reporting of Mrs Gandhi's shock defeat in the snap general election she had called in March 1977. This was a harbinger of what was to happen to Mrs Bandaranaike a few months later.

Back in Colombo, about nine months after he was jailed, 'influence' succeeded in getting Daddy transferred to a ward in the General Hospital. This was preferable to jail: he could receive visitors and home-cooked food daily. But he still had one ankle manacled to a bedpost, and a prison officer always stood guard close by.

~

Sri Lanka's general election of July 1977 was a watershed for the country – and for the Salih/Sally family. The choice was between more of the same under Mrs B's SLFP-led government and a new government under the pro-business UNP. If Mrs B won, Daddy would have had to serve out his full jail sentence; Uncle Razeen and other relatives would have had to stay out of the country. But freedom beckoned if the UNP won.

So, with bated breath, Aunty Zara, Rifky, Kyria, Mummy, Reyaz, Roshan and I huddled around the radio (TV had yet to arrive in Sri Lanka) in Bagatelle's upstairs sitting room on election night, 21 July 1977. Family jubilation erupted when the results rolled in: the UNP won a five-sixths parliamentary majority, never equalled before or since. It was a sweet personal victory for the UNP leader, Junius Richard Jayewardene – known to Sri Lankans as JR. A.C.S. Hameed, a family friend and fellow Muslim, became foreign minister. One of the new government's first acts was to pardon those who had been convicted of foreign exchange violations.

Daddy was released that August. The first thing he did, following family custom, was to go to the Dewatagaha mosque in downtown Colombo, where he prayed before the shrine of its Sufi saint, Sheikh Usman Waliullah. Then he went to see Mummyma. My aunts, who could always be counted on for emotional theatrics, duly spilled buckets of tears.

On our last visit to Razeena, in early December 1977, my twelve-year-old self realized I would not be back for some time. So I scribbled something on a piece of paper – something to the effect of 'I will be back' – and buried it next to the lemon tree by which I had morning class.

A few weeks later we left for the UK. That was the end of my Sri Lankan childhood.

3

Sri Lanka Absent

The War Years

Cry the beloved country.
 – Alan Paton

At first I pined for Sri Lanka: it took me a while to readjust to life in the UK.

In January 1978 we went back to Rhyl, this time not to live with Granny but to rent the house next door. Its proportions were exactly the same as Granny's house – three smallish bedrooms and a bathroom upstairs, a living room, dining room and kitchen downstairs, and with the same length and breadth of back garden. But we had spartan 1970s furniture compared with Granny's Edwardian and pre-World-War-Two clutter, and her profusion of flowers and shrubs, lovingly tended over decades, overshadowed our plain stretch of lawn. I started at Rhyl High School, just ten minutes' cycle ride away, on the site of the grammar school Mummy attended in the late 1940s and early 1950s. I did not like it. Many classmates were rough; some took against me, latching on to my foreign-sounding name, my accent and my religion. I encountered racism for the first and last time, sometimes addressed as 'Paki'. I got beaten up once, but not badly.

This daily source of anxiety evaporated when I changed schools. In summer 1979, Daddy decided to send me to St Mary's College, a private school in the small seaside resort of Rhos-on-Sea, about twenty miles from Rhyl west along the North Wales coast. St Mary's was much smaller than Rhyl High, without the latter's rough edges. Irish Catholic priests from the Oblate teaching order ran it, and most of my teachers were priests with different shades of Irish brogue. About a third of the pupils were boarders, many from abroad. There were only a handful of girls, because St Mary's had gone co-ed just a year or two earlier.

I stayed at St Mary's for almost five years, longer than at any other school. By the time I left St Mary's, aged nineteen, I had been to eight schools in two countries, and changed schools thirteen times. At St Mary's I forged the only school friendships that lasted into adult life. I still wasn't a mixer. I stuck to my lessons and books and spent most of my free time at home. I vegetated through my A-level years, uninspired by a second-rate public school, watching too much television at home. In summer 1984, I was lucky to get the bare minimum of grades to get into the London School of Economics.

During these later school years I returned to Sri Lanka just twice. On a short visit for a cousin's wedding in 1979, I discovered TV had arrived in Sri Lanka. In summer 1981, between O- and A-levels, I stayed again at Bagatelle, sharing a room with my cousin Rifky. I fasted the whole month of Ramadan for the only time in my life; this had much to do with a religious phase in my mid-teens, which replaced my ardent pre-teen Maoism. I had an exhilarating three weeks on the east coast with my new friend Naushaad, a nineteen-year-old Hafiz, the honorific given to one who knows the whole Qur'an by heart.

I accompanied Daddy on three short visits to the Maldives, only a few years after it had opened up to tourism. I found it strange. To me Maldivians seemed brusque and unfriendly, in stark contrast to my fellow Sri Lankans. They had only started to deal with foreigners in the late 1970s, and they were still clearly in adjustment mode. The resort owners Daddy did business with were enthusiastic alcohol-swillers – in a 100 per cent Muslim country, where alcohol was banned outside the resort islands – and had extensive smuggling side operations.

Daddy now split his time between Colombo and Wales. His work was mainly in Sri Lanka, though he embarked on business ventures in the UK so he could spend more time with the family. All of them failed. In Sri Lanka, he was in the early stages of accelerating professional decline, though he only recognized it as such in the 1990s, and never fully admitted it to his last breath. Without hotels to run, he switched to other businesses. In the early 1980s, it was selling beer coolers to hotels in Sri Lanka and the Maldives. When that failed he moved into garments, which occupied him for the rest of the 1980s.

He never really adjusted to the UK. There he was 'ordinary', living in a semi-detached house, just one of the crowd. In Sri Lanka he was a 'big man', known in high places, with a wide circle of friends, with underlings to direct, and favours to dispense to a large number of the less fortunate – poor relatives, employees, ex-employees and their dependants, and friends of friends of friends – who sought his help. That was his self-image: he felt wanted, needed, in Sri Lanka in a way that was never possible in the UK.

~

In that summer of 1981, I found that Colombo now had hustle and bustle; it became more crowded and noisier. The population grew eventually to about 4.5 million in Greater Colombo – almost a quarter of today's national total – and 0.5 million within the city limits. The huge gardens of upper-class houses disappeared as owners walled off their houses. There were new hotels, shops, restaurants, cafes, apartment blocks, even one or two new shopping malls. Suburbs sprawled. Geoffrey Bawa built a striking new parliament building in the suburb of Sri Jayawardenepura (otherwise known as Kotte, the capital of an old Sinhala kingdom). The old parliament, built in the Greek classical style at the Fort end of Galle Face Green, became the presidential secretariat.

Colombo's rapid commercialization was the showcase of the new, open, pro-business Sri Lanka under a UNP government, which was busy reversing the collectivist, inward-looking policies of Mrs Bandaranaike's government as fast as it could. This was very much a 'JR project'.

J.R. Jayewardene, a veteran politician from a prominent UNP family, was related to the Senanayakes and Kotelawalas, with experience stretching back to the pre-independence Donoughmore constitution. He took over the party when Dudley Senanayake died in 1973. JR was intelligent, polished, charming, mischievous and extremely wily – some would say without scruple; he was known popularly as the 'old fox'. From 1956, he embraced 'Sinhala Only' (to make Sinhala the sole official language, at the expense of Tamil and English), happy to play the Sinhala nationalist card to compete with the SLFP. He was remarkably similar to SWRD Bandaranaike, down to his gilded upbringing and 'coconut brown' ways. English was their mother tongue. Both reserved Sinhala for their servants and those they thought of as coming from other, lower orders. Both were power-hungry panderers to Sinhala chauvinism.

JR's government raced ahead with liberalizing economic reforms. It was the first to do so in South Asia, well before India opened up in the early 1990s. The most onerous foreign exchange controls were lifted and the rupee devalued. There was a bonfire of controls, including quotas and other restrictions on foreign trade. The economy was opened to foreign investment. New free trade zones (FTZs) were established, starting with one next to the international airport at Katunayake. Sri Lanka went quickly from being one of the most protected to one of the most open economies in the developing world.

In the private sector, long pent-up entrepreneurial energies were unleashed. A new garment manufacturing industry started to grow in the FTZs, employing lots of workers – especially young women – from the villages; it soon became Sri Lanka's leading export industry. In 1977, Sri Lanka was still a plantation-export economy: tea, rubber and coconut accounted for 80 per cent of export earnings. By the mid-1990s, plantation exports accounted for less than a quarter of total exports; garments had become by far the biggest export earner. Belatedly, following the East Asian Tiger economies, Sri Lanka began to industrialize through exports.

Market reforms dovetailed with a vigorously pro-Western – particularly pro-American – foreign policy. The government started the massive Mahaveli Project, the biggest irrigation project since the days of the Polonnaruwa kings. Western aid flooded in to finance it, fuelling inflation and corruption.

JR also used his thumping parliamentary majority to change the constitution. It further centralized power by establishing an executive presidency. JR became Sri Lanka's first executive president in 1977, a few months after his parliamentary election victory. He went all out to definitively neutralize Mrs B. She was deprived of her civic rights, expelled from Parliament and barred from contesting the presidential election in 1982, one which JR won handsomely. Then

Parliament's life was extended for another five years by referendum, without the bother of a general election.

JR was slower to deal with ethnic problems. Sinhala–Tamil riots occurred again, soon after the July 1977 election. Tamil militants preaching violence gained the upper hand over established Tamil political parties.

On the night of 1 June 1981, ethnic relations suffered a massive setback. An act of gross cultural vandalism occurred that, to Sri Lankan Tamils, is their equivalent of Hitler's *Bücherverbrennung*, when the Nazis staged ceremonial bonfires of books they disapproved of. Following the killing of three policemen in Jaffna, a Sinhala mob, led by policemen, burned down Jaffna's public library, destroying over 97,000 volumes of books and manuscripts. Centuries of Tamil literary culture, including age-old scrolls and palm-leaf manuscripts, went up in smoke. The government did nothing. It was widely rumoured that two senior cabinet ministers had instigated the event. To Tamils, nothing more powerfully symbolized Sinhala chauvinism. It was a gift to militant groups who believed Eelam, an independent Tamil state, was the only solution, and violence the only way to achieve it.

~

Sri Lanka started to fade in my existence soon after I returned to Wales in September 1981. I did not realize it then, but I was saying goodbye to the land of my childhood for the next quarter-century. The land, and my Muslim family there, gradually dimmed in my memory. I forgot the Sinhala I had grown up with as my second language. Gradually, Sri Lanka became a bothersome backwater in my mind. I returned infrequently – once every four or five years or so. My feeling for Sri Lanka would rekindle a little, only to flicker out soon after I left. On my trips back, I chafed at the restrictions, rituals and traditions I had grown up with. It was almost worse being in Daddy's shadow, trailing him from one interminable business meeting and family visit to another.

I became more judgemental about Sri Lanka as I rode up the escalator of Western education. 'Philistine' was the word that leapt to mind when I thought of Sri Lankan ways, and of local Muslim attitudes in particular. Take education, for example. Effort and expense went to educate the boys in my extended family. Some went to public schools in Britain; two of us went on to decent universities. But scant effort and expense went to educate the girls. They left school at sixteen and had marriages arranged a year or two later; by their early- to mid-twenties they had their complements of children.

I did not come from an extended family tradition of books and high culture and 'progressive' values. As I grew into my teens I felt this keenly, envying the odd upper-class Sinhala or Tamil family with such traditions. By my late teens, I had outgrown my religious phase and reacted against my Muslim upbringing – lots of unquestioned rituals, dos and don'ts, prayer meetings, talk of spirits and djinns, and following this or that guru or *bawa*. I wished I were nurtured in a more learned, inquiring religious tradition. It had not bothered me during childhood, when I was content to learn the Qur'an by rote, accompany Daddy to *jumma* prayers on Fridays, and fast a few days during Ramadan. But now it did.

I was changing, and so was Sri Lanka. On 23 July 1983, Velupillai Prabhakaran's LTTE, then one of many Tamil militant groups, killed thirteen soldiers near Jaffna. Anti-Tamil riots erupted the following day when their mutilated bodies were brought to Colombo. Sinhala mobs looted and burned Tamil-owned shops. By the second day of rioting, the mobs were more organized and became homicidal. Throughout Colombo, Tamil shops, factories and houses were burned down; Tamils were dragged out of their houses and vehicles, beaten and often burned alive. Sinhala bystanders egged on the mobs; so did many Buddhist monks. Sinhala shopkeepers applauded as their Tamil competitors were literally wiped out. The police and army looked the other way. The violence soon spread to other cities and towns.

One infamous photo from that 'Black July' tells a whole story. It shows a Sinhala mob singing and dancing around a naked, cowering Tamil youth, blood streaming down his lean body. Moments later, they beat him to death.

President Jayewardene was silent for four days. Finally, when he addressed the nation on TV, he seemed to side with the Sinhala mob; he did not express a word of regret for violence against Tamils. Worse, it emerged that at least one cabinet minister had instigated some of the mob violence, possibly with JR's tacit consent.

The rioting left 2000 to 3000 dead and 175,000 refugees and displaced persons; half or more of Colombo's Tamils had to leave their houses, many never to return. Many joined the LTTE. Others left the country and joined a new Tamil diaspora. Over more than two decades, this diaspora formed the LTTE's sinews of war, the source of its funding.

JR thought that giving the green light to anti-Tamil riots would teach Tamils a lesson and secure his Sinhala base. Instead, Black July turned a low-intensity ethnic conflict into a murderous civil war that would last twenty-six years. And it shut a window of golden economic opportunity: multinational companies cancelled plans to invest in Sri Lanka and went elsewhere.

Violence escalated in the Tamil north and east. The LTTE, nicknamed the Tamil Tigers, emerged as the dominant militia after systematically murdering leaders of rival groups. The Tamil parliamentary leadership, now in exile in Tamil Nadu, was marginalized as militias took over the Tamil cause. Its ranks were thinned by assassinations, mostly carried out by the LTTE. And India got enmeshed in Sri Lanka's ethnic conflict. After she was re-elected as prime minister in 1980, Mrs Gandhi armed and trained Tamil militant groups, believing she could exert hegemonic power over Sri Lanka.

In 1987, the Sri Lankan army was on the verge of retaking the Jaffna peninsula from separatist groups. Rajiv Gandhi, now India's prime minister after his mother's assassination, threatened to invade the north of the island. Then, without consulting his cabinet, JR announced the Indo-Lanka Accord. The Indian Peacekeeping Force (IPKF) would go to the north and east. In a major concession, he made Tamil an official language alongside Sinhala and announced the creation of provincial councils with devolved powers – what Tamil politicians had been fighting for since 1956.

Over the next three years, the 100,000-strong IPKF got bogged down fighting a bitter war with Tamil militants, especially the LTTE. Indian troops made themselves deeply unpopular with local Tamils. The Indo-Lanka Accord was also deeply unpopular with Sinhalese; it played into the hands of Sinhala nationalists. It split the governing UNP and fuelled a resurgent JVP.

~

Far away in Wales and England, I was preoccupied with A-levels, and even more so with new undergraduate life at the LSE from October 1984. I grew heavily involved in student politics, first as a Young Conservative in North Wales, and then in the Federation of Conservative Students at the LSE. Mrs Thatcher was my heroine, and I saw myself as one of her foot soldiers. I was in a new city, London, living away from home for the first time, with a new set of multinational friends, and a new world of global social science – politics and economics in particular – opening up before me. My political consciousness had travelled some distance from that day the CID raided our home and took Daddy away when I was only six.

But I related none of this to Sri Lanka. Daddy brought back family and political news on his UK visits, twice or thrice a year. I read about Sri Lankan happenings in newspapers and newsmagazines, and noticed the odd bulletin on the new civil war on TV. But I remained passive and detached, even when Black July engulfed the city of my birth and childhood.

For my summer holidays I preferred to take trains around Western Europe, discovering new countries, rather than go back to Sri Lanka. It was only in summer 1987, six years after my previous visit, that I went back for a short break with Mummy and my youngest brother Roshan. By now my centre of gravity was firmly in the West; Sri Lanka, for the first time, felt 'foreign'. My Sinhalese had gone to pot, I found it difficult to relate to relatives, and I could not wait to get back to London and take trains around Europe before starting my MSc.

I arrived just as JR announced the Indo-Lanka Accord. This time we stayed with Aunty Hilufa, Daddy's eldest sister, at her house off Hotel Road in Mount Lavinia, close to St Thomas', my old school, and Mount Lavinia Hotel at the other end of Hotel Road. One morning we drove into Colombo for family visits. A Sinhala riot broke out during the day, protesting against the Indo-Lanka Accord. On our drive back, for the first and (so far) last time, I had a ringside seat at a Sri Lankan race riot. Sinhala mobs – mostly pockets of youth and men in their twenties and thirties, turbocharged with alcohol, burned tyres and threw Molotov cocktails at Tamil shops along Galle Road. We drove very slowly, stopping frequently, and took circuitous side roads to avoid Galle Road as much as possible. In Mount Lavinia, back on Galle Road, I recognized the servant boy from the house next to Aunty Hilufa's. He was busy throwing stones at a Tamil shopfront. Just that morning, from his master's front gate, I saw him admonishing Aunty Hilufa for killing a snake in her front yard. 'We Buddhists don't kill snakes,' he told her in Sinhala. But Tamils were clearly a different story.

I noticed other changes in Colombo from my previous visit. The city was tattier. Army checkpoints popped up in central Colombo. Crime had increased. And everywhere, ethnic communities were retreating behind their parapet walls. The easy inter-ethnic and inter-religious mixing among Colombo's elite, the staple of my parents' social life in the 1960s and 1970s, was waning.

~

Daddy persuaded me to come back to Sri Lanka over the winter of 1991, just after I submitted my PhD at the LSE. This time, we went outstation – to Kandy, the hill capital, the tea country, and down the south coast. I climbed Adam's Peak, Sri Lanka's holiest of holy mountains, huffing and puffing behind my lithe, agile Sinhala guide. Daddy gave me a huge twenty-seventh birthday party, taking over the ground floor of Bagatelle, complete with a band and a cake in the shape of an open book with the LSE's coat of arms and motto, *Rerum Cognoscere Causas* ('Happy is he who knows the causes of things' – from Virgil's *Georgics*) inscribed on top. Well over a hundred guests turned up. It was a good old Sri Lankan bash, and the last time I had a proper birthday party.

The extended family had changed, much as Colombo had with ethnic strife and civil war. There were more squabbles, and occasional warfare, within and between different family branches. No longer were uncles, aunties and cousins in and out of each other's houses daily. Many cousins had left to study and work abroad. When I left for Berlin a couple of days after my birthday party, I was still more a Westerner than a Sri Lankan. This visit was a nice holiday, but not a reconnection. That had to wait another fifteen years.

~

Sri Lanka's modern tragedy continued to unfold before and after my 1991–92 visit. A second JVP rebellion broke out in 1987 – much more destructive than the first one in 1971. Between 1987 and 1989, the Sinhala part of the island was crippled by lightning protests and strikes, assassinations, arrests and disappearances. The JVP regularly declared hartals and intimidated businesses into shutting down for days and weeks at a time. Transport was paralysed; tourists fled the country. The JVP, on the one side, and the police and army, on the other, engaged in tit-for-tat atrocities. A 'fear psychosis' reigned.

JR retired as president in the midst of this conflagration. His long-serving prime minister, Ranasinghe Premadasa, succeeded him in 1989. Initially, Premadasa made overtures to the JVP. It did not work. He then set about destroying it. What materialized was Sri Lanka's 'Indonesia solution', reminiscent of how General Suharto wiped out the communist rebellion in 1965. The army and paramilitary forces went on a killing spree. Droves of young men were taken away in locked vans; there were mass arrests and torture in detention camps. Mutilated, charred, rotting corpses littered roadsides and floated down rivers, eaten by stray dogs when they washed ashore. This reign of terror resulted in about 40,000 deaths and disappearances. It culminated in the capture of the JVP leader, Rohana Wijeweera, with whom Daddy had shared a Welikada dorm when he was remanded in the early 1970s. Wijeweera was caught hiding on a tea estate. After he obligingly divulged the whereabouts of members of his politburo, he was taken to the Royal Colombo Golf Club; there, on the thirteenth tee, he was shot before dawn. That was the end of the second JVP rebellion.

Premadasa was the first head of government after independence who was not from the govigama caste (the highest in the Sinhala hierarchy) and not born with a silver spoon in his mouth. He came from the *dhobi* caste of washermen, grew up modestly in Colombo, and was genuinely self-made. He had to fight caste prejudice on every rung of his ascent up the political ladder, even as prime minister. A workaholic, he built a reputation as a can-do politician especially keen to spread welfare and prosperity to rural areas. But, as president, he had an imperial air, fancying himself a reincarnation of storied Sinhala kings of old. He moved quickly to centralize power and crush dissent. The methods he used against the JVP were deployed, in muted form, against other political opponents – within the governing UNP, in the opposition, and against journalists who criticized the government's human rights abuses.

Premadasa had, from the beginning, thought the Indo-Lanka Accord a bad idea. He even channelled arms to the LTTE to fight the IPKF. He demanded that the Indian government withdraw the IPKF from Sri Lankan soil; the last Indian soldiers left in March 1990. Then Premadasa attempted to negotiate with the LTTE. But that broke down and war resumed between the Sri Lankan military and the LTTE. A stalemate ensued.

Meanwhile, the LTTE proved to be among the deadliest terror groups in the world. Its leader, Velupillai Prabhakaran, exercised total control and had godlike status. His vision and methods were totalitarian. His pantheon of role models was a curious mix: it included Alexander the Great, Napoleon, Sylvester Stallone and Clint Eastwood. Eelam was to be a one-party socialist state run by him. Every soldier, male or female, had to swear a personal oath of loyalty to Prabhakaran, and was forbidden cigarettes, alcohol and premarital sex. He or she also had to carry a cyanide capsule, to swallow if captured by government forces. Parents were forced to give up one child to the LTTE; child soldiers became a staple of the war effort. Collaborators with the enemy were tied to lamp posts and blown to bits with explosives ignited by fuse wire.

From the late 1980s until the last years of the war, the LTTE had great success with targeted assassinations and bomb blasts. It assassinated numerous Sinhala public figures, including several cabinet ministers, opposition politicians and military commanders. An LTTE suicide bomber blew up herself and Rajiv Gandhi at an election rally in Tamil Nadu in 1991. There were spectacular bombings: of the central bank and World Trade Center in Colombo, killing over a hundred people and injuring about 1500 others; a fleet of airlines belonging to the national carrier on the tarmac of Katunayake airport; near a major Buddhist shrine in Anuradhapura, killing 146 monks, nuns and laypeople, including children; and at the Temple of the Tooth in Kandy. Premadasa, too, fell victim to an LTTE suicide bomber during a May Day rally in Colombo in 1993.

Elections in 1994 ended seventeen years of UNP rule and returned the Bandaranaikes to power. Chandrika Bandaranaike Kumaratunga, Mrs B's daughter, first led an SLFP-centred coalition to victory in parliamentary elections; then she won the presidency. She appointed her mother prime minister, giving her a third crack at this office. But the executive presidency had much diminished the premiership, and Mrs B was in poor health. This time, she was a figurehead while her daughter ran the show. The two had been estranged, but, in the early 1990s, Chandrika returned to the SLFP and wrested the party's leadership from her mother.

Chandrika had suffered personal tragedy twice, first when her father, SWRD, was assassinated, and then when the JVP assassinated her husband, Vijaya Kumaratunga, a film-star-turned-politician, in 1988. She was much less chauvinist than her parents and her two UNP predecessors as president. It seemed she wanted Sri Lanka to be a true liberal democracy again, especially after the authoritarian drift of the Premadasa years. A new sense of hope was in the air.

Chandrika, like Premadasa, made overtures to the LTTE. Once again, Prabhakaran proved an impossible negotiating partner. War continued, without either side gaining a decisive advantage. On the economy, Chandrika retained the market reforms of previous UNP governments and took liberalization further, despite having been a left-wing firebrand in her Paris student days.

Chandrika called an early presidential election in 1999, which she won, but only after narrowly escaping an LTTE assassination attempt on the eve of the election. The blast left her blinded in one eye.

The UNP won the parliamentary elections in 2001. Its leader, Ranil Wickremesinghe, became prime minister. Sri Lanka had 'cohabitation' for the first time: an executive president from one party, and a prime minister, commanding a parliamentary majority, from the major opposing party. A Bandaranaike occupied the presidency. Ranil, from a prominent UNP family and JR's nephew, was prime minister. Given Sri Lanka's bitterly polarized politics, sharpened by warring political families, cohabitation was bound to be strained. So it proved to be.

Ranil charged forth with an ambitious two-pronged agenda: negotiations with the LTTE to end the war, and market reforms to revive the economy. In early 2002, his government signed a Norwegian-brokered ceasefire agreement with the LTTE; six rounds of negotiations followed, facilitated by the Norwegian government. The shooting stopped, and Sri Lanka tasted peace for the first time in two decades. Tourism picked up, and the economy revived.

The LTTE's sincerity was always in doubt. They withdrew from negotiations in March 2003. Meanwhile, Chandrika, the SLFP and assorted Sinhala nationalists attacked Ranil's government for conceding too much to the LTTE. As it turned out, the LTTE used the ceasefire to build a de facto separate state, and to re-arm to prepare for a resumption of war. Its ceasefire violations increased rapidly after 2003. In 2005, it assassinated Lakshman Kadirgamar, Sri Lanka's highly respected foreign minister.

Ranil's economic reforms made eminent sense, but they failed politically. Ranil and his coterie were bad at communicating the need for market reforms to ordinary Sri Lankans. From the old

English-educated Colombo elite, Ranil was, and remains, an essentially reserved character. He is comfortable with others of like background, such as his schoolmates from Royal College, and in the company of policy wonks and in conversations about world affairs, as I discovered when I became a government adviser in 2015.

Chandrika dissolved Parliament in early 2004. Faced with popular opposition to market reforms and accused of selling out to the LTTE – 'peace at any cost' – the UNP narrowly lost the ensuing parliamentary election. The SLFP returned to power at the head of a multiparty centre–left coalition. This included a rehabilitated JVP, now in government for the first time. Chandrika reluctantly appointed the SLFP's rising star, Mahinda Rajapaksa, as prime minister.

While the ceasefire unravelled gradually, Sri Lanka suffered another body blow. On Boxing Day 2004, the world's most powerful earthquake in forty years, and its second most powerful in a century, triggered a tsunami that ravaged two-thirds of Sri Lanka's coastline. The south and east coasts were particularly badly hit. Thirty thousand people died or disappeared. Half a million were left homeless.

Presidential elections were held in November 2005, pitting Ranil for the UNP against Mahinda for the SLFP. The differences were stark. Ranil wanted a negotiated peace with the LTTE and further market reforms; Mahinda favoured the military option – to defeat the LTTE once and for all – and interventionist economic policies. The LTTE enforced an election boycott in the north and east. With Prabhakaran's help, Mahinda won narrowly.

Sri Lankans had made a decisive choice, and Prabhakaran his worst, indeed fatal, mistake. The ceasefire unravelled completely in 2006; Sri Lanka returned to war. The rule of the Rajapaksas had begun.

~

I saw hardly anything of Sri Lanka between January 1992 and December 2006. I went back only twice, and then mainly to Colombo. One such visit I spent almost entirely in and around the intensive care unit of a hospital, where Daddy was at death's door.

When I returned, for just over a week during Christmas and New Year 2006–07, Sri Lanka was getting back to war. In 2009, when I returned for two months, it was speeding towards its bloody end.

President Rajapaksa used this last phase of the war to solidify his rule, and that of his immediate and extended family. Like Premadasa, he did not come from the landowning elite that had been co-opted by the British and ruled Sri Lanka after independence. Rather, he hailed from the provincial bourgeoisie in the Sinhala heartland. A member of Parliament from the early 1970s, he came to national prominence campaigning against the Premadasa government's human rights abuses in the late 1980s. He had grown up in a political family in the deep south, centred on the coastal towns of Hambantota and Tangalle, a remote backwater until the Rajapaksas attained power.

Mahinda is the polar opposite of Ranil. His English, while passable, is far from polished. His interest in the outside world is limited. He is no policy wonk. But he is an acutely political animal with the common touch. He relates instinctively to the Sinhala small-town elite, the monk in the village temple and the Sinhala villager; he speaks to them in a language they understand.

Mahinda appointed his younger brother Gotabhaya as defence secretary to spearhead the war effort. For the first time since the beginning of the war, a Colombo government had a single-minded military objective – total victory. Defence expenditure skyrocketed. Huge arms supplies came from China, Pakistan and Russia. The USA and India helped with vital intelligence on the LTTE. The military more than doubled its manpower, from 125,000 personnel in 2005 to 300,000 in 2009.

Prabhakaran's hubris aided the government. First, he severely underestimated Mahinda, believing him to be, like his predecessors, someone who could be manipulated. He also totally misread the external environment after 9/11. Before 9/11, the LTTE could operate relatively freely abroad. Afterwards, it was branded a terrorist organization in country after country, and found it much more difficult to raise funds and procure arms.

The government's first big break came when the LTTE's two top commanders in Eastern Province defected. One, the LTTE's deputy leader, Karuna, had been responsible for bombings and political assassinations in Colombo. He gave the government a list of his Colombo-based operatives, none of whom were ever seen again. Overnight, Colombo became much safer. Later – I am not making this up – Karuna became a figurehead minister for national integration. By 2007, the army controlled Eastern Province, and the battle moved to the LTTE heartland in the north.

The new situation enabled Mahinda to accumulate and centralize power to a greater degree than any of his predecessors. Mahinda appointed his brothers to key positions: Gotabhaya as defence secretary, but also Basil as a senior economic adviser and Chamal as a cabinet minister. Others from the extended family circle got senior positions in government, the public sector and in embassies abroad. A Mahinda personality cult, orchestrated by a big government PR operation, took hold.

With the accumulation of power came an increasingly authoritarian streak. There were tight restrictions on reporting the war. Journalists and others critical of the government, whether on war-related or unrelated matters, were labelled 'unpatriotic' and accused of undermining the war effort. Journalists were hounded; some disappeared or were killed. In January 2009, Lasantha Wickrematunge, the editor of the *Sunday Leader* and a vocal critic of the Rajapaksas, was murdered. In a posthumous editorial, he predicted his own murder by the government.

'When I am finally killed,' he wrote, 'it will be the government that kills me.' He accused Mahinda, addressing him directly: 'For truth be told, we both know who will be behind my death, but dare not call his name. Not just my life, but yours too, depends on it . . . You will see to it that the guilty one is never convicted. You have no choice.'

The war's endgame took place in the first five and a half months of 2009. Before that the Sri Lankan army had regained full control of the Jaffna peninsula. In January 2009, it retook the LTTE capital of Kilinochchi, south of the Jaffna peninsula. Over the next four months, the remaining LTTE fighters, numbering about 15,000, retreated to the jungle around the town of Mullaitivu in the north-eastern corner of the island. They took with them more than 300,000 Tamil civilians to act as human shields between them and the army. By mid-April, they were trapped on a stretch of beach; the army shelled them relentlessly. The government announced Prabhakaran's death on 18 May. His wife and children had also been killed, as had other LTTE leaders and their families. Some had allegedly been carrying white flags. Sri Lankan TV displayed Prabhakaran's corpse. He was in crumpled fatigues, eyes open, his wilted torso propped up by jubilant soldiers, with a small piece of cloth covering the part of his head where the bullet had entered.

Subsequently, the UN and other critics accused the army of indiscriminate shelling, and of killing up to 40,000 people in the last three weeks of the war. A UK Channel Four TV documentary, *Sri Lanka's Killing Fields*, loudly publicized these allegations. 'Up to 40,000 civilians killed' became an international media factoid. Not surprisingly, the government denied the allegations outright. The Sri Lankan expat academic Michael Roberts estimated that perhaps up to 15,000 people were killed in the final stage of the war. He added that it was very difficult to come up with a precise number, and equally difficult to say how many were killed by the army and how many by the LTTE.

The war had ended. An editorial in a pro-government newspaper, *The Island*, triumphantly announced, 'Checkmate!' The pro-LTTE *Tamil Guardian* called it 'Holocaust'.

~

My absence from Sri Lanka in the 1980s and 1990s meant I was not close by to witness Daddy's decline. He did his best to mask it on my infrequent holiday visits, and during his stays at home in Wales, but succeeded only partially. Nor was I willing to acknowledge the total truth: that would have been too painful. Daddy doted on his children; and his pride in me, his firstborn, knew no bounds. He missed no opportunity to praise my academic accomplishments, far beyond their worth, to anyone who would listen. But I held back. My drift away from Sri Lanka was also a drift away from Daddy. His calamitous business ventures, which got worse over the years, ruined our family finances. Mummy had to bear the strain and pick up the pieces, just as she had to with Daddy's political problems in the 1970s. That angered me. Daddy never seemed to acknowledge or learn from his mistakes; his pride got the better of him. He harked back to his glory days and promised golden tomorrows, but made a mess of present reality.

Daddy's professional and material decline took its toll on his health, which he neglected flagrantly. He had been a chain-smoker since his teens, and for as long as I could remember he smoked forty-plus cigarettes a day, rapidly, one after the other, inhaling and exhaling in a rushed flow of nervous energy. He ate badly, wolfing down anything set on his plate without noticing what it was, almost as quickly as he consumed his cigarettes. He became more religious with age and worry, praying five times a day and making pious pronouncements. Until the 1980s he had been conventional: he went to the mosque on Fridays and on festival days, attended religious functions when necessary, and enjoyed his customary evening whisky with friends and acquaintances. By the 1990s he had a growing guilt complex about his alcohol consumption.

On a Friday night in mid-December 1996, I got back to my flat from a long session in the LSE bar with colleagues and students to a phone call from Mummy in Wales. Daddy had been taken ill in Colombo, and was in surgery, she said. It was life-threatening: he had a perforated bowel. We flew to Colombo the next day. For the next three to four weeks I spent most of my days hovering outside the intensive care unit of Asiri Hospital. Much of my day was taken up calling friends abroad to procure and send medicines the surgeon had requested on the next available flight, and then going to the airport to pick them up. It was touch and go: Daddy almost died several times. He had a second operation just before I had to return to teaching at the LSE, which lasted seven hours. In the middle of it the surgeon came out to tell us he was running short of blood: the hospital did not have enough of Daddy's blood type. Could we – the family – get some, and within the hour? A frantic search followed, finally getting a fresh supply from Colombo's General Hospital. Daddy survived. I returned to London; Mummy stayed on for another month to nurse Daddy back to health.

In its own way, Sri Lanka lightened the burden with sweet, even comic moments that would have been impossible in the West. Like other venues in Sri Lanka, hospitals, including intensive care units, are an excuse for a social gathering. Family and friends throng, insisting on going in to see the patient. They manage to get in through the day, disregarding visiting hours. Mummy and I had to take turns by the entrance to keep the flow manageable – often to turn back relatives and friends who were about to barge in. One day Daddy received sixty visitors, which gave him special pride. It fitted his self-image: he was still remembered fondly, indeed loved, by many in Sri Lanka.

Daddy recovered, only to resume his descent. On his first visit back to the UK after his operations, in April 1996, he was thin and drawn. He had lost most of his excess fat and looked aged, with folds of wrinkled skin hanging dejectedly off his frame. He drowned in his clothes. But this did not last long. He put his weight back on fairly quickly and resumed his smoking. The following year he got into trouble over an arms deal and was interned for a few months, but then released unconditionally.

In October 2002, late on a Friday evening – calamity seemed to strike Daddy especially on Fridays – Reyaz called to say Daddy had been rushed to hospital in Wales. Just as my youngest brother Roshan picked me up to drive to Wales, Reyaz called again to say Daddy had died. He had been to the mosque for jumma prayers that afternoon, and then gone to visit his eldest sister Hilufa, now in a retirement home close to our family home. Later that afternoon he was shrieking in severe pain, prompting Mummy to call an ambulance. He had suffered an aortic aneurysm. He was sixty-six.

I was given time alone in a hospital room, with Daddy's body behind a glass panel. I cried convulsively – enough to get it out of my system. We could not bury Daddy within twenty-four hours of death, as Muslim custom requires, because it was the weekend and the autopsy could not be done until Monday. It took us a while to find a suitable Muslim gravesite. On Monday morning, I accompanied two other Muslims – workers in a local Bangladeshi restaurant – to wash Daddy's body and wrap it in a white cloth. Luckily they, unlike me, had experience in this ritual. Then we went to the Rhyl cemetery, round the corner from where we lived when I was a boy, and there we buried Daddy, facing Mecca, in a section reserved for Muslims.

I haven't shed any tears since then, nor have I visited Daddy's grave. First came a wave of anger, for reasons going beyond what I feel able to write about now. But that passed, eventually. The Buddha says one should not accept someone else's present of anger, and let the other keep his anger. I think – I hope – I have learned that lesson. But forgiveness has yet to come. One day, before too long, I will go back to Daddy's grave and cry the tears that remain for me to shed.

~

And so I came to stand, just before Christmas 2006, at a bedroom window at Galle Face Hotel, looking towards the Indian Ocean through sheets of wind and rain, covered by a low-slung canopy of dark, brooding clouds. I was free now. Daddy was not in the room next door. I did not have to follow him around Colombo all day; nor did I have to go outstation on trips he so meticulously organized. I was free to conjure up Sri Lanka in my imagination, uninhibited, and roam and discover *my* Sri Lanka tangibly, at will.

Still, Daddy's shadow follows me wherever I go in Sri Lanka. It is ever-present in the houses of relatives and old family friends who recount their stories of yesteryear. It is at Mount Lavinia Hotel, and Hindu College Square and Borupana Road, Ratmalana. It is in the hotels and clubs of Colombo, and the Uva hills of his boyhood. After he died it stopped being an enveloping, constricting thing. But it still hovers over me, and my Sri Lanka would not be the same without it.

Part Two

Sri Lanka through Adult Eyes

A Travelogue

4

Home Town

Colombo Then and Now

More than anything, one is struck by the light. Light everywhere. Brightness everywhere. Everywhere the sun. Just yesterday, an autumnal London was drenched in rain. The airplane drenched in rain. A cold wind, darkness. But here, from the morning's earliest moments, the airport was ablaze with sunlight, all of us in sunlight.

– Ryszard Kapuscinski, *The Shadow of the Sun: My African Life*

Arriving from a European winter, Ryszard Kapuscinski's first tropical sensation was a sun-drenched welcome as he got off the plane in Delhi. For forty-five years, this has been my image of landing at Katunayake, Colombo's international airport. In my mind's eye, Heathrow landings are darkened by grey skies, rain-soaked and chilly. But I always anticipate an azure sky, a warm sun and blazing light as Katunayake approaches. Rarely am I disappointed.

Two aerial views of the approach to Katunayake are lodged in my

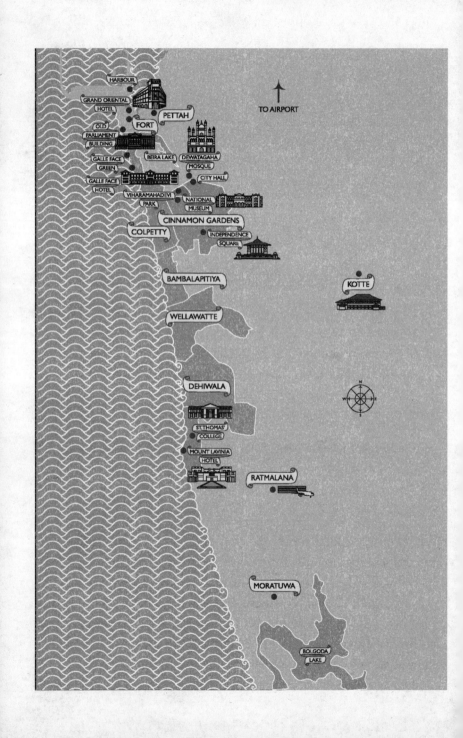

mind. The first is on flights from Europe and India. The parched, undifferentiated brown of the Deccan and the Tamil Nadu coastline gives way to the narrow Palk Straits that separates giant India from teardrop-shaped Sri Lanka. I look down to 'Adam's Bridge', the chain of sandbars that fills the fourteen miles between Rameswaram in India and Talaimannar in Sri Lanka. In the Ramayana, the monkey general Hanuman and his army used these sandbars as stepping stones to Lanka, where they went to rescue Sita from Ravana's clutches in the Uva hills. It takes almost no time to cross the Palk Straits by air, and high above I feel I could touch the two coastlines with the thumb and little finger of my extended hand.

We zip down the small, flat, bare island of Mannar, do an obtuse-angled turn and fly straight down the west coast of mainland Sri Lanka. The Kalpitiya peninsula sticks out its curved little finger at Mannar island to its north. Suddenly, the landscape becomes a lush, deep green – the abrupt transition from the dry zone of the north and east to the wet zone of the south and west. Groves of coconut palms, punctuated by the corrugated green roofs of estate bungalows, accompany us all the way to the airport tarmac. Before we land, I see the still waters of Negombo Lagoon. Just beyond, the breakers roll in from the Indian Ocean.

Flying from Singapore, where I now live, I get a different aerial view, this time east to west across the island. First we cross the coastline, bare, empty-looking compared with the west and south coasts. Then the flat, thinly vegetated, sparsely peopled land eases into thick green carpets of tea, undulating their way across the central hill country. Dirt-brown paths snake around tea carpets; grey-white tea factories and estate bungalows with green roofs perch on hilltops. Mid-sized mountains gird the central highlands – the natural fortress of the old Kandyan kingdom that protected it against Portuguese, Dutch and, for a short while, British invaders coming from the coast. Hill slopes to the west descend to low-country greenery of paddy terraces and coconut groves before we land at Katunayake.

As children, my cousins and I looked forward to the treat of a drive up to Katunayake to accompany travelling relatives. We went to see the first Boeing 747 land, ushering in Sri Lanka's age of mass tourism. Now no Colomboite thinks of an airport trip as a 'treat', but villagers from elsewhere in Sri Lanka still flock there, dressed in their Sunday best, when relatives arrive or depart. They see off or greet housemaids working in Saudi Arabia and the Persian Gulf, and pilgrims too – Muslims destined for Mecca for Hajj or Umra, Hindus visiting temples in South India, and Buddhists off to Bodh Gaya, in present-day Bihar, where the Buddha attained enlightenment.

The road from Katunayake to Colombo used to be narrow and quiet. It got wider and busier, especially after the Katunayake Free Trade Zone opened in 1978. It was the first and remains the biggest of Sri Lanka's FTZs, the centre of its garment industry. Catholic towns succeed each other along the road; ubiquitous crosses, Portuguese-style churches, images of the Virgin Mary and assorted saints, encased in glass, all dot the roadside – a first glimpse of the colourful drama that is Roman Catholicism in Sri Lanka. Running parallel to the airport road, between it and the ocean, is Hamilton Canal, constructed by the Dutch to transport cinnamon from up the coast to Colombo. Catholic fishing villages line the canal's banks, their rubbish strewn there and in the water. At the top of the lagoon is Negombo, the main Christian settlement north of Colombo. Negombo and its surrounding towns are Sri Lanka's 'Little Rome', packed with churches in vibrant blues and yellows and pinks, their high-arched fronts and sides open to the elements, and full to bursting for weekend Mass. An Islamist suicide bomber blew up one of these churches, St Sebastian's, during Easter Sunday

Mass, 2019, killing about a hundred worshippers, including twenty-seven children.

It used to take at least an hour to drive between the airport and Colombo's city limits, a journey that can now be done on a new highway in fifteen minutes flat.

In the 1970s, I invariably felt a pang of loss when we drove from the city to the airport. And the anticipation of returning 'home' when we drove in the opposite direction. Returning home after a spell abroad had a fixed ritual. We would drop in first at the Dewatagaha mosque to pray at the shrine of its Sufi saint, then go to see Mummyma, the matriarch of the family, and only then go to our own house. After my teens, infrequent visits did not feel like returning home. But, for the last decade, with frequent visits and rediscovered familiarity, that childhood sense of Colombo as home town has got under my skin again. But I am older by half an average lifetime, and Home Town is a different place, though not changed out of all recognition.

～

Architecturally, Colombo today is a jumble of the twentieth-century modern and late nineteenth-century–early twentieth-century British-colonial. Nothing is left of Arab Colombo before its European conquest in the early 1500s, and hardly anything of subsequent Portuguese Colombo.

But a few vestiges of Dutch Colombo remain. The British razed what was left of Dutch fortifications in the mid-1800s. But two landmarks stand out. One is Wolvendahl Church, built on a hilltop between 1749 and 1757 – a prize specimen of Dutch tropical architecture, gabled, solid and heavy, with a Doric facade. For two centuries it was the first landmark ships sighted when they entered

Colombo harbour. Soon after independence, a Buddhist stupa was erected near the harbour. Sinhala nationalism dictated that the first sighting from the sea should be a Buddhist, not a Christian, landmark.

Wolvendahl Church was the main place of worship for Dutch high society. Under its flagstones are the remains of Dutch governors, high officials, their wives and children. Many children died young, mainly from malaria. Under the British the church had a mainly Burgher congregation. Framed photos show light-brown-skinned besuited men with their hatted and befrocked womenfolk. Now poor Sinhalese and Tamils from the surrounding area make up the small congregation.

In nearby Pettah is the Dutch Museum, formerly the home of Dutch governors, now incongruously stranded in streets of Tamil and Muslim shops heaving with everyday commerce. Its sloping roof has generous eaves supported by thick round yellow-cream pillars; the Dutch called the resulting veranda effect a *stoep*. Large fanlighted doorways lead to rooms with high ceilings and dark, heavy Dutch period furniture. Gravestones line the garden at the back. The Dutch elite lived in high style in Colombo, full of pomp and ceremony and with a large retinue of slaves. Like the British after them, they were riven with class distinctions. Marriage with locals was permitted, but those who did so were not allowed to return to the Netherlands.

In 1679, fresh from his escape from nineteen years' captivity in the Kandyan kingdom, Robert Knox spent a few days in Dutch-controlled Colombo en route to Batavia (now Jakarta) and thence back to England. In his *Historical Relation of the Island Ceylon*, he referred to the city's original name, Kolamba, an abbreviation of 'Kola-Amba' – the leaf of the mango tree in Sinhala. Folklore has it that a leafy mango tree stood high above the hook at the south-east end of the harbour, a useful guide for incoming ships. The Dutch made the mango tree an emblem in the city's coat of arms. Ibn Batuta, visiting in 1345, referred to 'Kalambu – one of the finest and largest (towns) in the island'. Knox wrote that the Portuguese Christianized the city's name to Colombo to honour Christopher Columbus.

The other pre-colonial name for Colombo is Kolontota – a port or anchorage or ferry on the Kolon, a rivulet that carried floodwater from the Kelani river to the sea. The Portuguese dammed it up in the 1520s to create Beira Lake, then on the edge of Colombo but now right in the middle of the city.

Colombo was one of the island's major trading ports before the Portuguese muscled in. Tamil-speaking Muslim traders, of Arab and South Indian descent, set the tone. They exported gemstones, elephants and, above all, cinnamon, which grew wild in jungles in the western part of the island. The king of the surrounding Kotte kingdom authorized them to collect customs duties and regulate shipping in the kingdom's ports. Chetties, people of South India's moneylending caste, also settled in town.

Cinnamon was the allure for European invaders: the Portuguese, Dutch and British craved it. Ceylon, more than anywhere else, had it in luxuriant abundance, but Arab traders monopolized its export to Europe. The lust for cinnamon drew the Portuguese from Goa, their Asian capital, to the island they called Ceilão, and to Colombo in particular. In 1505, on the first Portuguese voyage to Ceylon, Lourenço de Almeida concluded a treaty with the king of Kotte. The king gave the Portuguese rights to trade in cinnamon and establish a trading fort in Colombo. But they faced resistance from established Muslim traders. They returned in 1517, this time with a flotilla of twenty-seven cannon-laded caravels. Only in 1519 were they able to build a fort, which they named Fort Santa Barbara. Pressured by the Portuguese, the Kotte king expelled Muslim traders in 1526. But, for the Portuguese, Colombo was not totally secure until they destroyed and gobbled up the Kotte kingdom in the 1590s.

The Dutch East India Company captured Colombo from the Portuguese after a seven-month siege in 1656. King Rajasinghe of Kandy came to aid the Dutch, thinking they would present the city to him on a plate. That the Dutch had no intention of doing. Even more than the Portuguese, they wanted to control Colombo as headquarters for a cinnamon export monopoly. Rajasinghe and his troops, rebuffed, retreated to Kandy. Just over a century later, Governor Falck created the first cinnamon plantation, just outside Colombo Fort in what is now Maradana, a down-at-heel commercial district. Cinnamon was later cultivated in today's Cinnamon Gardens, Colombo's poshest residential area – now totally bereft of cinnamon trees.

An early Dutch governor, Ricklof van Goens, thought Ceylon a superior prize to Java, and counselled that Colombo, not Batavia, should be the VOC's chief seat of government. But at that stage the Dutch did not control the whole coastline, let alone the whole island. They faced competition from English and Danish merchant fleets on the east coast.

On one side of Beira Lake was Kaffir's Veldt, where lived enslaved Africans, descendants of captives brought over from Mozambique by the Portuguese. Their descendants no longer occupy what came to be called Slave Island. The country's remaining Afro-Sri Lankans live in Sirimbadiya, a village near the town of Puttalam, farther up the west coast. No trace of African culture survives except their kaffrinha music, with its distinctive beat. For the last two centuries Slave Island has been a total misnomer. It holds no slaves, and it has never been an island.

The British took Colombo from the Dutch in 1796, with hardly a shot fired, following the Napoleonic invasion of the Netherlands and the retreat of the Dutch Stadtholder to exile in Britain. It became the official capital of the new Crown colony after the fall of the Kandyan kingdom in 1815. The Reverend James Cordiner, writing in 1807, described a town with about 50,000 inhabitants. The British lived in a still-intact Dutch fort with seven bastions. The remaining Dutch and their mixed-blood descendants, the Burghers, lived in adjoining Pettah, while Sinhalese inhabited the suburbs. The last Dutch governor, van Anglebeck, sold his house to the British, who made it Queen's House, the official residence of British governors. Now it is Janadhipathi Mandiriya, the official residence of the president of Sri Lanka.

The Colebrooke–Cameron reforms in the 1830s triggered British Colombo's transformation. Age-old mercantilist restrictions, including monopolies (not least on cinnamon) and *rajakariya* (compulsory non-wage, caste-based labour that Sinhala kings relied on), were abolished in the laissez-faire and free-trade spirit of the mother country. Administrative innovations introduced a new judicial system and a Legislative Council. These liberal reforms sparked a rush of private (mostly British) capital to invest in the new plantation economy – rubber and coconut in the lowlands, and coffee, and later tea, in the central highlands. British trading houses set up shop in Colombo.

A local professional class of English-educated Jaffna Tamils and Burghers emerged. So did a Sinhala low-country bourgeoisie, coming from the govigama and karava castes (the former the highest Sinhala caste of landowning cultivators, the latter the fishermen's caste, further down the caste ladder). The first generation made their fortunes in plumbago, coconut, rubber and liquor. In Colombo, they built palatial mansions with grand lawns and high trees. Their sons led the incipient nationalist movement, establishing the Ceylon National Congress and then the UNP. Such was the political trajectory of the interrelated Senanayakes, Kotelawalas, Jayewardenes and Wijewardenes, the ruling families of the 'Uncle Nephew Party'.

Hindu Tamils and Tamil Muslims from South India, and Borhas,

Sindhis, Khojas, Memons and Parsis from Bombay and Gujarat came over to establish new businesses. New roads and railways fanned out from Colombo to different parts of the island. The British built a modern port in the 1870s, which made Colombo a leading entrepôt in the British Empire in Asia. It became an obligatory port of call for P&O steamers on the voyage between Britain and Australia.

Leonard Woolf, fresh from Trinity College, Cambridge, sailed into Colombo harbour in 1904 to take up his new position in the Ceylon Civil Service. His first impression of turn-of-the-century Colombo was this: 'Before the motor car Colombo was a real Eastern city, groaning with human beings and flies, the streets full of fleeting rickshaws and creaking bullock carts, hot and heavy with complicated smells of men and beasts and dung and oil and food and fruit and spice.'

This Colombo scene changed only gradually, even with the advent of the motor car. But the next fifty years turned the city inside out. They saw the rise of a mainstream, mostly pro-British nationalist elite as well as left-wing radicalism. A small industrial workforce emerged that existed nowhere else in the country. By the 1920s, it became the base of a new union movement and the Ceylon Labour Party. New Marxist parties came to replace the Labour Party and controlled the unions. They organized strikes and opposed the constitution, agreed between the British Colonial Office and D.S. Senanayake, which took Ceylon to independence in 1948. But this was still minority opposition. At independence, Colombo continued to have an orderly, colonial feel to it.

Bevis Bawa sketched the post-independence Colombo of the 1950s and 1960s in his 'Briefly by Bevis' newspaper column. He saw the ruling elite mouthing nationalist and socialist slogans and implementing nationalist and socialist policies, even as they continued to live in the mansions and tread the grand lawns their capitalist fathers and grandfathers had built. They had lots of servants, who they treated as chattel, and lots of fresh air. Being socialists, they cut down the tall trees on their lawns to 'give them greater vision'. They wore the national dress in the style of SWRD Bandaranaike, but livcried chauffeurs drove them around in huge American cars. The avant-garde built American-style ranch houses with semi-detached roofs. The men of this elite continued to patter away in a mimicked idiom of 'great chap', 'good fellow', 'old boy' and 'what ho'. But, to Bevis, the old integrity and courtesy had disappeared, replaced by the ill-mannered and self-important lording it over social inferiors.

~

Bevis Bawa's Colombo was the city into which I was born in the mid-1960s. Until the late 1970s, it remained verdant, spacious and airy, a capital with a decidedly small-town vibe. The *Handbook for the Ceylon Traveller*, published in 1974, describes Colombo's private gardens as a riot of anthuriums, roses, chrysanthemums, caladium, multicoloured bougainvillea, coleus and croton, generously shaded by jacaranda, spathodea, tulip, gold mohur and padouk trees. But that was before property prices skyrocketed and the wealthy knocked down their mansions, dug up their lawns, felled their trees and built back-to-back apartment blocks.

The years of my absence from Colombo coincided with a construction boom, complete with condos and shopping malls and five-star hotels. It densified and expanded suburbs that morphed into satellite towns, such as Ratmalana and Mount Lavinia, where I used to live and go to school. Parapet walls sprang up around houses and gardens and public buildings to deter rising crime. Traffic and pollution got worse.

From the mid-1980s to 2009, Colombo was also a city at war.

It had burned in Black July 1983, set alight by its singing, dancing Sinhalese mobs. Security checkpoints and troops were ubiquitous. The Fort, the political and commercial heart of the city, became a barbed-wire no-go zone, ravaged by LTTE bombs and bomb threats. Its Victorian and Edwardian buildings slipped into dilapidated neglect. Galle Face Green, the oceanfront maidan of the city, was where I used to fly my kite and take pony rides, and where we used to go on family promenades to catch the evening sea breeze and watch the Indian Ocean sunset. It was green in my childhood. By the 1990s it had turned parched brown. Pimps and drug peddlers stalked stray tourists. The wan warehouses of the old trading companies along Beira Lake emptied of goods and human activity. Only Pettah, the cash-rich bazaar of Muslim and Tamil traders, carried on its sweaty bustle regardless.

One night, two months before the war ended, an LTTE kamikaze light aircraft crashed into an office building in central Colombo. It was aiming for Army HQ, but it hit Inland Revenue HQ instead on the opposite side of the road. Many locals cheered, hoping their tax files had disappeared in the flames. Symbolically, that closed Colombo's war chapter.

~

When I arrived in early 2009, just before the war ended, Katunayake airport was semi-deserted. I counted just ten flights on the arrivals board between 10 a.m. and 5 p.m. Colombo hotels were almost empty in the tourist high season, and offered magnificent discounts for room and board.

Soon after the war the opposite became true for both the airport and hotels. Colombo was 'beautified', and Gotabhaya Rajapaksa, one of Mahinda Rajapaksa's younger brothers, was the architect of this beautification. After the war he became head of the Urban

Development Authority. Ruling by diktat, and with un-Sri-Lankan speed, he deployed the military to clean streets, carpet roads and paint buildings, and drew up grand plans to clear slums and start megaprojects. The Rajapaksa government's star project was Port City: 270 hectares of land reclaimed from the sea, between Galle Face Green and the harbour, with new high-end financial, retail and residential districts. The contract went to a Chinese state-owned company, which promised to inject more foreign investment than Sri Lanka had for any other project.

The army retreated from the streets to its bases. The city became one of the cleanest in South Asia. Colonial buildings looked spruce, with fresh coats of white paint and free of their parapet walls, affording unobstructed views from the road.

The National Museum is a typical specimen. A Victorian neoclassical pile, it was built at Governor Gregory's initiative in 1877. During and even before the war, the building looked tired and forlorn: chipped plaster scarred its walls; overgrown grass, piles of rubbish and stray dogs completed the effect in the grounds. After the war it acquired a sparkling white facade and a presentably mown lawn. But, wandering round the back, I noticed a few mounds of rubbish, two stray dogs and loitering labourers. Some things in Sri Lanka do not change.

A few minutes' drive away, long-neglected racecourse buildings were turned into a mall; around it, and extending to Independence Square, a new track became popular with early-morning and early-evening walkers and joggers. Viharamahadevi Park (formerly Victoria Park) looked clean, tidy and inviting. Children returned there, to play their myriad games just as they had before the war. At one end of the park is the domed and pillared Colombo Town Hall, built in the 1920s to look like a cross between the White House and the Capitol Building in Washington, DC. Now it radiated lily-white, at least on the outside. At another end is Nelum Pokana, a new arts performance complex shaped like a lotus pond, another of President Rajapaksa's prestige projects built with Chinese money.

From my room balcony at the Hilton Residence, where I sometimes stay, I take in the panorama of Slave Island and Beira Lake, and beyond of Colpetty, the Fort, the harbour and the sea. The view now includes luxury condos and five-star hotels rising over what was a very low-rise skyline. The Fort has sprung back to life, with some of its colonial buildings getting welcome facelifts. The harbour has been extended, with a complement of brand-new cranes. Port City proceeds apace, round the clock, with imported Chinese labour. Ten minutes' drive inland, the walkway around a section of Beira Lake is not bespattered, as it used to be, with droppings from the lake's long-time residents, its flocks of pelicans who commute between the water and treetops surrounding the lake. The warehouses of the old trading companies backing on to another section of the lake are busy again with goods and workers. One section of Slave Island's rabbit warren of tiny houses, home to poor Muslim labourers and their families, has been demolished to make way for modern apartment blocks. And on lakefront land, where there used to be a squatter settlement, a spectacularly ugly tower, Nelum Kuluna, or 'Lotus Tower', rises, dwarfing everything else in the city like Gulliver in Lilliput.

I see many more foreign faces around, mainly tourists, but also Chinese workers on infrastructure projects around the island. Chinese tourists, too, have finally discovered Sri Lanka. Tourists flock to Barefoot to buy Barbara Sansoni's vibrant, multicoloured woven fabrics and lounge in the courtyard cafe behind the shop. They come to Gallery Café nearby, formerly Geoffrey Bawa's architectural practice. And as always, Galle Face Green is the most accurate barometer of the city's vigour. Here, boys fly kites, youths play cricket, couples court demurely on the esplanade, families frolic on the beach, stalls sell the local snack of *annasi* and *kadala* (pieces of pineapple and chickpeas, liberally sprinkled with salt and chilli) – just as they did in my childhood. The Green is no longer as green as it was back then, though.

These scenes I enjoy best when, twice a year, Colombo scintillates with night-time illuminations. Through the second half of December and early January, expat Sri Lankans fly back for the 'season' – Christmas and New Year holidays, family gatherings and endless rounds of parties. Humidity is low, and cool, salty breezes blow in from the ocean. Festive decorations light up the city at night. Incongruous-looking Santas, dark-brown faces smothered in snow-white beards, ring their bells in front of shops and in malls.

Then there is Vesak, the full-moon day in May which commemorates the Buddha's birth, enlightenment and death. Temples overflow with white-clad devotees, and *peraheras* (religious processions) take place around large temples, a festive throng of drummers, dancers and caparisoned elephants. Public buildings and private homes are strung with brightly lit paper lanterns. *Pandols* are mounted in prominent public spaces, large illustrations of the Jataka stories, relating the Buddha's past lives, in bright paint and encircled with neon lights. Buddhist associations and commercial organizations compete to sponsor the biggest, brightest and most elaborate pandols, prompting periodic complaints that Vesak, like Christmas and Christ, is becoming more about commerce and less about Buddhism. Still, for a week leading up to the big day, Colombo, and other cities and towns in Sinhala Sri Lanka, bathe and blaze in multicoloured night lights and street parties for ordinary folk, sanctified by religion and its rituals.

~

Mahinda Rajapaksa enjoyed an extended post-war honeymoon, which ended only in the months before his shock defeat in the presidential election on 8 January 2015. Most Sri Lankans, especially

Sinhala Buddhists, still credited him with winning the war and securing the peace. That included Colomboites, rich, poor and middle class, who could move about the city unobstructed by security checkpoints, without fear of bombs going off in office blocks, railway stations and bus stops.

Mahinda used this honeymoon to centralize power as never before. And power was a one-family affair. A quartet now ran Sri Lanka – the brothers Mahinda, Gotabhaya and Basil, and Mahinda's son and presumed successor, Namal. Then came an outer circle of numerous relatives and hangers-on. An overpowering Mahinda personality cult took hold. His presence was ubiquitous. Outsize posters and billboards displayed his perfectly coiffed, jet-black hair, his wide moustachioed grin, and his trademark crimson shawl draped over the national dress of long white banian and sarong. A giant billboard at the entrance to Katunayake airport depicted him thus, with the caption 'You are the Pride and Glory of the Nation'. The government's PR operation evidently had the image of Sinhala kingship in mind, and Mahinda as a reincarnation of Dutugemunu or Parakramabahu, redeeming and renewing Sinhala Buddhist civilization.

The Colombo media was not straitjacketed as it had been in the last few years of the war, but the atmosphere was still oppressive. Critical journalists and NGO workers were harassed and threatened. The occasional extrajudicial 'disappearance', to which the government turned a blind eye, continued to occur. The government and its business allies controlled Sinhala newspapers, radio and TV totally. Self-censorship was the norm, especially when covering the Rajapaksa family.

Decades of violent conflict had also transformed the military. The armed forces' budget and manpower did not decrease after the end of the war. The army went into business – in farming, roadside cafes and restaurants, hotels and construction. It even took charge of Colombo's beautification and gave compulsory 'leadership training' to university students. The air force went into hairdressing (a salon called 'The Clippers'), veterinary care (Sky Pet Animal Hospital), golf resorts and helicopter tours. The navy conducted whale-watching tours. Senior military officers were parachuted into state-owned enterprises, private companies and embassies abroad. Sri Lanka became the most militarized country in South Asia.

In the language of political science, Sri Lanka became an 'illiberal democracy' under the Rajapaksas. It was less like India and more like Russia and Venezuela. The president and his coalition were elected by popular vote. But individual rights and freedoms, an impartial rule of law, and checks and balances on power were another matter. All public institutions – the civil service, legislature, judiciary, police, military, local government, media, NGOs – became subordinate to the Rajapaksas. Politics infected everything, including business, schools, universities and hospitals; political connections were even used to rig beauty pageants.

The Rajapaksa government was never serious about genuine reconciliation with the Tamil minority. Rather, military victory and 'national reconciliation' were considered synonymous. Military victory made Sinhala Buddhist chauvinism shriller and more jingoistic. It pervaded Colombo conversations. Buddhism and the Sinhala race were visibly conjoined and wrapped up in the national flag. More outsize Buddha statues popped up, often next to national flags and patriotic slogans.

Most visibly, new militant monk-led organizations stormed on to the political stage. The Boddhu Bala Sena, or Army of Buddhist Power, was the most prominent. It targeted Muslims and Christians. It accused Muslim traders of commercial exploitation; and Muslims and Christians of religious fundamentalism, forcibly converting Buddhists, and generally attempting to destroy Buddhism in Sri Lanka. Monk-led mobs attacked mosques and Muslim shops, and even a few churches, in Colombo and elsewhere. The Boddhu Bala

Sena enjoyed the patronage of Gotabhaya Rajapaksa. Defeating the Tamil threat was not enough; Sinhala Buddhist Sri Lanka had to be protected from other predatory minorities as well.

The minorities' response to Sinhala chauvinism was to retreat into their fortresses. That was true of Sri Lankan Tamils, but I saw it also in my own Colombo Muslim community. In my childhood, Muslims had their separate religious and cultural traditions, and kept marriage within the community, but otherwise mixed well with Sinhalese, Tamils and Christians. But I noticed something had changed when I started coming back just over a decade ago, particularly with the generations after me – those now between their late teens and forties.

Colombo mosques became much bigger, including the Colpetty mosque where Daddy took me for Friday jumma prayers, as if to show non-Muslim Sri Lankans that we had wealth and power on our side. Many younger Muslims dressed differently, women in hijab and abaya, and even the niqab. This seemed to cut across the class divide: I saw it as much among the rich and upper middle class between Colpetty and Mount Lavinia as among the poor Slave Island Muslims who came to relax on Galle Face Green on weekday evenings and on weekends. Muslim children increasingly went to Muslim-only schools.

A new dour, segregationist minority took its cue from Wahhabi and Salafi strands of fundamentalist Islam. It denounced Sufism – the mystical branch of Islam with its galaxy of saints and shrines and itinerant singing, dancing bawas – as the practice of heretics and idolaters, and sought to rid Islam of South Indian 'impurities', such as the Tamil wedding custom of tying the *thaali* (usually a gold necklace) around the bride's neck. Such Muslims were quick to find fault, particularly with other Muslims who deviated from their 'pure' version of Islam – who sent their children to schools which included non-Muslims, whose womenfolk did not cover themselves, and who generally mixed too freely with non-Muslims. From a minority, with less than 10 per cent of Sri Lanka's population, these traits were a red rag to the Sinhala chauvinist bull.

I saw the same signs on my travels around the island, at its most extreme among Muslims on the east coast. It made me increasingly uneasy, fearing something nasty was brewing. But I had no idea it had already incubated a terrorist cell, linked to Islamic State, whose suicide bombers blasted three churches and three Colombo five-star hotels on Easter Sunday 2019, killing over 250 churchgoers, tourists and hotel staff.

～

The Rajapaksas made the most of the 'peace dividend' for which they gained credit after the war. Annual economic growth averaged about 6 per cent. Inflation and interest rates came down. Tourism boomed, with record arrivals year after year. Extreme poverty (those living on less than two dollars a day) came crashing down, and unemployment almost halved in a decade. With typical braggadocio, the Rajapaksa government advertised Sri Lanka as the 'Miracle of Asia' and the 'Emerging Wonder of Asia'. Morgan Stanley's Ruchir Sharma heralded Sri Lanka as a 'breakout nation', an imminent emerging market star.

It reminded me of women at Colombo society gatherings who slathered make-up on their puffy faces, layer upon thick layer, to mask blotchy, oily, pimpled skin, the result of lifetimes of pampered, over-indulgent living. Post-war economic growth was literally borrowed – increasingly from Chinese development banks and international capital markets – to finance runaway public expenditure on defence, infrastructure and lots of pet projects. The bloated public sector expanded further, crowding out the far more productive private sector.

The Rajapaksas' big-man politics and illiberal democracy seeped ever deeper into the economy; its glue was a parastatal network of insider politicians, favoured businessmen, senior military officers and Mafiosi. Like the media, leading businessmen were co-opted by a combination of fear and rewards: fear of ostracism or worse; and rewards of political patronage and commercial gain. Sri Lankan businessmen had always been good at 'doing puja' (performing ritual obeisance) to politicians. But it became especially craven under the Rajapaksas.

The Rajapaksa government also realigned Sri Lanka's international relations. Relations with the West chilled due to alleged human rights abuses, especially in the last stages of the war. The government delighted in thumbing its nose at the US and at European governments whenever they expressed public criticism. Relations with India remained ambivalent and testy. Harsh, melodramatic criticism came, as always, from Tamil Nadu, home to over sixty million Tamils in India.

But Sri Lanka gained new friends to replace old ones. These included Iran, Colonel Gaddafi's Libya, Russia, Pakistan and, above all, China, which emerged as 'first friend'. Pakistan and China supplied arms aplenty to finish the war. Chinese loans paid for new infrastructure and vanity projects; and Chinese state-owned enterprises were rewarded amply with infrastructure contracts. The Port City, Nelum Pokuna, the Lotus Pond arts centre, and Nelum Kuluna, the Lotus Tower, all were built with platoons of mainland Chinese workers. China's ascendancy also kept the Indian defence establishment awake at night, worried that Sri Lanka was now one of China's 'string of pearls' around India's neck.

~

Until the last quarter of 2014, the Rajapaksas seemed set to rule for years, if not decades. Flush with hubris, and on the advice of his astrologer, Mahinda Rajapaksa called a presidential election over two years before the end of his term. But nemesis followed, in the guise of an unassuming politician from his own ranks.

As soon as the election was called, the hitherto feeble and divided opposition rallied around a common presidential candidate. This was Maithripala Sirisena, a veteran SLFP politician, who, until the day he defected, was secretary general of the ruling party and minister of health in Mahinda's cabinet. He allied with the UNP and other opposition parties. Meanwhile, Ranil Wickremesinghe, the veteran UNP leader, and Chandrika Bandaranaike Kumaratunga, the former SLFP leader and Mahinda's predecessor as president, patched up their age-old enmity to unseat Mahinda. The opposition's common programme pledged *Yahalpalanaya*, 'good governance', to restore constitutional democracy and root out the corruption of the Rajapaksa years.

I met Ranil in Singapore a few days before Maithripala Sirisena's defection. Over dinner at the Singapore Cricket Club, Ranil talked grandly of the reforms he would initiate when he returned to office. At the time, I thought he was deluded. The Rajapaksas' lock on power was still unbreakable, I thought, and I wrote off Ranil as a spent force. But I knew nothing of Colombo backroom political manoeuvres.

In the preceding years I had been very critical of the Rajapaksa government, writing in local newspapers, and in occasional public lectures and TV interviews. During the campaign, I wrote a column in the *Wall Street Journal* calling for the end of Rajapaksa rule. Ranil quoted from it at a press conference; Sri Lanka's ambassador to the US, on behalf of the government, replied defensively and aggressively in the *Journal*'s letters page. A Sri Lankan English-language newspaper accused me of being a British spy 'of Sri Lankan

Muslim origin'. That, I must admit, is the closest I ever got to an association with James Bond.

Still, I sat out the election campaign in Singapore. The British high commissioner in Colombo advised me to stay away, at least until the election was over.

The election, on 8 January 2015, delivered a shock victory to Sirisena. The minorities – Tamils, Muslims and Christians – voted against the Sinhala Buddhist chauvinism to which the Rajapaksas pandered; Sinhala Buddhists voted against corruption and assorted abuses of power. The young and aspirational, fed up with quasi-feudal, dynastic politics, flocked to 'Maithri's' banner. If Mahinda had won, Sri Lanka would have slipped further into authoritarianism, Sinhala Buddhist chauvinism and ethnic strife, economic nationalism and dependence on China. So Maithri's victory was a golden and wholly unexpected opportunity for a fresh start – perhaps the best since the end of Mrs B's rule in 1977. Once again, Sri Lanka had the chance of a liberal efflorescence.

As the results rolled in, I also got caught up in new-found enthusiasm. But the words of my Colombo friend Tissa Jayatilaka kept reverberating in my mind. 'Sri Lanka has a history of missing buses,' Tissa told me, again and again over our periodic lunches. Would this time be different?

~

President Sirisena appointed Ranil Wickremesinghe as his new prime minister – Ranil's third go at the job. The new government – an SLFP president and a UNP-dominated cabinet – announced a hundred-day programme. At its core was constitutional and political reform. They intended to abolish the all-powerful executive presidency and restore a Westminster-style parliamentary system. They pledged to re-establish the independence of institutions such as the police, judiciary and public service, set up independent commissions to make public appointments, and introduce a Right to Information Bill. Parliament passed the Nineteenth Amendment to the Constitution, which curtailed the president's powers (though they remained significant), restored term limits, and increased the powers of the prime minister and cabinet.

Parliamentary elections in August 2015 confirmed the people's choice. For the first time since independence a national unity government was formed, comprising a UNP-led coalition and the Maithri faction of the SLFP. Never before had the UNP and SLFP been in government together. Ranil continued as prime minister.

Sri Lanka enjoyed a liberal political spring from January 2015. Some kinds of fear disappeared – fear of vilification, ostracism, and even physical harm and disappearance, if one criticized the government too loudly, and especially if one crossed a member of the Rajapaksa clan. Individuals spoke more freely. Civil society activists and NGOs breathed easier, and became more active. Gone were the pomp, gaudy glitz and imperious ways of Mahinda and his courtiers.

Symbolic steps were taken on the road to ethnic reconciliation. On National Day, less than a month after he was elected, President Sirisena read a 'peace pledge' in all three national languages, Sinhala, English and Tamil, expressing sorrow for *all* victims of the civil war. He replaced the governors of the northern and eastern provinces, both military men, with highly respected retired civil servants. The chief justice, a Rajapaksa lackey, was forced to resign. His successor was Tamil. The government pledged to restore land seized by the military in the north to its former owners, and to review the list of detainees held under the Prevention of Terrorism Act. The military presence in the north became much less obtrusive.

But Sri Lanka was still far away from genuine reconciliation. Substantial land restitution, devolving powers to provincial councils, reducing the military presence in the north and east, investigating and prosecuting wartime human rights abuses – these Tamil-minority issues remained stuck, unresolved. Sri Lanka's post-independence history is replete with false starts on this count. Every government in Colombo has to watch out for a backlash in the Sinhala Buddhist heartland.

The unity government quickly mended relations with the US, Europe and India. But money talked: Chinese state-backed projects were the only really big investments in Sri Lanka, and the government owed China at least $8 billion in loans. China remained 'first friend'. Economic growth plummeted to just above 3 per cent a year. Fiscal incontinence continued, with public sector salary hikes and other new spending entitlements, leading to more foreign commercial borrowing, and then a new IMF loan to prevent another balance of payments crisis.

The government was consumed by corruption scandals, shambolic decision-making, a breakdown in relations between the president and prime minister, and between the UNP and the Maithri faction of the SLFP. That led President Sirisena to sack Ranil as prime minister in October 2018 and appoint Mahinda in his place. But Mahinda could not secure a parliamentary majority, and the Supreme Court ruled the president's action unconstitutional, thereby restoring Ranil to the premiership.

~

Colombo is many things to me: childhood, absence and return; the ocean and sea breezes; its still-abundant green spaces – Galle Face Green, Viharamahadevi Park, the many school and club cricket and rugger grounds that occupy so much of Colpetty and Cinnamon Gardens; its architectural hotchpotch of colonial buildings and modern shopping malls, old and new hotels, grand old Colpetty and Cinnamon Gardens houses, new luxury condos, and the poky dwellings where the poor huddle in Slave Island, Maligawatta, Mattakkuliya, Kochchikade, Kotahena and Grandpass. But, above all, my Colombo is about people and encounters. In Sri Lanka there is a 'character' around every street corner, a writer's dream; in Colombo, there is one in every house and every office. My Colombo characters are a tropical kaleidoscope of Sinhalese, Tamils and Burghers; Buddhists, Hindus, Christians and Muslims; plus an occasional agnostic and atheist for good measure.

I will start with my relatives and be selective and brief, for fear of being declared an outcast in Colpetty, Bambalapitiya and Mount Lavinia. Mine is a family of non-stop talkers – hardly exceptional in Sri Lanka. Many relatives remind me of Michael Ondaatje's mother: 'She belonged to a type of Ceylonese family whose women would take the minutest reaction from another and blow it up into a tremendously exciting tale, then later use it as an example of someone's stain of character. If anything kept their generation alive, it was this recording by exaggeration.'

My cousin Rifky has, from pre-teen childhood, had a nice line in ripping yarns. The ones I enjoy most he collected long ago from Daddy, Uncle Razeen and their siblings about their Badulla childhood. These stories of yesteryear, no doubt embellished over the decades, he recounts with the force of his large, dark frame, vivifying narrative twists and turns with practised facial and gesticulatory animation. I picture him telling his tale while a factotum massages his legs and feet vigorously. The tale is long and meandering, punctuated by Rifky's grimaces and elongated gasps of 'Ahhhh' when the masseur's fingertips probe a sensitive spot. But he is in full flow – not to be deterred: the tale continues to its inevitably absurd, hilarious conclusion.

Then there is Rifky's sister Kyria, whose childhood expression, 'If you don't know don't talk,' has stayed in my mind all these years.

'So when are you going to get married, men?' she used to ask me, admonishingly, with mock exasperation, whenever I saw her. 'Aiyo, how boring,' she replied to my stock non-committal answer, with an upturned nose and a dismissive wave of her hand. But she stopped asking me that question when, eventually, she saw no prospect of a change in my circumstances.

Faraz, another cousin, is a well-known Colombo TV journalist. He was matchstick-thin in our childhood. Now, in middle age, his face and girth are very generously proportioned. He appears on his talk show bespectacled and snappily attired in a bold pinstripe shirt, tie and suspenders, rather like CNN's Larry King in the 1990s and early 2000s. There he opines forcefully and grills his politician interviewees vigorously, sometimes aggressively.

On Valentine's Day 2013, three thugs barged into Faraz's bedroom, shot him in the neck and ran away. He survived, narrowly: foreign guests staying with him drove him to hospital just before he lost too much blood. It was all over the local news, and even reported on the BBC. President Rajapaksa assigned a police guard outside his hospital room. When he had recovered sufficiently, he retreated to the safety of Colwyn Bay, North Wales, where his family lives ten minutes' walk from my family home. In Colwyn Bay he marked time, bored, far away from Sri Lanka, itching to get back, despite the danger.

In more ways than one, Faraz reminds me of my father. Like Daddy, Faraz loves to tell a tale. In temporary Welsh exile, only a few months after his dance with death, he popped round almost daily to see Mummy. One evening, when I was home, too, he gave us his version of the shooting. One assailant tried to suffocate him with a pillow while another strangled him from behind and the third aimed the pistol at his forehead. 'And still they bungled it,' he said incredulously. He was neither successfully suffocated nor strangled, and the bullet, fired inches from his forehead, lodged non-fatally in his neck. 'Typical Sri Lankan incompetence,' Faraz concluded. How can such a country hope to get anything right?

~

Three years ago, I gave a talk on the Sri Lankan economy and its prospects to a group of youngish senior executives from Sri Lanka's most reputed family-run businesses; they are the generation who will take over their fathers' and uncles' businesses. We gathered in a meeting room at Galle Face Hotel. There must have been just over twenty round the table that evening. I did some quick, silent ethnic profiling. About fifteen were Sindhis, Borhas and Memons. There was one Parsi, one or two Tamils, and two or three Sinhala Christians, but only a couple of Sinhala Buddhists. That was fairly representative. Most of Sri Lanka's successful, genuinely entrepreneurial companies are owned and run by its ethnic minorities.

Colombo's minority trading castes – Sindhis, Dawoodi Borhas, Khojas (Ismailis), Memons and Parsis – really do stand out. Their numbers are tiny – perhaps 5000 to 10,000 in all. Sindhis are Hindus; Borhas and Khojas are offshoots of Shia Islam; Memons a minuscule branch of Sunni Islam; and Parsis are, well, Parsis. All form tight-knit communities of extended families, embedded in worldwide community networks that are good for business and serve as intramural marriage markets. They keep a low profile, generally avoiding political involvement. They do not flaunt their wealth. Their children, including, in the last couple of generations, their daughters, go to the best universities abroad before returning to the family business.

Soli Captain, a Parsi, is Sri Lanka's second-richest man, putting a few politicians to one side. He is the main single shareholder in John Keells, the country's leading conglomerate. Borhas, Sindhis and

Parsis own corporate brands familiar to Sri Lankans: Abans for white goods, Chands for sports goods, Akbar Brothers for tea, Hemas for hospitals. Four family-run companies, MAS, Hirdaramani, Brandix and Timex, dominate Sri Lanka's garment industry, its outstanding export performer since the 1980s. The first two are Sindhi-owned, the third and fourth Memon-owned. They are hardy survivors of Sri Lanka's political turbulence, ethnic war, inflation, rigid labour laws, erratic electricity, Byzantine bureaucracy, high and unpredictable taxes, and corruption. They are oases of world-class efficiency. They have internationalized, offshoring much of their cheap labour production to Bangladesh and Vietnam. Their industry association, the Joint Apparel Association Forum, is by far Sri Lanka's most effective business lobby.

Hanif Yusoof is the CEO of Expolanka, Sri Lanka's leading logistics company, specializing in freight forwarding and supply chain management. He is a Memon. When I visited him in his office he was dressed exactly like his staff, in black pants and black polo shirt with the company logo. We were supposed to talk about the local shipping industry, but something in his round, bearded face – perhaps the soft, liquid eyes and kindly smile – told me he was in the mood to talk of other things besides. We started with shipping and logistics, but before long Hanif moved on to his family history, the state of Islam in Sri Lanka, and what it meant to be Sri Lankan.

Hanif's Memon forefathers came from Porbandar in Gujarat, where Mahatma Gandhi was born and raised. His family faced threats from local Hindus during Partition in 1947. That prompted his father to decamp to Colombo, where he had a relative, to set himself up in business. But his fortunes hit rock bottom by the late 1970s, and he died aged only fifty-two. Hanif had to give up higher education to deal with creditors and provide for the family. Soon after, he borrowed 25,000 rupees to start Expolanka; another Memon family came in as investors. Thirty years and 3000 employees later he sold the company to a Japanese multinational, staying on as its CEO 'to take us global'. 'My ambition,' he said, 'is to create Sri Lanka's first global company.'

Hanif wanted the government to open up the local shipping industry to international competition, so Sri Lanka could become South Asia's shipping and logistics hub, halfway between Singapore and Dubai. 'I'm happy to have the big guys come in and eat into my local market share. If we become a hub, that will be my platform to take Expolanka global and compete with the big guys internationally.'

The first thing that struck me, listening to Hanif, was how different his outlook was, compared with that of other Sri Lankan corporate captains. His counterparts in the local shipping and logistics sectors lobbied the government to keep foreign competition out, or only allow it in through limited joint ventures controlled by local business houses. Hanif had visions of something bigger and better; a comfortable status quo frustrated him intensely. I couldn't help thinking he must have an entrepreneurial gene, conditioned in his family and the Memon community over generations and centuries – a gene his fellow businessmen clearly lacked.

The economist Joseph Schumpeter said the most successful entrepreneurs have complex motives. 'Animal spirits' drive them, but these cannot be reduced to a narrow, all-consuming desire to make money through rational calculation and what economists call 'utility maximization'. So it is with Hanif. Somehow our conversation crossed the line from business and economics to religion and culture.

Hanif is a practising Muslim, and his spirituality infused much of what he told me. But he had no problem reconciling his Islam with modern life, and particularly a shared understanding with Sri Lanka's other religions. To begin with, his wife is a Burgher. While other Sri Lankan Muslims succumbed to Wahhabism and Salafism,

shrouded their girls and women in black from head to toe, erected
walls against non-Muslims, and attacked Sufism and other 'deviant'
practices within Islam, Hanif spent time and money to promote
interfaith understanding.

His eyes lit up and his smile broadened when he talked about
sponsoring a Sufi festival in Galle, in which a Buddhist monk
participated. To him these cross-faith encounters were the essence
of being Sri Lankan: 'putting Sri Lanka first' in his language.
Colombo's minority trading castes shy away from controversial
public issues: this must be an ancient instinct. But Hanif felt too
strongly about this pet issue – the heart and soul of Sri Lankan
identity – to keep quiet and just go on making money.

~

If I had grown up elsewhere, I probably would not have met as many
politicians as I have. But I met several in my childhood Colombo.
Daddy had friends and acquaintances in the UNP, including a
few Muslim politicians, but also on the far left, including the JVP
rebels he befriended in the remand wing of Welikada jail. Other
political bigwigs I had not met, especially Mrs B and members of
her government, hulked in my pre-teen imagination as omnipotent
Molochs, destroying and devouring everything in their path.

Before independence, the dominant Colombo political type
was the 'brown sahib' – the landowning patrician, Ceylonese
on the outside, British on the inside. Such coconut-brown types
commanded politics well into the 1960s and 1970s. The assassinated
SWRD Bandaranaike was a prominent example; J.R. Jayewardene
was the last to ascend to the very top. His enemies accuse Ranil
Wickremesinghe of being the last brown sahib, though he doesn't
quite fit.

I cannot recall meeting many brown sahib politicos in my

childhood – just one or two from the Communist Party and the Trotskyist Lanka Sama Samaja Party (LSSP) who lived in Cinnamon Gardens bungalows, patronized Daddy's clubs and preached class revolution. The breed is now near extinct. A few epigonal versions survive – less than a handful – not in positions of great power, but enjoying its baubles nevertheless.

Of these, Professor G.L. Peiris is perhaps the most prominent. He was a Rhodes scholar at Oxford, a law professor and later vice chancellor of the University of Colombo, and entered politics in the 1990s. He held several ministerial portfolios in Chandrika Bandaranaike Kumaratunga's government, then defected to the UNP and was Ranil Wickremesinghe's chief negotiator in peace talks with the LTTE, before defecting again, this time to Mahinda Rajapaksa and serving as his foreign minister. Now he is chairman of Sri Lanka Podujana Peramuna, Mahinda's vehicle to return to power at the next general elections.

Professor Peiris catapulted himself from negotiating peace with the LTTE to prosecuting all-out war to defeat them. At a time when most Sri Lankan politicians speak appalling English, men like him stick out with their intelligible, grammatically correct sentences. Hence the Rajapaksa government, not famed for its English-language competence or Western graduate polish, trotted Professor Peiris out to defend its case in international official forums, and on the BBC and CNN. But this type is now a mere appurtenance, addicted to the backside smell of power; the real thing escaped its clutches long ago.

A different but related political type – a generic son or daughter of the brown sahib – only slightly larger in number, is more Sri Lankan on the inside, with a coating of education and polish. They are also children of landowning privilege, speak English at home and with their social equals but Sinhalese with the lower orders, and also consider themselves born to rule. Ranil and Chandrika, both products of political dynasties, were conditioned into this worldview from the cradle. Some were educated abroad; a few, like Chandrika, had their youthful left-wing ideology burnished in Paris in the 1960s and 1970s. But this type is also dwindling closer to extinction, and Ranil may be the last of the line.

Now the more familiar political type is the home-grown Sinhala 'big man'. He comes from the second-tier cities and towns of the Sinhala Buddhist heartland. He may be self-made, a first-generation politician, but often he comes from an established local political family, a pillar of the small-town bourgeoisie. He speaks Sinhala at home, with friends and at work – with fellow politicians, civil servants, businessmen, minions and constituents. He is not well educated or outwardly polished. The Rajapaksas and their circle fit this type, more or less, and so does President Sirisena, who comes from Polonnaruwa district in north-central Sri Lanka and does not speak English, either in private or in public.

Some years back, during Mahinda's presidency, a rich cousin invited me to dinner at his house in Colpetty. When I turned up, there were a dozen jeeps parked outside; in his front yard were at least twenty armed bodyguards, a mix of policemen and soldiers. Inside Fawzi, my cousin, had a VIP guest, a prominent cabinet minister. I will call him 'X'.

Minister X swaggered from the sitting room to the dining table. He was fat, seasoned by power and its perquisites; dissolute living was written all over his face. He was bejewelled: a gold watch, gold chains and gold rings, studded with precious stones, adorned his thick wrists and pudgy fingers. His hair was dyed jet-black. Over dinner, he regaled us with stories of power: how he helped Mahinda win the war, and the famous statesmen he had met on numerous official trips overseas. His flunkeys around the table, all political advisers attached to his ministry, nodded vigorously, donkey-like, in assent at his every word and laughed loudly at his attempted witticisms. Fawzi kept addressing him as 'Honourable Dr X'. X was a high-school graduate, but he did have an honorary doctorate from a Sri Lankan university.

Minister X reminded me of the typical look of Sri Lankan politicians on posters and billboards that litter roadsides all over the island. They are men in customary pure-white sarongs, never trousers. They are nearly all overweight or obese with jet-black hair. They take care to visit temples and be seen in the company of monks. Their gaze down on passing pedestrians and motorists is invariably smug. The Rajapaksas and their acolytes projected this billboard persona; Mahinda himself radiated all-knowing, far-seeing confidence from his billboards, and visibly expanded, physically, the longer he remained in supreme power.

Harry Hopkins, the journalist who visited Ceylon in the early 1950s, had this to say about the Burmese character in the early years of independence after British rule:

> A taste for melodramatics, the juvenile striking of poses, the individualism that turns to dacoity or political privateering, the oversensitive national pride that becomes first a morbid resentment of all criticism, then xenophobia . . . It all added up rather disastrously to a tendency to anarchism, to a preference of the florid gesture to the dreary but effective business of getting down to the job.

He could have been speaking of Sri Lankan politicians. The exceptions are all too few.

~

My favourite Colombo characters are a mix of friends and local heroes. They show the better human side of Sri Lanka; my Colombo would not be complete without them.

Charmaine is a Dutch Burgher. She speaks correct, clipped, Received Pronunciation English. Her look and tone are authoritative; she does not suffer fools gladly. With a cigarette at hand, the message she signals is 'don't mess with me'. A beauty in her day, she harks back to the 'good old days' – when Sri Lanka was Ceylon. She knows her Burgher cooking. Her speciality, *lamprais* (correctly pronounced 'lampraai'), is rice boiled in stock with a special curry, accompanied by cutlets, all wrapped in a banana leaf and baked in the oven. This laborious process she performs daily, early in the morning, for her lamprais is the most popular dish at the Dutch Burgher Union, the citadel of what remains of Burgher society in Colombo. She cooked it on TV for Anthony Bourdain, the globetrotting celebrity chef, and refused to give him her grandmother's recipe.

Charmaine has firm views. 'Sri Lankan men are hopeless, Razeen,' she declares, puffing intently on her cigarette. 'They are so boring these days. All they do is talk about work and get drunk.' 'Firm but fair' is how I would describe Charmaine. No doubt those who get on her wrong side would describe her as forbidding, especially if they have been on the receiving end of one of her withering looks or put-downs.

But Charmaine has a very soft side. Her governing passion is animals. Sri Lanka is one of those poor countries where animals are treated cruelly; the Buddhist injunction to respect all living beings does not seem to make any difference. Charmaine is a veteran animal welfare campaigner. Just outside Colombo, she has a small property where she keeps well over a hundred dogs and cats (in separate sections, of course), strays she has rescued and rehabilitated. 'It's the animals that keep me here, Razeen. Otherwise I would have joined my relatives in Australia. Besides, over there I'd miss nature here – the birds, the trees, the low-country vegetation – and my home comforts. No loyal helper to make my morning tea over there, you know.'

Last Christmas season I popped over to Charmaine's to collect two large Christmas puddings to take upcountry the following day. I found her slouched in her favourite *hansi putuwa* (a local reclining armchair) in her TV room, binge-watching Netflix. She looked wan and dejected, recovering from a bout of heavy flu and pneumonia, unable to puff on her cigarettes and missing her beloved Sunday poker game. Two days later, on Christmas night, high up in the Uva hills, Mummy, some friends and I polished off the richest, most scrumptious Christmas pudding I have ever tasted, jam-packed with succulent fruit and probably marinated in a fair amount of alcohol. It dissolved on my tongue like the best quality butter or honey. In a warm glow of Yuletide good cheer on that cool, clear upcountry night, I thought of Charmaine and her old-fashioned Burgher ways and her animals, and wished her a speedy recovery.

'Tissera' was his family name, what we all called him; in all the decades I knew him I never got to know his first name. He was our family driver in the 1970s, devoted to Daddy; we missed him much when he had to leave us to work elsewhere.

Tissera was a fixture of my childhood Colombo. He drove me to and from school, Mount Lavinia Hotel and the Cabanas; he drove Mummy into town for shopping, and all of us on our Colombo house calls to relatives and friends; he drove us to visit Daddy when he was locked up at CID HQ, the Paget Road House and Welikada jail. He drove us to Razeena estate and back the year Daddy was jailed, when Mummy homeschooled Reyaz and me. He was always lean and wiry, with skeletal forearms and wrists. But he had a huge appetite, effortlessly levelling a mountain of rice on his lunchtime plate. In his prime he had the spare, stripped-down springy look of the long-distance runner, and a pencil moustache to match.

Back in 1971, when the CID came home and took Daddy away, the local police took Tissera to Mount Lavinia police station and beat him up, hoping to extract information on Daddy. They never laid a hand on Daddy, given his status and connections, so they picked on poor Tissera instead. At one point they drilled a pencil into his ear, puncturing his eardrum. His hearing got gradually worse over the next three decades, until it was extinguished.

Over the past decade I visited Tissera and his family – his wife, son, daughter-in-law and two teenage grandchildren – in his small, sparsely furnished house in a poor Ratmalana neighbourhood, and made a special point of taking Mummy to see him on her annual visit. Usually I called ahead to say we were coming. As we turned into Tissera's lane there he was, in his neat shirt and sarong, standing outside his door waiting for us. Now in his seventies, he was still lean and wiry, but he looked his age and more, his face wizened and his hair and moustache gone completely grey. He was housebound, stone deaf, and had dizzy spells if he walked outside for too long; he spent his days reading the newspaper from cover to cover.

Once inside, we communicated through gesticulation and scribbling notes on scraps of paper. Mummy wrote down family news from England – of Reyaz and Roshan and their families – and of Colombo relatives, and showed him recent photos. I could see Tissera transported back to his time with us in the 1970s, remembering people and places of yesteryear. Occasionally he would ask a question about someone in his now croaky voice, speaking the English he once spoke daily but now only on our annual or biannual visits. When we said our farewells he always gave me a hug, and teared up.

We saw him for the last time in February 2018. He was critically ill, having caught meningitis, and had been in and out of hospital for a month. We saw him at home. He was in bed, shrivelled down to sagging skin and bone, coughing and wheezing constantly, gasping for air and spitting out thick phlegm from his lungs. He was in great pain, and clearly could not talk, but he still motioned to his family, repeatedly, to get drinks for Mummy and me. His condition was so bad his son had to call an emergency doctor, and an hour later he was taken back to hospital.

Tissera died a few weeks later. I always thought of Tissera, and his sweet, loyal, rock-solid wife, as simple, decent Sinhalese – the best of the Sinhala Buddhist heartland, always smiling, warm and giving. One more fixture of my childhood had departed, no longer stepping on Colombo's pavements or breathing its sea air.

Vasantha is my favourite Colombo journalist. He is sparky and articulate, his writing direct and punchy. He is a model journalist, born to speak truth to power. Journalists are paid badly in Sri Lanka, and their social standing is not what it used to be. But Vasantha does the job for the love of it. His choice of profession, though, was just about the most frustrating and dangerous during the Rajapaksa years. It certainly was to Vasantha, who wrote long, detailed investigative stories that exposed corruption and assorted abuses of power.

Before the change of government in 2015, Vasantha vented his frustration to me whenever he held his punches and censored himself on this or that story, especially ones that touched on the ruling family. Then he felt soiled, not living up to his principles. But he had a wife and three small children to think of. Once we met soon after he had come back from a trip to the north, about two years after the war ended. He had story after story of poverty, homelessness, rape and damaged mental health. Compared with that, 'the beautification of Colombo means nothing, nothing to me', he said. The last time we met during the Rajapaksa years he confessed to being 'really depressed . . . They know how to get to you.' He thought he saw police detectives parked outside his house. Other detectives had been to see his parents in Galle and inquired about his personal finances.

Vasantha and his tribe breathe easier since 2015. Vasantha got a promotion and is now a respected senior journalist. But will it last? If the Rajapaksas, or another 'big man' in their mould, regain power, won't they clamp down on journalists the way they did before? And maybe worse next time – 'like a boot stamping on a human face', in George Orwell's immortal words? I don't know what will happen to Vasantha then.

Ranjini belongs to the Colombo 'middle-middle' class. Her father is a retired mid-ranking civil servant, and her mother a retired government schoolteacher; Ranjini herself is a private sector economist. She has a wide outlook on her country and the world, but her ways are those of the sweet, innocent small-town girl – nothing of the pretentious urban sophisticate in her. That is no accident, for Ranjini grew up outside Colombo. Her English is fluent and lively, delivered in a girlish high pitch, always smiling. But Sinhala is her mother tongue, what she speaks at home with her husband and relatives.

Economists' shop talk fills much of our lunch conversations – Ranjini is one of my go-to people on the Sri Lankan economy. But more revealing for me are her thoughts on Sri Lankan society and culture. Like my friend Charmaine, she thinks Sri Lankan men are hopeless, unless they have a strong female authority figure at home – a mother, wife or elder sister – to lean on and prop them up. 'The problem, Razeen, begins in childhood. Sons are thoroughly spoilt by their mothers, while the daughters get firm discipline and help with housework. So the boys grow up to be arrogant and incapable, bossing everyone around and expecting everything to be done for them. And so the cycle continues.'

A subject that interests us both is that of rural Sri Lankan girls and women who go abroad to work as housemaids, mainly in the Middle East. Ranjini tells me this is not just for money. 'They could get decent wages as domestics in Colombo or as trained machine operators in a garment factory, instead of going for years to an unknown land, facing unknown risks. But Sri Lankans are very status-conscious, even in the village. A maid will sacrifice two years abroad in order to come back for one month, when she will be queen of the village. She's the centre of attention; she showers presents on family and friends. In her mind, doing shift work in a garment factory is inferior, demeaning.'

In a land full of fake Buddhists, Ranjini is the real thing. She cleaves to the Buddha's philosophy: live a simple life, do not get attached to material things, do good. She shuns elaborate temple rituals and pampered monks. She abhors the money and politics that have polluted organized Buddhism. To me she represents the better face of Sinhala Buddhism, rooted in her culture, language and religion, but without a smidgen of communalism.

I visited Ranjini and her husband Chaminda at home in Gampaha district, about an hour's drive from Colombo off the Kandy road. Gampaha town is a sprawling little city now, but its surrounding district still has little villages in lush low-country vegetation. The town and district are close to Colombo as the crow flies, but mentally much further away. Colombo is multi-racial, multi-religious and polyglot; on the sea, it looks out to the world (though not nearly as much as it should). Gampaha is overwhelmingly Sinhala Buddhist, with few traces of the minorities, especially Tamils; Sinhalese is all one hears on its streets and country lanes. It looks inland, to Sri Lanka's interior, not to the sea and the world beyond.

Ranjini and Chaminda live away from Gampaha town, next to paddy fields, surrounded by coconut trees and twittering birds. A little village temple, with a small white stupa at its centre, is just down the road. Chaminda greeted me with a shy smile. Ranjini told me she was learning Tamil; Chaminda showed me his photos of birds. Ranjini said Chaminda, like most Sri Lankan men, was hopeless in the home. 'He doesn't know how to operate the washing machine,' she said. On weekends he still had his meals at his parents' house, a few minutes' walk up their road.

'There's a lot of indolence, drunkenness and cockeyed priorities,' Ranjini said of life in the village. 'I know a woman, totally destitute. She came to me asking for a big loan for her daughter's wedding. So you see, she was willing to beg and borrow to spend 50,000 rupees on one day's festivities.' She added, 'In Gampaha town, the Sinhala shopkeepers drove out their Tamil competitors in '83; they still prevent non-Sinhalese from setting up shops in town. But a lot of people go to shop in a Muslim village nearby; there they get good service. Sinhalese have no idea of service, unlike the minorities.'

Chaminda said there was little criminality in the village; people left their doors unlocked. 'That is because all the criminals are at the top of society, not at the bottom,' he added with his shy smile.

Gilbert Paranagama was one of Daddy's closest friends – perhaps his closest, longest-lasting friend outside his circle of air force buddies. Uncle Gilbert was perhaps the most decent adult I knew in my childhood. He hailed from Kandyan nobility. His wife, Aunty Krishni, came from an almost identical background: they were cousins, and she was a Ratwatte, a close relative of Mrs Bandaranaike. She and her daughters, with their moon faces, strikingly resemble Mrs B and her daughter Chandrika; Nandanie, the youngest daughter, was for a time Mrs B's private secretary. They are a devout Buddhist family, with strong Kandyan traditions. Nandanie, bless her, introduced me to Buddhist meditation. They live simply, unshowily. Our families have been firm friends since the 1960s.

Uncle Gilbert schooled at Trinity College, Kandy, the hill country equivalent of Royal College and St Thomas' College in Colombo. Three-quarters of a century later he is still remembered there, for he won Trinity's Ryde Gold Medal for 'Best All-Round Boy' – its highest honour – in 1942. (Kumar Sangakkara, Sri Lanka's cricket legend, won it in 1996.) Soon after independence, he was in the first batch of University of Ceylon students to move to the new Peradeniya campus, just outside Kandy. Later he was prominent in Colombo corporate life as a senior director of an old British trading house. Daddy made him a director of Mount Lavinia Hotel; from then on they became the fondest of friends.

Uncle Gilbert had a reputation for unfailing honesty, fairness and humanity; good manners, grace and warmth were his hallmarks. He was always sweet and avuncular with my brothers and me. He and his family were among the few who stood by us during Daddy's Calvary in the 1970s. While others shunned us, the Paranagama home was always open, warm and welcoming. As a child I always looked forward to visiting them. Aunty Krishni made English-style finger sandwiches and Sinhala sweets of *kokis* and *mung kevum*. Avuruddu – Sinhala New Year – which falls in April, was a special treat; in the morning the family lit their ceremonial oil lamp, boiled milk in a large clay pot till it overflowed and served a huge spread of Sinhala sweets.

After Daddy died, Mummy and I kept going back to see the Paranagamas, though Uncle Gilbert was now an invalid, mostly confined to his room and sleeping much of the day. We reminisced about the old days – Sunday sea-baths at Mount Lavinia Hotel and seafood lunches on the beach; Daddy's non-stop smoking and how he was constantly on the telephone; his hours-long chats with Uncle Gilbert in the Paranagama sitting room.

Uncle Gilbert died a few years ago after a long illness, and Aunty Krishni followed him in 2017. The last time Mummy and I saw Uncle Gilbert he was wheelchair-bound, almost blind, his eyes wandering aimlessly; his hand kept moving to slap his chest and stroke back his hair. His dementia was already advanced. The family had not told him Daddy had died almost a decade earlier. I held his hand. He smiled seraphically when he recognized Mummy and me, in the fleeting moments when his mind switched on. But he kept asking about Daddy: 'Where is Farouk?'

Vinita was Indian, raised in a military family in Delhi and cantonments elsewhere round the country. She married Sarath, a Sri Lankan, and came to live in Colombo in the late 1970s. I met her first in December 2006, when I started coming back to Sri Lanka. Then she was full of life. She had a rich speaking voice and that cut-glass, mellifluous, wonderfully expressive English one comes across in the well-heeled colonies of South Delhi. She was very active in charity work and delighted in the company of children; that was when her face and eyes lit up.

A year later, Vinita was limping slightly; her fingers and toes curled inwards, and her speech slurred a little. Two years afterwards, she could barely walk or speak; she had to take her food in liquid form through a straw. And two years later she was housebound, imprisoned in a wheelchair, skeletal, her complexion turned pallid-brown, almost off-white, from lack of sunlight. She had lost her voice and could only speak through a voice machine; she called it Winston – she thought it made her sound like Winston Churchill. Then her hands became totally rigid and she had to give up Winston. For her last five years she was bedridden, her body frozen, her mouth agape, her eyes blank; she could only breathe through a ventilator. Sarath cared for her at home, devotedly and stoically; four nurses took it in turns, two at a time, to minister to her round the clock. Vinita suffered from Lou Gehrig's disease, a degenerative motor neuron disorder; Stephen Hawking was a fellow sufferer. Stephen Hawking lived with it for a half-century; for some sufferers it is over in two or three years. For Vinita it took a decade, for the second half of which she could not twitch the slightest muscle.

Before she lost all movement, Sarath and friends helped Vinita put a little book together; *Go Slowly Lovely Moon* is its title. In it Vinita recounts her life in India, how she met Sarath, what she made of family life in Sri Lanka, and how she got used to Sri Lankan English expressions such as 'bugger', 'body wash' and the obligatory prefix of 'put a . . .' (as in 'put a walk', 'put a sleep' and 'put a body wash'). Her book's highlight is her credo of living in the present, thanking God for what she has, always seeing the good in people. As she writes, 'The moon is lovely but I also know it will move across the sky and vanish in the West. I only want it to go slow. Don't we all?'

Chandra is a retired corporate captain, a former CEO of a large insurance house and a former chairman of the Ceylon Chamber of Commerce. He and his wife Rohana live comfortably in Colombo. They could easily have a retirement life in clover, complete with large house, cars, servants, clubs and parties. But that is not what animates Chandra. He is an indefatigable citizen-activist, a one-man NGO. And a true patriot: he loves his country and wants the best for its people. Gross public failure – the degeneration of Sri Lanka's institutions, its rotten public life, cronyism in business, human rights abuses, politically orchestrated ethnic conflict – appals him. But armchair criticism is not what he does. Rather, he fires off public letters to persons in authority, exposes high-level corruption and nepotism, organizes good works, and gets people together to discuss problems and find solutions. He goes out of his way to help people individually, always with courtesy and a smile, never with a hint of ego.

Chandra puts his neck on the line, and did so even in the Rajapaksa years, when others kept quiet, conformed and collaborated. Then he convened the Friday Forum, a group of like-minded professionals and citizen-activists. They shone a light on sensitive issues a cowed media generally shied away from: government corruption and public sector mismanagement; the plight of poor, war-damaged civilians in the north and east; the government's oppression of the media, judiciary and other public institutions; its pandering of Sinhala Buddhist chauvinists, including troublemaking monks, who used incendiary language and incited violence. And Chandra kept berating his fellow corporate captains for keeping quiet and looking the other way; worse, he said, they brazenly kowtowed to the Rajapaksas, soliciting lucrative business deals.

Chandra, like other Colombo liberals, celebrated the end of Rajapaksa rule in January 2015. But he also found new crimes and misdemeanours to expose, new causes to defend. Those guilty of gross corruption during the Rajapaksa years had to be brought to justice. And there were new corruption scandals, starting with two central bank bond auctions hijacked by a huge insider trading operation. The new government came to power on their Yahalpalanaya or 'good governance' platform, but new cronies merely replaced old cronies. Chandra continued to fire off public letters to the president, prime minister and ministers, petition for information under the new Right to Information Act, and write and talk in the media. He is a walking, talking definition of civic courage.

Dil and Elmo are the best-matched couple I know, and they have the most wholesome family I know. They are a study in contrasts, but complement each other beautifully.

Elmo is exuberant, witty, loquacious, with a very Sri Lankan way with words, full of tropical light and colour. He is a whirlwind of energy, but always seems unselfconscious and relaxed even when he is frenetically busy. He is endlessly curious about people and places. And he is a born communicator, with an uncanny ability to connect with people from all walks of life. I have seen him do it so often: make direct eye contact with his dancing, twinkling eyes; initiate conversations with strangers, showing he is interested in them, putting them at ease, making them feel special; captivating an audience, small or large, with stories they relate to instinctively.

Dil is also a practical, can-do type. Like her husband, she is busy from early morning, with too many things to do in a single day. But she is different in every other respect. She is a worrier, a perfectionist, a details person, backroom organizer and administrator, not someone who commands the stage and wows the crowd. And she is a Christian with deep faith; it governs and suffuses everything she does, from caring for her family and friends to helping strangers in need. The word 'saintly' comes to mind, blasphemous though she may consider it. What unites Elmo and Dil, beyond love of family and friends, is a rare calling to help people in need, and a blessed talent to relate to the poverty-stricken and scarred. For Dil, it is her Lord's will, His purpose for her earthly life.

Dil and Elmo have travelled far in life. Both grew up modestly in Colombo's Christian suburb of Moratuwa. They met and married in their early twenties. Elmo put himself through flight training school, following in his pilot father's footsteps. Dil worked as a secretary and kept house. Elmo became a senior pilot, first with Air Lanka and then with Singapore Airlines. In middle age, he turned writer, fulfilling a boyhood dream, for he grew up devouring English literature. He wrote on his Singapore Airlines flight layovers in cities all over the world. Several books have flowed from his pen: a mammoth historical novel on the last days of the Kandyan kingdom, a novella, a collection of short stories, a coffee-table travel guide to Sri Lanka, a history of Sri Lankan civil aviation. He writes as he speaks: spontaneously, passionately, lushly, sometimes lyrically. Literary prizes have followed: the Gratiaen Prize, endowed by Michael Ondaatje for Sri Lankan English writing, and the State Literary Award for Lifetime Achievement.

Just over twenty years ago, Dil and Elmo and a small band of friends founded what is now Candle Aid, which does humanitarian work all over Sri Lanka. That is how I first met them, in Singapore, over a decade ago, just before Elmo retired from Singapore Airlines and they moved back to Sri Lanka. Aviation and writing were Elmo's childhood dreams. Starting an organization to help the poor and downtrodden and left-behind they had come across in Moratuwa and around Sri Lanka was the dream he shared with Dil.

Candle Aid is not a typical NGO. It does not have the bureaucracy, politics and gross waste of big international NGOs, nor is it like so many local organizations dining off foreign governments and international aid organizations, nor yet a token operation run by socialites and part-time philanthropists. Rather it brings together committed people, island-wide, who make time to do practical good in any way they can, whether sponsoring poor children's education, opening libraries in remote schools, helping children with disabilities, gifting meals to destitute families, or sponsoring a ward at Colombo's cancer hospital.

Candle Aid consumes Dil and Elmo's daily lives. Elmo lectures and writes, gets on the phone with influential contacts to raise money for projects and fix up jobs for this or that young high school or university graduate from the other side of the tracks. He seems to know everybody, and everybody knows 'Captain Elmo'. Sri Lankans generally have large circles of friends and acquaintances, but I do not know another Sri Lankan whose contact network is as extensive as Elmo's.

While Elmo strategizes and fundraises, Dil keeps Candle Aid's wheels in motion and on the rails. She runs the Candle Aid office, manages projects and corresponds with sponsors all over the world; she handles countless appeals for help, day after day, kindly, patiently and diligently. Both Elmo and Dil have a matchless empathy with, and practical compassion for, ordinary Sri Lankans, especially those at the bottom of the heap. Its burdens frequently weigh them down; but, every time I meet them, I see how it lights up their lives with meaning and purpose. For, as Elmo says, 'It is better by far to light a solitary candle than to curse the darkness.'

Dil and Elmo live in a house they built on the big, broad waterway that connects Moratuwa's Bolgoda Lake to the sea. It is in a Moratuwa suburb, off Galle Road running through the main town, at the bottom of a narrow side lane that was tarmacked only recently. Today, Moratuwa, like adjacent Ratmalana, feels like a busy, noisy extension of Colombo, at least on the main road. But here, at their 'river house', all is quiet and serene, with vistas of expansive water and low-country riverbank greenery, as if it were a hundred miles from the big city.

Their river house is the setting for Elmo's novella *Sam's Story*, based on his old servant boy, which was adapted into an award-winning film. It is where I stay sometimes on short trips to Colombo. From the rooftop terrace I take in early-morning river scenes and sounds: the play of soft, pale pink and then gradually brightening yellow light on the still water, small fishing boats coming back to the riverbank with their catch, myriad birdlife, *pirith* chanting (of the Buddha's words in Pali) from a nearby Buddhist temple, the muezzin's call to prayer from a nearby mosque; the roll call, in Tamil, at a Muslim girls' school on the opposite riverbank. A pelican stands sentinel on a wooden stilt in the river; Elmo christened him 'Jonathan Livingston Seagull' in a short piece he wrote. In the evenings we converse in their living room, with the French windows wide open, looking out to the darkened lawn and river. Elmo holds forth in his customary evening dress, wrapped in a sarong, barefoot, sometimes bare-bodied.

Mummy and I were over at the river house for dinner one evening in 2011. It was a gathering for Candle Aid office staff and their families – mainly Sinhalese, many Christian, a few Tamils. Everyone chatted away merrily, munching on short eats and with drinks at hand. As usual in Sri Lanka, it was very late by the time we sat down to dinner. Then someone started strumming a guitar and people sang their favourite baila tunes – 'Suranganee' and 'Mabalakale' from the days of my childhood, and others of more recent vintage with a faster beat. As we drove back, Mummy said the evening reminded her of Colombo dinner parties in the 1960s, when there was easy mixing of people of different races and creeds, all united in a Sri Lankan love of company and celebration. That evening, in such company, it was easy to forget the venal politicians, race riots and civil war that had disfigured Sri Lanka since the 1970s.

~

Home Town is not what it used to be. Manners and mores changed. Fraternizing still takes place across religious and ethnic lines, but much less so; more Sinhalese, Tamils and Muslims have retreated behind communal walls. Christians have always been best at inter-ethnic mixing – because Tamils and Sinhalese share the same faith. But even that changed with the war and its aftermath: more Christians in and around Colombo became Sinhala chauvinists.

Selina is a Tamil I know, a forty-something professional with striking dark looks. She left Sri Lanka after the 1983 riots, but returned much later to look after her aged parents. She bemoans how manners have coarsened in Colombo. In her eyes, people are more opportunistic, grabbing what they can when they can, imitating the greed of the elites.

My friend Tissa Jayatilaka echoes this sentiment during our lunches at The Capri and Galle Face Hotel. Tissa feels intellectually and culturally isolated in today's Colombo. He considers English his mother tongue and has a lifelong passion for English literature. His golden age was at the University of Peradeniya, where he studied in the late 1960s and early 1970s, before moving to live and work in Colombo. In his Peradeniya student days, and in his early years in Colombo, he had a wide circle of friends and acquaintances who spoke good English, looked out to the world and had gentlemanly values – before the descent into parochialism, vulgarity, philistinism and bad English. 'In those days I had about a hundred kindred spirits to talk to,' he says. 'Now maybe five.'

In one of his articles Tissa likens post-war Colombo, and the rest of the country, to the traffic:

> If one follows the road rules, observes etiquette and drives sensibly, one is abused by the majority of fellow road users. Might is right in this scheme of things. The bigger the vehicle they drive the greater their abuse of the road rules. The drivers of buses, the lorries, the jeeps and pick-up trucks are good examples of these law breakers as are those behind the wheels of government vehicles including those in security force and police vehicles. The Traffic Police studiously turn a blind eye as these latter day behemoths roll recklessly by. Meantime the grim statistics reveal that the number of deaths caused by road accidents is growing by the day.

Some things, though, have not changed. For all Colombo's expansion since the late 1970s, it retains a small-town feel. The novelist Shehan Karunatilaka writes, 'We may be a capital city, but our circles of association and our attitudes are very much small-town.' Now, as before, when dinner or barroom conversations turn serious, men interrupt each other constantly and go off on tangents, rarely allowing anyone to complete a sentence or a thought process. This I still have to get used to.

And Colombo is still a combustible mix. It remains a multi-ethnic city, indeed much more so than the rest of the country. According to the latest census, 55 per cent of residents within the city limits are Tamil speakers, a combination of ethnic Tamils and Muslims; island-wide, Sinhalese are 75 per cent of the population. This mix I consider a Colombo attribute; what vigour the city has would be much diminished without it. But the same mix can be a tinderbox, when Hermann Hesse's 'gentle doe-eyed Sinhalese' turn into a feral mob. Or when Islamist suicide bombers blow up churches and hotels.

Aunty Iyna, Daddy's youngest sister, lives in a neighbourhood of small, tightly packed houses on one side of Beira Lake, behind the Colpetty mosque. Buddhists, Muslims and Tamils live cheek by jowl. As I walked to her house, I passed a dove-white Buddha statue, encased in glass. As dusk fell, neon lights switched on to illuminate it; a loudspeaker blared out monks' chants from a nearby temple. Razana, Aunty Iyna's daughter, told me this public broadcasting of Buddhist chanting was new in the neighbourhood, intended to compete with the five-times-daily call to prayer from the mosque close by. A small Sinhala corner shop stood opposite the Buddha statue. Next to it was a Tamil house. And next to it a Muslim house. All seemed peaceful as I walked by. I wondered what little spark might, on another day, light a conflagration on this very spot.

5

A Turn in the South

And the place itself, the air, the trees, the sky itself were as different as those that I had left a few hours ago as the Sinhalese language from the Tamil. I had left behind me the bareness, austerity, burning dryness of the sands of Jaffna and now I was bathed, embraced by the soft, warm, damp, luscious luxuriance of the tropics. Here life was full of trees and changing leaves and . . . it seemed to be embowered in ferns and flowers.

– Leonard Woolf, *Growing*

My first serious journeys out of Colombo were in the south, the part of the island outside the city I knew best as a child. In childhood all I saw was Galle Road, which tracks the coast from downtown Colombo to the southern capital of Galle, several hotels, a few beaches and Galle itself, the place where the west coast ends and the south coast begins. My family hardly ever ventured to the other side of Galle, so I really was a stranger to most of the south. That I had to remedy. Many road trips followed, from Colombo all the way to the south-eastern tip of the island, starting in early 2009. My last

road trip to the 'deep south', the south-eastern part of the island, was in 2015, though these days I go as far as Galle and Matara in the south-west at least twice a year.

I had two regular drivers on these road trips, Joseph and Nihal. Joseph, a fluent Tamil speaker, drove me mostly in the north and east; Nihal drove me in the Sinhala parts of the country, including the south.

I have come to know Nihal well over countless hours and thousands of miles on the road together. He is sixty-odd years old, with at least forty years' professional driving experience, first in Oman and then in Sri Lanka. He lives and breathes cars, a childhood fascination inherited from his father that Nihal turned into his livelihood. His three younger brothers are also tour drivers. Nihal and his siblings are Sinhala Buddhists from the Colombo upper working class; they belong to the city, but their traditions, particularly religious traditions like temple rituals and pilgrimages to sacred sites, are those of the Sinhala Buddhist heartland. His wife is a highly sought-after German-speaking tour guide. Together, through hard work and diligence, they have moved up to the urban lower middle class.

'Nihal,' Mummy says, 'is a gentleman.' So he is: discreet, totally trustworthy and reliable, unfailingly courteous, constantly attentive, always anticipating the next item on the itinerary and the next stage of the journey. Like his compatriots, he is friendly, easy to chat with. But unlike many of his compatriots, he is quiet and restrained. He exudes calm and poise. In driver's downtime he reads detective stories, Mills Boon and Barbara Cartland novels to improve his already perfectly serviceable English. I bring fresh supplies from abroad.

My other perennial Sri Lankan road trip companion is a dog-eared copy of the *Handbook for the Ceylon Traveller*, now forty-five years old and in the family's possession since my pre-teens. After years of overuse its dust jacket has come off and its spine has all but fallen apart, like a wizened grandparent with severe osteoporosis. Its cover, typeface, layout, photos and ads are crude by today's standards. But it is one of a kind, oozing local charm and humour. It recalls bygone days of narrow, bumpy roads and sleepy towns; of rest houses in otherwise undisturbed rural idylls with extended verandas, slowly whirring ceiling fans, grand views, and full-spread rice-and-curry lunches for less than ten rupees a head. It holds dreams from before the post-1960s age of mass tourism, air-conditioned hotels and super-modern communications. Its chapters are really individual essays, gently perambulating their way through the country. They convey taste and erudition, in a light-hearted, quirky tone. And they are written in vivid, luxuriant, cultivated South Asian English, now rare in Sri Lanka.

Most of the south from Colombo around the coast is in the lush, deep-green wet zone. Up to the coastal town of Tangalle, its look and feel are as Leonard Woolf describes at the head of this chapter, before the barer, less rainy, paler-green dry zone unfolds in the south-east. The scene Woolf sketches is actually Polgahawela, in the approach to the hill country from the dry zone of Rajarata, and the Vanni and the Jaffna peninsula to its north. But he could equally be describing my route out of Colombo heading south on Galle Road. That is where this journey began.

～

My first stop out of Colombo was Kalutara, at the mouth of the Kalu Ganga (Black River). A prominent dagoba stands at one end of the bridge across the river. Like many towns, Kalutara these days seems two to three times the size it was in my childhood. Galle Road is four lanes wide as it runs through the centre of what is now a biggish, busy town. But veer off the main road on the land side and within minutes one enters a different world.

Nihal and I took such a side road, just past the dagoba, running alongside the riverbank. Suddenly village scenes appeared: greenery, paddy fields, little temples, makeshift roadside stalls selling fruit and vegetables, the odd village shop with a few small houses around it, fishing boats moored on the riverbank. In the rolling hills beyond, carpets of rubber trees stretched as far as the eye could see. When rubber was introduced to Ceylon in 1877, Kalutara district was home to its first plantations, before the crop spread elsewhere in the low country.

This abrupt Kalutara transition, from urban to sylvan, recalled a Colombo conversation with Bradman Weerakoon, a veteran civil servant who was secretary to seven prime ministers and served two presidents. After serving his last prime minister (Ranil Wickremesinghe) and finally going into retirement, Bradman wrote a little book about Kalutara, his home district. He told me about this retirement project one morning on his Bambalapitiya veranda, with the schoolboyish enthusiasm of someone just liberated from a lifetime of back-to-back meetings and never-ending short deadlines. That persuaded me to buy the book. In it he contrasts the expanding town's modernity with the village-centred life elsewhere in the district. Kalutara, Bradman contends, is Sinhala society in microcosm.

The temple and the sangha are the heart of village life. Temples are packed on monthly *poya* (full-moon) days with the young, middle-aged and old arriving in family groups, but elderly women are their mainstay the rest of the month. Monks are omnipresent in the village, officiating at every important public and family function – weddings, funerals, death anniversaries, shop openings; villagers defer to the 'authority of the robe'. Astrology exerts a powerful influence on people's lives. Land is often shared and collectively cultivated. Village homes have gardens full of low-country herbs, fruits and vegetables. To Bradman, this is Sinhala Buddhist heartland.

Kalutara town, on the other hand, is ethnically and religiously mixed. We passed a Muslim part of town: shops, a couple of large mosques, bearded men in sarongs and white prayer caps, older women in saris with the upper part draped loosely over their heads, many younger and middle-aged women draped in black from head to toe. Elsewhere in town are a few churches, mostly Catholic, testament to the European encounter that began with the Portuguese four centuries ago. The railway line runs close by, in between Galle Road and the shoreline, stretching from Colombo past Galle to Matara. It was the second railway track built in Ceylon, completed in 1895.

Nihal and I continued driving along the side road next to the riverbank. After a few miles we reached our side stop, Richmond Castle. A winding driveway took us past statues of semi-clad ancient Greek and Roman ladies, set in a crude copy of a European landscaped garden; then we reached the light-brown facade of the 'castle'. Don Siriwardene, a prominent landowning *mudaliyar* or headman under the British, built it over a century ago for his new bride. He spared no expense to ape the architecture of European aristocracy; Burma teak and Italian marble adorned the interiors. In a gloomy room upstairs, sepia-tinted photographs bore witness to the grand wedding, attended by the British governor. The large hall downstairs was the venue for lavish receptions, parties and dances.

But the marriage ended badly, apparently unconsummated, and Don Siriwardene became a confirmed misogynist. He retired to a room in Queen's Hotel, Kandy, and turned Richmond Castle into an orphanage, on condition that no girl orphans were to be admitted. An annex houses a boys' orphanage to this day. The building also houses a Montessori. The little boys in white shirts and blue shorts shouted 'hello-hello' from afar as I walked through empty, threadbare rooms that had once seen Sinhala nouveau riche high living under the British.

~

Just south of Kalutara lies the first recorded Muslim settlement in Sri Lanka, dating back to the eighth century AD. Arab traders, who knew it as Barberyn, took shelter here before riding monsoon winds west to the Gulf or east to the Straits of Malacca and beyond to China. Some settled permanently. This is Beruwela, home to Sri Lanka's wealthiest gem merchants. I stopped briefly at the Kechimalai mosque, at the tip of a little promontory where, it is said, the first Arabs landed.

All was quiet this afternoon in Beruwela and the adjoining Muslim town of Aluthgama; the lanes off Galle Road were empty and most of the shops shuttered. It was *Nombu,* the Muslim Tamil word for the fasting month of Ramadan. Two and a half years after this visit, in June 2014, a monk-led Boddhu Bala Sena mob attacked Muslim houses and shops in Aluthgama while the local police and the Rajapaksa government in Colombo looked the other way. Muslims feared it would escalate, like the Sinhala–Muslim riots in 1915 that started near Kandy, spread elsewhere and prompted the British colonial government to declare martial law. It might have, had the Rajapaksas not been voted out in 2015.

Sri Lanka's main tourist strip stretches from Beruwela to Galle; hotels and guest houses catering to Western sun-seekers popped up here and in Negombo near Katunayake airport first, in the late 1960s. Long-haired, stoned, culturally insensitive hippies came to the south coast before modern tourists. They sojourned, and some settled, in the fishing village of Hikkaduwa. Soon there were dope parties on the beach, and the Great Unwashed from the West had their way with local boys and girls.

Later came Germans on package tours. They rarely ventured outside hotel grounds; when they did it was for cheap beer, cheap food, cheap shopping and cheap sex. They complained loudly and gave hotel staff measly tips. They roasted on the beach from early morning, returned to Germany lobster-red, cultivated leathery nut-brown hides, and – poetic justice – developed skin cancer. A 'beach boy' industry emerged to service male and female tourists sexually, and some beach boys made good and now own local guest houses, shops and restaurants. Then came pedophile tourism, abetted by bribed local civil servants, policemen and judges. Sri Lankan society turned a blind eye, in the fashion of upper-class Colombo, which has a long tradition of high-born married men with catamites.

Only Western media exposure prompted a clampdown. Tourism is more varied and respectable along this coastal strip these days, but that tourist-trash look – loud, fat, white-turned-lobster-red – is still ubiquitous. And nowhere more so than in the erstwhile hippy heaven of Hikkaduwa.

A trope of foreign writing on Sri Lanka, over centuries, is the androgynous, even effeminate, allure of local boys and young men. Major Roland Raven-Hart, who lived in Ceylon in the 1950s and 1960s, could barely contain himself: 'Sinhalese countrymen are handsome and lovely, with straight classical noses and cleanly modelled lips; and both men and women have magnificent bodies and walk like happy gods.' He quoted similar sentiments from Robert Knox and Ernst Haeckel, the world-renowned German naturalist, marine biologist, philosopher and artist. Mark Twain, on a brief stopover on his round-the-world lecture tour in the 1890s, raved about his 'slender, shapely and . . . unmasculine' Sinhalese servant boy. Sir James Emerson Tennent, a Victorian prominence who was colonial secretary in the 1840s and subsequently wrote an acclaimed, over-thousand-page, two-volume book on Ceylon, said this: 'With their delicate features and slender limbs, their frequent want of beards . . . the men have an air of effeminacy very striking to the eye of a stranger.'

The same writers were not so complimentary about Sri Lankan women. Raven-Hart rubbed the point in. He quoted Haeckel: 'The stronger sex is also the most handsome.' And Hoffmeister, an earlier German traveller: 'The ugliness of the women is quite equal to the beauty of the men.' Raven-Hart had a well-known reputation for being partial to young boys. His Ceylon book, *Ceylon: History in Stone*, is rather good – historically super-informed, and observant and discerning on his island travels. But he was always befriending young village boys who accompanied him to remote temples and ancient ruins, went swimming with him in lakes and rivers and in the sea, and even stayed with him in his rest house bedrooms. The book is disconcertingly spattered with passages such as this: 'yet another weekend, with yet another youngster', 'with another schoolboy friend', and 'some of the most friendly small boys in Ceylon'.

As we drove along, I noticed the look of ordinary Sri Lankans had changed. Growing up, I was used to a paunchy look among the comfortably off and rich in Colombo. But, typically, those lower down the socio-economic scale, especially outside Colombo, were thin and wiry, the men often taut and muscled, habituated to hard physical labour and simple food. No longer. Since the late 1970s, rising living standards have created a new breed of Sri Lankans. Even in small towns and villages, men and women, boys and girls are running to fat. But they do so in a distinctively Sri Lankan way. When Sri Lankan men put on their pounds it tends to mass around the belly and hardly anywhere else; the resulting potbelly rises like a bubble-shaped dagoba from a flat Rajarata landscape. The new Sri Lankan woman is circular, like those old-fashioned alarm clocks, large, rounded and with a bell on top. The country still has its lithe, sleek boys and girls and twenty-something men and women, mostly from villages. But it tends not to last: marriage and children usually extinguish that look.

On a sombre note, we passed shells of abandoned houses and clumps of gravestones speckling the roadside – reminders of the tsunami that struck the east, south and west coasts on Boxing Day 2004. In the hamlet of Peraliya there is a giant standing Buddha, a gift from Japan built after the tsunami. Despite its size it has an austere, restrained beauty, unlike the crude, in-your-face Buddhas that have sprouted up all over the island to display triumphal Sinhala Buddhist nationalism. This Buddha has a quiet dignity. He is well proportioned, with angular features. One palm faces out in the *abhaya mudra* – the 'have no fear' gesture that signifies protection, peace and benevolence. Neat folds in his robe streak breadthwise from shoulders to feet.

The railway track runs just behind this Japanese Buddha. On that fateful Boxing Day morning, the giant wave crashed into a train passing by this spot, killing over 1500 passengers. Now there were fewer signs of tsunami wreckage along the coastline. The road was wide and smooth. New houses, schools, temples and mosques, built with aid money, stood by its side.

~

The coast this side of Galle is famous for resort hotel architecture, the legacy of Geoffrey Bawa. There are hardly any globally celebrated Sri Lankans, which is why the name of Bawa, and the admiration he elicits around the architectural world, means such a great deal. For Bawa is the father of 'tropical modernism'; his style has been copied and adapted all over Asia.

Geoffrey and his much older brother Bevis came from a rich, highly Anglicized and outrageously eccentric Burgher family. The brothers had a few traits in common. They were incredibly tall; both were artistically creative and gay, partial to young men; and both created stunning landscape gardens. There the similarities ended. Bevis was aide-de-camp to several British governors and turned to journalism; Geoffrey forsook a globetrotting playboy life for architecture. Geoffrey's persona was upper-crust English, comporting himself with imperial aplomb, while Bevis considered himself more Asian. Bevis would lounge around the house in banian and sarong; Geoffrey, always a trousers man, was very much a dandy in his younger days. The brothers saw little of each other right to the end of their lives, despite having country estates only a few miles apart.

Two Geoffrey Bawa creations stand out on this coastline. Bentota Beach Hotel, which opened in 1969, was his first on the south coast, and Sri Lanka's first resort hotel purpose-built for the modern tourist age. It set Bawa's tropical modern standard for hotels all over Asia, combining modern creature comforts with vernacular features.

The hotel stands on a spit facing the sea on one side and the mouth of the Bentara river on the other. Bentota is the traditional halfway stop between Colombo and Galle. The river marked the frontier between the Dutch, who controlled the coastline down to Galle and beyond, and the Portuguese, who controlled the coastline up to Colombo, during seven years of uneasy truce; the Dutch built a fort on their side of the river. In 1652, they crossed the river into Portuguese territory and fought their way up the coast to eventual victory in Colombo in 1656. Much later a rest house was built on the site of the old fort. Then, in the 1960s, the rest house was demolished to make way for the new hotel.

Driving over the river bridge the hotel looms above the trees fortress-like – a deliberate effect, as Bawa raised the front sections on a mound to mimic Dutch fortifications. One arrives at a massive stone bastion, and then a wide porte cochère – a porch leading to a courtyard. A short, tunnel-like stone staircase rises to an elevated lobby with a batik ceiling that covers the reception area – a riot of intricate design and colour, the handiwork of Ena de Silva, Sri Lanka's Mother of Batik and a long-time Bawa collaborator. Glass doors on four sides enclose an open-air pool fringed by three frangipani trees. The lobby reveals a straight-line view through this transparent inner garden, and the dining room and lounge beyond, to the outer garden's coconut palms and finally the sea. Bawa filled the hotel with his friends' and collaborators' artworks, as he did with his subsequent hotels. Laki Senanayake sculpted a giant bronze peacock to guard the staircase down to the pool bar; Barbara Sansoni created handloom ceilings for the dining room and lounges.

Bawa's lines are simple, straight and elegant. Huge terracotta half-tile roofs and broad eaves create large terraces and verandas as well as interior spaces open to the elements; open rooms interconnect seamlessly. The combination allows for maximum natural ventilation. What I particularly like about Bawa buildings is their creative use of fresh air and ceiling fans and minimal reliance on air conditioning. Bawa harmonizes the building with the landscape, opening it out, blurring the distinction between interior and exterior. His motto, always, was 'to run with the site'.

We popped into the hotel for lunch or tea, or stayed overnight, many times in the 1970s. Daddy's favourite spot was a shallow corner of the swimming pool in the outer garden, adjacent to the poolside bar. He stood in the water, his belly bulging above the waterline, smoking one cigarette after another, his whisky glass perched on the bar counter, chatting to friends who were also there for the weekend. The hotel was 'modernized' in the late 1990s, removing many original features, including the half-tile roofs, and imposing air conditioning on the dining room and main lounge. In 2017, the John Keells Group, the hotel's owners, announced they would demolish the hotel as it was getting too old, but promised to recreate the centre block exactly as Bawa had built it.

My other favourite Bawa hotel is The Lighthouse, just a mile before Galle, which opened in the mid-1990s. It is one of his last hotels. It sits on a rocky promontory with majestic views of Galle Fort, tipped by its lighthouse. From Galle Road it resembles a Portuguese or Dutch fort. A trademark Bawa porte cochère leads to a vertical drum enclosing the main staircase. This is a Laki Senanayake masterpiece. An elaborate copper-and-bronze handrail spirals up three flights – a swirling melee of interlinked, almost life-size human figures that recreates a battle between the Dutch and Kandyan Sinhalese. At the bottom of the staircase, the Dutch commander looks up through his long telescope. His soldiers with horses and cannon face off against Sinhala warriors with bows and arrows. At the top, the Sinhala king sits nonchalantly on a palanquin, fanned by his retinue. The upper levels interrupt this pitched battle, leading off to open-air lounges and verandas that face the sea and Galle Fort. Barbara Sansoni's pencil drawings of old Ceylon buildings hang on the walls.

Just past Bentota Beach Hotel, off Galle Road, is a typically narrow, bumpy low-country road that snakes its way into a hinterland of paddy fields, coconut groves and tiny villages. Dedduwa Lake, a lagoon fed by an estuary of the Bentara river, comes into view. A dirt track veers off this road to the main gate of a thickly wooded private property. This is Lunuganga ('Salt River' in Sinhala), Geoffrey Bawa's estate. He bought a plain bungalow with twenty-five acres of rubber trees in 1948; over the next half-century he remoulded it into a spectacular landscaped garden, fusing local with English and Renaissance Italian influences. He turned the bungalow inside out and added six cottages around the grounds. An army of gardeners (forty at one point) moved hills (the summit of one was lowered to create a view across Dedduwa Lake to a distant temple stupa), cut terraces and ponds, replanted trees, built pavilions, walls and statues, and opened up new vistas. Here, on weekends, Bawa choreographed landscaping and held court with friends and collaborators over Sunday or poya lunch. Prince Charles dropped in for tea in 1998. Lunuganga was Bawa's refuge in his final years, paralysed and speechless after a stroke. He got around the grounds in a specially made little vehicle, now displayed in one of the pavilions.

Bawa died in 2003. The Lunuganga Trust has run the estate since his death, and it is partially open to the public. When I visited it was too late for the ten-curry lunch, but I did get a decent tour of the grounds before being deposited on the bungalow terrace for tea and butter cake.

~

Galle Fort withstood the tsunami in 2004, which devastated the much bigger town outside the fort. Now the outer town looks much better – a wider road, a new bus stand, shopping complex and wet market, and a beautified promenade. The fort brings back happy childhood memories of scampering around the ramparts and weekend stays at New Oriental Hotel.

The NOH, as it used to be called, is a huge pile. It was the Dutch governor's office and army barracks combined before becoming an inn for visiting Dutch. It is Sri Lanka's oldest hotel, pre-dating Galle Face Hotel. Its veranda looks out across Church Street to a shaded green with four spreading rain trees and the ramparts just behind. In the old days the veranda had a row of 'loungers' facing the street and green. Imaginatively nicknamed Bombay Fornicators, their extendable arms allow reclining sitters to raise, stretch and rest their splayed legs. Framed photos of Queen Elizabeth and Queen Juliana (then the reigning monarch of the Netherlands) hung on the wall.

The queen of the NOH was the indomitable Nesta Brohier, née

Ephraims; a troop of Boxers (the canine variety) scurried constantly around her feet. Like my Dutch Burgher friend Charmaine in Colombo, she spoke in the clipped, authoritative tones of Received Pronunciation English. The Brohiers and Ephraims were the cream of Dutch Burgher society in the fort. The hotel had been in the family for a few generations; Mrs Brohier inherited it from her father, ran it first with her husband Hal, and then as a widow until she died in 1995. She, Hal and other members of the Brohier and Ephraims clans are buried in the Dutch church next door. That reminds me of my last memory of her, sitting on the NOH veranda, surrounded by her Boxers, sometime in the late 1980s. 'Next time I see you,' she said, pointing to the church, 'it might well be over there.'

For me the biggest treat at the NOH was to sleep in an outsize bed hung with mosquito nets, in a huge, high-ceilinged room with a gently whirring fan. The combination generated a deliciously soporific effect. In the middle of the adjoining bathroom, which seemed almost as large as the bedroom, was the biggest bathtub I had ever seen. E.F.C. Ludowyk, a Dutch Burgher, professor of English at Peradeniya University and historian of Ceylon, recalled the NOH in his childhood around the time of the First World War:

> What a realm it was, with steps leading down to cellars heavy with sawdust, muffling the heaviest footsteps, crooked corridors, little rooms which opened into larger ones, a small courtyard and the expanse of back garden with storerooms, sheds, clumps of bananas, breadfruit trees, an inexplicable confusion of boxes, and old furniture glimpsed through open doorways. All of it could have been a wonderland for any boy content to explore its unknown regions. But the eldest son of the family was blind, so too was his younger brother, and there was no one really to possess this kingdom.

Galle is linked to the biblical Tarshish, where King Solomon sent his ships to bring back gold, spices, ivory, apes, peacocks and pearls. The Arabs called it Kaleh. It was a major trading port going back to the fourteenth century. Even before, Arab traders in their dhows sheltered here on their Indian Ocean trading voyages, as they did in Beruwela. After the Portuguese conquered it they built the first fort, Santa Cruz. They called the town Punto de Gale – 'gale' deriving from 'gallo' or 'cock' in Portuguese, a corruption of the Sinhala 'gala' (or 'rock'); the cock takes centre stage in the city's coat of arms. The Dutch captured Galle in 1640 and vastly extended the fort, adding ramparts and bastions on a ninety-acre site. The British preserved the Dutch fort and added a clock tower on the ramparts. They renamed the town Point de Galle. It was the island's chief port and became a coaling station for steamships. But the port declined in the second half of the nineteenth century when steamships got too big to enter the harbour; from the 1880s, the new port in Colombo grabbed most of its trade.

Galle fell into sleepy decline; it remained 'as quiet as asleep' (the subtitle of a book on Galle) for well over a century. Most Burghers left after the 'Sinhala Only' policy was introduced in 1956. Thereafter Muslim traders and shopkeepers, descendants and co-religionists of people who had lived in Galle for centuries, well before the Europeans arrived, set the tone inside the fort. Galle started to revive from its prolonged slumber in the early 2000s, during the brief ceasefire between the government and the LTTE. Tourism picked up. Foreigners bought Dutch-style houses in the fort, and new hotels and guest houses catered to a budding market in heritage tourism. The NOH was thoroughly refurbished and became Amangalla, part of the Aman group of luxury hotels. The Amangalla's prices are, of course, multiples of what they were in Mrs Brohier's day, but it retains the old look, and some of the feel, of the NOH.

And Galle boomed after the end of the war. The Southern

Expressway, which opened in 2011, made it a two-hour journey
to or from Colombo – less than half the time it took on the coast
road. The fort became busy with tourists all year round. It had a
transformative facelift. Until the end of the war I remembered it as
somnolent, its buildings crumbling with neglect, their back gardens
overrun with weeds. Afterwards, rich foreigners and Colombo-ites
bought and refurbished old Dutch houses; new boutique hotels, cafes
and restaurants surfaced. Property prices became by far the most
expensive in Sri Lanka.

Tourists now flock to the gabled Grote Kerk, the Dutch Reformed
Church next to Amangalla. It was built a few years after Wolvendahl
Church in Colombo. Services ceased from 1958 for over half a
century due to Burgher emigration; then weekly services resumed,
but only in Sinhala for a much smaller congregation. Heavy
flagstones with elaborate coats of arms commemorate high society
buried here during Dutch rule. Gravestones on the outer side wall
indicate more recent burials; inscribed on one are the names of
Brohiers and Ephraims, including Nesta, Hal and their children.

On the other side of Church Street is the vast, solid Kornhuis,
the main warehouse in Dutch times. Cut into the middle of it is an
arch – the Old Gate of the fort. The British coat of arms is inscribed
above the arch on the outside wall. The VOC's coat of arms is on
the inside wall; Galle's emblematic cock struts on top, flanked by
two lions. 'ANNO 1659' is inscribed above it. In the Kornhuis the
Dutch stored cinnamon, harvested inland just a few miles from the
south coast; from here it went through the Old Gate to the jetty
close by, where ships waited to take it to Europe for sale.

In the renovated Kornhuis, now home to the National Maritime
Museum, one artefact stands out. It is the copy of a stone slab
Admiral Zheng He brought over on one of his voyages from China.
It has lettering in three scripts – Persian, Chinese and Tamil – and
was presented to the Vishnu temple in Dondra, farther down the

coast. The original is in the National Museum in Colombo, but a little description next to the exhibit announces its relationship to this place: it says, 'Found on Cripps Road, Galle, in 1911'. Here, if you like, is a choice specimen of premodern Chinese 'soft power': a Ming dynasty, Chinese Muslim naval superstar gifts a stele in three trade languages (including Farsi and Tamil) to a Buddhist temple honouring a Hindu god. Then again, on another voyage, Zheng He abducted a Sinhala king and took him back to Beijing to pay obeisance to the Son of Heaven – power not so soft this time.

The law courts and lawyers' offices cluster in a corner of the fort at one end of the Kornhuis. They surround a large square shaded almost completely by huge, unfolding banyans and rain trees; a Dutch pavilion, supported by thick, round pillars at its corners, nestles on one side. Youths played cricket as I walked by. I carried on down a side street, popped into a jewellery shop and chatted to its owner, who knew some of the Salih clan.

He sounded ambivalent about the new Galle. 'Many Muslim families – maybe half of those who used to live here – have sold their houses to foreigners, bought big houses outside the fort or apartments in Colombo, and can now afford big dowries for their daughters. That's good. But the culture has changed here. People are more money-minded; the old sense of community has gone. It's not right for our young to be exposed to scantily clad Western women all the time. Now there are gay tourists who stay at the hotel over there (he was referring to Galle Fort Hotel on Church Street). They advertise on gay websites. We feel uncomfortable; it's against Muslim culture.'

He reminisced about the old Galle – a 'sleeping city'. And he regretted the loss of the old multi-ethnic Sri Lanka. 'We all went to mixed schools, had Sinhala and Tamil friends. Now we send our kids to segregated schools. Muslims invite trouble sometimes, you know. All those flashy cars and women dripping in gold jewellery at weddings – makes local Sinhalese jealous and angry. No need to flaunt our wealth like that, no?'

At the end of the street, the main mosque stands round the corner, just before the ramparts. What looks like an outhouse with toilets is the 'Ladies' Prayer Section' – an enduring sign of Islam's degrading attitude to women in its houses of worship. The small lighthouse stands diagonally across at Point Utrecht Bastion. Townsfolk and tourists promenaded on the ramparts just as the sun set. This is a favourite Galle pastime: standing on the ramparts or a bastion, taking in the cool, salty breeze, and watching the reddening sun slip away slowly under the ocean horizon.

The walk back to Amangalla via Lighthouse Street offered a great contrast to the decrepit fort of only ten or fifteen years ago. So many new cafes, restaurants, guest houses. So many people on the streets. So many of the old Dutch houses renovated by the Colombo and expat rich. Typically, they have one storey and a narrow front. The veranda is a stoep – high, shady, with extended eaves and supporting round pillars, some with lattice screens across them. An elaborate fanlighted door leads to interior rooms, and these, further, on to a courtyard around which family life revolves. I recalled one or two of these houses from childhood visits to Muslim families in the fort. They looked deceptively small from the street, but, once past the veranda, one large room led back to another and another, before reaching a garden with fruit trees and a vegetable patch.

It was good to see Galle awake, architecturally restored and commercially buzzing. It is good for employment in the south, especially for youth from interior and coastal towns and villages. Galle today reminds me of Luang Prabang in Laos and Hoi An in Vietnam – and far superior to Cochin in Kerala, whose army of importuning touts never leaves you in peace. But, like Luang Prabang and Hoi An, it has lost the relaxed, lived-in authenticity it had in my childhood. Now freshly renovated Dutch houses set the tone, with shiny brass plates next to their front doors, shuttered doors and windows, uniformed staff and fancy cars parked outside. But, just next door to a few of these will be some plain house with open doors and windows, revealing poorly lit, sparsely furnished interiors, as its Muslim family mingles with neighbours on the veranda or on the street outside. How many of these will be left in five or ten years' time?

~

My next stop was Koggala, less than a half-hour drive down the coast from Galle. We passed Unawatuna beach, once empty except for Arthur C. Clarke's beachside house, now full of guest houses, budget hotels and backpackers. *Walauwes*, Sinhala manor houses, came into view on both sides of the road; their large lawns led up to whitewashed gingerbread villas with elaborate fretwork hanging off the eaves. We passed the runway of the Koggala airbase and the free trade zone next to it, driving on to the Martin Wickramasinghe Museum.

The museum is in the small, simple home where Martin Wickramasinghe was born and to which he returned in later life. He is the father of modern Sinhala literature, best known for his trilogy of village life in the first half of the twentieth century, set right here in his ancestral village. *Gam Peraliya* (Uprooted), the first part of the trilogy, is the most famous, and widely considered the first modern Sinhala novel. Its action revolves around the *mahagedara* (big house) and its high-caste family. The mahagedara family cleaved to old traditions and its status and privileges, but this was the losing battle of the unadaptable against encroaching modernity. Caste differences governed their universe, and their fellow villagers relied on Ayurvedic medicine, and on shamans, spells and exorcisms for both physical and spiritual needs. But the progressive force of the town and city gradually, but inevitably, defeated the occupants of the big house. Its agent was the lower-caste village schoolteacher, once in love with the mahagedara family's daughter but rebuffed; he left for Colombo, learned English and became a successful businessman, before returning to the village to build a bigger house for his mother.

Wickramasinghe, a Romantic, celebrated Sinhala Buddhist village culture with its rituals, religious festivals, myths and superstitions. To him these were ties that bound people, not the austere, doctrinaire 'Protestant Buddhism' of Olcott, denuded of tradition and colour. Wickramasinghe wanted to preserve village culture from urban modernity's ravages. But the village he celebrated vanished long ago, too. The British destroyed it to make way for an RAF base during the Second World War. Besides, nothing in Sri Lanka is black and white. This father of modern Sinhala literature, who Sinhala nationalists consecrated after independence, was English-educated and steeped in the English literary canon. English-language education exposed him to the Russian greats, who suffused his Sinhala romanticism.

A half-hour drive along the coast is Weligama Bay with its wide arc, calm turquoise-green waters and multicoloured fishing boats. Paul Theroux, who alighted here on his train ride from Colombo, described the bay as 'lovely as any in the South Pacific'. Fishermen display their tuna catch on the roadside; rows of plump black tuna sparkle in the sun. In the bay, a stone's throw from the shoreline, is a little island called Taprobane. Count de Mauny, a Frenchman with an invented name, bought it for next to nothing a century ago. My friend Elmo Jayawardena writes coyly that the count's marriage to a high-born Englishwoman failed due to 'possible conflicting incompatibility'. The locals called the island Galduwa (rocky island); they used it as a dump for stray cobras. De Mauny christened it 'Taprobane'; and here he built a house with an open veranda facing the South Pole and created a landscape garden. Rumours of homosexual orgies circulated among local villagers.

In England, the writer Paul Bowles saw photos of a dome-shaped island with a strange-looking house at its top flanked by terraces lost in the shade of great trees. He bought Taprobane in the 1950s. When he arrived he thought de Mauny's house 'an octagonal fantasy in a pseudo-Pompeiian style which he proceeded to decorate in a manner we should now associate with mild megalomania'. From the house Bowles savoured Ceylon's 'magical mornings and incomparable sunsets', and stayed awake at night listening to the sound of the big waves booming against the rocks below. His cook made him meals with twenty side dishes. Other servants – with whom the cook was constantly at war – went down to the rocks to catch enough lobster for the next day's fiery curry. From his back veranda he could see sharks patrolling the reef beyond the bay, but never venturing closer to shore.

On Taprobane Bowles wrote his Tangier novel *The Spider's House*, and here he ran a ménage with his nerve-wracked wife and a male Moroccan painter called Yacoubi, who was constantly stoned on hashish. Bevis Bawa said the local fishermen became hostile to the interlopers, hooting and throwing stones at the house after dark. Bowles and Co. had to up sticks and leave Ceylon.

Robin Maugham, nephew of Somerset, saw Taprobane for the first time in the 1960s and fell in love with it immediately. He wanted to buy it, for here he thought he could find 'nirvana'. But when he came a second time, in the early 1970s, he found the house dilapidated, denuded of its old furniture, and too costly to renovate.

Slightly inland on a side road, just past the Dutch-style rest house, is a large rock with a tall standing image carved into it. Its dhoti, belt, bracelets, and jewellery round its neck and crown are richly carved. Locals call it Sri Weligama Kustaraja. Legend has it that it is the image of a 'leper king', a monarch from a distant land who came to Sri Lanka in search of a cure for his skin disease. Others say it is the Mahayana bodhisattva Avalokiteshvara. Ven S.

Dhammika, in his book *Sacred Island: A Buddhist Pilgrim's Guide to Sri Lanka*, says it is the bodhisattva Samantabhadra. Most likely the image is evidence of Mahayana Buddhism; it dates back to the eighth or ninth century CE, when Mahayana was at its zenith in Sri Lanka, and when Weligama rivalled Galle as a flourishing port.

I like to stop at the rest house, have lunch or tea on its veranda and gaze at the bay and Taprobane. Ernst Haeckel stayed here on his six-month Ceylon visit in 1881–82, and here he set up his zoological laboratory. He went out to sea in fishing boats to collect jellyfish and larvae from the ocean surface. He had four servants in Weligama. One he called Socrates, and another Ganymede, after the youth who had the honour of serving the Olympian gods. Haeckel seems to have been smitten by Ganymede, 'a charming, naked, brown statue . . . since not even the boy beloved by Zeus could have had a nobler build, a finer harmony of comely limbs'. Haeckel returned to Europe with thirty crates of specimens – the seed for his internationally acclaimed *Kunstformen der Natur* (Art Forms in Nature), published in 1899, richly illustrated with lithographs and prints of marine organisms.

But Weligama was not always this tranquil. In 1988 and 1989, at the height of the second JVP rebellion, disgustingly mutilated corpses littered the roadside, hacked-off heads, torsos, arms, legs and genitals piled in heaps. These were alleged JVP activists and sympathizers, murdered by the army, police and government paramilitaries. They did to the JVP what was done to them: 'an eye for an eye, a tooth for a tooth' was what government forces scrawled on posters plastered on walls. The south was the JVP's heartland; the rebellion, and the government's quashing of it, was especially vicious here. The south is still JVP heartland, but now the JVP is legal, contests elections and has parliamentary representation.

Matara, the second largest town in the south, is a short drive along the coast. Like Galle, it was a prosperous Muslim merchant town before the Western encounter. The Portuguese raided it, massacring its 'Moor' traders and confiscating their goods. The Dutch occupied it soon after they took Galle – and spotted an opportunity to build yet another fort. Matara's river makes straight for the sea; then, at the last minute, it does a right-angle turn and runs parallel to the sea, leaving a narrow spit of land across from the river's turn to its mouth. The Dutch put a wall across the spit to make a new fort. On the landside of the main road, before entering the old fort, is the small, six-pointed Star Fort, still intact and freshly renovated. The Dutch built it after the Kandyan king briefly wrested the old fort from them in 1761.

Tourists rarely stop in Matara. Little remains of the old fort. Part of the old wall still stands next to a large open lawn with a clock tower. On the other side of the lawn is a small, gabled yellow-cream Dutch Reformed Church, a miniature version of its sister churches in Colombo and Galle. It was empty when I entered, save for a smiling Sinhala village woman in a frock and slippers. She showed me around, trilled wonderfully in sing-song Sinhala, and offered me a cup of tea. She told me she was a housemaid in Singapore for ten years, and that she converted from Buddhism to Christianity. 'God bless you, *Mahaththaya* (Sir),' she said as I left.

I continued walking to the residential area of the old fort, behind the church. It is much smaller than Galle Fort, but reminded me vividly of what the latter used to look like: sleepy lanes, and dilapidated Dutch-style and art deco houses with jungly gardens. But now, on the corner of Dutchman Street, I noticed a new smattering of hideous boxy guest houses with garish, opaque, dark-blue windows. Matara's old fort waits to be 'discovered', restored and beautified, just as Galle was nearly twenty years ago.

A little way past Matara is Dondra. Tourists usually make a beeline for Dondra Head, the southernmost tip of the island, with its lighthouse the British built in the nineteenth century. Slip a hundred rupees to the lighthouse keeper and one can ascend to the top for a 360-degree view. The uninterrupted dark green of the low country stretches as far as the Uva hills on the landside. Look the other way and nothing except fishing boats, the odd container ship and the horizon disturb the eyeline all the way to the Antarctic.

Dondra is 'Devinuwara', city of the gods, to the Sinhalese. It is, aptly, home to a major temple, Sri Vishnu Mahadevale, yet another example of Buddhist syncretism. A shrine to the Hindu god Vishnu has existed on this site since the seventh century CE. Ibn Batuta stopped here in the fourteenth century, en route from Adam's Peak, the holy mountain in the central highlands, to Galle. He found it a large town of merchants, and a 'vast temple' with a life-size golden statue with ruby eyes, 1000 priests and 500 dancing girls. The Portuguese destroyed the temple in 1588. A member of the raiding party subsequently wrote about a large pagoda with vaulted roofs and many chapels around it, all enclosed by a quadrangle of verandas and terraces. Having destroyed over a thousand idols, they ransacked the temple's stores for ivory, gems and spices. Finally, they killed cows in the temple to complete its desecration.

All that remains are a few stone pillars and seven *kovil*s, or chapels, to one side, each housing a deity. A newish tall standing Buddha faces the road. As I went in, the chained but reclining temple elephant was giving itself a mid-afternoon bath in a well, using its trunk to spray water sideways and above and behind its head. The main *devale* (a Hindu image house in a Buddhist temple) is rectangular and pagoda-style with a tiered roof; its external walls are jet-blue with white stripes. A plaque on a side wall says it was built in 1958, on the site of the original temple. Inside are murals displaying Vishnu's many incarnations. A thick curtain at one end hides the main image; Sinhala worshippers thronged around it with offerings of fruit. A devale lay priest, clad in white, recited prayers. Outside, devotees cracked open coconuts.

~

Justin is my favourite character in this part of the south. He and his wife lived in their ancestral walauwe just past Koggala off the coast road. I first visited Justin in late 2011. Prompted by my friend Elmo in Moratuwa, who had visited him a couple of years earlier, I brought along a bottle of Teacher's whisky – Justin's only very occasional 'strong drink', as he liked to call it.

On a late November morning, as Nihal and I drove into the grounds and approached the house, we saw a shortish, spare, wiry man, dressed in a T-shirt, shorts and slippers, attending to his plants on the large veranda. He moved lithely, with light, springy steps; his face and limbs were leathery, his black hair neatly combed. He had the fresh look of someone who spent a lot of time outdoors. Justin approached and greeted me cheerily, with a twinkle in his eye. We sat on planters' chairs on the veranda. I took Justin to be a fit sixty-something; I could hardly believe it when he told me he was eighty-four. 'I have always lived a simple, healthy life,' he explained. 'I cook for myself, I take care of the house and the garden without servants. We have three acres, you know, coconut trees at the front and back. I drink two litres of water a day. I climb up and fix the roof – why pay a young chap a thousand rupees to do it badly when I can do it perfectly well myself?' Justin told me he was a qualified swimming instructor, walking over to Koggala beach for a regular morning swim.

Justin went over his ancestry and the history of the walauwe. He came from Sinhala nobility. An ancestor, Don Bastian Jayewardene, was sent to Mauritius to look after Ehelapola, the Kandyan noble who plotted with the British to overthrow the last Kandyan king, aspired to the throne himself and was subsequently exiled. Justin's wife was an Obeyesekere, another high-caste Sinhala clan. The house dated back to 1650, when a Portuguese settler who married a Sinhala woman was given this plot of land. Arches fronted the Dutch-style veranda. Above the central arch was the British coat of arms with its trademark lion and unicorn; Justin said his grandfather got special permission from Edward VII to display the coat of arms.

We went inside the house. It was battered and crumbling; I saw cracks and holes all over the walls and in the high vaulted roof. A place like this required massive expense, but Justin was not rich: he lived off his pension as a retired salaried official of the Galle Port Authority. Whisky bottles filled with filtered water stood on the dining table, sufficient for Justin's daily requirements. Behind the dining area was the *meda midula,* an inner open-air courtyard surrounded on three sides by bedrooms, bathrooms and the kitchen.

The walauwe was a storehouse of memorabilia. A coffee table displayed a photo of Mrs Bandaranaike as a baby; next to it was one of SWRD and Mrs B visiting the house in the 1950s. The Bandaranaikes were relatives on Justin's wife's side of the family. Faded newspaper cuttings – reviews of the walauwe and its history – were pinned up on the walls, partially covering large patches where paint and plaster had peeled off over the decades. Hanging on the living room wall was a framed wide-angle photo of Justin's father and grandfather, taken over a century ago. They were in ceremonial uniform of cocked hat, waistcoat and thick black baubled overcoat, looking very status-conscious as they stood alongside British colonial officials. Three generations of Jayewardenes – Justin's father, grandfather and great-grandfather – served the British as senior mudaliyars. The remains of the one-room courthouse from which they once administered justice in these parts – now just a shell of the original building – stood next to the house.

Justin carefully unpacked and showed me a treasured family heirloom – the ceremonial overcoat worn by his forefathers. It was threadbare, over a century and a half old; its material was thick and heavy, suited to a British winter – who knows how they could bear to wear it in this tropical heat. The mudaliyar line ended with Justin's father, for the institution was abolished on the eve of independence.

We went back to the veranda. I wondered if Justin was tempted to sell the walauwe and move to Colombo, where his daughter and family lived. 'Never,' he replied. 'My family duty is to be its guardian and pass it on to the next generation.' Then he complained about the state of Sri Lanka. 'The country has gone to the dogs. People see what the politicians do, so they imitate. All are rogues.' 'When was it better?' I asked. 'Under the British,' he replied, without missing a beat.

Back in the late 1980s, during the JVP rebellion, Justin was still working in Galle. It became too dangerous for him to commute in an official car with a driver. So he decided to cycle all the way to Galle and back, every working day. 'There were days,' he said, 'when I passed thirty to forty bodies piled up on the roadside, by the Koggala airfield. All mutilated.'

We drove down to Koggala Lake just a few minutes away, where Justin picked a boat and boatman to take us out. It was early afternoon, the sun still high and beating down on the still, windless water. Justin stepped into the boat and moved around with feathery lightness, making me, thirty-five years his junior, feel shamefully creaky. We passed Madol Duwa, an uninhabited islet in the lake – a short, clumpy dark-green canopy with branches of screw pine reaching down to the water – immortalized in Martin Wickramasinghe's *Gam Peraliya*. Then Justin told me about the 'flight of the double sunrise'.

During the Second World War, after Singapore fell to the Japanese, Qantas Imperial Airways had Catalina flying boats brave the contested skies between the Swan river, near Perth, and Koggala Lake. It was twenty-eight hours of non-stop flying, a world record, taking in two sunrises. Singapore was their refuelling stop on the flight between London and Sydney via Calcutta; Koggala replaced it for the last two years of the war. Justin's family had a little house on an islet in the lake known locally as Kurullu Duwa (Bird Island). From that vantage point, as a boy, he saw the Catalinas take off from and land on the clear stretch of water across the breadth of the lake. Now he pointed to the rock in the middle of the lake where the windsock used to hang.

After we skirted round Kurullu Duwa, on the way back, we saw a bird in distress. I scooped it out of the water into the boat. But it was too late: moments later it convulsed, squirted blood from its beak and stopped moving. We laid it to rest on the banks of Madol Duwa. 'That was its lifespan,' said Justin matter-of-factly. He repeated it a few times. It occurred to me he was thinking of his son who had died, not yet fifty, a few months earlier.

I said goodbye to Justin and promised to come back. 'Come any time,' he said with his customary good cheer and that twinkle in his eye. 'I'm here twenty-four hours a day, 365 days of the year.'

This was my first visit to Justin. The last time I saw him at the walauwe, he had changed his mind about selling up and moving to Colombo. With his son gone, there was no one to whom to pass on the walauwe; his daughter had no interest in inheriting it. His other relatives had pressured him to sell, and he relented. How, I wondered, would he cope in the city, away from the simple, bracing country life that had kept him evergreen?

~

The 'deep south' starts on the other side of Matara and stretches all the way to the Yala National Park on the south-east coast. This is the heart of Ruhunu, a sub-kingdom founded around 200 BCE that lasted almost 2000 years. It was founded by Mahanaga, the brother of the first Sinhala Buddhist king, Devanampiya Tissa, in Anuradhapura. Mahanaga and his successors established their capital, Mahagama, near the south-eastern tip of the island. Over the next 150 years, this collateral branch of Anuradhapura's royal house unified Ruhunu and gained control of the whole island. Dutugemunu, son of King Kavan

Tissa and the most storied Sinhala king, launched his conquest of the rest of Lanka from Mahagama. First he had to secure Ruhunu for himself and see off Sinhala rivals; then he waged a fifteen-year campaign against the Tamil king Elara. This the *Mahavamsa* dramatizes as a Sinhala Buddhist holy war against Tamil invaders. It culminated in a battle between the two kings, fought on elephants according to kshatriya rules of chivalry just outside Anuradhapura; Dutugemunu killed Elara, entered Anuradhapura and reunited the island under Sinhala Buddhist rule.

For most of Sri Lankan history before Western colonization, Ruhunu remained a functioning sub-kingdom, jealously guarding its local interests and identity. The authority of Rajarata (the Sinhala Buddhist kingdom in the north-central plain) prevailed only loosely and indirectly. Ruhunu was the refuge of Sinhala kings overthrown by South Indian invaders and the launch pad for their reconquest of Rajarata. Vijayabahu I launched his campaign against the Cholas from here in the tenth century CE, retaking Rajarata and its capital Polonnaruwa for the Sinhalese. His successor Parakramabahu I was a centralizer, determined to maintain an iron grip on the whole island; unlike previous Sinhala kings, he did not tolerate regional particularisms. He quashed a Ruhunu rebellion brutally, killing his own relatives in its royal house, and eliminated its former autonomy. This proved fatal after his reign: Ruhunu lost its ability both to provide refuge to deposed Sinhala kings and as a base for reconquest. When Magha of Kalinga (in eastern India) conquered Polonnaruwa and laid waste to Rajarata in the thirteenth century, he destroyed the ancient edifice of Sinhala kingship in one stroke.

~

The deep south used to be a poor, remote, thinly populated backwater compared with the west coast around Colombo and the south coast up to Galle and Matara. Even just over a decade ago, when I first came back to Sri Lanka, the other side of Matara felt like old Ceylon – quiet, bumpy roads, few people, small, sleepy towns, a very slow pace of life. Not any more. The deep south is Rajapaksa heartland, and the Rajapaksa government lavished spending on it like on no other region in Sri Lanka. The main roads are new and smooth. It takes much less time to drive from Colombo to Tangalle and Hambantota, the main towns in the deep south. The Southern Expressway is being extended to Hambantota and beyond, and so is the Colombo–Matara railway line. New infrastructure spawned new activity. Roadside stalls cropped up, selling fruits, vegetables and drinks to travellers. New hotels and guest houses catered to new tourists as part of Sri Lanka's post-war tourist boom. The towns became bigger and more lively, the paddy fields greener with much better irrigation; people looked better off.

We stopped in Tangalle, whose bay is among the island's most breathtaking. A sharp bend in the coast road announces its vista all at once, without warning, drawing gasps of appreciation and wide-eyed wonder from all who see it for the first time. The road curves along the corniche above the bay. Halfway along, jutting into the bay, is the newly refurbished Tangalle Bay Hotel, where I stayed the night. Its modernist architect, Valentine Gunasekara, designed it in the early 1970s to look like a ship beached on the cliff, splicing the bay in half, its prow facing the sea.

The hotel was fairly busy with tourists this time. The last time I came here was for Christmas Day lunch, before the end of the war; we were the only non-local guests that day. The building was rotting away after decades of few tourists and lack of maintenance, compounded by tsunami damage.

Tangalle town is just the other side of the bay. It also looked better: 'beautification' arrived here, too. The lotus pond was clean now; five years earlier, on my last visit, it was strewn with rubbish.

On that visit, the small black-stone Methodist church on the main road looked abandoned, with broken windows and long-unmown grass out front; now, this Sunday morning, the church and grounds were presentable and busy with worshippers. The main junction around the clock tower and the market next to it were bustling with locals, tourists and day trippers. The town centre was plastered with posters and billboards of Mahinda Rajapaksa, his brothers Basil, Gotabhaya and Chamal, and his son Namal. Mahinda was depicted in various guises: Mahinda the Pious visiting temples, bowing to monks and giving them alms; Mahinda the Munificent bestowing his blessings on an adoring village grandmother, with rays of sunshine in the background.

Rajapaksa posters were ubiquitous island-wide before the government changed. Then they disappeared mostly, as always happens with regime change in Sri Lanka – except in the deep south. Mahinda returned to Carlton House, the family's ancestral home in Tangalle, down a side road past the lotus pond, the day he lost office. The house was bursting with well-wishers for several weeks afterwards. Tangalle remained the Rajapaksas' ultimate refuge, where they retreated after heavy defeat, waiting to launch their reconquest of Lanka – just like ancient Ruhunu kings.

We drove down past the old rest house, the colonial administrator's house in Dutch times, to the little harbour with its fishing boats and small patch of beach. It was busy with local day trippers. But, as I stepped on the sand, I recalled a photo in Victor Ivan's *Paradise in Tears*, a photographic guide to conflict in Sri Lanka. This photo was of the charred remains of a corpse set alight on this spot in September 1987. The victim was Sathyapala Wannigama, a sociology lecturer at Ruhunu University and, allegedly, a prominent member of the JVP. Government paramilitaries abducted and killed him, leaving his body stripped and burnt on this beach.

Tangalle, not by accident, was a cauldron of JVP ferment. The

Top left: Mummy in Wales, just before leaving for Australia, 1955

Top right: Daddy in the UK for air force training, 1959

Bottom: My parents' wedding photo, Colombo, July 1961

Top left: Mummy and I in the garden at the Hindu College Square house, Ratmalana, 1966

Top right: Granny in front of the New Oriental Hotel, Galle Fort, 1969

Bottom: Mount Lavinia Hotel and beach in the 1960s

Top: The Sally/Salih extended family and friends at my brother Reyaz's fourth birthday party, Mount Lavinia beach, September 1972

Bottom: Mummyma, Daddy, his siblings and I at my twenty-seventh birthday party, Colombo, January 1992

Top: Taprobane, Weligama Bay, February 2009

Middle: Joseph and I on the road, Eastern Province, March 2015

Bottom: Nihal, Mummy and I, Kalametiya beach, the deep south, November 2011

Top: The shelled ruin of Stanton Villa, Kayts, Jaffna peninsula, December 2011

Middle: The Lilliputian stupas at Kanthorodai, Jaffna peninsula, December 2011

Bottom: The victory memorial, Kilinochchi, Northern Province, December 2011

Top: The standing and recumbent Buddhas, Gal Vihara, Polonnaruwa,
December 2011

Bottom: Polonnaruwa rest house, December 2011

Top: The Razeena estate bungalow, Uva, December 2014

Bottom: Uva hills in the mist, December 2015

Top: The bullet-ridden wall of the jumma mosque, Kattankudy, Eastern Province, February 2018

Bottom: The Colombo skyline across Beira Lake, with the Lotus Tower in the foreground, December 2018

JVP leader Rohana Wijeweera was born here. His father was a Communist Party sympathizer, assaulted in 1947 by political opponents, who left him paralysed for life. This marked young Rohana deeply. He got a scholarship to study in the Soviet Union in the early 1960s. When he returned to Ceylon he got involved in the Communist Party, but was expelled for schismatic activities. He founded the JVP a few years later. His mix of Marxism, Sinhala nationalism and armed revolution appealed to alienated youth – nowhere more so than in this poor, remote part of the country.

Back at the main junction we turned on to a side road and drove inland for an hour. My destination was the rock temple at Mulkirigala, and I was making this detour for a special reason. In 1826, George Turnour, the government agent at Ratnapura, came here on horseback. He had to cut through thick jungle; back then there were no proper roads, only dirt paths and enveloping jungle this side of Matara. Turnour was the sort of bookish, history-minded British colonial who immersed himself in local culture, to the point of all-consuming passion. A monk in Galle had taught him Sinhala; the same monk told him about Mulkirigala. When he came he made the discovery of his life – a discovery that unlocked over 2000 years of Lankan history.

The monks who showed him round the temple pointed to a bookcase full of palm-leaf manuscripts. Turnour realized immediately this was the tika (or prose-key) that could decipher the *Mahavamsa*, which his monk friend in Galle had told him about. Given Buddhism's decrepitude after three centuries of Western colonialism, not many monks knew the *Mahavamsa*'s contents, but even the ones who did found it impossible to make sense of its metrical, mystifying Pali verse. The tika that Turnour chanced upon could be fitted into the verse to render it into a common-sense narrative. Turnour spent the next decade doing precisely that. He taught himself Pali with the help of a few monks and translated, edited and arranged thirty volumes of the *Mahavamsa*. These were published first in English and only later in Sinhala. Turnour did not live to see the whole of the *Mahavamsa* published, but he opened the way, as he did to the translation of Pali inscriptions among the monuments in Anuradhapura and Polonnaruwa.

Mulkirigala is still remote, surrounded by low-country vegetation with little habitation in sight. My temple guide was a local villager, a middle-aged man of dignified bearing, in national dress of immaculate white long shirt and sarong, with luxuriantly sprouting ear hair. He told me he taught himself English when he was twenty-one and had a career as a junior clerk in a government office. The temple dates back to the first or second century BCE and was a monastery for meditating monks; Kandyan kings restored it in the eighteenth century. Caves on two levels of the rock face contain reclining Buddhas and murals depicting Jataka stories (from the previous lives of the Buddha). Then, on the upper level, my guide pointed to a bookcase, next to a cave entrance. This was the bookcase Turnour saw. Now it was empty, dirty and half-broken.

~

We returned to the coast road and headed towards Hambantota. Suddenly, a little way out of Tangalle, the scenery changed: we entered the dry zone. Behind us was what Leonard Woolf called the 'gentle soft liquid' world of the wet zone, full of air and trees, all coated in a deep dark green. Ahead were wider spaces, more economical vegetation, fewer people, bigger skies, and a paler shade of green. Still, it is much greener than it used to be. Even after independence it was mostly scrub jungle, dry and desolate, with isolated *chena* (slash-and-burn) cultivation, ancient temple ruins and irrigation works abandoned centuries ago. But decades of irrigation have made the dry zone much less 'dry'; here in the deep south, rice and vegetable cultivation is no longer restricted to a few months of the year.

My next stop was the village of Hungama, where I was going to stay with my friend Renton, who I first met at a dinner party a few years ago when he still lived and worked in Colombo. He was waiting by his porch as we drove in, his customary banian and sarong enveloping his considerable girth. Next to him were his man Friday Nalaka, a quiet, shy Sinhalese man from the hill country, and Nalaka's two young children, who clearly had the run of the house.

Renton showed me round the house, his retirement home, which he had remodelled to resemble a walauwe. The interiors were simple and spare, but tastefully decorated with period furniture and curios. At the back was a three-sided veranda with rooms and a kitchen; enclosed within the veranda was a pond, bordered by vegetable and herb patches and a little pavilion behind it. I hardly had time to catch my breath: Renton talked of the house and his various local projects in a torrential flow. He is a true Sri Lankan: an inveterate talker, talking a mile a minute, full of opinions. He has that Sri Lankan habit of cutting you off at the beginning of your sentence – or, if he is indulgent, in mid-sentence – and going off on his own tangent. When other Sri Lankans do this, I get frustrated and bored. But I listened intently to Renton's relentless monologues, for he had much to say that repaid listening.

Renton retired as chairman of the Sri Lanka Tourist Board after a long career in the travel and tourism industry. When he turned sixty he gave it all up; he 'let go', as Buddhists say. He forsook Colombo bright lights and society for this distant village. But he did not come to Hungama to 'retire'. Far from it. As he told me, 'I realized I couldn't change Sri Lanka in the big things. For most of my life I thought I could. I tried. But I failed. Like everybody else. It's a waste of time: nothing ever changes. So I stopped and changed tack. Now I try to make a difference in small things, here in the village. I have my local projects. I have an impact on about forty families. If I can make a positive difference to twenty young people, I'm happy.'

Renton called his late calling in life 'The Power of One' – what a single person can do on the ground. 'My way of doing this is to spend small amounts of money to get maximum effort from those who receive it. No waste and no handouts. NGOs have so many overheads; they create so much waste and breed a dependency culture. You must insist on something in return for whatever you give. If I give 2000 rupees a month to a poor student in the village, I insist she gives free tuition once a week to a younger child. And I have to monitor it carefully. There is so much to do in the village. There is work and money enough for most. The men can earn 1200 rupees a day from casual labour. But they might give their wives 400 rupees of it; they spend the rest on drink and gambling. People have low expectations. They are satisfied with a secure public sector job, say, as a file clerk or a bus conductor. In the fishing communities here, the men drink all the time and marry their daughters off at sixteen. People lack a dream. I want to show the village children and youth a wider horizon, raise their ambitions – so they can have a "dream".'

I asked Renton if he missed Colombo. 'I don't miss it at all, Razeen. So much time is wasted – traffic, noise, society gatherings, meaningless talk. Now I only go back once every four months to see my GP; I drive back the same day if I can. I think my Colombo friends have forgotten about me by now. But I have no regrets.'

Our conversation took place over a long meal in the all-purpose living room. After dinner he showed me his projects on his PC, using digital photos, videos and assorted web content, all projected on to his TV screen. He spent much of his time preparing and teaching classes, right here in his living room, for bright kids from two village schools.

I rose early the following morning for Renton's Saturday 'masala' class, his potpourri of 'English, computers and values'. This morning's class was for thirteen- to seventeen-year-olds. Ten arrived, all girls. They looked spruce and demure in blouses with long skirts or long trousers, their raven hair combed straight back into a long plait. Renton said the boys had dropped out gradually. This, I thought, was Sri Lanka in microcosm: the boys prioritized their weekend leisure time, but these girls strived for something more in life, something Renton could point them towards.

The class started with a simple Buddhist prayer. All the girls were Buddhist. Renton told the class I lived in Singapore, which prompted him to talk about Singapore, illustrating what he said with Wikipedia entries and YouTube clips. Then he moved on to the topical story he had chosen for this week: President Sirisena's visit to Japan for the G7 summit – the news hook to talk about a new country, its people, language, food and culture. He asked questions along the way. But the girls were shy and barely audible, even more so with me around. Renton said it was incredibly difficult to get them to talk. The whole culture worked against it – deference to elders at home, and deference to teachers and rote learning at school. But he persisted, kindly, gently, addressing each girl by name with the suffix *dua* (daughter).

Renton moved on to other topics: English listening and comprehension based on a TV news clip, and English grammar with multiple-choice questions. At the end of class, the girls approached him individually and prostrated themselves as a mark of respect to their teacher; he touched them softly on their heads and said 'Buddhusarana' ('May the Buddha protect you').

Over lunch I asked Renton how he incorporated Buddhism into

his teaching. In Sinhala Buddhist Hungama, village life revolved around the temple and its monk. Renton's Buddhism also ran deep and was purposefully lived out. 'I have no time for temple rituals and monks' moneymaking schemes,' he said. 'But I think it is important to promote Buddhist values and Sinhala Buddhist culture. I hope at least some of my students will grow up to be independent-minded and be genuine Buddhists. When I talk about Buddhism I tell them what the dhamma says and hope it will guide them to be good Buddhists. I don't tell them how they should behave when they go to the temple and what sort of offerings they should give to the monk.'

After lunch came the masala class for fifth graders, a small group of ten-year-old boys and girls. And Sunday afternoons were for music classes. Renton bought instruments for the children and hired two music teachers from a nearby school. Class began with a Buddhist prayer, and then a few minutes' meditation followed by a yoga breathing exercise. Then the music started: boys and girls on tablas and flutes, and drumming the sides of clay pots with little sticks. They ran through several Buddhist devotional songs. A boy led with ringing, lilting solos. Class ended with everyone standing ramrod straight, chests out, arms down and fists clenched, to sing the national anthem.

Over dinner, on my last evening at Renton's, I told him I got the sense he was happier, more fulfilled, than he had been in his previous life. 'Oh yes,' he said without a flicker of doubt. 'Before I used to be anxious about so many things. Now not at all. I have no worries. I sleep soundly. I feel *light*. I am giving back for the free education I had. These days I put more into teaching than anything else. Other things are for my own pleasure; teaching is about giving to others, which is more satisfying.'

~

Hambantota is Sri Lanka's 'Malay town', though it has many Sinhalese as well. Greek navigators knew of its natural harbour going back to the time of Alexander. Local lore has it that Malay seafaring traders came here in *sampans* centuries ago, stopping on their way to and from East African ports; 'Hambantota' (Malay port) is a corruption of 'Sampantota'. The Dutch brought over Malays from Java as soldiers and slaves; in the nineteenth century the British even had a Malay regiment, the Ceylon Malay Rifles, whose soldiers and their families retired here. The more educated Malay settlers in Hambantota formed a professional class of legal executives, court interpreters, police officers and *kachcheri* (local government office) staff. Hambantota is also the salt capital of Sri Lanka; there are large *lewaya*s (salt pans) just outside town, fringed by rain trees. Salt officials were exclusively Malay. According to the 2012 census, there are about 44,000 Malays in Sri Lanka; several thousand live in Hambantota.

Hambantota is also the cradle of Rajapaksa vanity projects, all located outside the town. These I wanted to see. But first we had to drive into town for lunch.

Until regime change in 2015, the approach to Hambantota and the town itself were plastered with billboards advertising the chubby, grinning face and short-cropped, spiky hair of Namal Rajapaksa, President Rajapaksa's son and heir apparent. We stopped at the small locked-up colonial cemetery. It was thoroughly neglected: uncut grass grew as tall as the headstones, which stood precariously fissured and crumbling; some had collapsed into little heaps of rubble. The oldest tombstone, still just about intact, dated back to 1836. Next to the cemetery was a large, empty concrete space leading down to the beach. This area was once a crowded settlement of Malay fisherfolk, until the tsunami washed it away in 2004. Hambantota was among the worst-hit areas: around 3000 people lost their lives here.

Up the hill and down to the beach on the other side is a poor part of town, a warren of narrow, dusty lanes and tumbledown, packed-in houses. It is also Malay. I noticed several moon faces with blue eyes and fair complexions – rare sights in Sri Lanka, even among Muslims. The men and boys all wore prayer caps. The older women were in saris with their heads covered; the younger women and girls were in salwar kameez with shawls draped over their heads. All this lay in sight of the Hambantota rest house, a large bungalow just over the hill's brow.

The rest house looked woebegone, like other state-run rest houses around the island. It was not the place to be at in the evenings, when police officers and other municipal officials arrived after work to get rat-arsed. But the building was still charming, one wing with generous eaves and solidly pillared in the Dutch style, the other wing a boxy art deco, both with broad verandas and planters' chairs facing the back garden and the wide, wide sweep of Hambantota Bay down below. From the lawn you could look down to fishing boats behind a breakwater, built after the tsunami, then go back inside for a very good rice-and-curry lunch. Rest house rice and curries are generally better than the hotel version, because they are spicier and come with a wider variety of side dishes. This was rice and curry for locals more than tourists, and it reminded me of rest house lunches on childhood holidays.

Up the road are two old kachcheri or municipal buildings, in cream-pink with a typical Dutch stoep, and the government agent's bungalow. On my previous visit, in 2011, the kachcheri buildings were still functioning, just as they were when Leonard Woolf was assistant government agent here over a century ago. But now I found one building rotting away, full of broken windowpanes and engulfed by weeds and a troop of monkeys. The kachcheri, I discovered, had moved to a large new administrative complex way out of town on the road to the new airport.

Beyond the kachcheri, near the cliff edge, is the government agent's bungalow, which commands a sweeping panorama of the ocean in front and bays on both sides. This was where Leonard Woolf lived for over half of his seven years in Ceylon. Hambantota was where he did his most productive work as a colonial official and where he felt most fulfilled. The bungalow had a high parapet wall now, but, peeking through the main gate, it looked much as it did in Woolf's day. In *Growing,* he wrote that he would take his breakfast on the lawn; as regular as clockwork, flocks of pink flamingos, in perfect V-formation, flew high above the cliff, took a sharp right-angled turn, and made a beeline for the salt pans outside town.

Woolf led a solitary and work-filled existence here. 'I became almost fanatically interested in the country and the people and in certain aspects of my work,' he wrote. He became obsessed with good administration and drove his kachcheri staff hard; indeed he comes across as a Kiplingesque role model, taking the White Man's Burden to heart. He said if he had stayed in Ceylon he would have buried himself in Hambantota district until retirement, striving to eradicate disease, build schools and irrigate paddy fields. It was the Sinhalese that interested him, not fellow Europeans. He saw only three or four other white faces during these years, once or twice a month during his visits to Tangalle and Tissamaharama. But it was also during his time in Hambantota that he turned anti-imperialist, realizing the absurdity of lording it over a foreign race.

Unlike other foreigners, in colonial times and afterwards, Woolf did not idealize or romanticize the Sinhalese. In *Growing*, he presented them warts and all, their charm mingling with their inclination for superstition, and village life as a hotbed of infighting and caste oppression. These traits came together imaginatively in his *Village in the Jungle*, written soon after he returned to England. The novella is set in the jungles of Madampattu, east of Hambantota, where Woolf walked, tracked and shot game. It is the antithesis of a

Somerset Maugham short story. The characters are nearly all natives, and their world – of grinding poverty, disease and superstition, all the while fighting a losing battle against the encroaching jungle – is seen from their point of view. Generations of Sri Lankan schoolchildren were weaned on the book, and it was turned into a popular Sinhala film in 1980.

Growing sparkles with lyricism. Woolf wrote that his time in Ceylon 'left a mark upon my mind and even character which has proved indelible, a kind of reserve or withdrawal into myself which makes me inclined always to stand just a little to one side of my environment'. Of his Hambantota period, he wrote, 'I find this kind of complete solitude, with the necessity of relying absolutely upon oneself and one's own mind, is, when one is young, extremely good for one . . . I acquired a taste for it which I have never lost.' These were 'interludes of complete isolation . . . wordless and soundless meditation and savouring one's own unhurried existence'.

Fortified by a rest house rice-and-curry lunch, Nihal and I headed out of town to see the Rajapaksa projects. The first and largest project was the new port, built with Chinese state-backed loans, totalling over $1 billion, and by Chinese engineers and labourers. The Rajapaksa government wanted to turn Hambantota port into a South Asian hub for maritime commerce on the ancient trading route between the Gulf and the Straits of Malacca. Thus it would recreate the magic of Galle in centuries past. The commercial logic, however, was always dubious. Colombo port is the obvious candidate, and it is unlikely another port would add much to Sri Lanka's shipping business. That is the way it has turned out so far. The port here has hardly any business save for imported cars, which are required to enter here, even though most are destined for Colombo.

We drove along the new road to the port entrance, past the grounds of the newly opened Shangri-La hotel. There was literally zero activity when we arrived: no vehicles at the port entrance, no ships docked, no containers on the quayside. The multistorey glass-fronted Port Authority building was also empty; its translucent windows revealed totally unfurnished upper floors.

In 2017, three years after this visit, the government and China Merchant Port, a Chinese state-owned company, concluded in essence a debt-for-equity swap: China Merchant Port got the port operation, plus 15,000 acres of adjoining land for an industrial zone, on a ninety-nine-year lease. The price was $1.1 billion to the Sri Lankan government. I have doubts that the port-cum-industrial zone will make commercial sense. But it does entrench Sri Lanka's dependence on the Chinese government. The Indian and American governments are particularly worried China will sneak in military activity under cover of a supposedly commercial port operation. In 2017, they insisted the Sri Lankan government revise the lease agreement to ensure the Sri Lankan authorities manage port security, and to expressly forbid any foreign country using the port for military purposes.

Once back at the main coast road, we turned on to the new multi-lane highway that skirts Hambantota town. It was eerie, reminiscent of movie footage of Hitler's new autobahns in the 1930s. Driving just a few miles outside town there was virtually no traffic, just miles and miles of broad empty road cutting through scrub jungle where wild elephants used to roam freely. Nihal told me it could be unsafe to drive on these new highways at night because of elephants crossing. We passed the new Mahinda Rajapaksa International Convention Centre. It looked vacant: no delegates, no staff and no cars in the grounds. The lone human being I noticed was a security guard at one of the two main entrance gates; he lay asleep this afternoon, his legs hoicked up on a spare chair. A half-hour drive out we came to the Mahinda Rajapaksa International Cricket Stadium near the village of Sooriyawewa – also bare and silent. It was used four or five times a year for international matches, but deserted otherwise.

What I really wanted to see was the new airport, the Mattala Rajapaksa International Airport, named for the small settlement outside Hambantota where it is located. It is Sri Lanka's second 'international' airport, also built with Chinese labour and with a Chinese loan of close to $300 million. It opened with great fanfare in 2013, but not three years passed before it was being written up as the world's emptiest airport in Western magazines.

We passed the control tower and went up to the viewing platform; a vanload of Sinhala villagers from another part of the country was already up there. The view was surreal. I saw a long runway, an expanse of tarmac and a mid-sized terminal building. But there were no planes on the tarmac, none landing and none taking off. We walked to the terminal building. The car park was empty except for three or four minivans with local tourists. I did not see any passengers. Inside, I counted about fifty staff – security personnel, customs officials, check-in staff, airport management, cleaners – in various attitudes of repose; they had nothing to do all day, most days of the week. A cafe, an information desk, a travel agent's counter and a bureau de change lay unmanned. All was revealed by the Arrivals and Departures screens. The Arrivals screen showed two flights arriving the next day, one from Colombo, the other from Male in the Maldives; the Departures screen also showed two flights, one destined for Colombo, the other for Shanghai. The state-owned national carrier, Sri Lankan, and the state-owned budget airline, Mihin Lanka, operated all flights. That was it: four flights on two days of the week. I was reminded of Renton's comments about waste. This was a spectacle and a monument to tinpot Third World vanity.

The post-Rajapaksa government got the Paddy Marketing Board to store rice in Mattala airport's unused air cargo terminals. In 2016, over 300 soldiers, policemen and volunteers were deployed to chase away wild animals who had strayed on to the airport from the surrounding jungle; firecrackers were used to scare them off. By 2018, there were zero international flights. To allay Indian concerns about Chinese influence, the government is trying to persuade its Indian counterpart to operate the airport as a Sri Lankan–Indian joint venture. Might this, together with the port, see halfway decent commercial life after all? Perhaps – or perhaps not. But hundreds of billions of rupees have been wasted along the way, leaving a debt mountain and outsize Chinese influence.

~

About an hour's drive east of Hambantota is Tissamaharama, now a mid-sized town, but all jungle in Leonard Woolf's day. Until the mid-nineteenth century there were few people here. The Dutch tried to persuade locals from Matara to settle here, to no avail. Only with the restoration of the large *wewa* (an ancient man-made tank), starting in the late nineteenth century, was irrigation, viable rice cultivation and colonization possible.

Tissamaharama stands on the site of Mahagama, the ancient capital of Ruhunu. The wewa, with a bund around it, is just off the centre of the town. We drove to The Safari, right on the lake; it was the old rest house – where Mummy and Daddy stayed on a trip to the deep south in the early 1960s – but the Galle Face Group, its present owners, expanded and modernized it. On the lawn, just before sunset, I saw flocks of white herons flying to their night-time shelter in the trees of Kurullu Duwa, in the lake not far from The Safari. There were so many – in the thousands – that, in this tropical twilight, their mass converging descent created the effect of snowfall. Their cackle reverberated around the lake before they rested for the night.

From here, a good road leads to Kataragama, one of the three most venerated Buddhist sites in Sri Lanka. Kataragama has been a major centre of pilgrimage going back to the fifteenth century, known as far afield as Thailand. It is said that Dutugemunu came to worship here before setting off to conquer the rest of the island, culminating in his defeat of Elara in Anuradhapura.

Leonard Woolf supervised the annual pilgrimage here in 1910, just before he went back to England for good. Then it was just a clearing in the jungle, accessible only by a dirt track. Pilgrims were plagued by disease and in constant fear of wild animals. Woolf came back in 1960, on his only visit to Ceylon after his time as a colonial official. But Kataragama's galloping commercialization repelled him, particularly its 'rapacious priests'. Roland Raven-Hart, visiting around the same time, thought it 'a scruffy place, like most places that are parasitic on pilgrims or tourists, with rows of shabby, haphazard booths and eating-sheds'.

Historically, Kataragama has been religiously eclectic, attracting Hindus and Muslims as well as Buddhists. Until a few decades ago, most pilgrims were Tamils, some coming from South India, and many from the Jaffna peninsula along an age-old pilgrimage route down the east coast. That stopped during the war. Now Kataragama is overwhelmingly a Buddhist pilgrimage site, with a bustling bazaar and stalls full of religious paraphernalia, though it still attracts large numbers of Hindus and some Muslims.

We crossed the Menik Ganga (River of Gems) to the temple enclosure, which remains an object lesson in Sri Lanka's history of religious mixing and matching. At one end is a small mosque with the shrine of a Sufi saint. A sand path runs down the middle of the compound; Shiva image houses border it on both sides. At the other end are devales, housing Hindu deities incorporated into the Buddhist pantheon. The main devale is devoted to Kataragama. To Hindus he is Skandah, also known as Murugan, Subramaniam and

Kandeswamy, son of Shiva and Parvati, brother of the elephant-god Ganesh. Sinhalese believe he turned into the Buddhist deity Kataragama ages ago. His reputation is that of a fearsome warrior and ardent lover. He carries a *vel* or trident, one of Shiva's most potent symbols, and his mount is the peacock. Inside the devale, at the evening puja, nearly all the devotees were Buddhist.

~

Kataragama borders the Yala National Park, home to sambar, bears, wild boars, leopards and elephants. It became an animal sanctuary in 1938. Before it attracted big-game hunters; Leonard Woolf, as assistant government agent of Hambantota district, issued them licences. My final destination on this southern tour was not Yala but Kirinda, a coastal village on Yala's southern tip.

Kirinda was where some Malay soldiers and their families settled when the British disbanded the Ceylon Malay Rifles in the nineteenth century. Here they became fisherfolk. But Kirinda is best known for its ancient temple, atop a rock facing the sea. The temple's founding legend is the Sinhala Buddhist tradition's most romantic.

Around 200 BCE, King Kelani Tissa, who ruled a sub-kingdom near what is now Colombo, put his beautiful daughter Viharamahadevi in a small boat, all alone, and cast her out to sea. He did this as a sacrifice, to propitiate the gods who were enraged by his execution of a Brahmin. In revenge they caused the ocean waters to surge and submerge his kingdom – the last time a tsunami hit Sri Lanka before 2004. The boat drifted down along the south coast before washing up at Kirinda. King Kavan Tissa of Ruhunu saw the boat and its beautiful princess, fast asleep; he fell in love at first sight and later married her. Their son, Dutugemunu, unified Sri Lanka under Sinhala Buddhist rule.

I climbed the stairs on the rock face, its surface scorched by the noonday sun. The temple enclosure at the summit provided immediate relief, as I entered its canopy of cool, scented shade; flowering frangipani trees, also known as *araliya* or temple trees, formed a ring around it. Stray dogs lounged in the shade. Up another small rock face was a gleaming white bell-shaped stupa, with a statue of a slender, elongated Viharamahadevi next to it. A small Vishnu devale perched on another rock down below. There were just a handful of local worshippers around – and me. Everything felt remote, still, serene. Alone on the rock, standing next to the stupa and Viharamahadevi, I took in the panorama: the big azure sky, the flat scrub jungle, the deserted beaches on both sides, the expanse of the Indian Ocean.

Kalutara was where I started my turn in the south; Kirinda was where it ended.

6

Kandy Road

To the Hill Capital and Tea Country

All he could see in the half-light before dawn was the figure of a man standing at the edge of the lawn, peering through the mists at the mountains far away waiting for the sun to break through . . . But it was how Sanji himself began the day, standing on the same spot on which the man stood, watching the mists unveil the sun, and the sun unveil a cluster of green hills and mountains, from the folds of which sprang streams and rivulets and waterfalls that caught the sun in flight. For just that minute, though, for no sooner caught than it was gone, high into the sky, refusing to be looked at, but lighting up now the tangle of trees and shrubs and creepers in the valley below, to the greetings of a thousand birds and a hosanna of colours from the jasmine, the jacaranda and the frangipani. Day had broken, and the onlooker's eyes, returning closer home, would look immediately below him and see again the serried ranks of tea bushes and, breaking among them now, a swarm of cumbly-clad tea pluckers.

– A. Sivanandan, *When Memory Dies*

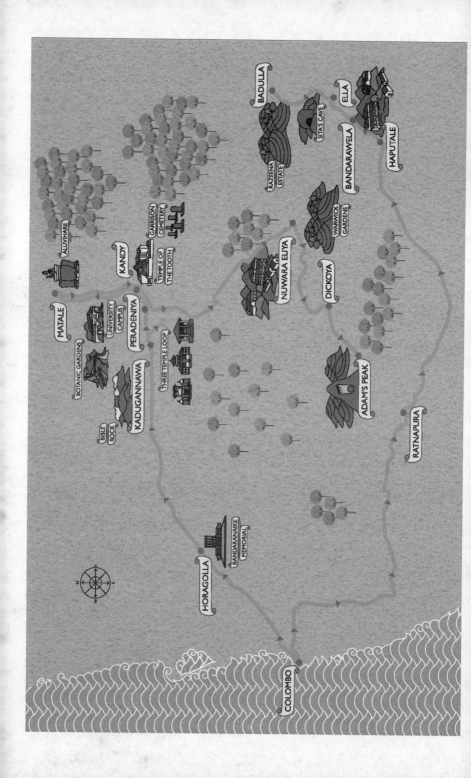

The 'upcountry' became my favourite part of Sri Lanka during school holidays spent on my uncle's little tea estate, Razeena, in the Uva hills. I grew familiar with this patch of the island during Daddy's year in prison. Roughly once a month, Mummy piled my brothers and me into our Peugeot 504 station wagon, and Tissera, our driver, motored us up to Razeena's little bungalow. In those days bad roads meant the journey took all day, with pit stops for a rest house lunch and last-minute shopping in the hill station of Bandarawela.

Razeena meant mornings of homeschooling on the lawn with Mummy, afternoons traipsing all over the estate, and evenings of playing cards in the living room and listening to the radio. The Uva hills had manicured dark-green teascapes, and a just-so climate – slightly chilly in the early mornings and nights, hot but without humidity in the day, and crisp fresh air. There was the twee colonial upholstery of estate bungalows, landscape gardens, half-timbered planters' clubs, miniature Gothic churches, and the single-track railway snaking around hillsides. How I relished the estate bungalows, perched on hilltops and shaded by cypresses, flamboyant trees and flame trees. Inside were large rooms with wide bay windows; outside were flowers – roses, foxgloves, anthuriums, agapanthus, hibiscus, marigolds, petunias, cannas – from wall to wall, in all colours of the rainbow.

Here I devoured meals of Western-style 'courses', invariably accompanied by the veg of the mother country – beets, leeks, cabbage, carrots – and topped off with pudding of apple crumble with custard or cream caramel. The beef and chicken were not the best in 1970s' Sri Lanka, given its raw material of scrawny cattle and fowl. The fish upcountry was not, and still isn't, as fresh and succulent as it is on the coast. But the vegetables were heavenly, even simply boiled, without adornment, for they came straight from the bungalow garden.

The bungalow kitchen was the domain of the *appu*, a Tamil estate bungalow head cook, who took special pride in the 'courses' he prepared. At Razeena, we borrowed the services of a cook and a cleaner from families who lived in the estate 'line-room' close by. But going to the superintendent's bungalow for lunch on a large estate was a different matter. There the table was laid with crisp white linen and an assortment of shiny cutlery; the appu, casually uniformed in a white short-sleeved shirt and white sarong, and his helpers came back and forth with piping hot dishes, serving us individually, padding the highly polished concrete floors on feet toughened and cracked by work, toes splayed.

Leonard Woolf wrote of that 'delicious one-and-a-half hours after dawn' in the upcountry. Early mornings were to savour, walking on lawn grass damp with dew, looking out to tea bushes sheeted with mist, and to hills and valleys and mountains beyond, inhaling the scent of mist and dew on the flora. But there were also cool clear star-studded nights bathed in moonlight, without a sound in the world except for the wind rustling through trees, the rush of a waterfall, and the occasional stray dog barking in estate line-rooms. I felt as the young Michael Ondaatje did on his tea estate holidays in the 1940s. As he wrote in *Running in the Family*: 'The most beautiful place in the world . . . If we lived here it would be perfect.'

In my long years away, it was the tea country I missed most. When I pined for Sri Lanka, images of Razeena would first crowd my mind. And when I returned to get reacquainted with Sri Lanka, I knew a homecoming would not be complete without going back to Razeena.

~

The A1 is the perennially congested trunk road between Colombo and the hill capital of Kandy. In my childhood it was a much more scenic ride. Low-country greenery of paddy fields and coconut groves started soon out of Colombo and climbed, largely uninterrupted, to forested hills just before Peradeniya, the town before Kandy. Now, Colombo and Kandy suburbs sprawl farther along the road, and the villages and towns in between have also inflated. The A1 feels semi-urban now. Since the end of the war, proliferating giant billboards plonked on the edges of paddy fields have disfigured its views.

My first stop out of Colombo, just before lunchtime, was the Bandaranaike Memorial, on the A1 at the family's ancestral estate of Horagolla. It is a pretty setting, bordered by frangipani trees; SWRD and Mrs B are laid to rest side by side. Given their legacy, neither deserves such prettiness. Their epitaphs ring false, couched in what George Orwell calls Duckspeak – when there is no connection between the brain and the vocal chords. SWRD is lauded for forsaking his heritage to serve the Common Man; Mrs B sacrificed herself for the country after her husband was assassinated; and so on. Sri Lankan encomiums are florid and bombastic. Here are two prize specimens.

Across the road, on a hillock, is another memorial, topped by the cross of Christ. Unlike the memorial to SWRD and Mrs B, this one is unkempt, its stonework cracked and hemmed in by weeds and unmown grass. Here lies Sir Solomon, SWRD's father and maha mudaliyar in early twentieth-century British Ceylon. Sir Solomon was the most senior native official under the British and a man of vast landed wealth, which he displayed lavishly. He was Uncle Tom-in-chief to the British, not least in his steadfast display of Anglican faith. The Bandaranaikes' family tree can be traced back to Tamils in South India who migrated to the Kandyan kingdom and became Sinhala Buddhists, changing their name along the way. They came to the low country to serve the Portuguese, Dutch and British, gaining wealth and influence as they climbed to the top of the co-opted Sinhala establishment. Along the way they changed religion, too, to Anglicanism under the British.

SWRD rebelled against his father and what he stood for, riding the tide of nationalism in early twentieth-century Ceylon. He converted to Buddhism, and Sinhala Buddhist nationalism became his vehicle to the premiership in independent Ceylon. Mrs B, a Ratwatte from Kandyan nobility, always displayed the imperious ways of her stock. The Ratwattes are *radalas*, one of the two highest Kandyan sub-castes in the govigama (the top Sinhala caste) hierarchy. They were courtiers to Kandyan kings; one of Mrs B's ancestors signed the Kandyan Convention that formally ended the Kandyan kingdom and ceded sovereignty to the British. Kandyan nobles eventually made their peace with the British, but remained more conservative and traditionalist than the low-country Sinhala elite. Unlike her husband, Mrs B was born a Buddhist, and was immersed in Sinhala Buddhist traditions and rituals throughout her life. The Bandaranaikes' marriage in 1940 was a Kandyan and low-country alliance of wealth and power at the pinnacle of Sinhala society. The political dynasty that resulted from it became one of the most powerful forces in Sri Lanka.

In July, the rambutan fruit, a cousin of the lychee, grows in abundance at the start of its short season. We passed innumerable roadside stalls heaped with rambutan, their hairy, bright red and yellow skins creating extra splashes of low-country colour. After a while the road started to climb, bend and wind. We entered Udarata – 'upcountry' in Sinhala. We passed a roadside *ambalama*, a resting pavilion for wayfarers built during the Kandyan kingdom, and then Nihal stopped the car so I could take in the view at the Kadugannawa Pass. A variegated scenery of forests, wild flowers, terraced paddy fields, rubber and tea spills a thousand feet down to the low-country plain. Framing it in the far distance is Bible Rock, called Coffin Rock by the Dutch, a solid squarish mass of rock jutting out in splendid isolation from its surrounding hills. Up around the bend is a tunnel the British cut into sheer rock when they built the Kandy road in the 1820s. And at the top of the pass is a single tall column in memory of young Captain Dawson, the engineer who oversaw the completion of the road. It opened in 1832 and was the first mail road in Asia. By building this road, the new British rulers ended Kandy's natural isolation – its chief defence from foreign predators – forever.

~

Robert Knox deserves the title of Sri Lanka's foremost expat. After all, he lived in the country for nineteen and a half years, admittedly in captivity, though it was not too onerous much of the time. He best evoked life in the Kandyan kingdom, and wrote one of the greatest books on Sri Lanka – probably the best written by a foreigner. In his *An Historical Relation of the Island Ceylon*, published in 1681, he gave a detailed, acutely perceptive account of the Kandyan kingdom in the mid-seventeenth century, encompassing its politics, people, flora and fauna. The book is all the more extraordinary because Knox wrote it entirely from memory, without preparatory notes. In his nearly two decades in Ceylon he never had access to pen and paper.

Knox led a wildly interesting and varied life. From England he went to sea, on his father's trading ship, in his late teens. In 1659, Knox and his father were on the *Anne*, destined for Madras, then run by the British East India Company. They lost the *Anne's* mast in a storm off Ceylon's east coast, and had to put ashore in Koddiyar Bay, near Trincomalee. But before they could set sail again, they, along with their shipmates, were captured by soldiers of the Kandyan king and taken to Kandy. Knox's father died just over a year later. Knox was held prisoner until he escaped in 1679, though his cage was commodious – he was allowed to roam relatively freely around the kingdom. And there he survived, made his living, indeed prospered, observed everything attentively, and schemed to escape. Eventually he escaped to Dutch-controlled territory on the north-west coast, and made his way back to England. On the voyage back he wrote his account of his experiences. *An Historical Relation of the Island Ceylon* became an instant bestseller.

After his escape Knox spent the next twenty years captaining ships for the East India Company and, on his own account, venturing around the African coast to the Gulf, India, the East Indies, and across the Atlantic to the Caribbean. On these voyages he carried goods and slaves, and even raided ships belonging to the Mughal Empire. He overcame destitution and near-death many times. Serious illness, enforced movement from one abode to another during his captivity, mutiny by his crew at sea, imprisonment and assault by a king in Madagascar, near-fatal accidents at sea – these were all part of his life experience.

In all this Knox presented a self-portrait of dour Christian piety and relentless resourcefulness. Early in his Kandyan captivity, with great difficulty, he procured a King James Bible, which remained his constant companion. While fellow European captives ran taverns and succumbed to drink, he knitted caps for sale, built his own houses, cultivated a garden with coconut trees, raised pigs, chickens and goats, and walked the length and breadth of the Kandyan kingdom as a pedlar. He planned his escape patiently and meticulously, finally walking barefoot for days through jungles full of wild animals before reaching Dutch-held territory in the north-west. We know Daniel Defoe read Knox's account of his captivity; and Knox – not Alexander Selkirk, as is commonly believed – was probably the model for the ever-resourceful Robinson Crusoe.

Knox's description of Kandyan politics is a reminder that the worst excesses of modern Sri Lankan politics have a long pedigree. The king, Rajasinghe II, was an absolute tyrant. He delighted in wanton cruelty and invented gruesome methods of torture and execution. He imprisoned and executed his subjects, nobility and commoners alike, according to his whim. There were no private property rights and no rule of law. Justice, which the nobility administered, was for sale: 'For it is a common saying in this land, That he that has money to fee the Judge, needs not fear nor care whether his cause be right or not.'

Knox detailed the feudal nature of Kandyan society, 'there being many Ranks or Casts among them', divided into royalty, nobility and several occupational castes. The dominant-caste govigamas, forming over half the population, gave Kandyan villages a homogeneous feel. Only nobles were allowed to sit on stools, and only the king had the right to sit on a stool with a back.

Knox described a pagan culture, worshipping a cornucopia of gods, idols and spirits, full of black magic and age-old beliefs in *yakka*s and *raksha*s, devils and demons – in other words, holdovers from the island's pre-Buddhist past. 'The Religion of the country is Idolatry,' he stated emphatically. 'Buddhou', who delivered the salvation of souls, was but a 'great God' in a large pantheon. Astrology, devil dances and exorcisms were common. But it was this pluralism in religion and superstition that made Kandyans so tolerant of other religions. 'Moor' (Arab Muslim) and 'Malabar' (Tamil) merchants, and Catholic exiles from Dutch rule, practised their religions freely, indeed with royal patronage; Christians were held in particularly high regard and treated on a par with nobles.

Knox read his Bible religiously and chose celibacy during his captivity. He disapproved sternly of sexual licence among the natives. Adultery, premarital sex, separation and divorce were common, without social stigma. Men offered their wives and daughters to show hospitality to honoured house guests and those of a higher station. 'Youth are bred up to Whoredom . . . I do think they be all Whores,' he wrote.

Knox was at his most picturesque when describing the leisure habits of the 'Chingulays', as he called the Sinhalese. They liked nothing better than to sit on their mats, chew betel, and indulge in endless talk with friends and neighbours:

> All these things the Land affords, and it might do it in much greater quantity, if the People were but laborious and industrious. But they are not, For the Chingulays are Naturally, a people given to sloth and laziness: if they can but anyways live, they abhor to work; onely what the necessities force them to do, they do, that is, to get Food and Rayment. Yet in this I must a little vindicate them; For what indeed should they do with more Food and Rayment, seeing as their Estates increase, so do their Taxes also? . . . Yet such is the Government they are under, that they are afraid to be known to have anything, lest it be taken away from them. Neither have they any encouragement for their industry; having no Vend by Traffic and Commerce for what they have got.

Those looking for classic stereotypes of the Sinhalese will find a rich lode in Knox. Here is a tasty morsel:

> They are crafty and treacherous, not to be trusted upon any protestations; for their manner of speaking is very smooth and courteous, insomuch that they who are unacquainted with their dispositions and manners, may be easily deceived by them. For they make no account nor conscience of lying, neither is it any shame or disgrace to them, if they be catched in telling lyes: it is so customary.

Knox added that they were 'very proud and self-conceited'; that 'a Christian's word will be believed and credited far beyond their own, because, they think, they make more Conscience of their words'; that they were 'in discourse courteous and full of Flatteries, naturally inclined in temperance in meat and drink, but not to Chastity'; and that they were 'in their Promises very unfaithful, approving lying in themselves, but misliking it in others; delighting in sloath, deferring labour till urgent necessity constrain them . . .'

~

Kandyan society remained much as Knox portrayed it well after his escape. But religious reform, at least, came with the four Nayakkar kings who ruled Kandy from 1739 to 1815. The Nayakkars were Tamil Hindus from Madurai, in present-day Tamil Nadu, who were related to Kandyan kings through their marriages to South Indian princesses. When the last, childless, Sinhala king of Kandy died, his Nayakkar brother-in-law succeeded him. He and his successors went out of their way to reinvigorate Buddhism. As South Indian Hindu imports, this was how they legitimized their rule over Sinhala Buddhist subjects. Kirti Sri Rajasinghe, the second Nayakkar king, engineered a Buddhist revival whose institutional cast survives to this day, restoring temples all over the kingdom and bringing over monks from Thailand to restore the *upasampada,* the higher ordination of monks.

He established a new *Siyam Nikaya,* or 'Siam order', and divided it into the co-equal Asgiriya and Malwatte chapters, both headquartered in Kandy and with exclusive rights to higher ordination. They are still the apex of the Sinhala Buddhist hierarchy. Crucially, the king insisted only govigamas be admitted to the Siyam Nikaya. This allowed the nobility, who came from the highest govigama sub-castes, known as *radala* and *mudali,* to cement their control of Buddhist institutions, including vast temple lands with their lucrative revenue.

Economic and social reform began only after the British conquered the Kandyan kingdom in 1815. The Kandyan chiefs rebelled in 1817. After they quashed the rebellion, the British clamped down on the

Kandyan nobility's power and privileges. Soon, they changed the face of the old Kandyan kingdom with new roads, a new railway and a new plantation economy. But later in the nineteenth century, and in the first decades of the twentieth century, successive British governors played the imperial game of divide and rule: they turned unreconstructed Kandyan nobles into collaborators to check the movement for self-government, led by members of the low-country Sinhala elite and high-caste Jaffna Tamils.

Tamils, Muslims, Burghers and low-country Sinhalese took advantage of the new commercial and educational opportunities that British reforms opened up. But Kandyans were left behind. Few Kandyan nobles became capitalists and plantation owners; they remained the most conservative element in the country. So they kept their distance from the emerging nationalist movement and what became the Ceylon National Congress, rather looking to the British to defend their privileges. No group hankered after official positions and honorific titles more than Kandyan nobles. Right up to independence, the Kandyan elite was the bulwark of political reaction against liberal and democratic reform.

This was also true in religious matters. The Buddhist revival that gathered steam in the second half of the nineteenth century was a low-country affair. Lower-caste, non-govigama monks from the *Amarapura Nikaya*, created in reaction to the Siyam Nikaya, played a prominent part in it. The Siyam Nikaya stood apart, primarily concerned with safeguarding its temple lands and privileges.

~

My earliest memory of Kandy is of the annual perahera (religious procession), which reaches its climax on Esala Poya, the full-moon day in August. I must have been four or five. We stood on the balcony of Queen's Hotel to watch the procession from the Temple of the

Tooth, right in front of the hotel next to Kandy Lake. Everything – caparisoned elephants, bejewelled nobles, priests holding umbrellas, drummers, trumpeters, pipers, dancers – glittered in the night. The dancers wore elaborate headgear and bangles on their wrists and ankles that jingle-jangled as they walked; they danced as they walked with sharp, precise, angular movements of their heads, limbs, hands and feet. And in the procession's midst was the giant temple tusker, richly caparisoned and bejewelled, carrying the temple relics on its howdah.

Robert Knox described the perahera when it was just a series of processions to and from the four devales that house Kandy's guardian deities, Pattini, Natha, Vishnu and Kataragama, all Hindu gods incorporated into the Sinhala Buddhist pantheon. Buddhist Kandyan subjects seemed happy enough with this Hinduesque spectacle after one and a half millennia of syncretism. Since the early centuries of the Anuradhapura kingdom, Tamils from South India had come over as traders, invaders, mercenaries, courtiers, priests and princess-brides to Sinhala kings, and their gods and rituals had flowed, seemingly without great obstacle, into Sinhala Buddhist practice. That syncretic river was at its widest and deepest in the Kandyan kingdom, before and during the rule of the Nayakkars.

Today's perahera season differs from that in Knox's day in one important respect: it culminates with a procession of the 'tooth relic' from the Temple of the Tooth after the four devale peraheras on preceding days. This was King Kirti Sri Rajasinghe's innovation in the eighteenth century, after visiting Thai monks voiced opposition to a spectacle with little Buddhist content.

The Temple of the Tooth is Sinhala Buddhism's most hallowed ground. The tooth relic it houses – supposedly one of the Buddha's teeth – gave essential legitimacy to Kandyan kings for over two centuries. The Kandyan chapter of the tooth relic's extraordinary peripatetic story started in the 1590s. A local warlord, an erstwhile

Catholic and Portuguese ally known as Dom João da Austria, expelled Portuguese intruders from Kandy and had himself crowned as King Vimaladharmasuriya. He founded the last major Sinhala dynasty. Minor kings had ruled from Kandy since the fifteenth century, constantly battling rivals for territorial control. But Vimaladharmasuriya refounded a unified Sinhala kingdom that came closest to the stature of the Anuradhapura and Polonnaruwa kingdoms. The *Culavamsa* (the sequel to the *Mahavamsa*) gives him high praise for this, and for two other reasons. He re-established the sangha, which was on the verge of extinction after Portuguese depredations, with the help of senior monks invited from Burma. And, significantly, he brought the tooth relic to Kandy and had it enshrined in a newly built temple, the Sri Dalada Maligawa, literally, the 'Glorious Tooth Palace'.

According to the Sinhala epics, an Indian princess, Hemamali, and her consort, Prince Dantha, had brought a tooth of the Buddha to Lanka in 312 CE. It became an object of worship and the most potent symbol of Sinhala kingship: possession was seen as essential for gaining and retaining the throne. And it led a wandering life, moving from Anuradhapura to Polonnaruwa and subsequent Sinhala capitals. In the sixteenth century, a Portuguese commander seized it and took it to Goa, where it was ceremonially crushed in a mortar, burned and thrown into the sea. But, miraculously, it reappeared in Sri Lanka. One Sinhala story is that the Portuguese captured a replica, with the original tooth hidden for safekeeping. Another says it was smuggled to Buddhist Burma and thence returned to Lanka. Vimaladharmasuriya brought it to its final resting place in Kandy, where it became the cynosure of Sri Lankan Buddhism.

The temple stands in what was a royal palace complex, of which little remains. The Natha devale, the oldest building in Kandy, surviving innumerable sackings of the town going back 650 years, lies directly in front of the temple. The Hindu deity Natha, a form of Shiva, is also the Mahayana bodhisattva Avalokiteshvara. This is Kandyan Buddhist syncretism at its most potent: an alloy of Hinduism and Mahayana sits yards away from Theravada's inner sanctum, all in the same temple enclosure for Sinhala Buddhist worship. Next to the devale is the Audience Hall, a rectangular Kandyan pavilion on a raised stone plinth, open on all sides, supported by intricately carved wooden pillars, and topped by a typically Kandyan 'hipped' roof, double-sloped and steep-pitched. This is where the British and Kandyan nobles signed the Kandyan Convention in 1815, which formalized British sovereignty over the old Kandyan kingdom.

There is little to see in the Temple of the Tooth. The entrance is fairly new. In 1998, an LTTE truck bomb detonated right here, killing over twenty people and causing extensive damage to the temple. Inside, on the upper floor, the tooth relic is held in a locked golden casket in a special enclosure; it is hardly ever displayed. But, every day, white-clad worshippers throng in front of the enclosure; they bring offerings, sit on the floor and pray silently. An old photo of the relic shows it is too long and pointed to be a human tooth. When he was stationed in Kandy just over a century ago, Leonard Woolf showed the tooth to the visiting Empress Eugénie of France; to him it appeared more canine than human. Sir James Emerson Tennent, visiting in the 1840s, thought it looked like a crocodile's tooth or a piece of carved ivory – but definitely not a human tooth.

The last king of Kandy, Sri Vikrama Rajasinghe, added an octagonal tower to the temple to house a library of 700 palm-leaf books. The tower looks out to the lake – the real delight of the city – also created by Sri Vikrama Rajasinghe on what used to be paddy fields. It was built with forced labour under the ancient rajakariya system, by which subjects performed unpaid services for the king in return for land tenure. Sri Vikrama Rajasinghe added a royal pleasure house in the middle of the lake, and the Queen's

Bath, a two-storey pavilion that juts into the lake, opposite the Octagonal Tower. The British later built a walkway and parapet around the lake.

I was not alone in finding the Temple of the Tooth underwhelming. Hermann Hesse stopped for a few days in Kandy on his Asian sea voyage in 1911. He stayed at Queen's Hotel and popped over to the temple one night for all of twenty minutes – in a 'dreamlike, half-conscious' state, for he had dysentery and had dosed himself with red wine. He found the temple's atmosphere oppressive: guides crowded around him, and rushed him through a melee of priests, servants and worshippers. He thought the temple's images – its statuary, carvings and wall paintings – distastefully idolatrous. And, echoing Knox, that was his abiding impression of worship in the temple, 'where beautiful, luminous Buddhism has developed into a truly curious form of idol worship, compared to which even Spanish Catholicism seems quite spiritual'. He continued, in a reekingly condescending passage:

> But I felt a deep sense of empathy and compassion for the kindly, gentle Indian (*sic*) folk, who over centuries had turned a magnificent pure teaching into an utter caricature and built this immense edifice of naïve gullibility, foolishly sincere prayers and offerings, and movingly misguided all-too-human ignorance and childishness. The feeble, blind vestige of the Buddha's teaching that in their simple-mindedness they were capable of understanding they honoured, cared for, hallowed and ornamented, made offerings to costly images – what are we to do, we smart and spiritual people from the West, who are much closer to the source of Buddha's teaching and to all knowledge?

~

From the Temple of the Tooth I ambled over to a side street with decrepit nineteenth-century buildings, all peeling plaster and roofs that looked like they were about to cave in. One block housed dark, poky, single-room lawyers' offices with ancient blackwood signboards hanging on the front facade, many aslant, their wood cracked, and their English and Sinhala lettering fading into borderline invisibility. Opposite was the Anglican red-brick, single-tower St Paul's Church, which the British started building in 1816, the year after they conquered the Kandyan kingdom.

I circled back to Queen's Hotel. Then Nihal and I drove all the way round the lake to the back entrance of the Temple of the Tooth. The lakeside road, a quiet, easy drive in my childhood, is congested most of the day these days, as are the town's other main roads.

On the other side of the lake from the Temple of the Tooth and Queen's Hotel, forested hills were being rapidly denuded by construction sprawl. As we drove along the lakeside road we passed the headquarters of the Asgiriya and Malwatte chapters of the Siyam Nikaya, and then several buildings dating back to British times, including the charmingly faded Hotel Suisse, which reminded me of Mount Lavinia Hotel. Until the 1980s, the hillside above these lakeside buildings was a thick green carpet, dotted here and there with stately bungalows. Now, a profusion of hotels, guest houses and private homes fanned upwards and outwards, marring the view from the lake and the town.

After we negotiated the traffic, Nihal parked the car near the back entrance to the Temple of the Tooth, and I walked round the corner and slightly uphill to see a vestige of British Kandy. Tucked into a narrow strip of land, slightly above and adjacent to the temple complex, is the Garrison Cemetery. It contains the graves of the British in Kandy up to 1871. The first person to be buried here, in 1817, was a young soldier who walked all the way from Trincomalee on the north-east coast and contracted malaria. Lady Gregory, the wife of a governor, is buried here, too. So are planters who, according to their epitaphs, had tragic misadventures. One died because his house collapsed on top of him; another impaled himself on a stake while dismounting his horse. Yet another was trampled by an elephant. I took all this at face value until I read George Orwell's *Burmese Days*. There were plenty of epitaphs along these lines in the Christian cemetery of the godforsaken Burmese town where the story played out – all euphemisms for colonials who died of alcohol poisoning. 'Mauled by a tiger' or 'Trampled to death by an elephant' sounds far more respectable than 'Liver pickled by drink'.

The lone caretaker of the cemetery showed me round. He told me his name was Charles Carmichael. He was a lighter shade of brown, and dishevelled; his cheeks had heavy stubble, his shirt and trousers were threadbare and dirty, and he walked barefoot. I took him to be in his mid- or late forties, but he could have been younger: he had the look of someone life's knocks had aged prematurely. His manner, though, was winningly shy and gentle, his eyes downcast when he spoke. Softly – barely audibly – he related the stories behind the gravestones in a mechanical voice; he knew them all by heart and churned them out for visiting tourists.

The most famous and intriguing resident of the cemetery is Sir John D'Oyly. He came from an upper-class British family and was educated at Westminster and Corpus Christi, Cambridge. He seems to have developed an early fascination for Ceylon, for he used his father's connections to secure an appointment in the newly formed Ceylon Civil Service; he went out in the first batch of British officials when the Crown took over Ceylon from the East India Company in 1802. From 1805 he was the British governor's point man for dealings with the Kandyan court and nobility. A decade of intrigue followed, and then came the crucial breakthrough – the British conquest of the Kandyan kingdom and the unification of the whole island under British rule.

D'Oyly's role was instrumental, as he detailed in his diary, found in the Kandy kachcheri, or municipal offices, a century after the Kandyan kingdom's collapse. He cultivated a network of spies and contacts in Kandy, and he persuaded its most important nobles to conspire with the British against the king. That was why the British entered Kandy unopposed. Then he drafted the Kandyan Convention, which preserved much of the power and privileges of Kandyan nobles, and became the first British Resident in Kandy. But D'Oyly went native, even before Kandy fell. He eschewed the society of fellow Europeans, became a strict vegetarian, devoted himself to the study of Sinhala and Buddhism, and dressed like the locals, going around town barefoot, in a sarong, with his long uncut hair drawn back and tied in a bun. Rarely has a senior colonial official's immersion in local culture run so deep, and one can only imagine the reaction of British society in Ceylon, with its aloof and superior ways.

After the British takeover D'Oyly tried to protect Kandyan autonomy as best he could, but this was a battle lost after the Kandyan nobles' rebellion of 1817–18. The British quashed it at the cost of over a thousand British lives and ten times that number of Sinhalese. Martial law was imposed. Nobles implicated in the rebellion were arrested, and some executed. Ehelapola, the rebellion's figurehead, was exiled to Mauritius for the rest of his life. The nobility's powers were severely curtailed. From then on the governor and military officials interfered constantly in D'Oyly's administration of Kandy. He retired in 1820, but never returned to England, despite entreaties from his family. His mother implored him to return to see The Travellers, the London club of which he was a founding member but had not yet set eyes on. D'Oyly was no longer interested. He died of cholera in Kandy in 1824, not yet fifty, a reclusive and marginalized figure.

D'Oyly intrigued me. First as an Empire type: the educated,

sensitive British colonial who immersed himself in local culture. George Turnour and Leonard Woolf were like that, but they did not 'go native' in D'Oyly's manner. Then there was his profound ambiguity. He disdained European society, but he also intrigued to topple the Kandyan kingdom and secure it for the British, thereby ending two millennia of Sinhala Buddhist kingship and establishing, for the first time, Western overlordship of the whole island. Did he regret his actions in his final years, after the British quashed the 1817–18 rebellion? I wonder.

I was also intrigued by Charles, the mixed-race caretaker, so I asked him about his background. His grandfather, it turned out, was a British tea planter who fell in love with a fifteen-year-old Tamil estate girl, the daughter of the priest at the local kovil. He wanted to take her with him to India when he was posted there, but she refused. He put his illegitimate son (Charles's father) through St Anthony's, a leading Christian school in Kandy. Misfortune must have befallen Charles somewhere along the line, for he worked as a security guard on a building site before ending up here. But here, among the graves of nineteenth-century white men and women, he seemed content with his modest lot in life.

～

Beyond Kandy town's surrounding hills nestle lovely villages in a green sea of terraced paddy and fruit orchards. Kandyan village life, with its gentle manners and lotus-eating ways, charmed Leonard Woolf, as it did D'Oyly before him. Dotted among these hills are Buddhist temples that vividly display Hindu–Buddhist syncretism. Tourists usually visit the 'three temple loop', a trio of temples near Kandy within minutes' drive of each other, built by kings of Gampola (now about an hour's drive from Kandy) in the fourteenth century. All have devales devoted to Hindu gods. Lankatilleke, the

most scenic, stands on a rock commanding a superb panorama of
the Hantane range and surrounding villages; it has a Buddha shrine
back-to-back with a circular gallery of shrines to Vishnu, Ganesh,
Kataragama and Saman. Gampola kings brought over architects
and craftsmen from South India to build all three temples; their
families became Sinhalicized and Buddhicized in a few generations.

The temple near Kandy I was keenest to see was Aluvihare, in
the town of Matale, about an hour's drive from Kandy. Matale
is nondescript, but Aluvihare is special. In the first century BCE,
King Vattagamini Abhaya commanded 500 monks to gather at
Aluvihare. They came from Anuradhapura and took refuge here
during South Indian invasions of Rajarata, the centre of the kingdom
farther north. Their mission was to commit the whole of the Pali
Tipitaka, the Buddha's collected teaching, to writing, which they
did on palm-leaf manuscripts. Generations of monks had passed
down the Buddha's discourses orally in the four centuries after his
death. And during this period there were probably attempts to write
them down. But no written record survived. Aluvihare is hallowed
Buddhist ground precisely because it is where the first recorded
writing of the Tipitaka took place. And it must have taken many
years, for the Tipitaka, even without its voluminous supplemental
commentaries, is many times the length of the Bible.

Aluvihare is famous for other reasons, too. The Indian monk
Buddhagosha sojourned here in the fifth century CE, and wrote,
in a temple cave, the *Visuddhimagga,* the prime commentary on
Theravada Buddhism. Aluvihare was also the epicentre of the
second, and last, Kandyan rebellion against the British, in 1848.
Kandyan chiefs, colluding with the sangha, proclaimed a new
king; a rebellion broke out, centred in Matale. British troops went
on the rampage. They burned the temple, destroying ancient Pali
manuscripts in its famed library.

Aluvihare's setting is captivating. The temple enclosure is a series of caves and rocks with passages cut into them, surrounded by the Matale hills and groves of coconut, breadfruit and jackfruit trees. But modern Aluvihare is a pale imitation of what it must have been like before the British destroyed it. I found it downright tacky. One cave temple with a reclining Buddha has a gut-churning antechamber. Its murals depict yakkas perpetrating horrible acts on human beings. One yakka spears a woman's vagina from behind. A man is impaled through his anus and the top of his head. Another is impaled in crucified form, with stakes going through his body horizontally and vertically. A woman has a nipple pulled by a pair of pincers. Genitals are hacked off and chopped up. Eyes are burned with hot irons and gouged out. Flames of hellfire fill the background scenery. Opposite, another cave contains a diorama of people being tortured and executed in different ways according to medieval Kandyan custom. A man hangs upside down, his legs tied to two coconut trees held together by rope; the rope is cut, tearing him apart, starting at the groin.

A large building by the main entrance houses a 'Buddhist International Library and Museum' – the successor to the old library the British destroyed. It is a joke. When I popped in, the 'library' comprised a single set of the Tipitaka, completed in 1981; tacky photos and bric-a-brac filled the rest of the ground floor. The attendant showed visiting tourists how to write on palm leaves.

~

Foreigners associate Peradeniya with its luxuriant botanical gardens, and rightly so. It was also Lord Mountbatten's headquarters for South East Asia Command after the fall of Singapore in the Second World War. But for me Peradeniya is its lovely university campus, born and brought to fruition in the fertile mind of Ivor Jennings. In his memoir, *The Road to Peradeniya*, Sir Ivor said 200 pages of delegated legislation were needed to establish the university here – all of which he wrote. His ambition was to make it 'one of the finest small universities in the world'. The site he chose was the Meda Oya valley, looking out to the Hantane ridge. 'No university in the world would have such a setting,' he wrote.

Arguably, no foreigner had as much impact on twentieth-century Ceylon as Jennings did, though his story is largely unsung. He was a working-class lad made good. He grew up poor in Bristol, in a nonconformist family that held to the typical virtues of hard work, thrift and self-improvement through education. Like his contemporaries Neville Cardus, the cricket commentator, and Anthony Burgess, the novelist, he was a 'scholarship boy' who made the best of a grammar school education. He became a distinguished constitutional expert and authority on British politics before he came to Ceylon.

Jennings arrived in 1941 to take charge of the University College of Ceylon, with its campus in downtown Colombo. He found a 'government cram shop', a glorified vocational college; by the time he left in 1955, it had become one of the leading universities in Asia. He played a crucial, albeit back-room, role in the run-up to independence in the 1940s, and remained a highly influential government adviser until his departure.

Jennings also left behind a large body of published work on Ceylon. His memoir, *The Road to Peradeniya*, is one of the very best books about Ceylon. It reflects its author's character: utterly unsentimental, detached, often hypercritical, full of sound sense – and sardonic and condescending. I picture him writing feverishly late into the night, chain-smoking, hunched over his desk with his horn-rimmed spectacles, sunken cheeks, pallid complexion and cadaverous frame. He wrote in plain, short, sharp sentences that would have pleased George Orwell or V.S. Naipaul. He gave his all for Ceylon, driving himself to perform to punishingly high self-imposed standards. But the Ceylonese, with their laid-back ways, exasperated him precisely because they rarely came close to his standards.

Between 1943 and 1947, Jennings collaborated closely with two of independent Ceylon's founding fathers. One was Oliver Goonetilleke, who became a senior cabinet minister and ultimately governor general. The other was D.S. Senanayake, the leader of the State Council, founder of the UNP, and first prime minister of independent Ceylon. Jennings was their 'unconstitutional constitutional adviser'. He drafted the State Council's Declaration of 1943, and the subsequent Ceylon Ministers' Constitution that was submitted to the Soulbury Commission, which the British government set up to examine constitutional reform in Ceylon. The latter adopted it with slight amendments, giving Ceylon independence with dominion status. Thus Jennings was the draughtsman of independent Ceylon's first constitution. It is known as the Soulbury Constitution, but it should be called the Jennings Constitution.

Jennings had high praise for Oliver Goonetilleke, and even more so for D.S. Senanayake's leadership qualities. But he was scathing of the rest of Ceylon's political class. The 'undergraduate politicians', the 'Bloomsbury Boys of Cinnamon Gardens' he came across at the University of Ceylon – the country's future leaders – were champagne socialists from upper-class families. They spoke in clichés and parroted slogans; they made good speeches but were academically mediocre. They took themselves very seriously. Jennings thought similarly of their adult counterparts, 'a group of wealthy agitators, drawn from a society based on race and caste, with no experience of government or of elementary economic principles ... Capable talkers who had done little but pass exams, who wanted to convert themselves into a nice little oligarchy.' Nepotism, bribery, exaggerated notions of prestige, flatulent oratory: these were all local, not colonial British, traits. The political class, he said, 'condone the breakdown of fundamental principles of civilized behaviour – bribery, corruption, nepotism – because they believe that man is vile'.

Such descriptions captured, with pinpoint accuracy, the post-independence political class – to this day. *The Road to Peradeniya* has an undertone of anxiousness and foreboding – that Ceylon's political class would, one day, ruin the country. Read today, Jennings's prescience about developments in post-war Ceylon and Sri Lanka is astounding. But where his prescience failed him concerned the strength and durability of his brainchild, the Soulbury Constitution. It had weak safeguards to protect the minorities. Jennings, and the rest of the departing British, put too much faith in one man, D.S. Senanayake. Without DS, the minorities were vulnerable, lacking constitutional protection.

~

The University of Ceylon opened officially at Peradeniya in 1952. It is a vast, verdant site of lawns, playing fields, gardens and forest canopy rising to the Hantane hills; frangipani trees and massive banyans shade the main road and the roads that lead off it. Its buildings are a fusion of mid-twentieth-century modernism – boxy structures with straight, perpendicular lines – and swooping Kandyan roofs and patterned columns. They light up the campus in splashes of cream-yellow and bright pink.

Over lunch at The Capri in Colombo, my friend Tissa Jayatilaka reminisced about his Peradeniya student days. 'How wonderful it was in the 1950s and 1960s. It was such a well-kept campus. Our lecturers were erudite and cultivated; they taught with real moral authority. They were true role models. And there was an easy rapport between staff and students. Many professors used to invite us to their homes. We enjoyed open-air evening plays and long, long discussions into the night. Halcyon days. But everything coarsened in the 1970s.'

The campus is not so well tended these days. The buildings look rundown; they could do with replastering and fresh coats of paint, and the grounds have lost the manicured look they had in campus photos of the 1950s and 1960s.

My first visit was to the Catholic Chaplaincy, another bright-pink building that made me think of a flock of flamingos in a watery expanse. I came here to see the veteran chaplain, Father Egerton Perera SJ. Everyone who had anything to do with the university knew of Father Egerton, and those who knew him personally said he had a special rapport with the students. He greeted me in a bit of a rush; the phone rang constantly and he had to prepare for Mass. But he preserved his kindly demeanour. Father Egerton was knocking on eighty, bearded and plump, with his extra pounds massing around his posterior – he was the first to admit how much he loved his food. He became a Jesuit at forty after studying at Peradeniya in the late 1950s and then following a career as a chartered accountant.

We chatted before he said lunchtime Mass, which he did in English with Sinhala and Tamil thrown in. The phone kept ringing; he was always busy trying to sort out students' material problems – money issues, jobs and so on – in addition to ministering to their spiritual needs. 'I feel sorry for the students these days,' he told me. 'They are under so much pressure – exams, extra tuition after class, IT courses, applying for jobs. Their education is so narrow. They don't get the liberal education we did in the 1950s – no rounded education to become a good person and good citizen in later life.'

I left Father Egerton to say Mass and headed to the other end of the campus. On my way I passed the Students' Union building. Posters of the hammer and sickle, Marx, Lenin, Trotsky and Che Guevara carpeted the walls; JVP posters were everywhere, too. Peradeniya acquired a strong left-wing reputation soon after Ivor

Jennings left in the mid-1950s; in the 1960s it became a JVP hotbed and was a breeding ground for recruits in both the 1971 and 1987–89 armed rebellions. The university was shut down several times as a result. In 1983, a Sinhala mob set upon Tamil students here. Jennings's creation, which began as one of the finest universities in Asia, careened into militancy and mediocrity.

My next visit was to the Faculty of Social Sciences to see Inoka, a lecturer in sociology. We met in the threadbare faculty lounge, and drank tea local style – milk boiled with strong black tea and a lot of sugar. Inoka, who was in her early forties, came from a rural Sinhala background. She got a Fulbright scholarship to do her PhD in the US and taught there for a few years. She returned because she felt isolated, cut off from her homeland and culture. 'I had a good position, a comfortable home, the kids went to a good school. We had a very comfortable college-town life. But my research was all here; I felt I was marking time over there. I really thought I could be more use back home.'

She felt ambivalent about her return. 'I'm not sure it was the right decision to come back. I have mixed feelings. It's very difficult to survive on a lecturer's salary. My eldest boy misses the life back in the States. I have a much heavier teaching load here. There's hardly any time for research. On the other hand, the students are worth it. I didn't feel I was making a difference to the students in the States, but here it's different. Mostly they come from poor village backgrounds; their fathers, typically, drive three-wheelers. They get a bad school education. They have little or no English. When they come here they have very little basic general knowledge of the world; their horizons are so limited. So there's a lot of catching up to do. But they are naturally intelligent; they have promise. We have to nurture them.'

Inoka lowered her voice when talking about politics in the university. 'There's a fair amount of self-censorship in the faculty.

Especially during the war. Maybe a little less afterwards. Some are very good at currying favour with politicians to get promotions and senior positions.' To Inoka, the real problem was the highly politicized university administration. 'The vice chancellors and UGC (University Grants Commission) people are political appointees; many are unqualified. They kowtow to politicians. Jennings warned us about this. He said the rot would set in when vice chancellors became political appointees. He got it mostly right. What he feared has come to pass. It took me a while to realize this, since I come from the Left. But there it is.'

The left-wing nationalism that came to dominate Peradeniya had no truck with the university's founder, of course. Even while Jennings presided here, student leaders resented his condescending tone. There is no statue or portrait of him on campus. Only half a century after his departure was something – a hall of residence – named after him, and only after vociferous opposition.

~

Nuwara Eliya is Sri Lanka's main hill station, 6000 feet up in tea country. The British pronounced it 'Newrailia'; it was where they retreated for the 'season', when Colombo got too hot and humid in April. The Colombo elite still goes there for the April and Christmas seasons, taking over the Hill Club, the Golf Club, the two main hotels, The Grand and St Andrew's, and choice cottages; the less advantaged crowd into hundreds of other small hotels and guest houses.

This part of the hill country, in the old Kandyan kingdom, was mostly virgin jungle and grassland until the British came. From the 1820s, the Crown requisitioned vast tracts of land – jungle, grassland, as well as temple land and common land used by villagers for grazing – parcelled it out and sold it to private (mostly British) buyers. Here, over the next four decades, coffee was planted on an industrial scale. The coffee plant had grown wild and in village gardens before the British came, but it was not used for drinking, only for flavouring dishes. Its flower was given as a temple offering. The Dutch concentrated their coffee cultivation in Java, not Ceylon. But the emancipation of slaves working on coffee plantations in the Caribbean, and British removal of export restrictions on other coffee-growing regions, opened up the market for Ceylon coffee. This drew in British smallholders as well as poor seasonal labourers from South India, willing to do the back-breaking work at which Kandyan villagers baulked, and which they found demeaning. British governors, members of their Executive Council, military officers, judges, clergymen and half the Ceylon Civil Service bought land cheaply for coffee cultivation. Roads were built to transport coffee to the coast and thence shipped abroad.

But disaster struck with a leaf disease in the 1860s; it destroyed the coffee crop in less than a decade. Salvation came with tea, which was planted in the old coffee-growing areas. A British director of the Royal Botanical Gardens in Peradeniya had experimented with tea seedlings from China and Assam. Ceylon tea cultivation took off quickly, producing the Indian-type black-brown fermented tea, not the Chinese-type unfermented or semi-fermented green tea, which was becoming popular in Britain. British trading companies bought up smallholdings and turned them into large tea estates. From the 1890s to the 1930s, Sir Thomas Lipton stood at the summit of the tea industry. He owned a big chunk of Ceylon's tea estates. Tamil labourers from South India arrived in droves, this time for permanent settlement, again willing to do the daily toil on the estates that was foreign to Sinhala hill country villagers. The population of these 'Indian Tamils' rose to 750,000 – 14.5 per cent of the national total – by 1931. Inevitably, it triggered enormous disruption in the hitherto isolated, feudal Sinhala village society of the hill country.

Soon after they started clearing land the British built a road from Kandy to where Nuwara Eliya lies today; then they went up in bullock carts to create their replica English home-counties hamlet and plant coffee and, later, tea. This was the road Nihal and I took, past Peradeniya campus, before we started winding round ever-steeper bends. As children, my cousins and I always got queasy curving round these bends on what was then a narrow, bumpy road. Now the road was broad and smooth, making the journey comfortable, if less adventurous. Before long we were in dramatic, picture-postcard high tea country.

The air got cooler as we climbed. The look of people changed, too: they were darker-skinned, and dressed differently. Women wore the Hindu *pottu*, the circular red mark in the middle of their foreheads; many men had their foreheads streaked with white ash. Estate labourers wore padded jackets, battered sweaters and woolly hats, or cloth wrapped around their heads, to guard against the early evening chill. But still they walked barefoot. We passed red-and-white striped Hindu kovils. Now we were in Indian Tamil country.

We stopped at the tea shop next to the Labookelle factory, part of the second-largest tea estate in the country. The aroma of toasted tea leaves wafted over from the factory. There were coachloads of overseas tourists here today; when I was last here, just before the war ended, there were very few. The roadside was much busier, too: many more stalls selling upcountry vegetables – swede, marrows, radishes, cabbages – flower stalls, the odd nursery, new guest houses and cafes. As we approached Nuwara Eliya we passed one of Sri Lanka's market-gardening hubs – nurseries that dispatched flowers and vegetables to Colombo and elsewhere around the island. We drove through town, past the pretty golf course, cheek by jowl with the town centre, turned the corner and arrived at the Hill Club.

Governor Barnes, the pioneer of coffee planting and road-building in Ceylon, founded an embryonic hill station here in

1828. His residence, Barnes Hall, is now the Grand Hotel. But Samuel Baker, who later co-discovered the source of the Nile, was the real architect of this English home away from home. Over the next few decades Nuwara Eliya acquired the appurtenances of a classic hill station: a grand hotel, a planters' club, a church or two, a golf course, a landscape park, a racecourse, a gingerbread post office, a department store, a botanical garden just outside town, and twee cottages with rose gardens and patches of strawberries and vegetables. The railway line was extended from Kandy to Nanu Oya in 1885; the rest of the journey to Nuwara Eliya was done in bullock carts. 'Natives' were not allowed to own property here until 1903.

The Hill Club is the nearest thing Sri Lanka has to a St James's Club or an Indian equivalent; it still has the feel of bygone 'Newrailia'. Planters founded the club in 1876, but the present clubhouse was built in the 1930s in the arts and crafts style. A sweeping lawn with perfectly tended shrubs and rosebeds leads up to the porch. The clubhouse's greystone and timber facade resembles a Scottish baronial hall. Inside, the reading room has sofas, coffee tables and lampshades out of *Country Life*, and framed photos of the Queen and the Duke of Edinburgh above the fireplace. The dining room is all dark wood with crisp white linen and candles on the tables; it has a jacket-and-tie dress code in the evenings. Waiters wear starched white tunics and white sarongs, and glide across the hardwood floor barefoot; in the evenings they don white gloves to serve 'courses'. Until recently, the bar was split in two: the 'casual bar' (men only) on one side, the 'mixed bar' on the other. Mounted hunting trophies hang on the walls of the main hall. The club retains its tradition of sticking a hot water bottle in one's bed at night. It also has a tradition of retaining staff, mostly from estate-labour families, for decades. Three waiters, Raja, Anthony and Kesan, have been here ever since I can remember: between them they have over a century of service. Club membership was 'Europeans only' until 1970, twenty-two years after independence. Non-Europeans and women could only enter by the tradesmen's entrance round the back.

The next morning I went for a long walk around town. Pidurutalagala, Sri Lanka's highest peak, towers above the town and Lake Gregory close by. Hermann Hesse walked all the way from the town to the summit in 1911, which must have taken him the best part of the day. At the top he took in a view of 'a thousand mountains, broad valleys, narrow gorges, streams and waterfalls'. He was transported: this, to him, was Eastern spirituality embodied, 'the fullness and lush abundance of an all-natural bounty; (where) we find the plain, simple, childlike people of paradise'. But, he added, 'we (meaning Westerners) are other; . . . we have long since lost paradise, and the new paradise that we have and seek to build is not to be found on the Equator and in the warm seas of the East; rather it lies within us and in our own northern future'.

I walked across to the Golf Club, right opposite the Hill Club, and then took the public footpath that runs down the middle of the main fairway to the town centre on the other side. Old photos show a tidy hill station village built around its bank, post office and department store. The town has since sprawled to resemble other urban centres in Sri Lanka: colonial buildings lie neglected; newer buildings press against each other in various states of disrepair; roadside litter and stray dogs complete the effect. But, for all its modern sprawl, Nuwara Eliya looked better than it did on my visits before the war ended: it has had its share of post-war beautification. Victoria Park, next to the town centre and opposite the Golf Club, was presentable once more. Lake Gregory, just outside town, was tidied up and got a neat new pathway round half of it; tourists paddled pleasure boats in the water.

Narrow lanes, past old cottages and flashy new guest houses, lead up the hill to Holy Trinity Church. Its walls have memorial tablets commemorating planters who died in the Boer War, the Great War and the Second World War. The Queen and Prince Philip came here for service on Easter Sunday, 1954. The cemetery has the graves of local Anglicans, mostly British planters and their wives, and a small section for members of the Dutch Reformed Church – Ephraims, Bartholomeusz, Graetians. I stopped a few minutes by the grave of Jessie Turner, eternally shaded by the drooping branches of a nearby tree. She was a planter's wife who stayed on after independence and died in the 1970s. Her epitaph read: 'I fought the good fight, I stayed the course, I kept the faith.'

~

My next stop was Warwick Gardens, about a half-hour drive out of Nuwara Eliya and one of the highest tea estates in the country. The bungalow, run separately from the estate, is part of Jetwing, one of Sri Lanka's leading hotel chains. The vistas are as dramatic as they come in hill country: high ridges on three sides enclose the estate like a protective shield; tea bushes slope down and fill the valley below. We spiralled down a bad dirt road to the bungalow, deep in the valley bowl. Fareed, the bungalow manager, met us and led us to the sitting room with a crackling fire. It was already getting dark.

I rose early the next morning, resolved to do a proper tea estate walk. First I spent the cool dawn hour walking slowly around the bungalow garden, relishing the sights, sounds and scents of a new up-country day. At the end of the lawn was a large monkey puzzle tree. Standing next to it, I looked straight down the tea-filled valley to a plain of terraced paddy beyond and mountains on the horizon; tea bushes rose up hillsides to the right, left and behind the bungalow. I spotted a lone white tea factory perched on the ridge behind the bungalow; standing sentinel in front of it was an African tulip – a flame tree – in full scarlet bloom, and next to it, for contrast, a flamboyant tree with its paler green leaf and flower a lighter shade of red. Rows of agapanthus, painter's palettes, roses and marigolds bordered the bungalow. To one side was a large vegetable and herb garden with a motley crew of two- and four-legged creatures – ducks, chickens and goats.

I set off on my walk after a big Sri Lankan breakfast. By now the day was clear and hot. I followed dirt-brown paths that snaked their way round carpets of tea. In the midst of tea bushes were shade-giving windbreakers gently swaying in the breeze – albisia, dedup, screw pine and, most common of all, silver oak. After a while I approached the estate lines, walking past neat vegetable patches bordered by white elderflower, hibiscus, red cannas, and angels' trumpets drooping pendulously like tobacco plants. Just ahead were two rectangular, single-storey white-painted blocks with corrugated iron roofs, divided into individual family units. The dwellings were tiny and basic, but how they had improved from what I saw as a child. No longer were they dark one-room hovels without electricity, running water and toilets. No longer were the drains outside spattered with human excrement. Now there were satellite dishes on the roofs; TV sets were in all the front rooms. All the adults were armed with mobile phones. A little away from the main lines were small stand-alone houses – about half of upcountry estate families live in such housing these days.

As I walked through the lines my ears echoed with the cacophonous din of Tamil pop music; it blared out from estate lines continuously and could be heard miles away. Then I chanced upon a pack of dogs, who took an immediate dislike to my intrusion and started to growl menacingly. I beat a hasty retreat.

My walk continued high up to a ridge above Warwick Gardens where the tea line gave way to copses of eucalyptus and pine. Out of the woods, near the highest point on the ridge, I found a lone tree close to a brook. In the tree's shade was a small stone shrine with white chalk marks and a yellow ribbon tied around it, and next to it an iron *trishula* (or trident), Shiva's three-pronged spear in Hindu mythology. These are common sights of worship on tea estates. Here, I sat to eat my packed lunch, enjoyed the cool breeze and took in the panorama of the whole estate. I slipped into a reverie of sorts, which took me back to afternoon walks around Razeena all those years ago. I felt a compound of elation and inner rest and contentment. Here, now, I felt totally concentrated and present, intensely aware of everything around me. I wished I could have held on to this moment, though I knew it was fleeting.

Walking back to the bungalow, I came across a band of neatly uniformed pre-teen children heading back to the estate lines after school. They smiled broadly and addressed me exuberantly with 'hello-howareyou-whatisyourname-wheredoyoucomefrom'. One little fellow stepped forward spontaneously, put his chest out, and announced: 'My name is T. Shiva Selvam. I am eleven years old and I want to be English teacher.'

Back at the bungalow I found Fareed on the lawn, lounging in a chair, his head covered by a floppy hat and deep in a book. He beckoned me over as I approached; I pulled up a chair and ordered a pot of tea. We chatted.

Fareed is a hill country Muslim with a wife and baby in Kandy. He is a jack of many trades. He trained as a vet, became a planter – he was assistant superintendent of Warwick Gardens (the surrounding tea estate) a few years ago – and worked at St Andrew's Hotel in Nuwara Eliya before coming back here. His interests are eclectic: wildlife, botany, the history of Nuwara Eliya, and the restoration of old cars and motorbikes. He told me he completed his PhD in botany last year. 'What did you specialize in?' I asked. 'Three species of lizard on Horton Plains,' he replied. I did not ask him to elaborate. Horton Plains is close by, and convenient for Fareed's fieldwork.

Fareed, in his quiet way, is a natural storyteller. He gave me a potted history of the estate. 'A Scotsman carved it out of the jungle in the late nineteenth century and built the bungalow. After sixty years, soon after independence, he sold it to a low-country family and went back to England. According to rumour, he went back heartbroken because his daughter married a Ceylonese. The estate was nationalized in the early 1970s, but the family kept the bungalow plus fifty acres. When Jetwing took over, the bungalow was in a bad state, thoroughly neglected.'

Fareed told me stories of 'wild oats' – of British planters impregnating Tamil estate girls, kept as their concubines. On this theme: 'I once worked on an estate near Bandarawela. My servant boy told me the bungalow I lived in used to be haunted. A previous occupant, who lived there on his own, heard noises all the time. So he called a priest in to exorcise the ghost – or whatever it was. The priest pointed to the wall next to the fireplace and ordered it to be broken down. When it was, they found the remains of a newborn baby. They say it was "half-half".'

And on the same theme: 'Did you walk past the Sinhala village at the top of the road, just before the turn-off to Warwick Gardens? Did you notice some villagers have fair hair and blue eyes? British troops passed this way during the Uva rebellion in 1818; they had their way with the village girls.'

I asked Fareed about conditions on the estates. 'It's difficult to make a profit out of tea these days. Fixed costs are so high; wages keep going up. The estate owners have to spend much more than in the old days on housing and school facilities. The CWC (Ceylon Workers' Congress, the estate workers' trade union-cum-political party) keeps the pressure up; they deliver a block of half a million votes at elections. But productivity is low. Tea pluckers do six hours a day in the fields, not twelve hours the way they used to. They get days off every week and retire at fifty-five with a pension. The young do proper schooling, not like before, and they want clerical jobs in the city, not this kind of work, so there's a severe labour shortage. Alcoholism has always been a problem on the estates. Now you find it among the women, too. Half the wages go on drink.'

Fareed's description of Indian Tamil estate life took me back to what I saw at Razeena and nearby estates forty-plus years ago. Estate labourers and their families were the lowest of the low in Sri Lankan society. They lived on a pittance in unsanitary hovels, and worked outdoors in sun, wind and rain more than half the day, every day of the week. Most were illiterate and remained uneducated; children followed parents into full-time work before their teens. The men squandered their little spare cash on *kasippu* (local moonshine), *beedi* (cheap local cigarettes) and *ganja* (marijuana), and abused their wives and children. Estate life was suffocatingly self-contained, cut off from the rest of society – from nearby Sinhala villages, from faraway urban centres, and from the rest of Tamil life in Colombo, the north and the east.

All this suited the British trading companies and the odd rich local who owned the estates. It particularly suited the British planters who ran them, who treated estate Tamils as pliant serfs and docile children – and as concubine fodder. Conditions changed little through most of the last century, even after the estates were nationalized in the 1970s and the remaining British planters left the island.

Most shocking to me was the way Colombo Tamils and Jaffna Tamils looked down on Indian Tamils, treating them contemptuously as primitive, ignorant, lower-caste transplants whose ancestry in Sri Lanka went back just two or three generations, not centuries and millennia. They did not lift a finger when D.S. Senanayake's government disenfranchised the estate Tamils in 1949, the year after independence. Nor were they much concerned by the 'Sirima–Shastri Pact', the deal Mrs Bandaranaike struck with the Indian prime minister, Lal Bahadur Shastri, in 1964. India agreed to the compulsory repatriation of half a million estate Tamils. 'Repatriation' was hardly the right term, since most of these poor souls had never seen the Ceylon coastline, never mind their ancestral villages in Tamil Nadu. A few hundred thousand were forcibly packed off to Tamil Nadu until the programme was stopped in the late 1970s. In 2003, the Sri Lankan Parliament extended Sri Lankan citizenship to all Indian Tamils who had remained in Sri Lanka after 1964. It took a while, but this righted a grievous historical wrong.

Conditions on the estates are better today, as I saw on my Warwick Gardens walk. The younger generation is getting educated, moving to towns and assimilating into Sri Lankan society. The last thing they want is to return to estate work and life in the line-room. But that leaves ageing, decaying communities on large, mostly unproductive and loss-making estates. Indian Tamils remain confined at the bottom of Sri Lankan society.

~

Many journeys are not complete without climbing a holy mountain. Mine was no different.

My destination was Adam's Peak, called *Sri Pada* or Buddha's Foot in Sinhala. In Bogowantalawa, tea country two hours' drive west and downhill from Nuwara Eliya, tea is still high grown, with scenery to match. We passed Hatton, the main hill town in the region, and headed to the estate bungalow I rented in Dickoya. Joining me for the climb up Adam's Peak was Alex, an American friend who is also a photography buff. He came laden with fifteen kilos of fancy camera equipment.

We set off for Adam's Peak just after midnight, rounding Castlereagh Dam, with its water shimmering in the moonlight. Wild boar and mongoose darted across the road in front of us, caught in Nihal's car headlights. At the base of the mountain, we drank fortifying cups of strong sweet tea before starting the climb. Just as we began, two small friendly strays sniffed around our feet and decided to adopt us. They stuck with us, more or less, all the way to the summit.

The surrounding land was pitch black, except for a string of lights that traced a wavy line to the summit, 7400 feet above sea level. There were about 5500 steps to the top, illuminated at night during the pilgrim season from the poya day in December to Vesak, the poya day in May when the Buddha's birth, death and enlightenment are celebrated. The lights ascending to night-time heaven reminded me of a story told by an Italian friar, Marignolli, who visited Sri Lanka in the mid-fourteenth century, en route to China as the Pope's emissary to the Great Khan. He wrote:

> And from Seyllan to Paradise . . . is a distance of forty Italian miles; so that, 'tis said, the sound of the waters falling from the fountain of Paradise is heard there . . . And straightaway the Angel took Adam by the arm and set him down beyond the lake on the Mountain of Seyllan . . . And by chance Adam planted his right foot upon a stone which is there still . . . And the size, I mean the length thereof is two-and-a-half of our palms . . .

Sri Pada has been a Buddhist pilgrim destination for over 2000 years. To Buddhists, its summit is where the Buddha planted his foot on his third visit to Lanka. But other religions have their claims, too. A Christian legend, dating back to the Portuguese occupation, attributes the summit's footprint to St Thomas in the first century CE, around the time he went to Kerala. To Hindus, it is *Sivanadi Patham* or Shiva's Footprint. Muslims believe it is Adam's footprint – where God set Adam down, to make the shock of banishment from Eden less terrible. Muslim pilgrims have been coming here possibly since the time of Prophet Muhammad. Ibn Batuta came to Sri Lanka specifically to go on pilgrimage to the 'Mountain of Sarandib', to see the footprint of 'our father Adam'. He was but following in the footsteps of sheikhs and dervishes before him. On the way up he saw rhododendron trees in bloom, wild monkeys and lots of leeches.

Sinbad the Sailor came here in *The Tale of the Thousand and One Nights*. Sri Lanka would have been on his route: he was a seafaring trader from Baghdad, after all, sailing in goods-laden dhows between the Arabian Gulf and China. Arab sailors used the mountain as a navigational landmark. Marco Polo wrote that Kublai Khan, the emperor of China, heard that 'Sogomombar Khan' – the *Sakyamuni* or historical Buddha – was buried on the summit with a mound of treasure, which he wanted to procure from the king of 'Zeilan'.

In the Buddhist tradition, the mountain is also associated with Saman *deviyo*, the reigning deity of this region. In the *Mahavamsa*, the mountain is *Samantakuta* (Samanta's Abode); in modern Sinhala it is *Samanala Kanda* (Saman's Mountain). Indeed, Saman and the mountain were linked long before Buddhism came to Sri Lanka. Saman doubles as the bodhisattva Samantabhadra, so there is a Mahayana connection as well. In Sinhala, 'samanala' also means 'butterfly'. White and pale-yellow butterflies swarm in unending streams and perform their ethereal mid-air dances for days around the mountain during the pilgrim season, before they descend the mountain as their brief lives come to an end.

The first two hours of the ascent were fairly easy. Our canine advance guard faced off occasionally against other strays defending their territory, engaging in mock fights and the odd minor scuffle. This mountain's strays, I noticed, were strictly race-conscious: they seemed to adopt fair-complexioned tourists and avoided locals, who shooed them away or even threw stones at them.

Roadside refreshment stalls go most of the way up; pilgrim's rests offer food, shelter and even medical assistance, part of Sri Lanka's long tradition of hospitality to pilgrims. The path was full of pilgrims. Some, out of shape and struggling, were clearly city types. A few groups of young men treated the ascent as a party outing; they were tipsy and loud from the arrack they drank on the journey here. There were Muslims, Hindus and Christians. But, overwhelmingly, pilgrims were from the Sinhala heartland, small-town and rural folk, here for devotional duty. Fathers carried sleeping babes across their chests and over their shoulders; small children held their parents' hands; the old were aided by their children and grandchildren.

The disabled went up on crutches, in slow, laborious motion. Bent and wizened grandmothers and grandfathers dragged themselves up sideways, one leg at a time, gripping the railings fiercely. Most ascended barefoot or in plain slippers. It was a simple testament of faith. Only the blinkered and fanatical, whether atheist or religiously fundamentalist, could not be moved by this scene. Sir James Emerson Tennent, on his ascent in the mid-1840s, was struck by how amiable relations were among pilgrims from different religions, unlike the bickering he saw among Christian denominations at the Church of the Holy Sepulchre in Jerusalem. What a sweet metaphor for Sri Lanka at its best.

The final hour was tough. The climb grew very steep, up a narrow flight of steps with a railing down the middle. Alex was rangy and fitter than me, but he was weighed down with camera equipment; all I had to do was carry his tripod. Masses of pilgrims huddled together close to the summit, standing, sitting, crouching, with woolly hats pulled down over their ears and sheets wrapped around them against the cold. It was 4.30 a.m.

There are two small shrines at the top. One contains the Buddha's (or Adam's, Shiva's or St Thomas's) footprint, invisible to the public since it is totally covered by a slab. It is outsize. Tennent, who saw the actual footprint, described it as a 'natural hollow artificially enlarged, exhibiting the rude outline of a foot about five feet long'.

And almost as wide. He added, 'But it is a test of credulity too gross even for fanaticism to believe the footstep is either human or divine.'

Next to the footprint is a shrine to Saman. Pilgrims thronged around the shrines, praying and making offerings. Alex and I secured our places next to the short wall around the summit edge. A smiling young pilgrim offered us fruit and Sinhala sweets, as he did to those around us. We waited an hour or so for the sunrise.

At 5.45 a.m., a faint pink hue emerged from behind faraway mountains against a clear sky turning gradually into lighter shades of blue. Pink turned to red-orange and then orange-yellow. Monks started chanting. We heard the sound of drums. A bell started pealing from the summit's belfry. Everyone now stood ramrod straight, facing east. Finally the sun's rim appeared, then rose slowly, shimmering, radiating sharp, penetrating yellow-gold light, illuminating the land. It revealed the encircling hills and mountains of the Kandyan kingdom, the valleys and lakes and rivers in between, and the plains beyond.

I felt as if half of Sri Lanka was laid out before me. On a super-clear day, I was told, one could see all the way to the south coast and the sea. As Castlereagh Dam came into view, ringed by slopes of tea, everyone dashed to the western side of the summit. At one point, as the sun illuminated this side of the mountain, it created a 'shadow', a perfect pyramid, that moved serenely across the landscape like a trail of meditating monks. Alex clicked away madly as the shadow juxtaposed itself with perfect symmetry against another mountain directly opposite.

Soon after, a Japanese monk appeared from the path we ascended. He circumambulated the Buddha's footprint several times, striking his drum with a stick and bowing every few steps. I could hardly believe my eyes as I saw four strays accompany him in lockstep, two in front and two behind in perfect formation. Clearly they came with him all the way up. When he finished his circumambulation, they followed him all the way down to the Japanese temple with its World Peace Pagoda at the base of the mountain.

After hours of expectation, and then the unbroken exhilaration of the sunrise and the mountaintop rituals it occasioned, Alex and I began our descent. This proved harder than the climb: our knees stiffened and our legs turned to jelly, but there was the solace of the unfolding teascapes below. We returned whence we had started, surrounded by the tea gardens of Dalhousie estate. One stray was still with us, though his companion had forsaken us for other tourists. We rewarded him with biscuits and took our leave. Our exhilaration persisted on the drive all the way back to the Dickoya bungalow. A huge late-morning breakfast awaited us – hoppers, stringhoppers, sambals, curries, fruits, curd and treacle, prepared by Suppiah, the bungalow's Tamil cook. And then we slept the rest of the day.

~

I left my favourite hill country journey for the last. It was mid-November, and the rains had started to descend upcountry.

We took the Colombo–Badulla road. The first major town out of Colombo is Ratnapura or 'City of Gems', Sri Lanka's gem-mining hub. These parts still have a low-country look – paddy fields, coconut groves, rubber estates, some low-grown tea. Gradually, the road climbs to Belihuloya, where high-grown tea starts, and which has a beckoning rest house where I never fail to stop for lunch or a pot of strong Uva tea.

From Belihuloya we gained considerable elevation until we reached Haputale. In the middle of town the road appeared to end abruptly, right on the cliff. But it was only a hairpin bend, a sharp right-angled turn, and the road and the town continued around the corner. Most of the time, Haputale is shrouded and smothered in a giant fluffy ball of thick, damp mist. But, if it is clear, one must

stop, for Haputale Gap affords as splendid a view as any in Sri
Lanka. On one side rises the amphitheatre of the upper Uva hills
with its endless rolling carpets of deep-green tea; on the other side
the lower Uva foothills slope down to Ratnapura; and straight ahead
the southern plains stretch to the sea. W. Dahanayake, briefly prime
minister, once told Bevis Bawa, 'What is the point of emigrating to
Australia when you can't enjoy a Haputale sunset?'

The next stretch, from Haputale to Bandarawela, has some of
the loveliest teascapes in the hills. It is classic Uva. It lacks the high
drama of Nuwara Eliya tea country, 2000 feet higher up. Its beauty
is subtler: tea estates spread, curve around and spill down hillsides,
mingling with Sinhala villages and small white, bell-shaped stupas
in valleys of terraced paddy, vegetable gardens and fruit orchards. We
passed Diyatalawa, a mini hill station with 2000 acres of military
camps, where army, navy and air force recruits train. It figures in
the family history in a minor way: Daddy was stationed here for
a few months in the late 1950s. Close by is the much bigger hill
station of Bandarawela, which is twice or thrice the size it was in
my childhood.

I love the little Bandarawela Hotel. It is retro heaven, an old
planters' club turned into a hill station hotel, all timber cross-beams,
interior courtyards and polished brown wooden floorboards, with
a porch and a manicured lawn and easy chairs out front. In the
reception area hangs a framed excerpt from an obscure law journal,
penned by Sir Oliver Goonetilleke, minister of finance in Sir John
Kotelawala's cabinet and later governor general. Sir Oliver wrote
that Ivor Jennings and he holed themselves up here in 1943 to write
the Ceylon Ministers' Constitution, which, a few years later, with
minor changes, became the Soulbury Constitution for independent
Ceylon. They worked late into the night in Oliver Goonetilleke's
room. At one point a sleep-deprived planter barged in and declared,
'Why don't you buggers go to bed?'

In my favourite nook of the hotel, its cosy little bar, I met Bruce. He was a rare British planter who stayed on after the estates were nationalized and retired here. When he started planting, in the 1960s, there were about 400 British planters in Ceylon. Nearly all had left by the 1980s. Bruce was ancient, but still had that look of rude health – compact, muscled limbs, ruddy cheeks – that came from decades of fresh-air living, striding around tea estates.

On this evening, his eyes were bloodshot after several whiskies, but he retained the gruff periya dorai authority of his working days. His opinions were fixed. The Sinhalese – villagers near the estates and shopkeepers in hill stations – were lazy, capricious liars and cheats who played out credulous foreigners. The latter fell in love with Sri Lanka, bought land, set up little businesses – hotels, guest houses, even estates – but got bamboozled and left with their tails between their legs. But not Bruce: he knew how to look after himself. He respected Muslim shopkeepers and traders in Bandarawela: they did not play him out. Estate Tamils were fine, but they were eternal children who needed a firm guiding hand.

Somerset Maugham never made it to planters' clubs in Ceylon. If he had, innumerable Bruces would have provided him with extra writing fodder. But his nephew Robin did visit Ceylon in the 1960s and 1970s, and became besotted with Taprobane island in Weligama Bay. Robin Maugham travelled upcountry and met British planters in their estate bungalows and clubs. In his memoir, *Search for Nirvana*, he invented a character, Jack Phillipson, a composite picture of a tea planter based on those he met: a lonely, hard-drinking fellow who preferred 'Oriental' girls to his own kind, but could not hold on to the young woman – and then the young man – he installed in his bungalow.

~

One day, Mummy, Nihal and I drove down the valley that connects Bandarawela to the Muslim village of Hali-Ela. In Hali-Ela, we drove past the mosque and stopped next to a row of tiny tumbledown houses. We were here to see Fareeda, ayah to my brothers and me in the late 1960s and early 1970s. Fareeda was now a great-grandmother. Two of her grandchildren welcomed us; one, Razeen, is named after yours truly. This visit was unannounced, so when Fareeda came out the first thing she did was shout 'Madam!' before she hugged us joyfully.

It was dark and poky inside the house. The walls were unplastered, and a few chairs were strewn around the front room. Fareeda, her husband, one son, his wife and their three children lived in two small rooms, with a tiny kitchen and a squat toilet at the back.

Fareeda, always lively, cheerful and good-hearted, had come with us to England for a year when I was a child. But she left us to get married; she showed us the weathered black-and-white wedding photo from 1975. Now Fareeda looked much older than her years. Pink-white blotches ravaged her face and body – signs of vitiligo, the disease that destroys pigment cells in patches of skin, making it lose its normal colour. Most of her teeth were gone; grey tufts of hair protruded from her sari-covered head. There was sadness, a careworn look, written across her face; her little body seemed to sag under the weight of age and toil and worry.

She had a hard married life. After bearing her children, she worked as a housemaid in Saudi Arabia for over a decade. Her eldest daughter, herself a grandmother, now did what her mother did, also in Saudi Arabia. Fareeda's husband always complained of ailments and never did serious work; she was, for long, the expanding family's main breadwinner. One son used to work part-time in a local butcher's stall, but now had no work. Another son drove a three-wheeler in Badulla, but gave up because it was too far away – a half-hour drive.

So the women ended up doing the work and toiling for years in the Middle East, in addition to raising children, keeping house and supporting deadbeat men. And the cycle repeated itself in the next generation. This seemed to be common to all Sri Lanka's ethnic communities.

Mummy and I said goodbye to Fareeda and drove on to Badulla. It used to be a fine hill station, although even by the 1970s, when we used to visit often, it had become somewhat down at heel. That had not changed. It was bigger, of course, like other towns around the island. But it still felt remote, cut off. The rest house was awful, reduced to a drinking den for police and other government officials, complete with dirty toilets. St Mark's Church, where British colonial society used to worship, and its cemetery still looked pretty. On one side of it is Uva College, where Daddy went to school. Behind the church and opposite the school is a field where he played hockey. On the other side of the playing field is the town jail, a stone's throw from the public library. The Uva Club and its tennis courts, once the centre of Uva planters' social life, were long gone.

~

Mummy and I reserved a day to visit Aunty Jameela and Uncle Ranjith. Aunty Jameela is Daddy's first cousin, Badulla born and bred. Still in her teens, she defied her family to marry Uncle Ranjith, a Sinhala Buddhist. He was a planter for forty years, mostly in tea, but he also ran rubber and coconut estates; he was superintendent of some of the biggest estates in the hill country. They retired to an old estate bungalow that Uncle Ranjith painstakingly renovated.

On the hour's drive to their place from Bandarawela along the Poonagala road, we passed a couple of well-tended estates. Then the road became narrow and potholed. It descended and curved around a hill to reveal an arresting view: a spectacular deep valley of paddy fields, vegetable patches, fruit orchards and a Sinhala hamlet or two. There was a small temple with a gleaming white bell-shaped stupa sitting on the valley floor. Running up the slopes on the other side of the valley, directly behind Ella Rock, were patches of tea. Perched high up was a tea factory with a whitewashed front and sides, topped by a deep-blue corrugated iron roof; a grove of eucalyptus trees started where the tea bushes ended and rose to an undulating ridge of hilltops. We descended gradually, snaking our way downhill, passed a hamlet and turned off on a dirt road that led to the bungalow. Uncle and Aunty came out to greet us and we took our seats – planters' chairs, of course – on the wrap-around veranda.

It felt like the back of beyond: I saw only two or three other houses in the distance, embowered in greenery and shielded by a ring of hills. Ella Rock rose majestically to one side of the bungalow, just fifteen minutes' walk from here to its base at the rim of the valley bowl. Here, on the Poonagala side of the rock, all was quiet and still. This, I thought, was what the other, better-known side of Ella Rock must have been like when Mummy and Daddy honeymooned at the Ella rest house in 1961. That side now felt a world away – a lively tourist hub served by a railway line and railway station, an expanding little town of hotels, guest houses and backpacker cafes and bars, and a busy road down Ella Gap that runs past Sita's Cave and Ravanella Falls to the southern plain.

Uncle Ranjith started the conversation, and, over the next five hours, as was his habit, did 90 per cent of the talking. He was a man of many talents, all charmingly self-advertised; 'Ranjith by Ranjith' was Daddy's description of him. 'How I miss Farouk,' he said. They had been great friends who liked nothing better than a long session of mutual ribbing over whisky-sodas. All I had to do was press a few buttons, and off Uncle Ranjith went with stories of the old planting life.

He was 'spotted' young, by the British director of a Colombo-based trading house that owned tea estates. 'I was seventeen, at Trinity (the leading school in Kandy), mad about sports. This chap saw me playing in a rugger match and offered me a job. They never recruited the academic types, the bookworms. No, they went for sporty types like me who love the outdoor life – the best material for planting.'

I asked Uncle Ranjith about the days before the estates were nationalized. 'I was trained by Scots planters. One thing I learned from them was this. Whenever I went to take charge of a new estate, I had to establish my authority – had to keep discipline. So I would identify the main troublemaker among the labourers – usually the union man. I'd take him round the back of the shed and give him a good thrashing. That usually prevented any problems.'

Then, with a look of mock innocence, he added, 'I'm told you're not allowed to do that these days.' One Scotsman, a well-known planter, gave him this piece of advice: 'If you have a troublemaker, just put him to work in the foundry hammering nails into metal all day; after two years, the sound of ringing in his head will make him go cuckoo.'

Uncle Ranjith had to take permission from head office to marry Aunty Jameela. 'That was company policy those days. Planters' wives had to be "suitable"; they weren't allowed to work. No, they were expected to keep the bungalows and the gardens in tip-top condition. Every so often, a director from head office and his wife would come up for lunch – so that the wife could inspect the bungalow to see if it was tip-top. And I was given a large allowance and a large staff for the bungalow; I had four gardeners looking after my vegetable patches. I sold the veg at the market – that was my side income.'

Uncle Ranjith said the estates 'went to pot' after nationalization. 'The Scots left. They put in lots of unqualified people to run the estates – relatives and cronies of politicians. They stripped the bungalows of the old furniture to put into government offices and official residences in Colombo. The new generation didn't look after the bungalows and gardens. Their wives and children they kept in Colombo. And they didn't live and breathe planting; what they were really after was a cushy office job in Colombo – so they could wear a tie to work, sit behind a desk and be chauffeured around in a company car. That was also the end of the old planters' clubs. In my young days how much drink we consumed with the British planters in the clubs after work. Yes, we really got pretty.'

It was time for lunch. Uncle Ranjith pointed out that he personally supervised the cooking, just as he personally supervised the planting and tending of flower beds and shrubs in the garden. We sat down at the dining table next to a large bay window, with a high sloping roof above.

Still in full flow, he told me about his adventures during the war. He was a reserve officer and saw active service in the Jaffna peninsula. 'They sent me up there because I speak Tamil. So many narrow escapes. Artillery fire, snaking through grass, trying to avoid LTTE snipers in the palmyra trees. Of my batch of fifteen planters, I was the only one who survived.' His friend, Lieutenant General Denzil Kobbekaduwa, was blown up by a landmine. The LTTE murdered another friend, Ranjan Wijeratne, a veteran planter and later senior cabinet minister.

Then there were escapades during the JVP uprising in the late 1980s, when rebels set fire to estate bungalows and factories. One day Uncle Ranjith had to drive down to Colombo from Kegalle (on the Kandy road), which was a JVP hotbed. 'Mine was the only car on the road – not a dog on the road, but lots of mutilated bodies. I drove to Colombo and back on the same day – with a flat tyre most of the way back.'

For pudding we had cream caramel with lashings of burnt brown sugar, an Uncle Ranjith speciality. It was already close to 6 p.m.,

and time to get back to Bandarawela before nightfall made it dicey
to navigate these narrow upcountry side roads.

~

This Uva trip, indeed all these trips of rediscovery in Sri Lanka,
would have had a gaping hole without one particular return. So, on
our final day in Uva, Nihal, Mummy and I set off for Razeena. A
side road from Hali-Ela took us past remote Sinhala hamlets and
two large tea estates, Queenstown and Sarnia, familiar from the old
days. At a village junction, the road got so bad we had to get out
of the car and hire a three-wheeler for the rest of the journey. For
the next three-quarters of an hour we bobbed and weaved around
loose stones and potholes.

We headed towards Keenakelle, the factory where Razeena tea
was sent for processing, which was burned down by the JVP in the
late 1980s. Behind it was Narangala, the highest peak in the area,
which Mummy led us up one fine afternoon in 1977. We passed two
disused tea factories and several rundown bungalows, surrounded by
hundreds of acres of straggly tea bushes. The decline of tea in these
parts reminded me of what Uncle Ranjith said about nationalization
in the 1970s: the damage done was long term, despite privatization
of most estates from the mid-1990s. Just before Keenakelle, the
three-wheeler did a sharp turn down a side road and we arrived at
Razeena.

What a dramatic difference in the intervening thirty-five years:
the estate was almost unrecognizable. It was going back to the
jungle, returning to what the land must have looked like before the
British started planting coffee and then tea after they conquered the
Kandyan kingdom. What had been carpets of tea rising up hillsides
were now patches of long grass and weeds, punctuated by the odd

scruffy bush of overgrown tea. The driveway leading to the bungalow was too rutted for vehicles to pass, so we walked up. The bungalow was in a terrible state: the walls were riven with deep cracks; the corrugated roof was battered and looked like it might soon collapse. The trees around the lawn had disappeared. And there was no lawn, no flower beds: everything had been dug up to grow vegetables.

As we stood in front of the wooden gate, a woman in village dress – a blouse and long skirt that spilled down to her bare feet – came out of the bungalow, shyly, reluctantly. We exchanged a few words in Sinhala. Then her husband came out and invited us inside. The interior was as dilapidated as the exterior. The walls had not been painted in decades, aged mercilessly with cracks and peeling plaster. The living room was bare except for a few threadbare pieces of furniture and a simple Buddhist shrine in one corner. Our host told me his name was Janaka; he was the estate caretaker and had lived here with his wife and two children for the past five years. Relatives from Galle owned the estate, which they bought over twenty years ago. They thought it uneconomical to revive it. Up until five years ago there were five estate labourers who lived with their families in the lines nearby. But they left: there was no tea to pluck. Mummy and I took our leave and made our way back to Bandarawela. Our return to Razeena was bittersweet.

My mind kept switching between yesteryear and today. The look of the bungalow, the garden, the tea bushes, the paddy fields back then. The tough daily routine of the prematurely aged tea pluckers. The Tamil pop music blaring out from transistor radios in the line-room. School on the lawn, walks in the afternoons, hunting for coffee plants in the midst of tea bushes. Bathing under waterfalls, my body tingling with the rush of ice-cold mountain water down my back. The sunrise view from the back of the bungalow, across misty hills and valleys, to the hazy outline of the eastern plain, illuminating, in the far, far distance, the tip of Mahiyangana's temple stupa. I felt sadness for what had become of Razeena, but the setting was everlasting: the remoteness, the Uva hills, the cool, clean air, the scent of tea leaves outdoors and of tea dust from the factories. And Narangala high up, dominating the landscape. Yes, I was glad I returned; it was a homecoming.

7

Rajarata, Land of Kings

His commanding personality is made dazzling to the eyes of the world by the fact that at his coronation he dispersed the clouds that gathered in the sky by merely frowning at them. His great majestic power is such that once when hunting in the forest, a fierce she-bear sprang at him with a snarl and he fearlessly killed her and her cubs. He possesses the powers of a lion-king who can extract water from any spot he likes while travelling in the wilderness. His power of command is such that it cannot be transgressed. For example, once when he was swimming in the sea, a huge dragon appeared before him and he said to it, 'Your presence is unwelcome. Be off and ascribe to yourself a fit punishment!' The dragon then bit itself and died.

– The *Galpotha* (Stone Book), Polonnaruwa,
on the virtues of King Nissankamalla

Rajarata is the cradle of the original Sinhala Buddhist kingdoms, centred first in Anuradhapura and then in Polonnaruwa, from the third century BCE to the thirteenth century CE. It lies in what is now

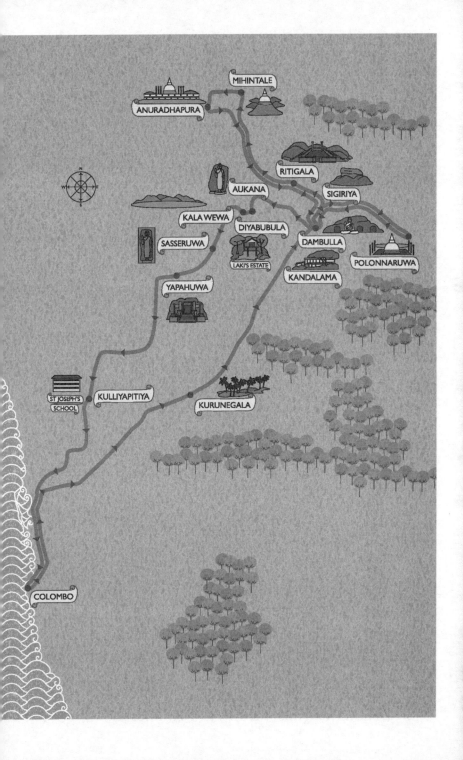

North Central Province, the stretch of the dry zone sandwiched between the Kandyan hills to its south and the scrub jungle of the Vanni to its north. The passage inscribed on the *Galpotha* in Polonnaruwa's Sacred Quadrangle echoes the last gasp of ancient Lankan glory. Here Nissankamalla, that most solipsistic of Sinhala kings, advertised his fantastical feats. But nemesis – an all-destructive invasion from India in 1215 (the year of England's *Magna Carta*) – followed hubris: everything fell apart after Nissankamalla's reign. For centuries, Rajarata lay abandoned. What few pockets of people remained were sparse, scattered and ill nourished. The jungle smothered dagobas, temples, monasteries and palaces in the ancient capitals, their history lost in the thick fog of Sinhala collective memory.

It took British rule to resurrect Rajarata's history. George Turnour's decryption of the *Mahavamsa,* followed by the decryption of other Sinhala chronicles, illuminated Lanka's ancient past, though through the distorting prism of the Theravada Buddhist establishment. Colonial officials discovered the ruins of Anuradhapura and Polonnaruwa, starting in the 1820s; proper excavation and restoration began only towards the end of the nineteenth century. But attempts to resettle Rajarata failed due to pervasive malaria, spread by mosquitoes that infested ruined wewas, the man-made tanks that sustained ancient Lanka's hydraulic economy.

After seven centuries, Rajarata started to be peopled again in the 1930s, by which time DDT was on hand for the mosquitoes, and new tank restoration projects irrigated the land once more. Successive governments, before and especially after independence, resettled Sinhala villagers, including many landless peasants, from farther south. The war against the LTTE brought a large influx of military camps and personnel – Anuradhapura was just an hour's drive from the front line, on the edge of the Vanni, which separated Sri Lankan forces from the LTTE. New roads and villages were built; more Sinhalese came to settle, not least as an extra buffer against the Tamil rebellion north and east of Rajarata.

My driver through Rajarata was Joseph, who knows Sri Lanka's byways like no other driver I have come across. Like Nihal, he is a consummate professional, although he differs from him in every other respect. He is dark and stocky, with forearms like tree trunks; a hearty appetite for spicy, oily food and strong liquor fortifies his solid belly. He is a Catholic from Negombo, just north of Katunayake airport. Sinhala is his mother tongue, but he speaks excellent Tamil, and he likes nothing better than to declaim loudly, with gesticulatory accompaniment, in its ear-shattering tones.

Joseph is a supersized character. While Nihal speaks softly and moderately, Joseph is high volume and gregarious. He delights in human company; and he is as street-savvy as they come. His guttural chortling punctuates his monologues on all manner of subjects. His witticisms – invariably pithy one-liners – are funny and perceptive. He does not need to work – his sons are all abroad earning good money. He says he does so because he loves the freedom of the open road and the company en route. His loquacity might grate on others. But I find Joseph endearing, for he is all natural, not merely comfortable in his skin, but inhabiting it with aplomb.

~

Joseph and I set off from Colombo on the Kandy road, then turned off it in the direction of Kurunegala. We entered coconut country – everywhere coconut estates, little factories for processing coconut, and piles of discarded coconut husks in factory yards. It reminded me of Robert Knox's encomium on the coconut tree. What abundance it provides: nourishing drink (water and milk) and meat (the soft, fleshy inside of the shell); cloth, mats, brooms, brushes and rope from its fibrous husk; timber, thatch, cups and spoons, vegetables and herbal medicines; not to mention honey, toddy and oil. Joseph told me coconut trees were shorter than they used to be, to make it easier for tappers to shin up to the top. Better living standards made labour scarce: tappers demanded more money for less arduous work.

We crossed rivers in which village children frolicked and women bathed, covering themselves demurely with wrap-around cloth knotted above their breasts. We passed fields with farmers ploughing their paddy with Japanese mini-tractors, while buffaloes lay idle, surrounded by white egrets, their constant daytime companions. This prompted Joseph to philosophize: 'British gave independence to Sri Lankans, but Japanese gave independence to the buffalo.' And as we drove through the odd Muslim settlement, cheek by jowl with Sinhala habitation, Joseph pointed and said, 'Mixed fruit, mixed fruit.' He did this occasionally when we passed mixed-race areas. Joseph grew up in 'mixed-fruit' Negombo, alongside Sinhalese and Tamils, Buddhists, Catholics, Muslims and Hindus, and as I discovered on our journeys, he was happiest in mixed-fruit company.

We stopped for lunch by the lake in Kurunegala, looking out to the large gneiss rock that hulks over the town. An outsize bleach-white Buddha, seated on the rock summit, gazes over the town and its lake. Less than a couple of hours after lunch we arrived in Dambulla.

Dambulla's claim to fame is its rock temple. Monks lived in caves on the rock and in the surrounding area as far back as the second century BCE. King Vattagamini Abhaya, who commissioned the writing of the Tipitaka at Aluvihare temple, took refuge here during a South Indian invasion; he had the temple restored after he reclaimed the throne in Anuradhapura, just forty miles north-west. The Kandyan king Kirti Sri Rajasinghe restored it again in the eighteenth century. Dambulla is where the 1848 rebellion against the British started: a pretender to the Kandyan throne proclaimed himself king here and was crowned by the abbot of the temple.

At the rock's base is a flashy golden temple with an outsize Buddha, the sort of total kitsch only money can buy. Behind it, frangipani-fringed steps ascend to the rock summit. Here are five caves carved into the rock, all packed with statues of kings, Buddhas, bodhisattvas and Hindu gods – over 150 of them. Fantastically colourful murals of epic scenes from the Buddha's life and from ancient Lanka cover the cave walls and ceilings.

On a broad terrace before the caves, an ancient bo tree stands, guarding a tiny Vishnu devale squeezed between two caves, generously spreading its cooling shade and calm. Hundreds of small white cotton flags dangle off its branches and flutter gently in the breeze. The terrace faces north: a flat pale-green landscape with low-cropped vegetation unfolds, punctuated by sudden rock spurs. It is a great contrast to the wet zone landscape, dense, dark-green and tree filled, bursting with fruits and vegetables and spices, that starts just a few miles south of Dambulla.

From Dambulla a short drive took us to Kandalama, Geoffrey Bawa's most spectacular hotel. His motto – 'I run with the site' – is nowhere more on display than it is here. The hotel is built around a rocky outcrop close to the bund of the ancient Kandalama wewa. The approach through thick foliage ascends to what looks like an impenetrable ridge. Suddenly the hotel's entrance appears, carved mouth-like into the ridge, enveloped in vegetation, seemingly without an attached building. From it a winding tunnel bores through the rock; turning the corner, it opens out to the main lobby, a terrace and a swimming pool that look directly out to the wewa and, beyond it, to Sigiriya, the huge flat-topped rock that rises 650 feet out of the jungle. Four floors of rooms below snake around the cliff face; foliage spilling down from the rooftop garden drapes them in a vegetal screen. The whole structure looks like it has been carved out of the rock, and seems to merge with the surrounding jungle.

As dusk fell, birds and bats glided and swooped through the upper lounge and its adjoining open-air terraces and corridors. Nature and ceiling fans provided abundant ventilation. Just as the land and sky darkened, heavy clouds gathered quickly, then burst open with loud thunder, piercing flashes of lightning and crashing rain. Suddenly it was pitch black outside, but the lightning, in short, sharp snapshots, revealed dramatic silhouettes of the lake and Sigiriya.

I woke the next dawn to the sight of monkeys – armies of them – trooping across my balcony. Fishing boats were out on the wewa; birdlife and birdsong filled the air around Kandalama's terraces. Sigiriya was clearly framed in the early morning light.

Sigiriya is a syncopation of *Sihagiriya* – 'Lion Rock' in Sinhala. It was the setting for the Sinhala version of *Macbeth*, a tale of parricide and fratricide preserved in the *Culavamsa*. In the fifth century CE, Prince Kasyapa murdered his father King Dhatusena – he had him pasted alive to a mud wall and left to die – and usurped the throne. But he retreated from Anuradhapura to Sigiriya in fear of his half-brother Mogallana, the king's chosen successor. There, on the summit, a flattish forty-acre expanse, Kasyapa built a palace and lived for seventeen years; and around the rock he created an outer city of vast landscape gardens, moats and ramparts. Mogallana returned from Indian exile with an army of South Indian mercenaries. The two brothers' troops battled it out near Sigiriya; Kasyapa was defeated and, before he could fall into his brother's hands, slit his own throat. Mogallana returned to Anuradhapura and turned Sigiriya back into a monastic complex. It had been a monastery as far back as the second century BCE, before Kasyapa commandeered it to build his palace.

But there is another history of Sigiriya, long forgotten, that pre-dates the Kasyapa saga. This is a Mahayana story, which may be why the *Culavamsa* overlooked it: at the time of writing, in the twelfth or thirteenth century CE, Mahayana had disappeared from Sri Lanka. According to Ven S. Dhammika's *Sacred Island*, a Buddhist pilgrim's guide to Sri Lanka, Sigiriya was for centuries a representation of Mount Potala in northern India, the cosmic abode of the bodhisattva Avalokiteshvara. It was a large branch of the Abhayagiri monastery in Anuradhapura, the citadel of Mahayana in Rajarata. It continued to function as a monastery, with a vast network of inhabited caves, until at least the tenth century CE, after which it was abandoned to the jungle until it was rediscovered and restored in the late nineteenth century.

Kasyapa may have been a parricide, but he had great artistic taste. His Sigiriya is an astounding feat of engineering and creativity, on and around a gigantic rock mass. At the base, an immense boulder, cracked in half, leads to stairs that wind their way diagonally up the rock face to a side terrace. Here the giant sculpted paws of a lion, of T-Rex in Jurassic Park dimensions, serve as a portal to another set of stairs that ascends steeply to the summit.

On the way up to the terrace, painted on the rock face, are frescoes of bejewelled females with ethereal smiles and mango-shaped breasts. Each one holds a pink water lily blossom in one hand, while an attendant stands by her side holding a tray of flowers. The conventional view is that they are court maidens or *apsara*s, the celestial nymphs of Hindu and Buddhist mythology. But, following the Mahayana story, *Sacred Island* says they represent bodhisattvas – probably Tara, Avalokiteshvara's consort, and her attendants – who dwell on Mount Potala's slopes. Directly above the frescoes, stairs lead to a 'mirror wall' in front of the rock face, an open upper gallery cluttered with inscriptions. This is ancient graffiti, poems penned over a thousand years ago to praise the frescoes. Up at the summit,

all that is left of Kasyapa's palace and ancient monasteries are the
bare foundations of temples, pavilions and gardens.

~

Laki Senanayake is probably Sri Lanka's most famous living artist.
He is a protean and prolific solo creator, and was a long-time friend
and collaborator of Geoffrey Bawa. One of his sculptures, a giant
sheet-metal flying owl, its wings at full span, towers at the top of
Kandalama's main staircase, threatening to swoop down to the
ground floor. Laki lives less than a half-hour drive from Kandalama.

Joseph and I drove up a side road, off the main Dambulla–Kandy
road, and arrived at Diyabubula, Laki's five-acre property where he
has lived since 1970. Outside the property the April sun beat down
mercilessly – it was the hottest time of the year; but inside the gate
it was jungle-like, tall trees crowding in everywhere, cool and shade
everywhere, with narrow shafts of sunlight here and there. Playful
naturalistic sculptures – a golden horse, a giant lizard creeping up
a tree trunk – surprised us as we advanced up the driveway. At the
end, behind a stone screen, was a raised wooden structure built on
an outcrop of rocks between two mini man-made lakes. This was
Laki's house-cum-studio.

There must have been a dozen people milling around: bare-bodied
men in sarongs, who I took to be Laki's workmen, and women in
blouses and long pleated skirts pottering about doing household
chores. The scene looked like a Sinhala village gathering. I ran up
the short flight of steps to the upper platform; and there, on the
extended open-air deck, was Laki, sitting in a wheelchair, cigarette
in hand, a bottle of arrack on the table, holding court with other
guests. I recognized him instantly from many photos: a squarish
bearded face, tousled hair now more grey than black, bare-bodied,
with a sarong knotted high up his belly.

'Ah, it must be Razeen. Come, come, sit. Join the party.' I had long wanted to meet Laki, having admired his objects, murals and paintings in Bawa hotels and heard of his eccentric reputation. I had emailed him in advance, having got an introduction from his brother Daya in Colombo.

As I sat down, Laki was holding forth on the irrigation system he designed for Diyabubula, losing me as he went into technical detail on how water pumps work. I took in the arresting views instead. Then he switched attention to me. 'We are exactly in the centre of Diyabubula,' he said. 'From here I have long views in every direction, with the two lakes on either side. I can walk, by the way. The reason I have this wheelchair is because I can rotate in whichever direction I please to take in the panorama. From here I see ever-changing life, in the water and on land – the birds, the plants, insects, animals. I can see fifty species of birds on the same day. At night I gaze up at the stars and the moonlight streaming down; I watch fireflies after dark, and listen to the raucous chatter of insects and the sounds of monkeys waging great battles. Some even crash into the water after fighting in the trees.'

The deck was also Laki's command post. From here he observed and instructed his workmen around the property. Laki's playful art was visible all around: a trademark owl sculpture perched atop his thatch roof, standing guard over the deck where we sat. A strutting cock, made of copper, stood next to us on the deck; a star-shaped object dangled over one of the pools from the overhanging branch of a tree.

Laki – the family pet name for Lakshman – was destined to be one of a kind. He was born into a planting family just before the Second World War, the seventh of eight children. Like others of his background, English was his mother tongue. His language was the second thing I noticed about Laki, after his unique physical presence: he spoke a lively, precise, full-bodied English, filled with a rich vocabulary and vivid description. His parents were socialist rebels against British rule, and founding members of the Trotskyist LSSP. His father was jailed during the war and died soon after; his mother was independent Ceylon's first female member of parliament. So politics was a staple of daily life in the Senanayake house, and political passion stayed with Laki into adulthood. But he was drawn to painting birds from the age of three, starting with birds he saw at a rural coconut estate. Later he discovered books on great painters, and classical music. He was useless academically, but good at swimming and diving.

Laki's independent streak formed early. Even in his twenties, in the late 1950s, he went around Colombo dressed as he was now, bare-bodied and in a sarong, but also with a flower in one ear and a flute tucked into his sarong. He joined an architectural practice, where he learned to become an excellent draughtsman, but – as he took special delight in telling me – from which he was sacked for organizing a new trade union. Geoffrey Bawa discovered him in the early 1960s and put him to work at Edwards, Reid and Begg, his architectural practice, where Laki continued his habit of organizing union strikes. Through Geoffrey he befriended his brother Bevis and the Australian artist Donald Friend. He began to experiment widely with painting and sculpture, and left Bawa's practice to work on batiks with Ena de Silva. From the mid-1960s, Laki and two friends roamed the island to view, measure and draw fine old buildings from Sri Lanka's colonial and pre-colonial past.

He turned away from city life in 1970, when he moved to Diyabubula to set up a farming collective with some friends and one of his brothers. Here he incorporated the natural life around him into his art, and here he became egalitarian, working alongside village boys who became lifelong friends. In fallow periods, waiting for crops to grow, he removed himself to the Botanical Gardens at Peradeniya, where he drew tree after tree.

The farm itself proved unviable. He continued to paint and sketch and sculpt – people, flora and fauna; he experimented in murals and in stuccoing walls for Bawa's hotels, designed a prize-winning set of currency notes, began a lucrative new career as a garden designer, and courted controversy with an exhibition of erotic prints.

All the while Laki pumped money into his consuming passion, Diyabubula. Having given up on the farm, he totally reforested and relandscaped the property, recreating a five-acre dry zone jungle full of trees, ferns, shrubs and animal life. Here he remained, with occasional forays to other parts of the island on work, or just to sit and paint in landscapes that enchanted him. 'As I age I hardly leave the property,' he told me. Google and YouTube connected him to the world now.

Laki's livewire talk – on his life, people he knew, his art, Diyabubula – took up much of the afternoon. The other guests had left, leaving me alone with Laki – plus cigarettes and the depleted arrack bottle – to enjoy the twilight hour. Insect sounds revved up to full volume; birdlife around the water entered its final frenetic burst before nightfall, just as it got to be time for Laki to retire. He told me to come back in the morning, 'not too early'. He meant about 6.30 a.m. He rose at 4 a.m. and worked solidly till 8 a.m. Then he had breakfast and a nap, and then pottered about the rest of the day. At night, before he went to bed at 9 p.m., he read and listened to music.

As Joseph and I drove off the lights came on around the house and the water, illuminating Laki's animal sculptures. And on came Laki's classical music, reverberating around Diyabubula. This evening it was an Indian number, a mix of the tabla and sitar. The previous evening, he told me, it was Stravinsky.

The following morning, soon after daybreak, I fetched up at Laki's room, on the upper platform a few steps from the deck where we talked the previous day. He was busy, cigarette and coffee at hand. This mid-sized room was where he worked, relaxed and slept: a bed in a corner, a PC in another, a few bookshelves, the bathroom at another end, and, dominating the room, a large worktable choc-a-bloc with paintings-in-progress, sketches and paints.

'Have you ever painted, Razeen?' he asked me. I had not, but he showed me around his works-in-progress regardless. Laki's eclecticism was breathtaking, and it expressed itself best in his painting. On the table were oils and watercolours, naturalistic landscapes and expressionist abstractions. On his PC he showed me a digital catalogue of drawings from the 1970s – incredibly precise, intricate botanical drawings, mainly of trees in Peradeniya Gardens. 'Loitering is one of my favourite pastimes,' he added. 'I highly recommend it, especially in Peradeniya Gardens.' Then he showed me another digital catalogue, this time of 'gestalt-like' vegetal abstract compositions of elephants, leopards and other wild animals. 'The eyes are the giveaway to detecting the frame,' he said.

Before I left Laki gave me a book which brought together his best-known works. In it I read:

Things don't inspire me to draw.
I'll draw anything that is there.
It's like the urge to eat or read –
I have the urge to draw.

Art is a journey, it is an adventure
And if it doesn't end up as anything good
As quite a few journeys don't . . .
You just paint over it . . .

And then:

I just start playing around and then I see shapes – perhaps a lovely thigh or a car. Of course, to do that you have to be passionately fond of thighs or cars. To produce anything that pleases you, you have to be fond of something . . .

It was 8 a.m. by the time I left the Sri Lankan genius in his little jungle. Time for breakfast – for him after a day's work, for me with the day barely begun.

~

Our next stop was Mihintale, directly north of Dambulla. Mihintale means 'Mountain of Mahinda' in Sinhala; according to the *Mahavamsa*, it is where Buddhism began in Sri Lanka. In 246 BCE, Mahinda, a monk said to be the son of Emperor Ashoka, descended here from India; in the *Mahavamsa* rendering he 'flew', just like the Buddha did on his three visits to Lanka. The reigning king, Devanampiya Tissa, and his entourage were out hunting. The king got separated from his group while pursuing a stag up the hill. Here he came across the saffron-robed Mahinda, who engaged him in a kind of Socratic dialogue. Satisfied by the king's answers, Mahinda delivered his discourse.

He converted the king, and subsequently his entourage, to Buddhism. Arahat Mahinda (*arahat*, meaning 'noble one', is the title given to someone who has attained full enlightenment) stayed on in the kingdom to preach the dhamma and guide the fledgling sangha before retiring to Mihintale for the remainder of his life. In time, Mihintale became the third largest monastic complex in the kingdom; when the Chinese monk Faxian visited in the fifth century CE, he counted over 2000 monks living there.

Almost 2000 frangipani-lined steps lead up to the rock summit. At the top, in the middle of the temple compound, is the Ambasthale dagoba, which is said to contain Mahinda's relics. Next to it is a statue of King Devanampiya Tissa. To one side a path leads down

to Mahinda's cave, where he slept on a granite slab. A few steps
from the dagoba is the Rock of Invitation, from which Mahinda
is said to have delivered his first sermon. Since this was a temple
compound, I had to clamber up this spur barefoot. It was midday;
my feet were scalded by the sunburnt rock. But the panorama was
worth the pain. All around the landscape was flat, the vegetation
even lower-cropped and paler green than what I saw in Dambulla
and Sigiriya.

On the way back down the nearly 2000 steps, my guide, who
came from the village nearby, told me Mihintale was rarely visited
during the war for fear of LTTE ambushes. Now, busy once again,
it gets most crowded on Poson Poya, the full-moon day in June
that commemorates Mahinda's conversion of Devanampiya Tissa.
Then the mountain is a sea of white; pilgrims converge on it from
all over the island.

Less than a half-hour drive from Mihintale is Anuradhapura,
Rajarata's capital for thirteen centuries. An expanse of royal palaces
and pleasure gardens, and monasteries with giant dagobas and
temples, it was built around Tissawewa, one of Rajarata's oldest
and largest man-made tanks that irrigated the fields around the
capital. It was home to colonies of South Indian, Greek and Persian
merchants. Elephants, ivory, precious stones, medicinal herbs and
spices were exported to the Middle East, Mediterranean, East
Indies and China. Local elites imported Chinese earthenware and
ceramics, while South Indian merchant guilds controlled trade at
Mantota, the kingdom's main port on the north-west coast.

South Indian invaders conquered Anuradhapura many times,
delivering the final blow in 993 CE. The city was abandoned for the
last time in 1073 CE. For almost a thousand years it was covered
by jungle, but never quite forgotten. A few monks continued to
live among the ruined shrines; a trickle of pilgrims came from

farther south. In the early years of British rule, Ralph Backhaus, a young assistant government collector, and a Buddhist monk led a small expedition to find the remains of the city, just as archaeology was becoming a science in Europe. Only in 1889 did systematic excavations begin. Significant resettlement of Anuradhapura had to wait until 1957, when construction of a new town next to the ancient city started.

My first stop was at my favourite Anuradhapura temple, Isurumuniya. It is smallish, compact and serene, quietly secluded at a distance from the main temple sites. It dates back to the early days of Buddhism in Devanampiya Tissa's reign. The small stupa sits atop a rock at the back of the enclosure. On one side of the rock is a square pool lined with stones. Next to the pool, directly under the stupa on the rock, is a little gallery of stone sculptures; its highlight is 'The Lovers', said to represent Prince Saliya, King Dutugemunu's son, and his bride Asoka Mala. She was a *rodhi*, an outcast, considered the lowest of the low in Sinhala society.

Rodhiyas were the Sinhalese equivalent of the untouchable communities of Hindu society. They were confined to segregated dirt-poor communities, eking out their living from ritualized begging and clearing upper castes' refuse, and forbidden to enter temples, draw water from village wells or wear anything above the waist. But their womenfolk were considered to be the most beautiful in Sinhala society. Prince Saliya's love, it is said, cost him the throne: he was banished among the rodhiyas for the rest of his life.

The following day I lunched at the Tissa rest house, on the banks of the sparkling wewa. Leonard Woolf broke his journey here en route from Colombo to his first posting in Jaffna in 1904; he continued to Jaffna in a bullock cart on what were still unpaved roads. The rest house had just been renovated; on my last visit, a few years earlier, just after the war ended, it was shabby, frozen in time.

The mark of passing time is everywhere in Anuradhapura, though. The ruins of its glory days are scattered over the ancient site, close to the rest house. Many are mere stone stumps in the hard ground, reduced to rubble by centuries of sun and rain and smothering jungle. But some landmarks survived sufficiently intact to be restored during the twentieth century. For me, as for any cultural tourist, four stupa visits were essential, each one an embodiment of Anuradhapura's politico-religious foundation, its alliance of Sinhala kingship and institutional Buddhism.

But Anuradhapura is no Venice or Florence, or Angkor or Borobodur, a museum piece of extinct civilization for coachloads of foreign tourists to gawp at. Quite the opposite: its temples, centred on their ancient storied stupas, live and breathe from the predawn hour to late at night with monks and pilgrims and local worshippers circumambulating the stupas clockwise, offering scented flowers at shrines large and small, lighting little lamps of coconut oil, sitting cross-legged and chanting prayers under the shade of trees. For tourists and devotees, this is what makes Anuradhapura come alive.

First up for me was Ruwanvelisaya dagoba, also known as the Maha Thupa or 'Great Stupa'. King Dutugemunu built it to celebrate his defeat of the Tamil king Elara in the second century BCE, though he did not live to see it completed. It was an outsize wonder of its age, dwarfing the famous stupa at Sanchi in North India, which was built around the same time. The huge bubble-shaped dagoba had been restored recently and was gleaming white; sculpted elephant heads ringed its surrounding wall.

Close by is the smaller, bell-shaped Thuparama, the oldest of Anuradhapura's dagobas, built by Devanampiya Tissa and said to contain the Buddha's right collarbone. It was the dagoba of the Mahavihara (Great Monastery), which grew into a vast complex of thirteen monasteries on a hundred-acre site. The Mahavihara was the cradle of Theravada Buddhism; it was the kingdom's religious centrepoint for over a thousand years. It had critical political influence, often making and breaking kings. One of its abbots, Mahanama Thera, the uncle of King Dhatusena (he who was murdered by his son Kasyapa of Sigiriya fame), is credited with writing the *Mahavamsa*. Now, though, scattered stone pillars around the Thuparama are all that remain of the Mahavihara's monasteries.

At the northern end of the ancient city is the Abhayagiri dagoba, built by King Vattagamini Abhaya in 88 BCE to commemorate his return to the throne. It is gigantic, one of the biggest stupas in the world when it was built, and has a curious ovoid shape that creates what the Sinhalese call a 'mound of paddy' effect. Sir James Emerson Tennent wrote that the bricks used to build it could have built a wall, ten feet high and one foot thick, all the way from London to Edinburgh. Faxian, who saw it one and a half millennia ago, said it was covered in gold and jewels. But, on my visit, it was still undergoing restoration, with most of its red brick exposed – a contrast to the impeccable dove-white cover of Ruwanvelisaya and Thuparama.

The dagoba was part of the Abhayagiri monastery, set up in opposition to the Mahavihara and which expanded to occupy a 300-acre site. Abhayagiri was much influenced by the new Mahayana sutras coming out of India, and became Mahayana's chief repository in Sri Lanka, reputed for being more open and liberal than the Mahavihara. Mahayana's emphasis on emotional aspects of devotion, such as worshipping Buddha and bodhisattva images, caught on with the laity, and indeed with Sinhala kings – many fancied themselves as *devaraja*s (god-kings) and bodhisattvas who would attain Buddhahood in a future birth. Abhayagiri had custodianship of the most sacred relics, including the Tooth Relic. Intermittently, it exercised great political influence, though underplayed in the *Mahavamsa* and other Theravada chronicles.

Swinging round to the west of the ancient site is Jetavanarama, the most recent and biggest of Anuradhapura's great dagobas. King Mahasena built it in the third century CE after he fell out with the Mahavihara. It took twenty-five years to build, weighs 657,000 tonnes, contains 62 million bricks and is almost 400 feet high. It was the world's biggest stupa; next to the Great Wall of China, it was the biggest structure made entirely of brick in the world. Monks who broke away from Abhayagiri established its adjoining monastery. Ideologically, Jetavana lay somewhere between the Mahavihara's doctrinaire conservatism and Abhayagiri's relative liberalism.

We drove past the ruins of smaller stupas dotted around the ancient site, and then past what little remained of King Dutugemunu's Lohu Prasada or 'Brazen Palace', once a nine-storey structure with, it is said, a thousand rooms, but now a forest of 1600 stone pillars. My last stop was the enclosure that contains Sri Maha Bodhi, the original bo tree in Sri Lanka. Sanghamitta, King Ashoka's daughter, came to Lanka with a group of nuns soon after her brother Mahinda established Buddhism here; she brought with her a sapling of the bo tree at Bodh Gaya under which the Buddha attained enlightenment. After it took root, thirty-two cuttings from it were planted all over the island. Even in the centuries when Anuradhapura lay abandoned to the jungle, monks tended to the bodhi tree and pilgrims visited it. Officially, Sri Maha Bodhi is the oldest recorded tree in the world, now some 2300 years old.

~

Polonnaruwa lies a couple of hours' drive south and east of Anuradhapura. It replaced Anuradhapura as the capital for just over two centuries, first under Sinhala kings, then under the Cholas for eighty years, and then again under Sinhala kings. Three of the latter – Vijayabahu, Parakramabahu and Nissankamalla – ruled its golden age before its sudden, precipitous decline and collapse. Previous South Indian conquerors had pillaged, as all invaders did, but they tolerated Buddhism and left Buddhist shrines intact. But Polonnaruwa's and Rajarata's ultimate destroyer, Magha of Kalinga, was the outstanding exception: his twenty-one-year reign of terror included the destruction of Buddhism and its monasteries, temples and sculptures, as well as the network of wewas that sustained the economy. The restoration of Polonnaruwa's splendours had to wait until the late nineteenth century.

Aesthetically, I prefer Polonnaruwa to Anuradhapura. The site is more compact and walkable, the buildings and sculpture more varied and with richer detail. Here one can feast one's eyes on some of the most sublime religious architecture and statuary anywhere in the Buddhist world. Anuradhapura, being much older, has lost more of its ancient architectural glory to the jungle. But Anuradhapura feels more real, its chief ancient monuments still alive as functioning temples; Polonnaruwa is more the museum piece now.

I am also partial to Polonnaruwa's little rest house and its magical setting. This is where Joseph and I headed. We drove past a small statue of D.S. Senanayake on the banks of the Parakrama Samudraya, Polonnaruwa's large wewa built by its greatest king, Parakramabahu I. The rest house lies a few yards ahead at the end of a short road. The front veranda leads to the dining room, a box-like structure with windows on three sides that juts into the lake, supported on stilts. Beyond it is a semicircular terrace looking out to the wewa, bordered by what looks like a ships's railing. It surrounds two large bedrooms; Room 1 is where Queen Elizabeth and Prince Philip stayed a night on their visit to Ceylon in 1954. Black-faced langurs congregate outside the front veranda, waiting to pounce and snatch food on coffee tables when guests are off guard.

The rest house is a popular lunch stop for travellers, but it is usually quiet and still outside of lunch hours, and just the place to slip into a reverie. What better spot to do so than on the back terrace facing the wewa, in a cane chair, sandwiched between frangipani and bottlebrush trees, feet propped up on the white railing? Birds in flight skim the waterline; the calm water laps the lakeshore with hushed, rhythmic delicacy. A soft breeze wafts from the water across the terrace.

I had been to Polonnaruwa's ruins before, but it was so long ago, on an outstation trip with Mummy and Granny, and all I remembered were gangs of menacing monkeys. This time I started at the Southern Complex, a short drive on the road around Parakrama Samudraya. Here the main sight is King Parakramabahu's statue, carved out of a surrounding block of yellow stone. It is a Sri Lankan icon, as familiar on banknotes and picture postcards as Sigiriya and its frescoes.

Parakramabahu and Dutugemunu, who ruled from Anuradhapura a good thirteen centuries earlier, are considered Sri Lanka's greatest kings. Parakramabahu, who saw himself as a Buddhist reformer-emperor like Ashoka, reigned for thirty-three eventful years. He had to put down a rebellion of his relatives who ruled the sub-kingdom of Ruhunu in the south, murdering many in the process. He built dagobas, monasteries and palaces. He reunified the sangha in one Theravada order, and laid out a monastic code that emphasized social seclusion, asceticism and meditation.

He also restored Anuradhapura after its destruction by the Cholas, and built over a thousand wewas and connecting canals. Exceptionally for a Sinhala king, he invaded South India and Burma, albeit without success. But, like most of his predecessors and successors, he was religiously eclectic. Hindu deities from the Chola period were preserved and worshipped; they came to be regarded as protectors of Buddhist shrines. Brahmins were welcome at the royal court, and there were matrimonial alliances with South Indian courts.

Some archaeologists date the yellow-stone statue before me to the ninth century, at least 300 years before Parakramabahu's reign. But no matter: it is imposing enough to evoke Parakramabahu's grandeur. He stands in the classic *tivanka* (thrice-bent) pose, bent slightly at the knee, hip and shoulder. This shows an earlier South Indian Buddhist influence, from Amaravati sculpture in what is now Andhra Pradesh. He is moustachioed, bearded and wears a tall rounded headdress; a long cloth covers his loins and legs, but his torso is bare, showing off an ample belly. His hands hold a concave object, what could be a palm-leaf book or a yoke of sovereignty. Local wags say it is a papaya.

Right next to the rest house, also on the banks of Parakrama Samudraya, is the Island Park complex built by Parakramabahu's successor Nissankamalla. Troops of langurs – those not delegated to steal guests' food from the rest house veranda – congregate around the ruins of the royal baths. Nearby, Nissankamalla's council chamber is guarded by stone lions.

From here I headed past the new town to the ancient city's main complex. Parakramabahu's palace was once a seven-storey structure with a thousand rooms, a wooden roof and large outer walls, according to the *Culavamsa*. Now it is roofless and no more than four storeys high. The royal baths and king's council chamber are close by. Here Parakramabahu's cabinet of ministers met, a model of multi-religious, multi-ethnic representation rarely equalled since. According to the contemporary Arab historian Idrisi, it had four Sinhalese, four Christians, four Muslims and four Jews; the non-Muslim majority were probably leaders of trading communities in the kingdom.

A five-minute walk leads to a Shiva devale, erected by the Pandyans in the thirteenth century after the collapse of Sinhala

Polonnaruwa. And a short walk from there leads to the magnificent Sacred Quadrangle.

The quadrangle encloses several temples and *gedige*s (image houses), which housed the Tooth Relic once it came here from Anuradhapura. The quadrangle's jewel in the crown is the stupendous Vatadage, a circular relic house built by Parakramabahu and embellished by Nissankamalla. Beautifully carved moonstones and *nagarajah* guardstones, with their figures of snake deities, announce the entrance to the upper terrace at four cardinal points. Friezes of dwarfs, lions, elephants and lotus petals adorn the outer wall – a riot of carved artistry. Around the circular enclosure are four *samadhi* Buddhas, in the seated meditation pose, at each cardinal point. It is said there was once a brick dagoba inside this ring of Buddha statues that housed the Tooth Relic.

Directly opposite the Vatadage is the Hatadage, which is also accorded the honour of having once held the Tooth Relic. And next to the Hatadage is the Galpotha, a twenty-six-foot-long stone slab with vainglorious and prolix inscriptions in praise of Nissankamalla.

I left my Polonnaruwa highlight for the last: the Gal Vihara (Stone Temple) – the acme of Sinhala eloquence in stone. It is one massive 170-foot-long granite block from which four exquisite Buddha statues are carved. At one end is a large samadhi Buddha with a Sanchi-style arch above its head. Smaller Buddhas, also covered by arches, hover above its head and shoulders like ethereal apsaras in the Buddhist cosmos. Further along the rock is a smaller samadhi Buddha covered by an arch in a cave-like recess. And on the other side of it is an inscription commemorating Parakramabahu's unification of the sangha in 1165 CE, with directions for its future conduct.

Then come the Gal Vihara's real stunners, two giant, ineffably sublime Buddha statues side by side. The twenty-two-foot tall standing Buddha is in the thrice-bent tivanka pose, like the statue of

Parakramabahu in the Southern Complex. His arms are crossed in front of his chest, and his gaze is one of eternal serenity. Thin films of black sediment striate delicately across his face and robed body, blending harmoniously with the whitened rock face. And completing the Gal Vihara's statuary quartet, at this end of Sri Lanka's mini Mount Rushmore, is the island's most famous Buddha, forty-five feet long and recumbent.

In the Tipitaka, the eighty-year-old Buddha and his disciples approached a grove of sal trees near the northern Indian town of Kushinara. This was the Buddha's last journey. He said to his disciple Ananda, 'Spread for me, I pray you, a bed between these twin sal trees. I am weary, Ananda, and wish to lie down.' And there, among his mourning disciples, he died, lying on his right side in the manner of a lion.

The Gal Vihara's recumbent Buddha lies on his side, facing out. The face is beautifully serene, the head rests on a cylindrical pillow, and a large blossoming lotus covers the sole of each foot. The Awakened One is close to death. Having already achieved enlightenment decades earlier, he will no longer be subject to rebirth and the endless rounds of suffering that plague unenlightened beings.

On a sloping rock in front of the last two Buddha statues, I sat and gazed in wide-eyed wonder. Half an hour went by before I knew it. So far on my travels through Rajarata, I was a cultural tourist, my *Handbook for the Ceylon Traveller* and Ven Dhammika's *Sacred Island* at hand, writing up notes afterwards on hotel and rest house verandas. At Gal Vihara, contemplating these two standing and recumbent Buddhas side by side, something felt fundamentally different. Their unshakeable inner stillness, their core of peace and harmony, manifest in the perfectly proportioned body draped in its flowing creased robe, and above all, in the gentle, smiling visage – all this radiated a kind of power from the mass of cold, hard, whitened rock. It seeped deeply into my being.

When my mind returned to external reality, I thought of how total destruction swiftly followed this apotheosis of Polonnaruwa civilization. Parakramabahu's and Nissankamalla's excesses – imposing a crushing burden of taxes and labour duties on their subjects to build these masterpieces, lavishing money on monasteries, centralizing their power and even fighting wars abroad – so weakened the state that it became ripe for takeover once they departed the scene.

~

The next morning Joseph and I headed back to Colombo, slowly and circuitously. Joseph decided to take byroads for 'interesting sceneries'. I have a habit of nodding off in moving vehicles, however. When I woke up, Joseph remonstrated that, after all the trouble he went to, 'Sir, what shame, no, you missed so many interesting sceneries.'

We stopped briefly at Kalawewa, one of Rajarata's largest tanks, built by King Dhatusena in the fifth century CE. On the roadside where we stopped is a little devale and King Dhatusena's statue. This is the setting for a famous story in the *Culavamsa*. Kasyapa, the future parricide and lord of Sigiriya, had already overthrown and imprisoned his father King Dhatusena. He had heard the king had buried treasure in Kalawewa, which he coveted. So he had Dhatusena led to this spot, now marked by the devale and statue, where he waded into the water. Knowing death was nigh, one way or the other, Dhatusena cupped water from the tank, held it high, and said, 'This is my treasure.' Then, incensed, Kasyapa had his father put to his gruesome death.

Joseph got talking to a Sinhala family from down south on their way to perform pilgrimage in Anuradhapura. The two sweetly smiling daughters, one probably in her early teens, the other a bit younger, came up to me offering home-cooked pilgrim food; it was delicious *mungkiribath,* milk rice cooked with green gram and sweetened with jaggery. It is customary for Sinhala pilgrims to offer food to those they meet on the journey; the mungkiribath reminded me of smiling pilgrims offering sweets to fellow climbers at Adam's Peak.

A side road off Kalawewa led us to Aukana. The standing Buddha here, forty feet high, is the tallest in Sri Lanka, and undoubtedly one of the finest statues in the island. It dates back to the fifth century CE, probably to King Dhatusena's reign. It stands on a lotus plinth, and it is free-standing, only lightly – hardly noticeably – attached at the back to the rock from which it is carved. One hand is upstretched to hold the robe in place. The other hand and forearm are raised and turned sideways, with the elbow bent. The visage is serene, the eyes open; the body is lifelike, slim and finely proportioned. It is a wonder to follow the line of each delicate crease on the robe.

From Aukana, Joseph took me down other byroads; I stayed awake to enjoy the 'interesting sceneries'. This was Sinhala village heartland: small towns, hamlets, paddy fields, fruit orchards, a slow, slow pace of life. Womenfolk were up and doing. The men in sight lolled around, sitting, chatting, sipping tea and smoking cigarettes.

~

My final stop before we returned to Colombo was not an ancient temple or statue but a school for the deaf, run by a remarkable Catholic nun.

St Joseph's School for the Hearing Impaired lies a few miles outside the market town of Kuliyapitiya, surrounded by paddy fields and coconut groves. It is a simple two-storey building with a small annex where boarders lodge. I came here because it was part-funded by Candle Aid, the charity run by my friends Elmo and

Dil Jayawardena in Moratuwa. Sister Therese, the school's founder and headmistress, greeted me and led me to her little office. She matched the office: small and neat. Her broad, generous smile was the window to her character. As she started to talk, her feet moved out of her slippers, crossed each other and oscillated gently, like a little girl on a swing.

Sister Therese came from Catholic country near Negombo. After she was ordained, she trained in Manchester and came back to work with deaf children at a convent school in Ja-ela, halfway between Colombo and the airport. She went on: 'But I was dissatisfied with the conventional method of teaching deaf children in Sri Lanka. They are treated as something apart; there is no attempt to integrate them into society. These children have so many creative talents, but they are suppressed. I want to bring them out, bring the children into society as much as possible. That is my calling. So I got some money from a Dutch foundation and started the school here.'

Her face became more animated, her voice more passionate, as she warmed to her theme. 'The children crave affection, so much more than normal because they are denied it. They are set apart, consigned to a world of silence. Parents, brothers, sisters and teachers don't know how to deal with them. They get bullied at school. The government schoolteachers don't stop it; they don't make the effort to teach them properly. So, here, we teach them useful things so that, when they leave, they can work, earn a living, contribute to society. I try to be kind and loving – they crave it so much, since they don't get it at home or in society. But I must also be firm. Kind but firm.'

Sister Therese led a small teaching staff – another nun, two young female teachers, and a male teacher who gave computer classes and drove the van. The school had about thirty pupils, from the ages of six to eighteen, many from Kuliyapitiya's surrounding villages. Seventeen were boarders, children from poor families in remote areas who could not afford the daily commute. Those who had better hearing went to the government school in Kuliyapitiya, but they did special classes here in the afternoons.

Sister Therese told me she was on the go the whole day, teaching and administering in the mornings and afternoons, helping the boarders with their homework in the evenings. 'I am so tired at the end of the day. Many times I feel it is such a burden on my small shoulders. Society can be very cruel. People are ignorant about the children's needs – they are unconcerned. Some get hit by drunken fathers. We have orphans looked after by old grandmothers. Sometimes I have to go to visit homes to sort out domestic problems. But I know this is my calling. God wants me to do this work. So, at the end of the day, when I put my head on the pillow, I go to sleep immediately. I don't think of all there is to do the next day. My sleep is sound, undisturbed.'

We went upstairs. Afternoon classes were in full flow. In one small room, children were having speech therapy, the little heads of the younger ones swaddled by large earphones. Another class had children learning computer skills. The two biggest classes, led by sari-clad young teachers, were busy painting, making cane baskets, and stitching decorative patterns on to pillowcases and tablecloths for the school's annual exhibition. Sister Therese showed me the paintings. They were mostly pastoral scenes, full of trees, birds and animals, all in a blaze of colour.

It was time to go. Sister Therese took me down to the car. A lone boy stood near the car and shot a shy, sweet smile at me. 'He is twelve, an orphan,' Sister Therese told me. 'He is so shy and withdrawn. He has a learning problem, so he still attends the Montessori in the town. He boards here, but he goes to the temple on weekends – his uncle is a monk.'

'God bless,' were Sister Therese's parting words, accompanied by her broad smile. That smile of the deaf orphan boy stayed with me all the way back to Colombo.

8

War Scars

The North and the East

The landscape is full of a bleak and bitter beauty such as you will find nowhere else in Sri Lanka.

– Handbook for the Ceylon Traveller

The 'bleak and bitter beauty' in my guidebook refers to Delft, the most remote inhabited island off the Jaffna peninsula. But it happens to be true of much of the north and east, setting it apart from the rest of the country. Here is harsh, flat, dirt-brown terrain with expanses of scrub jungle under vaulted skies that contrasts with the wet zone lusciousness of the south, west and hill country. The slender, bending trunk and tapering leaves of the coconut palm dominate the wet zone treescape. The palmyrah dominates in much of the dry zone, with its thick, vertical trunk and short, rigid, jagged leaves. The former sways gracefully in soft breezes; the latter stands martial and erect on more forbidding ground. But the palmyrah, like the coconut tree, has a hundred and one different uses.

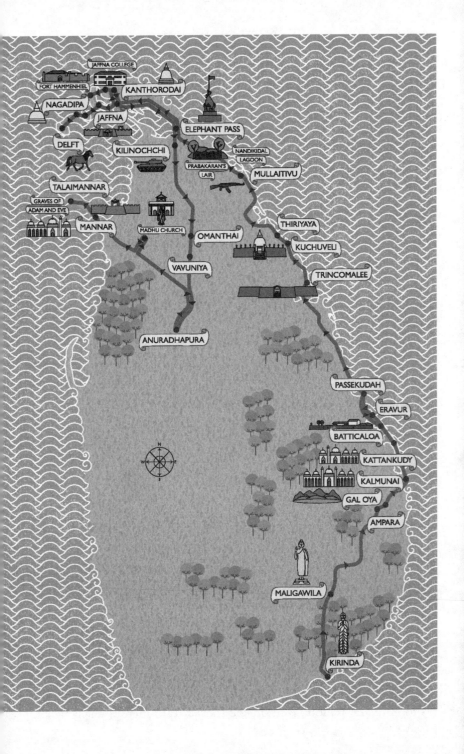

The people of the north and east are different too, predominantly Tamils in the north, and Tamils and Muslims, whose mother tongue is Tamil, in the east. They occupy one-third of the island's land mass, although they are just over a tenth of its population. These are by far the poorest parts of the country. During the war, while terrorist incursions and fear plagued the rest of the country, the north and east were the actual battlegrounds, places where the overwhelming majority of casualties, both combatant and civilian, occurred. This is the most scarred part of Sri Lanka, and will remain so for years and probably decades to come.

I travelled four times in the north and east, all after the end of the war. The last trip, in late February 2018, was my longest, retracing previous tracks and covering much new ground. It started where my last trip to the deep south ended, at Kirinda Vihara on the south-east coast. I went all the way up the east coast, cut into the Vanni, headed up to the Jaffna peninsula and the islands off it, and crossed over to Mannar island in the north-west on my way down to Colombo. This was my most extensive Sri Lankan road trip, and the most exhilarating.

~

From Kirinda Joseph drove me inland, skirting the Yala National Park and heading north and then north-east to the eastern town of Ampara. We made two stops en route, one a diversion west to Buduruvagala, the other at Maligawila. Both are temple sites dating back to the seventh or eighth century CE, but what really marks them out is their prominent Mahayana sculpture. At Buduruvagala, carved on a large rock face, is a tall standing Buddha flanked by bodhisattvas; on one side is Avalokiteshvara, in turn flanked by Tara and her sister Bhrkuti. Maligawila is a forest clearing a half-hour drive off the road to Ampara, remote, well off the tourist trail. Here is a spectacular, towering free-standing Buddha, the tallest in the island after the Aukana Buddha in Rajarata. But a five-minute walk away, on a raised terrace, is possibly the largest extant Mahayana statue in Sri Lanka, a richly bejewelled thirty-foot-tall Avalokiteshvara, arms extended in front of the torso, elbows bent, forearms raised, the palms facing outwards in the gesture of instruction.

From the Uva foothills we descended to the plain and reached Ampara after dark. Now we were properly in the east. Ampara town is predominantly Sinhala, but Muslims dominate the surrounding district, the only one in Sri Lanka where Muslims outnumber other ethnic groups. One-third of Sri Lankan Muslims live in the east. Traders from other parts of the Muslim world – the Gulf and Yemen, the Malabar and Coromandel coasts of South India, and Java – came and settled here, and their descendants continue to trade and run shops. But, exceptionally for Sri Lankan Muslims, many are farmers and some even fishermen. Their forefathers settled here in the seventeenth century or possibly earlier, when the east was part of the Kandyan kingdom. Eastern Province is Sri Lanka's most ethnically mixed region – two-fifths Tamil, over a third Muslim and almost a quarter Sinhalese. Until independence it had a Tamil–Muslim mix; then large-scale irrigation projects and government encouragement caused Sinhala peasants to flood in – a big bone of contention in Sinhala–Tamil politics since the 1950s.

Ethnic conflict surfaced later than it did in the north. The east's ethno-religious heterogeneity, the easy rapport between Muslims and Tamils, and contact with the rest of the island through roads and commerce, tempered the Tamil militancy that arose in the more ethnically homogeneous and isolated north. But tensions surfaced in the 1970s, and Tamil–Muslim–Sinhala conflict exploded in the late 1980s. The army and police battled it out with the LTTE, with atrocities on both sides. The LTTE turned its terror on local Muslims; massacres took place in mosques in the Muslim towns of

Kattankudy and Eravur. Muslims, in turn, formed vigilante groups that attacked Tamils. After two decades of fighting, the eastern leadership of the LTTE broke away from Prabhakaran in the north and defected to the government. Peace arrived three years before the war ended in the north.

The next day, Joseph and I drove around the district. We crossed the hamlet of Inginiyagala, an hour's drive out of Ampara town, and the gateway to the Gal Oya National Park and its dam. The latter was the first major irrigation project completed after independence, the brainchild of D.S. Senanayake. It accounted for the greenness of the surrounding national park, full of elephants, and of the cultivated land in Ampara district.

I got out of the car at the park entrance and walked along the long bund that bordered this end of the dam. Saw-toothed hills framed the western horizon beyond the water on this hot, cloudless day. On the other side lay Uva tea country. I passed two large groups of schoolchildren with their chaperoning teachers, one group Tamil, the other Muslim, the girls all shrouded in black hijabs and abayas.

Ampara district is home to many *aranyas,* remote forest hermitages where monks used to live and meditate in caves. They still do, though in smaller numbers and without the extreme deprivation to which they used to subject themselves. Here one finds Sri Lanka's more ascetic monks, who flee the busyness, worldly vices and petty jealousies in temples closer to human habitation, and come here to meditate.

I spent a good hour at one aranya, Buddhangala. It felt like the back of beyond, at the end of a narrow road full of signs warning of elephants crossing, even though it was not far from Ampara town. All was quiet, as befitted a meditation centre. I walked across to a squat rock with a tiny temple and a conical white stupa on its sandy surface; facing the footbridge was the statue of an emaciated, meditating hermit, shaded by a tree. Small sitting Buddhas garlanded the adjoining rock face, flanking a larger Buddha, shaded by a parasol. The landscape all around was flat scrub, dotted with rocky outcrops.

Joseph and I stopped at a lonely roadside stall on a country road for a late lunch. The woman at the stall had the welcoming manners and gentle conversation of Kandyan villages, and that is indeed where she hailed from. Joseph picked out papaya, bananas and *tambili* (king coconut) with an expert eye and a sure touch, and lost no time to chat and joke with our hostess. She had worked as a housemaid in Saudi Arabia for ten years and bought the plot of land behind the stall with her savings. She and her husband lived in the small house they built on the land, grew paddy and vegetables, and ran this stall. It is a common story of Sinhala countryfolk attracted by cheap and abundant land in the east.

∼

Back at my hotel I met Irfan, a Muslim politician from a prominent local family. Of the old stripe, Irfan was steeped in the culture of his faith, but also wedded to the ideal of an ethnically plural, harmonious Sri Lanka. He told me his kind of Sri Lanka faced a double threat – from Sinhala chauvinism and Muslim self-isolation.

'With the war over, the Sinhala lion has awoken and is on the prowl, pushing against the minorities. We have to live with it. Life is still better than it was during the war. East-coast Tamils feel the same: they prefer Sinhala rule in peacetime to the rule of northern Tamils in wartime. Peace has restored some of the old relations between Tamils and Muslims. Tamils from the villages come to buy goods in Muslim shops in the towns; Muslims buy agricultural produce from Tamil farmers.' But mutual suspicion remained. 'Tamils still feel Muslims betrayed them during the war. The SLMC (Sri Lanka Muslim Congress, the main Muslim political party) cut deals with successive governments and got a lot of patronage for east-coast Muslims, jobs and so on, but there was nothing for Tamils. They were left to face the brunt of military and police oppression and petty discrimination.'

'Muslim politicians are easily bought off with money and perks of office,' Irfan went on. 'Just look at the SLMC. And they squabble all the time, full of personality clashes. We Muslims are never united – only in prayer, nothing else.'

But what disturbed Irfan most was the virus of fundamentalist Islam. 'It started with university graduates in the 1970s. They started dressing the Arab way, grew long beards, had more austere, militant views. Then their women covered themselves in black. Maulanas and maulvis came back breathing fire after studying on scholarships in the Middle East. Saudi and Kuwaiti funding was showered on mosques and madrassas. From the 1980s it spread to poorer Muslims. They went to work in the Middle East and came back with a different version of Islam. Every Muslim family in the east has a relative, often several, who are working or have worked in the Middle East.

'Now nearly all the younger women are dressed in the abaya and hijab; many wear the niqab, even young girls. They face huge social pressure to dress this way. And Sufism is under siege. This is so tragic. We have a centuries-old Sufi tradition in east-coast Muslim culture. But the militants attack Sufi preachers and the *kandooris* (festivals of devotional singing and dancing in front of Sufi shrines to celebrate the death anniversary of a saint).

'All this is new identity politics. Some Muslims now claim we are a "nation", just as Jaffna Tamils claim nationhood for Sri Lankan Tamils. They want to keep their distance from other Sri Lankans, rewrite Muslim history in Sri Lanka, rid it of "impure" influences. This is destroying the community from within, and it's fodder for

Sinhala militant groups like the Boddhu Bala Sena that target Muslims. It weakens the traditions that held the community together and linked it to Sinhalese and Tamils. We were the natural bridge-builders of Sri Lanka through trade and racial mixing, marrying Sinhalese in Sinhala areas and Tamils in Tamil areas. Unlike Tamils and Sinhalese, we had no claims of nationhood.'

Irfan's observations resonated with my impressions of some Colombo Muslims, particularly the younger generation. They seemed to yearn for a purer Islam, in their perception closer to its roots in the Arabia of the Prophet and the two or three generations immediately after him. But from what I had heard before, this Wahhabi and Salafi-influenced Islam had struck its deepest roots on the east coast. Irfan's anxieties reinforced the point. Why? Was it because of the mass of poor east-coast Muslims, now over three generations, who had gone to work in the Middle East? Did the isolation and suffering of east-coast Muslims over two decades of war have something to do with it? Was it inciting a backlash among Sinhalese and Tamils? Where might it lead? I had only questions. And I hoped to find out more on my way through Muslim towns up the east coast.

Just over a year after this conversation with Irfan, suicide bombers linked to Islamic State blew up churches and hotels in Colombo, Negombo and Batticaloa, killing over 250 people and injuring about 500 others. All the attackers were Sri Lankan Muslims. The most prominent, Zahran Hashim, came from the east-coast town of Kattankudy, where he founded a radical splinter group, National Thowheed Jamath, in 2014 and preached hatred and violence against 'infidels', starting with local Sufi Muslims. The Easter Sunday 2019 atrocities dealt a body blow to Muslims' reputation for peaceful coexistence, which had stretched over a millennium. Sinhala revenge attacks followed. Suddenly, a national, indeed global, spotlight was turned on the recent radicalization of Sri Lankan Islam. Irfan's foreboding was on the mark, but even he did not imagine its consequences would strike so soon and so destructively.

~

From Ampara we headed to the coast and turned north. The coastal strip, from Batticaloa to Pottuvil farther south, is full of Muslim towns like Kalmunai, where we made a brief stop. Muslim shops and mosques with outsize bulbous domes lined the road, all packed tightly together. Shops were busy. Locals crowded the pavements: bearded men in prayer caps and sarongs; women in hijabs, abayas and saris with one part of the cloth draped loosely over their heads; schoolboys in prayer caps and neck-to-foot white tunics; and schoolgirls in a white version of the abaya and hijab.

We turned off the coast road and headed to the beach. My destination was Kalmunai's beach mosque, the site of the main Sufi shrine on the east coast. On the way we drove down narrow, dusty lanes jam-packed with modest little houses behind parapet walls. Occasionally, a house stood out with a grand gold-painted front gate and an additional storey or two on top of the original building, usually a sign of money remitted from a relative working in the Middle East.

Now I got my first close-up view of east-coast waters on this trip – a beach of bleach-white sand and a serene turquoise-green sea: not blue or bluish-green like on the west and south coasts, but brilliant green water, sparkling in the noonday sun. Multicoloured fishing boats were beached all along the sand. The mosque, right next to the beach, was painted pale green; in front was a stand-alone white minaret, from which the muezzin recited his call to prayer. It was between prayer times; no one was in the mosque except a grizzled old caretaker in a prayer cap and sarong. He led me to the *ziyaram* inside – the shrine of the Nagoor saint who visited here many centuries ago. The shrine was a simple green slab, cordoned off and illuminated by an oil lamp. The saint was buried in Nagoor in Tamil Nadu, not here. The shrine simply commemorated his visit. The old man raised and cupped his hands, recited prayers to the saint, and promptly put his right hand out for a tip.

Next to the mosque was a large sand-covered square with a shady tree at its centre. This was the site of the annual kandoori, when devotees came from all over Sri Lanka and even India. For centuries, bawas would dance themselves into a trance and perform blood-curdling acts of self-torture with the swords, knives and spikes they carried with them. That hardly happened now with the backlash against Sufism. The Kalmunai kandoorie was one of the few to survive in Sri Lanka.

~

Up the coast, churches, Christian missionary orders, kovils and Hindu spiritual-cum-charity missions occupy large plots of beachside land, their one-storey buildings surrounded by scrub and palmyrahs. I noticed several Pentecostal churches, small and modest compared with their Catholic counterparts.

Kattankudy, the main Muslim commercial town between Batticaloa and Pottuvil, is special, probably the most intensely Muslim urban space in the country. The municipal area covers one square mile, packed densely with about 50,000 inhabitants in 8000 houses. Every single one is Muslim. Within the square mile there are sixty-three mosques, including four large jumma mosques, where Muslims congregate for Friday prayers. Kattankudy had a long-standing reputation for piety, but, after the Easter Sunday 2019 bombings, it became infamous as the east coast's hotbed of fundamentalist Islam.

A giant Moorish arch, towering above and straddling the coast road, announced the religious composition of the town with loud overstatement. There was an equally giant arch to see us off at the other end of town. In between, running continuously down the middle of this road, was an avenue of date palms imported from the Middle East. I felt I had been whisked away on a magic carpet to an oasis in the Arabian desert. Nothing about Kattankudy's modern landmarks told me I was in Sri Lanka.

The town was heaving and bustling this afternoon. The cheek-by-jowl shops bulged with produce and customers; locals crowded the narrow pavements; and masses of motorbikes, interspersed with cars and vans, were parked uninterruptedly on the roadsides. Commerce was clearly booming. When I first passed through, in 2011, five years after the war ended in the east, I noticed these Muslim coastal towns were the first to recover from wartime ravage. But there were still many bullet-ridden shopfronts and the odd empy shell of a building. On my next trip, in 2014, most vestiges of war damage had gone. Now, four years later, none were visible, replaced by Muslim trading at full throttle. Even before the war, Kattankudy's denizens fanned out far and wide, in Sri Lanka and beyond its shores, to settle and trade.

In the town centre, still on the main road, was the newish Muslim Heritage Museum, another building that looked like an Arab transplant, all arches and domes with an ochre-brown facade. It was the brainchild of M.L.A.M. Hizbullah, Kattankudy's political Big Man, a veteran politician who had hardly been out of government since the 1990s. Like other Sri Lankan Muslim politicians he kept changing allegiance, from the SLFP to the UNP and back and forth.

On the ground floor were souvenirs from Minister Hizbullah's innumerable official overseas visits, but it got more interesting upstairs. The second floor contained household items from generations past of east-coast Muslims: betel-cutters and betel-leaf trays, spittoons, walking canes, saris, fez caps, Qur'ans and Qur'an stands, jewellery. There were mock-ups of a prosperous Muslim family relaxing on their home veranda; of an itinerant Muslim trader displaying his wares under the shade of a tamarind tree; and of a tiny one-room wattle-and-daub beachside mosque from the eighteenth century. On the top floor, displayed on boards hanging from the ceiling, was a history of Islam in Sri Lanka, focusing on the east coast.

My museum guide, a Hizbullah retainer, said he noticed the look of Kattankudy change during the 1980s, when locals started to flock to the Middle East for work. It changed again during the war, as a defensive backlash against Tamils and even Sinhalese. Muslim cultural reference points shifted from their age-old anchor in South Indian, particularly Tamil, culture to the Arab Middle East.

I could have lingered on the top floor for another half-hour or more, but Mrs Salma arrived to take me to the next stop. Mrs Salma was a dark, vigorous lady, clad in a black abaya and blue-and-white headdress. She was Minister Hizbullah's sister, personal assistant and a newly elected local councillor – the only elected female Muslim politician in the country.

At the nearby jumma mosque, on a side road just off the main road, Mrs Salma's husband joined us and led me inside. The building was modern, large and airy, big enough, at a pinch, to accommodate 5000 worshippers on a Friday afternoon. But the inside front wall stuck out, riddled with bullet holes from side corner to side corner and bottom to top, on both sides of the mihrab and dais in the middle. Here, on 3 August 1990, during jam-packed jumma prayers, LTTE fighters barged in from all sides, shooting indiscriminately. They attacked three other mosques in town at the same time.

Here they slaughtered 103 worshippers, from old men to young boys, the youngest just six years old. A black plaque outside commemorated the fallen, including the six-year-old and a doctor who was born a Hindu but converted to Islam. One of the mosque attendants, a grizzled man in prayer cap and sarong, told me his son was a victim, just thirteen on that fateful Friday afternoon. Opposite the mosque was a large patch of ground with the graves of the dead, without tombstones, just simple wooden sticks to mark where they were buried.

~

From Kattankudy it was a short drive to Batticaloa, one of the two main towns in Eastern Province (the other being Trincomalee, a few hours' drive up the coast). Batti, as locals called it, spread out along the banks of a magnificent lagoon fringed by coconut and palmyrah groves sprouting out of shallow, watery sand. Here nestled little one-storey houses and home gardens. These vegetal suburbs converged along lanes with crumbling art deco houses to a smallish town centre and a Dutch fort. We crossed Kallady bridge, which connected Batti's southern outskirts with its northern town centre and outskirts across the lagoon; then stopped briefly at the northern end of the bridge so I could get out and walk back along the older gridiron bridge right next to the one we crossed. This was the old bridge for motor traffic, now reserved for cyclists and pedestrians. In Batti lore, one could hear the lagoon's 'singing fish' from its mid-point. But that was only on full-moon nights – certainly not on a weekday late afternoon.

We arrived at Passekudah, on the coast, just in time for a crimson sunset over the bay. This was our stop for the next two days. In 2011, when I was last here, there was nothing on the bay but the rotting shells of two hotels from pre-war days that the LTTE burned down. Then the beach was dirty, abused by locals who liberally dumped their picnic rubbish on it, and full of stray dogs. Now there were seven hotels up and running, and the beach was spotless. Still, I felt that back-to-back hotel resorts strung around the bay had spoilt a little of its old charm.

That charm I savoured thirty-seven years earlier on three idyllic weeks in August 1981, just after I finished O-levels in North Wales. I stayed with the family of the local member of parliament, who was also a cabinet minister, but spent nearly all my time with Naushaad, whose family lived in Eravur, just outside Batti. Naushaad had just finished his A-levels in Colombo and lived at my Aunty Zara's house in Colpetty. He was a phenomenon: a poor east-coast Muslim boy who became a Hafiz – one who could recite the whole Qur'an from memory – at the age of eight and got a scholarship to study at one of Colombo's elite schools. He was a thin, angular boy, with a chiselled face that constantly lit up with a flashing, tooth-filled smile; and, most winningly, a sweet, innocent nature.

Over those three weeks in Eravur, I spent my days and evenings with Naushaad and his huge family – a father, seven brothers and four sisters – all packed into a two-room house with an outside toilet and a well for washing in the backyard. There we ate, played cards, visited innumerable relatives in town, and cycled to the local mosque at prayer times. We scootered to Passekudah for a swim in the bay almost every morning, had a picnic lunch on the beach, and scootered back to Eravur by mid-afternoon. The east coast was largely peaceful then, two years before Black July 1983.

Soon after, I went back to the UK, and Naushaad spent the following decade in the Middle East, going to university and then working. We drifted apart and lost touch – until the week before this trip, when Naushaad and I met in Colombo for the first time in twenty years. We salaamed and hugged, and spent the next four hours in non-stop talk, relating our life stories to each other.

Naushaad was now in his late fifties. The wide smile was still there, but he had filled out, with a little middle-age paunch. His hair was completely grey. He sported a trim goatee in the Muslim way. He looked his age. The mien of the worldly, confident man of action had replaced the winsomeness of long-lost youth. When he returned from the Middle East, he got married, started a family, quickly became very successful in business, leveraging his Middle East contacts, and went into Muslim politics. He was in the thick of intramural warfare in the SLMC before rejoining its leadership. Now he was a minister, and Eastern Province's leading Muslim politician. All seven brothers worked in his businesses, as did several nephews. My head reeled. I could hardly process how far he had travelled in life, how much he had accomplished, from such humble beginnings.

Naushaad was a self-confessed workaholic, and devoted himself full-time, he said, to bettering the condition of people in the east. 'Allah has blessed me with success, with riches. I don't need to earn more. It's my duty to help my people. I haven't earned a cent since I took office; all my time goes on my projects. I am on the go all the time, travelling between Colombo, Trinco and Batti. I'm always in meetings, always the phone rings. I can't remember the last time I spent even an hour talking to someone without interruption, like I'm doing with you now, Razeen.

'So many problems, Razeen,' he continued. 'Poverty in Batticaloa district is the highest in the country. The official rate is 23 per cent, but it's much higher. Families break down because relatives go to work in the Middle East, especially women as housemaids. The provincial council's budget is tiny, so I have to spend my own money on projects in the east.'

The next evening, at his office, Naushaad showed me promotional videos to attract investment and project proposals – for paddy and vegetable cultivation, animal husbandry and much else besides. Then we went to his home for dinner. Now I saw the trappings of the big-shot politician. We drove in one SUV while another followed. Flunkeys, presumably including bodyguards, surrounded him. My impression was they were all from Eravur; some were probably relatives. When we reached the house the first thing I saw were two shiny BMWs under the porch. The house was well appointed, the food overflowing; his wife and children had that soft rounded look of Colombo prosperity. I still found it difficult to reconcile all this with the Naushaad I knew during that brief, intense friendship thirty-seven years ago.

~

Naushaad could not join me in Batti as he had a business trip to the Middle East. But his 'coordinating secretary' Mr Jeyaratnam, a diminutive Tamil from Trincomalee, picked me up from the hotel after breakfast and led me to a jeep; sitting in front were a driver and a Sinhala police sergeant who was part of Naushaad's security detail. First we headed into the interior of Batti district – and into another world.

The landscape changed dramatically. Now we were in scrub jungle: hard, parched, stony ground, flat as a pancake, under an enormous sky. I saw a few skeletal cows here and there. The humans were few, too, and thin and bony, like their cattle. Their clothes were threadbare. They were on foot or rode clapped-out bicycles. They lived in scattered hamlets of huts with roofs of thatch or corrugated iron, set in little plots of land fenced off with *cadjan* (dried coconut-palm leaves) and iron sheets; many huts did not seem to have electricity or running water. We passed a remote school next to a clutch of small brick houses for resettled refugees, built with European Union aid. The roads were terrible, evidently not repaired since the end of the war. At one point our jeep gingerly crossed a war-damaged bridge with one corner upended, suspended in mid-air.

It was a stark contrast with the coast, which was only a half-hour drive away. This used to be LTTE-controlled territory; the wounds of war still festered in these faraway, scattered, thinly peopled interior settlements. This kind of poverty did not exist outside the north and east. I had not seen its like in Sri Lanka since driving through remote villages in the 1970s. Then, from the comfort of a Peugeot 504, my childhood eyes saw the occasional mud hut without electricity and running water, occupied by a family in threadbare clothes, and perhaps lacking a square meal some days of the week. Four decades later, this looked as bad, even before thinking of the bereavement and trauma that war must have brought.

From the barren interior we returned to the greener coast, lined with coconut and palmyrah trees. Post-war progress was visible, in the roads and shops, and the faces, bodies and clothes of the people who lived here.

At Eravur, Naushaad's home town, we went straight to his main compound. A madrassa – this one a religious boarding school for teenage Muslim boys, all uniformed in prayer caps and long white tunics – occupied one corner. Next door was Naushaad's mother's old house, which he had turned into an industrial park. His photo featured prominently on the signboard in front of the house, as it did elsewhere in town. Here ten instructors trained over 200 girls and women in various workplace skills – computers, basket-weaving, carpet-making, weaving of sarongs and saris, carpentry, cashew-making. Most trainees were Muslims, but there were a few Tamils. Ninety per cent of the Muslims were in abaya and hijab. Naushaad told me he paid for all this out of his own pocket.

Around 1 p.m., Mr Jeyaratnam deposited me at Eravur's main mosque. It was Friday, and jumma prayers were in my programme. It took me back to jumma prayers with Daddy in Colombo, part of my childhood rituals, and indeed to the last time I was in this mosque, with Naushaad, in August 1981. It was packed with local men and boys. The preacher delivered the sermon, a staff clenched in one hand, his head, neck and shoulders shrouded in a white cloth;

he barked in ear-piercing Tamil, interjecting the occasional religious word or phrase in Arabic. Prayers – the customary two *rakat*s on Friday early afternoon – were over in less than ten minutes.

Batti town nearby still felt like a small, slow-paced country town, well off the tourist trail, a place where visitors passed through rather than stayed – just like it felt on my first visit in 1981. Its lagoon setting is captivating, but its Tamil nickname is Matta Kalappu – muddy swamp; and the occupying Dutch thought it a 'vile and stinking place', its lagoon full of crocodiles.

From Kallady bridge we headed to a poor Tamil suburb of fishermen and toddy tappers on one of the lagoon's banks; cadjan and iron sheets fenced off the small houses from each other and the surrounding lanes – a hallmark of Tamil privacy and defence of individual property seen all over the north and east. And a metaphor for Tamil–Sinhala cultural difference. The gregarious Sinhalese like their dwellings to open out to their neighbours and the wider world. But these Tamil dwellings are fenced off and closed in, shielded from the world outside.

On another bank of the lagoon stands a small Dutch fort, with 'VOC 1682' inscribed above the front gate. When the Dutch first coveted Ceylon for its cornucopia of cinnamon, they eyed this stretch of the east coast as their back door. It was part of the Kandyan kingdom; unlike the west and south coasts, it was not controlled by their Portuguese enemies. Admiral Joris van Spilbergen made the first Dutch landing here in 1602; he and his party were carried on palanquins, accompanied by elephants and music, to Kandy for an audience with King Vimaladharmasuriya. The king and his successors sought a deal with the Dutch to parry the expansionist Portuguese. Deals, misunderstandings and false starts followed.

Then, in 1638, the Kandyan kingdom and the VOC joined forces to expel the Portuguese. In exchange for ejecting the Portuguese, the VOC demanded reimbursement and a monopoly of the cinnamon trade. That year the Dutch established their first fort on the island in Batti, after taking it from the Portuguese after a four-hour siege. They rebuilt the fort and promptly handed it over to the Kandyan kingdom, only retaking it in 1665. That gave them control of all the main coastal ports – and control of the Kandyan kingdom's trade with the wider world.

From the fort, it was a five-minute drive to the town centre. Like Colombo and other big towns, the Rajapaksa government 'beautified' it after the war. The clock tower got a fresh coat of paint; next to it came a new landscaped green space: Mahatma Gandhi Park. Down a side road past a row of shops lay a trio of buildings that formed the Catholic hub of Batti – a Jesuit church, all in blue, a convent and a boys' school, St Michael's College, one of Sri Lanka's leading Jesuit institutions.

I arrived at St Michael's on Expo Day, when it threw its doors open to the public to celebrate the anniversary of its founding in 1873. The grounds were full of schoolchildren with their relatives, and Tamil music blared from the speakers. The main building was a whitewashed Edwardian pile, all pillars and arches, now looking down-at-heel inside. At one entrance was a statue of Father Bonnel, the French Jesuit who founded the school and was its first headmaster. Generations of Jesuits came from afar to teach here. A couple of these foreign veterans remained, now in their nineties, settled in retirement in the seminary next door. Everyone in Batti knew of Father Miller, the American Jesuit who came here in the 1940s and taught English to generations of local boys.

I chatted awhile with Father Rajeevan, an old boy of the school who returned to teach English and Christianity. He told me the government took over the running of the school in the 1970s, but retained Jesuit priests to teach English. The school's medium was Tamil, with English taught as a second language. During the war, he said, the Jesuit fathers kept the boys safe from the predations of the army and the LTTE. They also kept teaching English, which enabled some old boys to get decent jobs after the war ended. 'I owe everything to them,' he added.

From St Michael's we drove along the coast back in the direction of Eravur. We passed Nivalady beach. It used to have a fishing settlement. Over 2000 people died in the tsunami in 2004, totally destroying the village. Now all I saw were a few stray huts and small memorials to the dead next to little chapels and kovils.

Mr Jeyaratnam pointed to a narrow sandbar separating the lagoon from the sea, from where a great wall of water came crashing through that fateful Boxing Day morning. It ripped through the lagoon and wreaked havoc on one side of the town. The tsunami killed 13,000 in Batticaloa and Ampara districts alone, nearly half of all tsunami-related deaths in Sri Lanka.

Back in Eravur, we drove down dirty, dusty side roads with ramshackle houses, men and boys riding bicycles, and goats roaming freely: a classic sign of a Muslim settlement, full of ravenous mutton-eaters. We passed a troop of adolescent schoolgirls, all shrouded in black and completely veiled. Eravur, I thought, at least off the busier, built-up main road, hardly looked different from my first visit in 1981, apart from women and girls imprisoned in their folds of black cloth. But it was different during the long war years, a Muslim town under siege, buffeted by the Sinhala army and the Tamil LTTE. In August 1990, LTTE soldiers rampaged through these dusty lanes, killing over a hundred local Muslims, a few days after they murdered 147 men and boys in Kattankudy's jumma mosques.

I woke early the following morning to see the sunrise over Passekudah Bay. Before dawn, the beach was deserted, save for three mainland Chinese tourists, whose loud chat and clicking cameras shattered the silence around us. The sun emerged gradually from a horizon fringe of light cloud and illuminated fishing boats coming in from their nocturnal trawl. The water was waveless, like a still forest pool. When I stepped in it was warm – 'as warm as tea', as my *Handbook for the Ceylon Traveller* promised.

~

After breakfast, Joseph and I took the coast road up to Trincomalee, the administrative capital of Eastern Province. Before the war this journey took ages but was full of romance, for five small lagoons had to be crossed by ferry. The war shut the road down and put the ferries and ferrymen out of work. Now the road had been repaired, and five new bridges smoothed the way across the lagoons. The journey from Batti to Trinco, as it is universally known in Sri Lanka, could be done in about three hours.

Past the mostly Tamil town of Valaichchenai the landscape became bleaker, changing from green to brown and dry as a bone. There were fewer people; they looked poor and ragged, though not as bad as their skeletal cattle and goats. We passed isolated hamlets, the odd roadside shop, and two little towns, Vakarai and Varengal. Army camps and soldiers lined the road, though their presence was not as numerous or obtrusive as it had been when I first passed this way in 2014. Joseph pointed to mud huts surrounded by vegetable patches – but fewer than what I saw last time, and many more standard two-room concrete houses built by Western NGOs and the Indian government for war refugees. We passed NGO offices, and the occasional UN or NGO white jeep. Just before Varengal was the turn-off to Seruwawila Raja Maha Vihara, its white stupa visible in the distance, rising bubble-shaped and isolated out of the scrub jungle. Ruhunu's legendary king Kavan Tissa founded the temple in the second century BCE, and it became a major pilgrim site before Tamil invasions from the north caused its disuse and decay. The stupa was only rediscovered and rebuilt in the 1920s and early 1930s.

The scene changed again as we approached the Muslim town of

Muttur and passed through a succession of sweeping bays linked by lagoons. First came Koddiyar Bay, where Robert Knox and his shipmates were taken captive in 1660. We crossed Marble Bay, where the air force ran cabanas on the beach and a fancy new hotel with an eighteen-hole golf course. Farther down the road was the China Bay air force base, established by the British in 1938, where Daddy was stationed in the late 1950s. In one of Mummy's albums is a colour photo of Daddy taken at China Bay. He is in uniform khaki shirt and shorts, his back propped nonchalantly against a wall, smiling for the camera. He must have enclosed the photo with a letter to Mummy in North Wales. It was just a year or so before Mummy came out to Ceylon to get married.

~

In ancient times Trincomalee was called Gokanna, the Polonnaruwa kingdom's main port in the east and a hub for trade in the Bay of Bengal and with Southeast Asia. The Dutch built one of their biggest forts here, on the site of a Portuguese fort they captured in 1639. When the British cast their eye on Ceylon, they coveted Trinco's deep-water harbour first: from here they could reinforce their naval supremacy to protect their territories in India. They tried to conspire with the king of Kandy against the Dutch. In the 1780s and early 1790s, Trinco changed hands between the Dutch and British, and even the French occupied it briefly. The British wrested control from the Dutch once and for all in 1795. They renamed the fort after Frederick, Duke of York, in 1803.

The Japanese had their eye on Trinco's deep-water harbour during the Second World War; they bombed Trinco just once, from the air, on the night of 9 April 1942. In the recent war, Trinco was a front line between government forces and the LTTE. The army controlled the town, but the LTTE controlled much of the surrounding countryside, especially at night. The town's resources were stretched to bursting as it was a holding centre for refugees.

Trinco town, in Joseph's words, is very 'mixed fruit'. Sinhalese, Muslims and Tamils live side by side in its residential lanes off the town centre. On my last visit I noticed a church, a kovil and a mosque, all a stone's throw from each other on a single small lane. Trinco's inhabitants enjoy the most magnificent urban setting in Sri Lanka. The town straddles two sweeping bays, Dutch Bay and Back Bay, separated by a rocky headland occupied by the fort and an ancient Shiva temple, all facing the Bay of Bengal and the Indian Ocean.

On a visit in 2011 Trinco still looked backward to me, dishevelled and frozen in time. Outwardly, it had changed little from what I saw during school holiday visits in the 1970s. Its colonial buildings were falling apart; the Esplanade next to the fort was scruffy; derelict buildings scarred its shopping thoroughfare. Now it looked a little better. The Esplanade was cleaned up after the war and a sports complex built next to it. The surrounding public buildings were given a fresh lick of paint. The colonial navy commander's residence, a ruin enveloped and strangled by an encroaching banyan when I saw it in 2011, was restored and reopened as a Naval and Maritime Museum.

Naushaad's nephew, who met us here, asked me what I would like to see. I wanted to find a colonial grave. I had read somewhere that Charles Austen, Jane Austen's 'problem brother' who ran away to sea, was buried in Trinco, but I did not know which cemetery he was buried in. So we traipsed around a few old cemeteries before finding the right one, St Stephen's, opposite the Esplanade. We were, however, without success. There were too many colonial tombstones, nearly all cracked and crumbling, smothered by uncut grass and weeds. Charles Austen's grave lay somewhere here, but not where I could spot it. My hosts were nonplussed: what on earth was this mad Englishman doing hunting for the grave of an old colonial who died almost two centuries ago?

After I gave up the chase, we drove to Fort Frederick and took the road inside the fort up to its summit, Swami Rock. Right on the cliff edge was Koneswaram temple, one of five Shiva temples on the island that had been pilgrimage sites going back to pre-Buddhist times. The Portuguese destroyed this 'temple of a thousand columns' in the early seventeenth century; they simply uprooted the edifice and threw it into the sea. Koneswaram was nothing special inside.

Frankly, what Leonard Woolf called the 'gaudy exuberance' of Hindu temples – their loud red-and-white-stripe exterior walls, their dark interiors furnished with statues of garlanded gods and their animal mounts, their stern-faced priests with bare pot bellies protruding proudly above their white *verti*s – has never seemed attractive to me. The simple, quiet aesthetic of a Sinhala Buddhist village temple – a plain, all-white stupa, an equally plain, all-white samadhi (meditating) Buddha behind a shrine with flower offerings, and a lone bo tree, all in a neatly swept sand-covered courtyard surrounded by shade-giving trees – draws me in far more intimately.

For all that, Koneswaram commands the best panorama in Trinco, looking down to Back Bay and Dutch Bay, and on the other side to the ocean. I walked downhill on the road whence we came back to the main gate. On either side were crumbling old Dutch barracks, one-storey pillared buildings in white and yellow-cream with broad stoeps, now occupied by the army. At the end of the road was the officers' mess, a two-storey colonial building with huge verandas, fronted by two giant banyans. Half-tame spotted deer roamed indolently around the grounds of the officers' mess and barracks, or lay in the shade undisturbed. And what shade! From Swami Rock to the main gate, Fort Frederick was full of spreading banyans, rain trees and frangipani trees, bestowing it a full canopy of shade.

As Joseph and I drove out of the fort and the town, I thought of Trinco as a case study of Sri Lanka's golden potential and chronic underachievement. Yes, Trinco looked better than it did in 2011. But, almost a decade after the war ended, I had hoped to see more improvement. It had Galle's potential, and more: a majestic, intact Dutch fort, other historic buildings, and deep-water bays that blessed it with the most stunning setting of any settlement in the island. It should be humming with heritage hotels, cafes, restaurants, shops and tourists.

~

After stopping overnight at Nilaveli, the beach resort strip just outside Trinco, we headed to the Tamil heartland in the north. My next stop was one of the oldest and most important temples in Sri Lankan Buddhist history, but one few Sri Lankans visited and most had never heard about. This was Thiriyaya, deep in the jungle, about a two-hour drive north along the coast from Trinco and then inland. It dated back to the second century BCE and was a major pilgrim destination for Sri Lankan and South Indian Buddhists for over a thousand years.

Buddhist legend has it that the main stupa housed a hair relic. The Buddha is said to have given a strand of his hair to his first two disciples after he attained enlightenment. After his death, the disciples placed it in a jewelled casket and brought it here. But Thiriyaya was abandoned during South Indian invasions over a thousand years ago, left to the jungle and forgotten. Until 1951, when the site was excavated. But treasure hunters had already broken into the stupa and made off with whatever relics were buried there.

Thiriyaya was only opened to the public after the war, the territory surrounding it having either been controlled by the LTTE or bitterly contested during the years of strife. We drove through the jungle and passed yet another army camp. A modest new temple with a couple of monks and a small cafe announced the entrance to Thiriyaya. Past a small reservoir, steps ran up a 200-foot rock face. On one side of the staircase were caves where monks used to meditate, and one had a Sanskrit inscription that dated back to the seventh or eighth century CE. Farther up were the ruins of the old monastery, spread across two terraces. And then the summit, with a vista so stunning it left me breathless. There were no other tourists or pilgrims. I was the only soul here.

The summit must have been flattened by the monastery's founders. At its centre was a Vatadage, a circular pillared image house, which rivalled the splendour of the famous Vatadage in Polonnaruwa. Guardstones with dragon-king motifs kept watch at the four entrances to the temple. The outer wall supported a ring of pillars. Further in were four altars at the cardinal points that used to support seated Buddhas; they encircled the central bubble-shaped red-brick stupa. Also on the summit, around the Vatadage, were the remains of six shrines. One was a large slab of stone, with an indentation where a recumbent Buddha used to be supported; another, encircled by stone pillars, had the severed head and fallen body of a standing Buddha, weathered by the elements for over a millennium. Everything was still and silent in the beating noonday sun. Up here I was magically alone, surrounded on all sides by the jungle; looking east, beyond the jungle, I saw the outline of the coast – a long strip of white sand – and the Bay of Bengal stretching to the horizon.

From Thiriyaya we drove to Mullaitivu, looping inland before returning to the coast. We were now in the heart of the Vanni, the stretch of scrub jungle between the Jaffna peninsula and Rajarata that the LTTE controlled for most of the war. We passed isolated, thinly peopled Tamil settlements, some with newly built small brick houses for war refugees, plus the odd new village school. But police stations and army camps seemed to outnumber civilians. For the next few days, wherever we went in the north, we passed innumerable army camps and many soldiers on the roads. The soldiers were nearly all Sinhalese, the civilians nearly all Tamil.

Not far from Mullaitivu, we drove through what appeared to be a Sinhala village: the look and dress of the villagers were unmistakably Sinhala – soft, rounded features, the men in sarongs, the women in blouses and long billowing skirts. Flowers and shrubs garlanded the house fronts. Well-irrigated paddy fields surrounded the village, and on the roadside was a simple little temple with a stupa and a Buddha shrine. The village exuded greenery and colour, softness and warmth. There was no cadjan fencing around the little stand-alone houses, none of the austerity and severity of Tamil settlements. Joseph stopped the car and chatted to an elderly woman. She flashed a Sinhala smile and told us the villagers came from the south and settled here forty-five years ago. She was Catholic. During the war, she and the other villagers were in refugee camps further south. She came back here, but not before losing her son in the war.

Just nine years earlier, Mullaitivu and its surrounds were killing fields, reduced to rubble by the government's final blitzkrieg against the LTTE. The LTTE's last 15,000 fighters and over 300,000 Tamil civilians – their human shields – were trapped in this north-eastern pocket. First the government declared a no-fire zone, but the army shelled it indiscriminately. The retreating LTTE corralled civilians on to the Nandikidal lagoon, just north of Mullaitivu. The government declared it the new no-fire zone, but the army also shelled it, including two makeshift hospitals in local schools. By this time, according to UN estimates, there were about 130,000 people left, cornered on a narrow strip of beach between the surrounding army and the sea.

LTTE leaders, their families and bodyguards were in a separate huddle, eating heartily while others starved. The army allowed civilians to cross the causeway to the mainland; many died on the way, fired at by the army in front and the LTTE behind trying to prevent their escape. In the last days, LTTE leaders crossed over. The army held survivors in a huge open-air cage, weeding out LTTE suspects from among civilians. Many of those taken away were never heard of or seen again. The remaining civilians were sent to refugee camps; the last camp closed in September 2012, three and a half years after the war ended.

I found Mullaitivu surreal. The Rajapaksa government clearly went all out to remove every trace of what happened. When I first visited, in 2014, the roads were new and smooth as a baby's bottom, the tarmac glistening under the relentless northern sun. The town still had a few shelled-out buildings, but not many. New public buildings – a bank, a police station and an administrative complex – surrounded the main roundabout. Normal life seemed to proceed on the side roads leading to the beach.

I stopped to take a photo of a private tuition college – a collection of windowless shacks packed with rows of desks and benches, all fully occupied by uniformed schoolchildren; scores of their bicycles were parked outside. It was mid-afternoon; they must have come here straight after school. There are tuition colleges all over Sri Lanka, after-school private tuition for which Sinhala, Tamil and Muslim parents all fork out. But Tamils strive for education and qualifications more than other communities, and it is most visible in the north and east.

We drove down to the small beach, packed with fishing boats. A few churches lined the landside of the road, a reminder this was a settlement of Christian fisherfolk. Most were Catholic, but I noticed one or two small Pentecostal churches. At one end of the beach was a church ruin, destroyed not by the war but by the tsunami.

Out of Mullaitivu, we drove past the signpost to Nandikidal Lagoon, still cordoned off by the army. Again, no sign that this beach drowned in blood in May 2009: everything looked bare, new, sanitized. But the shells of houses, riddled with bullet holes, lined the next stretch of road. Clearings in the scrub showed telltale signs of heavy bombardment – palmyrah trees sliced in half, tree stumps, little craters of water. We stopped at a victory monument in the middle of a lake. Here stood a statue of a helmeted soldier brandishing his AK-47, with a dove perched incongruously on it, against the backdrop of Sri Lankan and Buddhist flags. Figures of Sinhala lions stood sentinel at the corners of the square around the main statue.

Across the lake was a makeshift open-air war museum with a motley collection of crude LTTE armoury: rifles, pistols, bullets; a light aircraft and propeller; armoured boats whose prows were decorated with shark fangs; suicide boats with bombs attached, labelled 'Terrorist's Suicide Boat'; and two constricted iron cages for holding prisoners. The explanatory texts next to the exhibits were only in Sinhala. It was a museum for Sinhala war tourists from the south, not for defeated Tamils.

On my last visit, in 2014, Joseph and I headed to the hamlet of Pudukuduirippu, on the lookout for 'Prabhakaran's swimming pool'. Joseph stopped and, in Tamil, asked for directions. This took us deep into the jungle, and, at the end of the road, an army camp. The soldier on guard was initially suspicious, perhaps mistaking my off-white face for that of a foreign journalist. When he let us through after I addressed him in Sinhala, we walked through the camp, populated more by monkeys than soldiers. Around the corner was the infamous swimming pool.

We were now in what was Prabhakaran's lair. Here he had his bunker, a runway for the Air Tigers, and this pool. The army demolished everything else to prevent it becoming a shrine to the fallen *Thalaivar* (Leader), but they saved the pool. It was long and wide, waterless and full of rust. One half was very deep; the Sea Tigers used it for diving practice. A noticeboard told us that only the 'cream of the terrorists' had access to the pool. Metal rods overhung the pool with netting on top to camouflage it from aerial reconnaissance.

On this Mullaitivu visit I was told Prabhakaran's swimming pool was no more; it had been broken up and the ground filled in to prevent anyone turning it into an LTTE shrine. We headed back to the main road that took us to the A9, the trunk road up to Jaffna. This stretch, from Pudukuduirippu to Paranthan on the A9, was a multilane highway that reminded me of the new roads around Hambantota: a wasteful expanse of concrete in the middle of the jungle with little traffic.

~

The A9 bisects the Vanni on its way up to Jaffna. Over a century ago, Leonard Woolf rode in a bullock cart this way to take up his first posting as a colonial official. His impression of the Vanni was of 'sand and brackish scrub, flat and arid country, jungle, an enormous blue sky, immensely distant horizons, airless heat'.

The first thing I noticed in Paranthan was that it had a new railway station; a new railway track, courtesy of Indian aid and Indian engineers, now ran all the way to Jaffna, restoring the pre-war rail link with the rest of the island. Buses on the Colombo–Jaffna run crowded the road and raced ahead, ignoring all speed restrictions.

Soon after Paranthan we reached Elephant Pass, so called because, in ancient times, elephants caught in jungles further south were herded across the narrow isthmus here and thence shipped to India. Now a causeway cut across one end of the Jaffna Lagoon and connected the Jaffna peninsula to the rest of the island. It was almost sunset; the sky was a darker shade of blue, casting shadows on the lagoon. Birds flocked to palmyrah treetops in the peninsula, ready for their night-time slumber. The scenery changed dramatically:

the parched brown of the Vanni gave way to groves of black-green palmyrahs, paddy and vegetable plots in the peninsula.

During the war, heavy fighting bloodied this rustic scene. In one daring raid in April 2000, the LTTE overran the main army base at Elephant Pass, killing 3000 soldiers. One memorial, at the Vanni end of the causeway, commemorated Gamini Kularatne, a Buddhist monk who disrobed to enlist and fight the LTTE. On 14 July 1991, he ran right up to an advancing LTTE tank laden with explosives and blew it up with a hand grenade. A guard of honour played *The Last Post* by his statue just as we drove past. On the roadside was a rusted hulk, behind a sign that read 'Terrorist Bulldozer' – the LTTE tank that Lance Corporal Kularatne blew up in his last earthly moments.

At the peninsula end of the causeway we stopped at a victory memorial that commemorated the army's defeat of the LTTE at Elephant Pass in January 2009. Here was Sinhala triumphalism personified. Friezes of heroic soldiers wrapped around the base; the main statue had a circle of soldiers with upstretched arms holding an object in the shape of Sri Lanka. The writing on the commemorative plaque was full of bombast and vainglory; a semi-literate had composed the English version, replete with grammatical and spelling mistakes. Mahinda Rajapaksa was born 'to the glory of the nation' to defeat the terrorists, mastermind military victory and bring about national reconciliation, ably assisted by his brother Gotabhaya. And so forth.

On the road from Elephant Pass to Jaffna I noticed big changes from 2014, when I was here last. There were more shops, cafes, eating houses and guest houses, more street life, new reception halls, and temples that looked like money had been recently lavished on them. The new houses and reception halls had a characteristically garish Tamil Nadu style, all curved eaves and arches framing facades of shocking pink and orange. Tamil film music played from shops and cafes. We passed through Jaffna town, also much busier and noisier than it was on my first post-war visit. As we turned into Palaly Road, Joseph stopped and asked for directions every five or ten minutes. He hailed people over in his habitual shouting voice, mostly in Tamil, once or twice in Sinhala; it was *aiyaar* (for an older man) or *thambi* (a younger man or boy) for a Tamil bystander, *malli* or *rahlaami* if it was a Sinhala soldier or policeman. It was dark by the time we arrived at the Margosa, the bungalow guest house where we would stay for the next few days.

~

The east feels different from the rest of the country, but the Vanni and the Jaffna peninsula even more so. The peninsula is a culture apart; it feels more like South India – especially Tamil Nadu – than Sri Lanka. People are darker and dourer. Jaffna Tamils, the 'Scots of Asia', are renowned for their industriousness, thrift and thirst for education. Visiting in the late 1840s, Sir James Emerson Tennent remarked that 'Jaffna is almost the only place in Ceylon of which it might be said that no one is idle or unprofitably employed'. He found its bazaar a hive of activity, full of fruits and vegetables. But warm and welcoming Jaffna Tamils are not. The tourist charm of Sinhala culture – all smiles, friendliness, hospitality, gregariousness – is almost totally absent up here.

The north has a distinctive history. Its ancient inhabitants were the Nagas, who had friendly relations with the Sinhalese and paid tribute to the king in Anuradhapura. Many were Buddhists. In later centuries there were isolated Tamil Hindu settlements. But it was Magha of Kalinga's conquest of the Polonnaruwa kingdom in 1215, using Tamil and Keralite mercenaries, that led to concentrated Tamil settlement of the north. This set the stage for the Jaffna kingdom of the Aryachakravarti dynasty, centred on the peninsula, which ruled for almost four centuries. The peninsula, separated from the rest of the island by the Vanni, evolved its own language, religion and culture. The Portuguese first nibbled away at the Jaffna kingdom's coastal territory, converting fishing communities to Catholicism along the way, before conquering the whole kingdom by 1621. They set about destroying Hinduism, including Jaffna's famous Nallur temple. The Dutch took over in 1658, then the British in 1795.

Under the British, missionary activity in the peninsula started earlier and was more active than it was elsewhere on the island. This spawned an English-educated high-caste elite, the Jaffna vellalas, of the landowning cultivator caste, equivalent to the Sinhala Buddhist govigamas. They became influential in the professions, the civil service and in national politics. But this missionary-inspired English-language culture sparked a backlash, and an accompanying Hindu revival, that preceded the Buddhist revival down south by a generation.

The driving force of Jaffna's Hindu revival was a remarkably erudite and protean figure, Arumugam Navalar (*navalar* being the Tamil honorific for orator). He was educated at Jaffna's Wesleyan Central Mission by Father Percival, an American Methodist missionary, who noticed the boy's promise and nurtured it. Over seven years, Navalar helped him translate the Bible into Tamil. But, later, with a deep knowledge of classical texts, Navalar powerfully restated and revived Shaivite Hinduism to counter the missionaries' Protestant Christianity. He was Jaffna's Olcott, a gifted orator, grammarian, translator, editor and pamphleteer who also renewed the Jaffna version of written and spoken Tamil, and founded Hindu schools. Since Navalar, Jaffna Tamils have been famously proud and protective of their 'pure' Tamil. The schools Navalar founded provided a modern education in English, but in a Hindu, not a Christian, context. Navalar, like Olcott, used the missionaries' methods of writing, oration and sermonizing for his very different objectives.

But Navalar was also arch-conservative, a strict orthodox Hindu who defended a rigid caste system dominated by vellalas and Brahmins. That caste system had remained intact, even hardened, since the seventeenth century, for Portuguese and later Dutch occupation had cut Jaffna off from an evolving caste system in South India. Vellalas jealously guarded their feudal privileges, including restricting temple entry to lower castes. They also monopolized Tamils' political representation. Not least, Navalar hardly thought of or mentioned the rest of Ceylon, rather defining himself as a Tamil from Jaffna. He perpetuated Jaffna's self-isolation, its 'peninsularity of mind', that was to have such baleful consequences a century later.

There was an all-too-brief period, in the early years of Ceylonese nationalism, when Tamil and Sinhala leaders acted in unison, trying to forge a pan-Ceylon identity. But, from the 1920s, they went their separate ways. Tamil leaders, reacting to Sinhala majoritarianism, pursued a solely communal interest. They overplayed their hand in the quarter-century before independence, opposing key elements of the Donoughmore and Soulbury constitutions, while defending vellala privileges in Tamil areas. Democratization in the north and east was the last thing on their minds, given its threat to caste privileges. And they presumed to speak for all Ceylon Tamils, including lower-caste, east-coast and Indian Tamils. To quote Professor Kingsley de Silva, Jaffna Tamils were a 'minority with a majority complex'.

After independence, through the 1950s and 1960s, Tamil opposition politics, led by S.J.V. Chelvanayakam's Federal Party, was legal, moderate and non-violent. But Sinhala intransigence fed Tamil militancy, starting in the Jaffna peninsula. Within a generation, it mutated into full-blown terrorism, in the name of an independent Eelam.

Between 1983 and 1987, the LTTE controlled much of the Jaffna peninsula, until the Sri Lankan air force bombed Jaffna in

1987 in a concerted operation with the army to secure the town and the peninsula. Between 1987 and 1990, bitter fighting took place between the IPKF and the LTTE, and Jaffna suffered massive civilian casualties. The LTTE retook Jaffna town when the IPKF left and hostilities resumed with the Sri Lankan army.

In October 1990, the LTTE expelled the Muslim population of the north – 65,000 people in all – giving them forty-eight hours' notice. That included 24,000 Jaffna Muslims, who were stripped of their money, jewellery and deeds to their properties. In 1995, the army laid siege to Jaffna, and the air force bombed it heavily; thousands of civilians died. The army retook Jaffna town, but not before the LTTE evacuated it and marched its civilian population to the Vanni. From then on until the last months of the war, the army held Jaffna town while the LTTE controlled much of the peninsula's countryside.

~

I woke up to loud Tamil music from a small building across the road. This turned out to be a kovil, and the music – almost non-stop, round the clock – was prayer music, which reminded me of unremitting background music on estate lines in the hill country. To my untutored ear it sounded much like the music of Tollywood, the film factory across the Palk Straits in Madras.

Over breakfast I chatted with Manik, the Margosa's Sinhala cook. He hailed from Bandarawela and spent a decade circumnavigating the world as a merchant seaman. The captain of his first ship, a benevolent Norwegian, told him he needed to improve his English; so he gave him a thick pile of porn magazines, which was how Manik came to speak his serviceable English. Now he was a landlubber, with a wife and children down south. I asked him how he related to the Tamil staff here. 'No problems, sir. I had to learn a little Tamil so we can communicate. Then we get along fine. It's the politicians who make trouble between Sinhalese and Tamils.' This refrain I came across often on my road trips all over the country.

I spent my first full day driving around the peninsula and in Jaffna town. The Margosa was in a semi-rural part of the peninsula, a half-hour drive from Jaffna. Around it was watery, fertile countryside, planted with paddy and neat rows of chilli, onions and tobacco. Farmers still worked the land with hoe and buffalo – little sign of the mechanization one saw down south. I was told that before the war the peninsula supplied 30 per cent of the island's vegetables. Now it was 5 per cent. Off the main roads, the poverty was similar to that of the remote areas of the east: more thin, bony villagers living in mud huts surrounded by cadjan fencing. Back on the Jaffna–Kankesanthurai road, I saw bungalows of the Jaffna middle class. Some lay dilapidated, riddled with bullet holes, with caved-in roofs, overgrown tree trunks, roots and creepers cracking open walls and floors, and jungly gardens. Some had been abandoned, others walled off by their owners, now in Colombo or in the diaspora. But I also noticed several houses looking brand new or under construction, fronted by freshly painted ornamental gates and parapet walls.

On the road were lots of old bicycles, the dominant mode of transport I noticed on my first visit in 2011, though not as dominant now. A classic Jaffna sight is of a very spruce dark local girl, pottu on her forehead, dressed demurely in a blouse, long baggy trousers and slippers, her raven hair coiled in a long, tight plait and lashed together by a blue or yellow or red ribbon. She rides her bike purposefully, with a ramrod-straight back. Often she carries a passenger, a girlfriend or a younger brother or sister, riding side-saddle. On that first visit I thought there were no Sri Lankan women quite like the girls of Jaffna, lean and sharp-featured, with sleek, unblemished complexions. But this was perhaps a product of circumstance. Being poorer than their counterparts down south, they walked or cycled rather than taking three-wheelers, and ate fresh vegetables and herbs from the back garden, not processed food from the supermarket. But that changed after the war, as I noticed on this trip.

Near the village of Chunnakam is a most unusual Buddhist site; nothing like it exists elsewhere in Sri Lanka. In Tamil it is Kanthorodai. Soon after the war ended, Kanthorodai was renamed Kathurugoda, a Sinhala place-name. Now Sinhala villagers from down south came here in minivans; it became a pilgrim stop on their holiday trip to a part of the country they were seeing for the first time. Everything gave the appearance of a Sinhala Buddhist site. The signs were all in Sinhala; Buddhist pennants hung off lines strung between palmyrah trees; the visitors were all Sinhala (except for yours truly); so were the gun-toting soldiers guarding the site. The American Smithsonian Institution undertook the first excavations here in 1967; archaeologists dated it to the second or third century BCE – the early days of Buddhism in Sri Lanka. Surely, one would think, evidence of Sinhala Buddhists in the Tamil heartland, centuries before Tamil Hindus arrived here.

Dotted around the small site were about twenty diminutive mounds of black stone, arranged in neat rows; these were bubble-shaped mini-stupas, each between three and nine feet tall.

In Anuradhapura, it could be a doll's house, full of miniature representations of the ancient city's great dagobas. But, contrary to the Sinhala narrative on the signboard at Kanthorodai/Kathurugoda's entrance, these curious Lilliputian creations were not evidence of ancient *Sinhala* Buddhism. Hard conclusions are difficult when one looks back so far in time, but the expert consensus is that Kanthorodai points to *Tamil* Buddhism in the Jaffna peninsula, before Hinduism arrived and triumphed. This is plausible, for Kanthorodai as an active monastery and temple complex was contemporaneous with Buddhism that was widespread in South India. But now, millennia later, a war victory and Sinhala occupation led to a change of name, and with it a terribly unsubtle change of historical narrative.

On the way out I chatted briefly with a Sinhala middle-class family from Colombo. The wife was an army doctor during the war, based in Anuradhapura. Her husband complained of Tamil villagers encroaching on this site in years past. 'The Tamil people have no respect for our religion,' he said. But then he reassured me: 'After the war all is now okay.'

I spent the afternoon in Jaffna town. Before the war it was remote by Sri Lankan standards, quiet, sleepy. My first visit in 2011 revealed a town battered by decades of war. The shells of houses were everywhere, the shops and streets were quiet, there were no modern hotels, and generally few places for visitors to stay. People looked like they had the stuffing knocked out of them. Much appeared frozen in time. There were no modern taxis, and few three-wheelers. Morris Oxfords and Austin Cambridges served as taxis, kept going during the war with incessant mechanical tinkering.

Jaffna was still scarred, on the surface and even more beneath it, but it had bounced back to life. The streets around the main market were busy day and night. I saw many more motorbikes, three-wheelers and Tata Nano minicabs, and fewer Austin Cambridges and Morris Oxfords. The first mall in the north and east, Cargills Square, opened next to the main hospital four years after the war ended.

Roads leading to the town centre were chock-a-block with private tuition colleges, advertising courses in English, IT and whatever else looked good on a paper certificate. Even some Muslim traders who were thrown out by the LTTE in 1990 had returned. The late nineteenth-century Moorish Gothic clock tower, unveiled to commemorate a visit by the then Prince of Wales, got a fresh coat of paint. So did Jaffna's civic pride and joy, its public library. On my first visit, the Esplanade opposite the public library was empty, weedy and fronted by a headless statue of Sir Ponnambalam Ramanathan, the late nineteenth-century and early twentieth-century Tamil leader. The statue had gone, leaving just the plinth, but the Esplanade was now home to a new police station, a sports stadium and a municipal complex. Facing it is was a new gold-painted statue of S.J.V. Chelvanayakam, the post-independence Tamil leader. A Jaffna Cultural Complex was under construction close by.

I found the Jaffna Public Library a curious architectural mix of Indo-Saracenic and art deco, with Mughal cupolas on roof corners. It opened in 1954 and had a huge collection of centuries-old Tamil literature, all burned to cinders by a Sinhala police mob in 1981. A foundation stone round the back testified to the first effort to rebuild it in 1984. But the war intervened; rebuilding only finished during the ceasefire in the early 2000s.

From the Esplanade we drove down Main Street, the colonial heart of Jaffna. Down-at-heel buildings recalled Jaffna's Portuguese, Dutch and British past: the Catholic St James' Church, the Rosarian convent behind high walls, St Martin's seminary, the Anglican St John's College, and rotting Dutch-style villas of the old elite with their broad pillared verandas. Round the corner was Old Park, the creation of P.A. Dyke, who was government agent in the north for forty years in the second half of the nineteenth century. The trees he planted became majestic with age. They survived twenty-five years of war, but not the post-war bulldozer. They were felled to make way for new houses for the governor of Northern Province and other senior officials, and a new children's park.

We circled back to Jaffna Fort, sandwiched between the Esplanade and Jaffna Lagoon. It occupies a fifty-five-acre site and was the largest Dutch fort in Asia – even larger than Galle Fort. The Dutch seized the old Portuguese fort after a three-month siege; they completely rebuilt it in a star shape with thick walls and a large moat.

Inside they built the fort's crown jewel, the Grote Kerk, one of three main Dutch Reformed Churches in the island. In the nineteenth century, the British added a kachcheri, the main government office for Jaffna district, the government agent's bungalow, quarters for other officials, a jail and a tennis club. The fort was the centre of officialdom and elite social life in Jaffna; Leonard Woolf worked and lived here. But wartime shelling by both the army and the LTTE pounded all this to rubble. A major restoration effort rebuilt the huge outer wall. But inside there was nothing but green space and rubble; a large stone mound indicated where Grote Kerk once stood. It could hardly have looked or felt more different from Galle Fort, with its restored Dutch buildings, its boutique hotels, cafes and chi-chi shops, its recently arrived Colombo and expat rich and its daily tourist crowds.

On the way back to Margosa we stopped at the Nallur temple, the main Hindu temple in Sri Lanka, dedicated to Skandah, otherwise known as Murugan and, to the Sinhalese, Kataragama. Leonard Woolf would have found its loud exuberance distasteful. Red-and-white stripes lined its walls; one *gopuram* (a temple tower) was painted in a blindingly shiny gold. Non-Hindus could enter, as they could in all the Hindu temples I visited in Sri Lanka. Males could only enter bare-bodied, but I couldn't have the pleasure of taking my shirt off, as the temple was closed to the public when we arrived.

~

I spent the next two days in Jaffna conversations. I started on Main Street, at the house of the Anglican archdeacon of Jaffna, Father Nesakumar. Father Nesa, as he was universally known, was in Jaffna throughout the conflict, active in a Peace and Goodwill Commission, a group of local religious and business leaders who liaised with the army and the LTTE, depending on who controlled Jaffna at the time. Ordinary people brought their problems to him, mostly about requisitioned land and ill treatment by soldiers, policemen or the LTTE. He and his fellow commissioners followed up with the authorities as diplomatically as they could. He recounted stories from those years – the atrocities both sides committed, the forced marches to the countryside, once in 1995 and then again in 2000. His wife was pregnant when the LTTE marched them out of Jaffna in 2000, and his baby daughter was stillborn as a result.

After an hour's conversation Father Nesa drove me round the corner to 6th Cross Street, a side street of modest one-storey houses and corner shops. We were going to see his 'spiritual guide – the one I turn to when I feel my faith needs shoring up'. This was Father Jeyaceelan, an elderly Catholic priest. We entered the little house, Father Jeyaceelan's family home, where he was born; several dogs and cats – strays Father Jeyaceelan had adopted – seemed to have the run of the house. Father Jeyaceelan met me with a sweet, other-worldly smile and said 'Welcome brother' in a soft, gentle voice. The way he said 'brother', repetitively, so disarmed me, though I could not figure out why exactly. He was well into his seventies, if not older, bald, in a well-worn white cassock and barefoot. We settled to chat in his small, plain, mosquito-infested front room, its walls bare except for posters of the Virgin Mary and the Pope.

Father Jeyaceelan was a learned, cultivated man. He spoke an old-fashioned cultured English rare in Sri Lanka these days. He told me he taught Greek and Shakespearean drama at Jaffna University. 'I gave this up because my students were only interested in passing exams to get good jobs,' he said. 'I felt I was wasting my time; I could be more useful being with the poor. So that became my calling.' He had a regular Bible study group; its composition changed over the years – 'so many abducted, gone missing, killed'. On weekends he went to villages in the peninsula and the Vanni to give sermons, lead Bible study classes and teach a little English.

Father Jeyaceelan had a clear view of what spirituality meant for him. 'In the Church the leaders are from the middle classes; they are comfortable with elites, they do deals with our rulers. But they are distant from their flock. The real spiritual seekers are those with their people, the poor.' He related the harrowing story of the seven priests who elected to stay with trapped civilians in the killing fields around Mullaitivu: the poor souls the LTTE held as human shields in front of the advancing Sri Lankan army. 'They exercised their caritative option – to stay with their suffering flock. One of them – he was elderly and frail – was clubbed by a soldier with his rifle butt. He died. Another, whom the LTTE agreed to release, refused to go. He was in Prabhakaran's bunker. Next to him was a girl whose legs had been blown off. She was looking after a cat without legs. "How can I leave them?" he asked.'

Father Jeyaceelan's credo was anti-materialist. He advocated a return to a simple life of saving, eating healthily, spending economically, being self-sufficient. 'Be content with a small house, a little plot of land, the air we breathe, the sea out there. That is where the spiritual path lies – how we can shore up a threatened moral life.' He called the new post-war materialism 'consumerist spice'. Fewer people came to listen to his sermons in the villages now; he got a bigger hearing during the war, when people found solace in religion.

Both priests said a whole generation grew up spoilt and self-indulgent in the war years; their parents did everything they asked, gave them everything, to prevent them leaving home and joining the 'Boys' – the LTTE. Now they were only interested in consumerism and emigrating to join the diaspora. Generous remittances from diaspora relatives allowed them to be spendthrifts, diminishing the incentive to study hard, work hard and save. Too many, particularly male youth, descended into drugs, violence and petty crime. To Father Jeyaceelan this was a broken, lost generation, coarse, aggressive and nihilistic.

'After independence there were thirty years of uneasy truce,' Father Jeyaceelan said. 'But that was all about elites – the Tamil elite talking to the Sinhala elite. Tamils were obsessed with language and identity. Then came thirty years of armed violence. This ended in Mullivaikal and Nandikidal – the price paid by Sinhalese and Tamils to the Moloch. Now we have a negative peace: the war is over, but people here feel no benefit from peace. This is an occupation of a defeated people. Tamils have no stomach for another fight. But there is no genuine reconciliation. We have to go back to square one with Sinhalese and Tamils getting to know each other, and the religions opening up to each other.'

Father Nesa motioned for us to leave: Father Jeyaceelan was about to start his Bible study class. He bade me farewell with 'God bless you, brother.' I was moved, almost to tears. Somehow this encounter left a deep impression on me. I may not have agreed with all of Father Jeyaceelan's anti-materialist, perhaps utopian, views, but I felt, for once, just for this past hour, blessed by spiritual presence, in the form of a truly good man.

~

Tamil nationalism still dominated Jaffna University, which was once a hotbed of Tamil militant activism, but now there were more Sinhala and Muslim students on campus. After the war, until the government changed in 2015, the army, which closely watched campus politics, intervened at the slightest sign of student protest. It shut the campus down on War Heroes Day, the LTTE anniversary to commemorate its fallen soldiers. Rumours abounded of army spies, especially among Sinhala students on campus. But freer expression reigned from 2015, and students and professors celebrated LTTE anniversaries openly, untroubled by external intervention.

On previous visits to Jaffna, Colombo friends and acquaintances put me in touch with several university academics. Their complaints, when we spoke, were predictable: an obtrusive military presence; army land-grabbing for 'high-security zones' in the peninsula; infringements of civil liberties; Colombo businesses and Sinhala workers crowding out local businesses and local jobs. But they were remarkably uncritical of the LTTE. When I asked about the LTTE's influence on campus during the war, their answers were vague and evasive.

The tone was one-sided. Sinhala nationalism was responsible for all ills; Tamils were its victims. I got no sense of critical introspection. Wasn't it a disastrous mistake of the Tamil intelligentsia to support violent militancy from the 1970s, and then the LTTE exclusively from the late 1980s? Didn't they fuel the LTTE monster? Was it justified to overlook LTTE atrocities against other Tamils? These were questions to be evaded.

On this visit I got much more out of an off-campus conversation with Siva, an anthropologist from the diaspora who had returned to his childhood home to do fieldwork for his doctorate. Siva was stridently anti-'neoliberal'. He blamed the north's post-war economic travails on the depredations of a Colombo-dominated market economy. To me, this was nonsense. I thought the north needed more markets – domestic and foreign investment for more jobs and better incomes – to give ordinary folk life-chances they had been denied for so long. Siva's ideal of a self-contained economy of local cooperatives struck me as a romantic, faintly Gandhian illusion.

Nevertheless, I found Siva worth listening to, particularly his critique of the current Tamil political leadership. The Tamil National Alliance (TNA) ran the Northern Provincial Council after winning a long-delayed local election. But it had squandered its mandate. Its Colombo vellala leadership played to the Tamil diaspora gallery on human rights issues that hit international media headlines, but woefully neglected bread-and-butter local issues – jobs, public services, rural poverty and so on. The war had papered over caste divides, taking overriding priority. But caste had resurfaced. Vellalas had reasserted themselves; they excluded lower castes from good education and employment. Colombo Tamils and the Jaffna diaspora were of little help. They showered money on local relatives, elite schools (through old boys' associations) and temples, but not on investment projects and assistance for the poor. Most of the young wanted to leave to get jobs in the Middle East, to have marriages arranged with high-earning professionals in the diaspora, and, for the most desperate, to get on to smugglers' boats heading to Australia and Europe.

Siva hoped to become a local professor and contribute to reviving academic standards. Serious learning and open debate, however, was still actively discouraged. A cabal of opportunistic academics, former LTTE supporters and fellow travellers who switched to the Eelam People's Democratic Party (an erstwhile pro-Eelam terror organization that became the Rajapaksa government's proxy in the north), ran the university. They operated a patronage network that shut out dissent and talent.

Sri Lankan university standards were pretty low after decades of political interference. But I got the impression Jaffna University was stuck at an even lower peg, beholden to Tamil-nationalist professors and students still fighting yesterday's war, parroting old slogans and wallowing in collective grievance. Now their talk was empty, mere armchair nationalism that echoed that of the militant Tamil diaspora. They did not have the stomach for another real fight.

My last campus conversation left the deepest impression on me. It was with Dr Rajan Hoole, a mathematics lecturer in his mid to late sixties. He met me outside the science faculty building and led me to a simple, unadorned office he shared with a fellow mathematics lecturer half his age. Rajan was tall, quiet, with an unexpressive face. Once in a while, his brows furrowed and his face set into a mild frown. He walked slowly, with the look of someone who had aged prematurely and suffered a lot. He spoke English slowly, clearly, with surgical precision. The life story he related to me was full of drama and pathos, but he told it in a soft dry monotone, without emotion. He never laughed, but, very occasionally, when he said something he found amusing, a quiet, wry smile surfaced.

Rajan completed his education abroad and taught at the National University of Singapore, where I taught now. After the war broke out in 1983, when other academics escaped Jaffna for the security and comfort of the West, he returned and joined the university faculty. He and two colleagues set up University Teachers for Human Rights (UTHR), which documented and publicized human rights abuses by the LTTE, the army and, during the years of Indian occupation, the IPKF.

'By 1986,' he told me, 'the LTTE was in control of Jaffna, and they were set on a monopoly of power: they had no interest in a plural polity. They brooked no dissent. They showed their intentions on campus and clamped down; they made sure their supporters were appointed to the faculty. We (UTHR) came under pressure from both sides, but mostly from the LTTE.'

In a gory public spectacle, the LTTE assassinated his close colleague and fellow human rights activist Rajani Thiranagama, a professor of anatomy, in 1989. That was when he, a colleague and their families had to flee Jaffna. He and his wife lived for several years in safe houses in Colombo; he was prominent on an LTTE death list. Then they lived in Madras before returning to Colombo. During these years he published two books on wartime atrocities, *The Broken Palmyrah* and *The Arrogance of Power*. When war resumed in 2006, the Rajapaksa government bore down on him for publicizing the army's human rights violations. He spent a year at Harvard, courtesy of their Scholars at Risk programme. Then he returned to Jaffna, where he was reinstated to the lectureship from which he had been dismissed in 1991. Contrary to the equivocations of the senior academics I had spoken to earlier, he told me the LTTE continued to control the campus until the end of the war, even when the government nominally controlled Jaffna town.

After the war Rajan remained a thorn in the side of the powerful. The Rajapaksa government and military were clearly unhappy with his widely publicized calculation that about 100,000 people, mostly civilians but including about 15,000 LTTE fighters, were killed or disappeared in the last six months of the war. In 2015 he published *Palmyrah Fallen*, a reckoning of human rights abuses, and of the war generally, in the twenty-five years after Rajani Thiranagama's assassination.

Senior academics on campus were clearly discomfited by this gadfly in their midst. When we adjourned to the Senior Common Room for tea, I could not help noticing how Rajan's colleagues steered well clear of him. He pointed to framed photos of academics on one wall, all of whom died during the war. 'The only one missing,' he said, 'is Rajani Thiranagama.' His colleagues did not think it fitting to commemorate her, shot dead by LTTE assassins in front of her house as she cycled back home from her university office, just a few weeks after she, Rajan and a colleague had published *The Broken Palmyrah*.

As Rajan talked I realized I was in the presence of a rare being: someone who stood up for his principles and suffered the consequences. Academics wax eloquently about 'speaking truth to power', but most, especially in the West, never have to do so, not when their livelihoods and lives are at risk. Rajan had done so, repeatedly, over three decades. For that he had sacrificed security and ease, and been willing to pay the ultimate price. He maintained a quiet dignity that radiated from his frail-looking body. As an academic habituated to normality and creature comforts, first in the West and now in Singapore, I felt humbled.

Just before I took my leave Rajan made a final observation that rang true. 'Jaffna, nine years after the war ended, doesn't look or feel like a place where war occurred recently. The army isn't on the streets; its presence isn't obtrusive. It tolerates contrary opinions. Even before 2015 (during Rajapaksa rule), the situation wasn't as bad as Tamil nationalists make out.' And he added, with that rare surfacing of a slight, amused smile, 'The Sinhalese are lackadaisical even in their extremism. Not relentlessly thorough and systematic like the LTTE were.'

As we said goodbye I asked him if he went abroad these days. 'No,' he replied, 'I am content to pass the rest of my days in Jaffna.'

~

I first saw the islands around Jaffna on my visit in December 2011. We drove across the long, narrow causeway that linked Jaffna to Kayts, the largest of the islands the other side of the lagoon. Prawn-catching nets lined both sides of the causeway; fishermen, clad only in loincloths and cloths wrapped around their heads, waded in the shallow water, their leathery sunburnt backs bent low attending to their prawn nets. Army and navy checkpoints were strung out on the road. The landscape was flat and waterlogged, the terrain barren compared with the relative fecundity of the peninsula mainland. Everything induced a sense of bleakness and loneliness, even though the hulking walls of Jaffna Fort, and the town behind it, were just a short distance behind us. Palmyrahs grew here too; many seemed to sprout straight out of the water. We passed small kovils, Christian chapels, and several roadside shrines of Catholic saints encased in glass and mounted on poles. Kayts bore all the scars of heavy fighting and aerial bombardment: the shells of little houses and their outhouses were everywhere, the countryside littered with tree stumps and mini-craters where bombs fell.

We drove across the short causeway from Kayts to the island of Punkudutivu and reached a jetty. Here Mummy and I got into the lower deck of a rickety ferry, packed to the rafters with Sinhala pilgrims. They, and we, were going to Nagadipa (Nainativu in Tamil), the little island where the Buddha, on his second visit to Lanka, made peace between two warring Naga kings, or so the *Mahavamsa* tells us. The navy ran this ferry. Sailors gave passengers unusable life jackets; the ancient engine started and sputtered loudly, and after a rocky twenty-minute ride we arrived at Nagadipa. For all its fame there was little to see: a small, nondescript Buddhist temple built in the 1950s and recently renovated; next to it a big poster of a typically beaming Mahinda Rajapaksa, one arm raised triumphantly; an open-air market; and a kovil with a gopuram.

Back at Punkudutivu jetty, we did a longish drive back to Jaffna, around the peninsula coastline heading east, and across another causeway to the island of Karaitivu. On the way, just outside Jaffna town, was an enormous putrid rubbish dump; hundreds of used plastic bags were strewn along the roadside. We passed middle-aged and elderly men in sarongs riding clapped-out bicycles, and the odd farmer accompanying a herd of bony cattle or goats.

Across the causeway we drove to Karaitivu's north-eastern tip, which revealed another example of the military diversifying into post-war tourism: a small hotel run by the navy, next to a navy base. No other guests were here when we arrived, but the hotel had a full complement of uniformed staff – sailor-waiters and receptionists in regulation blue, and two officer-managers in regulation white. From the veranda, a short distance into the sea, we saw Fort Hammenhiel, a tiny Dutch fort the navy had restored and turned into four hotel rooms – all unoccupied at the moment. The water which surrounded it was as tranquil as a swimming pool, the afternoon air hot and heavy, the sky a cloudless blue. A lone short palmyrah stood rigidly erect in front of the veranda; its thick hard fronds made a strange crackling sound in the faint breeze, quite different from the soft swaying lullabies of coconut palms down south.

On the way back to Jaffna, back on the peninsula mainland, we stopped at Vaddukoddai. At the junction was a landmark in Jaffna history, a hub of missionary activity that gave Jaffna a head start in education and bred a local elite that played an outsize role in nineteenth- and twentieth-century Ceylon. We entered the large grounds of Jaffna College, whose origins went back to 1823. The British allowed American missionaries to operate in the peninsula – though not elsewhere on the island – in 1813: in the remote north they were at a safe distance; down south they would have rubbed up against British missionaries, anxious to preserve a monopoly of gospel-spreading in their new empire outpost. The missionaries – Methodists, Presbyterians and Episcopalians – came as the American Ceylon Mission. They founded the Batticotta seminary on this site in 1823, to educate the brightest local boys up to university level – and to convert them to Christianity; it became Jaffna College in 1871. For a century and a half, Jaffna College and its predecessor schooled those who became luminaries in the Tamil intellectual, professional and political elite. American missionaries ran the college until the government took over in the 1960s; a few missionaries continued to teach there until the war broke out.

The American Ceylon Mission was remarkably progressive for its time, keen as much on education as a means to escape poverty as on biblical instruction. It founded a counterpart girls' school in Uduvil, not far away, and a wider network of schools in the peninsula. It started a printing press and ran publications in English and Tamil. And it set up medical facilities, notably the Green Memorial

Hospital, Ceylon's first medical school. Just before independence, the American Ceylon Mission was amalgamated into the Anglican Church of South India.

Across the road from Jaffna College was a small parish church with an old history. It started as a Portuguese church, then a Dutch one (the name of a Dutch governor of Jaffna was inscribed above the front door), before the American Ceylon Mission took it over. It was now the unlikely 'cathedral church' of the Church of South India, Jaffna diocese. Next door was Bishop's House, about ten times the size of the cathedral church.

In February 2018, and on my last day in the peninsula on this particular trip, Joseph drove me all the way back to Punkudutivu jetty, from which Mummy and I had taken the ferry to Nagadipa in late 2011. This time I took a different boat to a different island. My destination was Delft, the remotest inhabited island off the Jaffna peninsula. The once-daily ferry took a full hour. Sitting next to me was Pushpakumaran, a Tamil from the hill country, a Badulla boy, from Daddy's home town. He spoke Sinhala, so we chatted about Badulla. Pushpakumaran was that rarity, a Tamil policeman; he was stationed on Delft. He told me the Delft police post had fifty officers among a local population of barely 4000. Only five officers spoke Tamil; the rest, all Sinhalese, presumably communicated little with local villagers, most of whom did not speak Sinhala.

Delft's landscape is unique in Sri Lanka, totally different even from that of the peninsula and other islands off it. It is wild, desolate, forbidding. Much of it is treeless, windswept and parched-brown across a flat plain; the sun beats down and bakes the earth from a gargantuan sky of cloudless blue. The ground is stony, the soil barren. Delft gets a little rain, when it gets any, for two months of the year. For the other ten, it is bone dry. Porous dry stone walls of local coral split up the land into individual plots, a feature not seen elsewhere in Sri Lanka; it reminded me, strangely, of the stone walls that demarcate farmland across the rolling hills of the British countryside. The population is scattered. Here and there I saw a small house on a plot of land fenced off with cadjan. I had never felt this hot or humid before in Sri Lanka, and nowhere else in Sri Lanka did I have such an intense feeling of being cut off, far, far away from human presence and interaction.

My three-wheeler driver took me first down narrow dirt roads to a Delft landmark, a baobab tree. Baobabs are extremely rare outside Africa and Australia; a passing Arab trader probably planted this one, many, many centuries ago. It stuck out like a gigantic sore thumb. The trunk was short and stubby, but with an enormous girth and spindly root-like branches, almost bereft of foliage, that extended horizontally, like a squat and many-armed scarecrow. The trunk was open on one side; its cavity was huge – wide and high enough to accommodate five adults, with room to spare.

We headed back to Delft's main road, next to the jetty. The *Handbook for the Ceylon Traveller* says the island has one bus, one jeep and one tractor. That was forty-five years ago. Now, in addition to the three-wheelers, I saw an old bus, a white van, a lorry, several motorbikes and lots of bicycles. This sole thoroughfare contained most of the island's public buildings: a navy camp, a small garment factory, two shops and guest houses near the jetty; and, down the road, two churches, one kovil, a school, a mini hospital, the police station and a small market.

Off the road were two of Delft's other tourist sights: a pigeon tower the British built in the nineteenth century (to house the winged carriers of messages to and from the mainland); and the ruin of a small Dutch fort. A drive to another side of the island took me to a grassy plain where wild ponies roamed; they were small and bony, clearly suffering for lack of grass and water. The Dutch introduced their ancestors to Delft; the ruins of the stables the Dutch built for them were close by.

On the journey back, the boatman invited me to sit at the prow for a chat. He was a Delft man, and we needed an interpreter who spoke Sinhala, for he spoke only Tamil. His young assistant obliged. He chewed betel while he talked and smiled through betel-stained teeth. I asked him about Delft during the war. The navy patrolled the waters around the island and cut off its food supply from the mainland, he said. Ferry services were stopped. Villagers starved. So, en masse, they got into their fishing boats and fled the twenty miles across the Palk Straits to India. The boatman spent fifteen years in a refugee camp in Dhanushkodi. Many islanders were still refugees in India; some, like him, came back; some ended up in the wider diaspora; and others 'went to the Vanni' – as LTTE fighters.

Life on the island was very hard now. The tsunami did something to the waters around Delft, he said. There were fewer fish to catch, and Indian trawlers grabbed most of it.

~

As soon as I got back from Delft, Joseph and I started the journey down to Anuradhapura. Back in the Vanni, we reached Kilinochchi, the LTTE's wartime capital. Joseph saw it when he drove foreign correspondents up north during the ceasefire, now over fifteen years ago. On our first trip he said the army had erased all traces of the LTTE town: its ministries, the courthouse, the parade ground, and the huge cemetery with graves and statues of its war dead.

Now Kilinochchi looked transformed. The A9 highway – dotted with army camps all the way down from Elephant Pass – expanded to four lanes through the town centre. There were gleaming new shops and showrooms. A large white Buddha, its head illuminated by neon lights, sat on the roadside in the middle of town. At one end of town was another victory memorial, as big and triumphant as the one at Elephant Pass. The design was bizarre: a large lotus (the floral symbol of Sri Lanka) with a bullet piercing its roots.

On our first trip to the north, Mummy and I visited two centres near Kilinochchi supported by Candle Aid, the charity organization run by my friends Elmo and Dil Jayawardena. One was a remote village school. We passed huts and backyards fenced off with cadjan; the government school was a basic one-storey, three-room building with a corrugated roof and open on the sides, without windows. It was the week before Christmas, and we were here to give the children their Christmas presents. They looked desperately poor – thin, ragged, barefoot, some with sores on their arms and legs.

The other centre we visited was a shelter for war widows and their children, run by Father Dominic, a Catholic priest. He trained in psychology and gave counselling to both mothers and children, as well as organizing tuition classes for the children. We talked to a group of mothers, all traumatized in one way or another; Father Dominic translated. One young mother had a goat and a few poultry to support herself and two children. Another's husband was killed out in the open while she and her children took shelter in a bunker; they watched him die. An older woman, aged about fifty, blind in one eye, had a son who went missing in 2006. I could not help noticing the endlessly deep well of sadness in her remaining good eye.

Father Dominic complained the government (still the Rajapaksa government when we visited) was not serious about genuine rehabilitation for war refugees. 'They release IDPs (internally displaced persons) and deposit them in the Vanni with four posts and a tent, and call it rehabilitation. Before farmers had land. But they had to flee during the war. The army took over the land and now farms it. People are left with nothing.' He added, 'We have to be very careful with counselling; the government is suspicious and tries to control what we do. Because it worries the truth will come out.'

~

Now, on the last full day of this third post-war trip to the north, Joseph drove me north-west of Anuradhapura to Mannar island. This took us back into the Vanni on the way to the coast. Our first stop was Madhu Church, one of the two main Catholic pilgrim sites in Sri Lanka. Catholics fleeing Dutch persecution came here in 1670, carrying the statue of Our Lady of Madhu. The LTTE controlled the surrounding area for much of the war and occupied the church. Before they did so, priests took the statue elsewhere for safekeeping.

A long driveway led to a large lawn-filled enclosure; in its centre was a sizeable Portuguese-style church, painted in yellow-cream with vertical blue stripes. A fair number of pilgrims were here today, but Joseph told me the site was jam-packed during the annual festival in August.

The church had large wooden doors and windows, wide open during the day to let in air and light. Like other country churches in Sri Lanka, one had to enter barefoot and sit on the floor – there were no pews. A central aisle bordered by wooden railings ran up to the altar with the holy statue. Pilgrims – Sinhalese, Tamil, rich, middle-class and poor – sat on the bare floor and crawled to the altar on their knees.

Mannar is relatively small, dusty and sleepy now. Time has passed it by, but it was Lanka's main port during the Anuradhapura kingdom. Then it was called Mantai (in Tamil) or Mahathitha (in Sinhala). According to the *Mahavamsa*, Vijaya, the legendary founder of the Sinhala race, landed with his 700 followers not far from here. It attracted Indian merchants and Arab traders, and it was the port of entry for invaders and mercenaries from South India. The island's Muslim population is the legacy of Arab traders sailing here in their dhows centuries ago. Until 1905, Mannar island had a famous pearl fishery that attracted divers and traders from India and the Arabian Gulf, and gave Georges Bizet the subject matter for his opera *The Pearl Fishers*.

We crossed the two-mile causeway from the mainland to Mannar town. Past its celebrated baobab tree, on the banks of the water, was a poor settlement of Christian fisherfolk. We stopped at a Catholic church, paint peeling off its pale yellow facade, with what looked like a midday service going on inside. I took my sandals off and stood quietly at the back. And there I stood for the next half-hour, captivated by a scene of simple devotion. The priest-less, impromptu congregation consisted mostly of elderly and middle-aged women, dressed in gaily coloured frocks, sitting on the floor praying and singing hymns in Tamil. Candles lit up the altar. One man, next to his wife and toddler son, was on his knees with his arms outstretched in prayer, like a bird in flight displaying its full wingspan.

Back in the town centre, next to the causeway, were the ruins of Mannar Fort. It was close to a ruin before the war, but it suffered additional wartime damage; the LTTE occupied it for a while. There was little to see inside except what remained of a small chapel, roofless and without an inner wall, open to the elements. One plaque, dated 1587, bore the name of a Portuguese commander's wife; a tombstone by the altar displayed the coat of arms of a Dutch commander of 'Jaffnapatnam', the old Dutch name for Jaffna. Another plaque commemorated a British couple who died in the nineteenth century.

We drove out of Mannar town up the finger-strip of land to the tip of the island that faced India. This was one of the most arid parts of the country, full of palmyrahs, sandy water and scrub. We passed the only copse of baobabs in Sri Lanka – several trees, not just one or two – and many, many scrawny donkeys. This brought us to Talaimannar.

Until 1983, a ferry ran twice weekly between Talaimannar and Dhanushkodi, on Rameswaram island, fourteen miles away at the other end of the Palk Straits. A Colombo–Talaimannar mail train linked up with the ferry. The war put paid to the ferry and the train link. Indian engineers rebuilt the track after the war, and there was a new station here now. The Colombo–Talaimannar train service had resumed. There were no immediate plans to resume the ferry service.

On the other side of the railway track, a small road led to Talaimannar village. It was a tumbledown Muslim settlement; a mosque and a few small houses and shops lined the dusty lane that led to the beach. Some of the houses looked abandoned. The LTTE expelled the island's Muslims in 1990, and only some had returned. The beach had a small, disused lighthouse and the pier where the ferry used to dock. It was now out of bounds because it was part of a navy camp. On a clear day one could see the gopuram of Rameswaram temple across the water. Adam's Bridge – the chain of sandbars across to Rameswaram – started just the other side of the pier, but this stretch was also out of bounds.

That left one final sight to see on this trip: the graves of Adam and Eve. I had read somewhere that they were buried near Talaimannar, in a Muslim shrine. So Joseph and I asked about 'Adam's grave'. We got directions to a Christian fishing village ten minutes' drive along the coast, and went down to the end of a dirt road. Here a glade, embowered by palmyrahs, revealed a tiny dome behind a white wall and a green flag fluttering next to it – telltale signs of a Sufi dargah or shrine. The signboard at the gate enjoined visitors to take off their 'shoes and sleepers'. A short, dark man with a weather-beaten face approached; he told us, in Tamil, that his name was Terence, that he was Christian, and that he took care of the shrine for the Muslim authority that owned it.

Inside were two extremely long graves – graves of giants – draped in green flags. Terence pointed to one and said *Appa* (Father), and then to the other, *Amma* (Mother). Or Adam and Eve. Actually there were five separate graves in each row, laid back to back; they contained the remains of Arab preachers and their wives (the husbands in one row, the wives in the other) who came here about 600 years ago. Next to 'Appa' was a small replica of a dhow.

~

The journey back to Colombo ended the last and longest of my Sri Lankan road trips for this book. It had been the one with the widest geographical coverage and the greatest variety of experience. It had the most intense contrasts of scenery, of culture and religion, of wealth and poverty. It had the pathos of war and its enduring scars, and, in the east, troubling signs of emerging Islamic fundamentalism, but also the buoyancy of post-war recovery. I returned to places I remembered from childhood, but much of what I saw was new, and much of that in parts of the country far from its metropolitan centres.

Joseph kept me entertained throughout. On this final stretch he was extra-voluble, full of stories. He came up with new terminology: 'spare-wheel' (a mistress) and 'doing jiggy-jiggy' (having sex) stuck in my mind. On our first trip, when the A9 was still very bumpy, only semi-repaired two and a half years after the war ended, he said he was giving us a 'free massage'. I reminded him of our last day in Jaffna on that trip. It was Christmas Day. His wife had died just a year earlier. I told Joseph we could leave later if he wanted to go to Mass. 'No need to go to church, sir,' he replied. 'I do self-service Mass.' Indeed he had, in the car first thing in the morning, complete with candles and his St Anthony's talisman.

Joseph dropped me off in Colombo. My Sri Lankan road trips, spread over almost a decade, were done.

Envoi

I began this journey standing by a window in Galle Face Hotel, looking out at a turbulent sea on a stormy morning in December 2006. Sri Lanka was still engulfed in civil war. Colombo was a maze of barbwire and security checkpoints. The hotel was almost empty in what was, in normal times, the tourist high season. It was my first day back in a decade, and I felt a stranger in the land of my birth and childhood.

That first brief visit, and the one a year later, persuaded me to return to rediscover Sri Lanka. Over the next ten years, I travelled not only across its geography, but in time. First, through my parents' shipboard romance, their six-year epistolary courtship and their early married life; next through my own childhood, which included the political convulsions that shook my family to its bones. An extended Muslim family, a colonial hotel, a pukka school, Daddy's clubs, a verdant slow-paced Colombo of big houses and even bigger gardens, school holidays at Razeena and family trips around Sri Lanka – these were my backdrops. The 1977 general election, Daddy's release from jail and our final departure for the UK, marked the end of my Sri Lankan childhood.

From my mid-teens to my early forties, I turned my back on Sri Lanka, just as it was tearing itself apart in ethnic violence. But since 2009, I made up for that prolonged absence. I familiarized myself again with Colombo, my home town, and criss-crossed the island, covering tens of thousands of miles, from the Kalpitiya peninsula on the west coast to Batticaloa and its lagoon on the east coast; from the Dondra Head lighthouse, with nothing between it and the Antarctic except a vast ocean, to Point Pedro, the war-scarred northern tip of the Jaffna peninsula. With Nihal and Joseph, my two regular drivers, and sometimes with Mummy in the back seat, I drove around nearly all Sri Lanka's coastline – in the south and deep south, past the deserted powder-white beaches and waveless, crystal-clear waters of the east coast, around the marshy, palmyrah-clad islands off the Jaffna peninsula, to Talaimannar pier and the graves of Adam and Eve at the tip of Mannar island.

I retraced the paths of Buddhist sages, Sinhala kings and Tamil invaders among the ruined temples, palaces and statues of Rajarata, and walked all over the tea-carpeted hills of Kandy, Nuwara Eliya, Bogowantalawa and Uva. Among a sea of pilgrims, I climbed a holy mountain to see the sunrise. In Colombo and on the road, I had hundreds of encounters and conversations. I studied and reflected upon Sri Lanka in a way I had never done as a boy. For nearly four years, from 2015 to late 2018, I even had a ringside seat as a policy adviser, watching Sri Lanka's disastrous politicians miss another opportunity for national renewal.

What have I learned from coming back? A lot, but it starts with the range and depth of my ignorance. The limitations of childhood and extended absence made me see Sri Lanka in black and white, with blinkers on. Now, with eyes wide open, I see it in a multitude of bright colours – not shades of grey, for grey is totally the wrong colour for such vivid people and landscapes. I think I am more alive to nuances; I am certainly more attuned to Sri Lanka's manifold paradoxes.

Much of what I saw – people, places, situations – reminded me of childhood. Even so, I felt I was on a journey of fresh discovery, seeing Sri Lanka for the first time. These were moments of pure exhilaration, an awareness, however inchoate, of something vital that had escaped me before. After all this time spent travelling, talking, reading and writing, I also felt I scratched the surface and started digging in fertile ground, with much more to do.

I have covered many sides of Sri Lanka in this book – landscapes and people, history and current affairs. Large gaps remain. I speak Sinhala of a sort, but it is still basic, not fluent. I do not speak Tamil. I have never lived the daily life of a Sri Lankan village or small town. I do not have much to say about food, since I hardly cook, though I do enjoy Sri Lankan food, and always relish a huge Sri Lankan breakfast of string-hoppers or hoppers, milk rice or coconut roti, with sambals, dhal curry and other vegetable curries. As a convert to vegetarianism, I find Sri Lanka's sheer variety of fruits, herbs and vegetables a matchless feast. I have hardly even mentioned cricket, since my interest in team sports is close to zero. But cricket, like politics, is a national obsession. And unlike politics, it is Sri Lanka's one unifying religion.

Those are but two examples of what is left to be explored. So how to sum up my take on Sri Lanka's past and present? And what pointers to the future? Finally, on a more personal note, how has returning to Sri Lanka affected me? When I set out on these journeys

I imagined, vaguely, they would be voyages of self-discovery. Did that happen? Has Sri Lanka really got under my skin? How?

~

I will start with lessons from the past. My abiding impression is of a heaven-and-hell country, often convulsed and sometimes consumed by its own extremes. Sri Lanka's glaring paradox is its mix of beguiling tourist charm – Hermann Hesse's 'Paradise island with its fern trees and palm-lined shores and gentle doe-eyed Sinhalese' – and astonishing record of violence. Foreign visitors who fall in love with the island cannot fathom how such a blessed spot could tear itself apart during Black July 1983 and for a quarter-century thereafter. Nor can they make sense of the two JVP rebellions in the early 1970s and late 1980s, both viciously prosecuted and brutally crushed. How could this land of serendipity, cradled by the world's most pacific religion, and with such sweet, smiling people, come to this?

Sri Lanka's story is blood-spattered, from royal massacres in the Anuradhapura and Polonnaruwa kingdoms, punctuated by frequent South Indian invasions; to Western colonization, in particular the orgiastic violence of Portuguese conquistadors, to the post-independence present. Yet ethnic mixing and religious tolerance, indeed syncretism, have been a great feature of this history. Sinhala kings had South Indian consorts, imported Tamil Brahmins, mercenaries and craftsmen, and incorporated Hindu rituals into their Buddhist practice. To this day, Hindu and Mahayana influences suffuse Theravada Buddhist devotion in viharas and devales all over the island. It is emblematic of the architectural splendours of Anuradhapura and Polonnaruwa, and of Sinhala Buddhist kingdoms thereafter. It reached its zenith during the Kandyan kingdom, whose Nayakkar kings from Madurai sought legitimacy by revivifying

Sinhala Buddhism. During their reigns, waves of high- and lower-caste South Indian migrants were Sinhalized and Buddhicized in two or three generations. As Professor Gananath Obeyesekere, a leading authority on this period, says, Sinhala–Tamil and Buddhist–Hindu distinctions are 'fuzzy', certainly not binary opposites.

Then there is the multicultural cocktail that comes from an age-old maritime trading heritage. Sri Lanka, halfway between the ancient trading hubs of the Arabian (or Persian) Gulf and the Southeast Asian archipelagos, was long open to the world through trade. It was once the Clapham Junction of Indian Ocean trade; and trade brought migrations, particularly of Arab and Tamil merchants. But this extraordinary cultural hybridity did not go unchallenged. The late nineteenth-century Buddhist revival did not challenge it directly, but Anagarika Dharmapala's later hitching of Buddhism to Sinhala nationalism did. To Dharmapala, 'hybridity' was a dirty word. His legacy to Sinhala Buddhism is a mythical revisionist history, and a political programme that is exclusive and supremacist, chauvinist and racist.

But bigotry is not exclusive to Sinhala Buddhism. Elite Christians displayed it during colonial times; Dutch Burghers were notorious for it. It finds its echo in the caste-riven, self-isolating Hinduism of the Jaffna peninsula, perpetuated by Arumugam Navalar and following generations of the vellala elite. Their 'peninsularity of mind' has a long history, with disastrous consequences since independence. More recently, another echo comes from a fundamentalist minority in my own Muslim community. Their attacks on Sufism, their attempt to rid Islam of South Indian 'impurities', their jet-black shrouding of women and girls – these are outbreaks of identity politics that vitiate Sri Lankan Islam's pragmatic, outgoing, ethnic bridge-building heritage. This was the Wahhabi and Salafi breeding ground for the terrorist cell that blew up churches and hotels on Easter Sunday 2019.

With or without Dharmapala's noxious influence, Sinhala

Buddhism suffers from its ancient umbilical link to the state and its arch-conservative Theravada tradition. Since its founding, organized Buddhism in Sri Lanka has expected the state to elevate it over other religions. This has corrupted the sangha and laity, politically, financially and spiritually. It destroyed D.S. Senanayake's vision of a secular, multi-ethnic Ceylon.

Conventional Theravada remains spiritually impoverished. It has never had a proper reformation. This is the central message of the Venerable Shravasti Dhammika's *The Broken Buddha*. Ven Dhammika is a clear-thinking, direct-speaking Australian scholar-monk I got to know when I moved to Singapore in 2012. He has travelled extensively in Burma, Thailand, Laos and Cambodia, the Theravada countries of Southeast Asia. Knowledge and wisdom permeate his precise writing, and humour livens his talk. He was ordained in India and lived for over a decade in Sri Lanka, staying in temples, building his *kuti* (a monk's cell) on a hillside in the Dumbara valley near Kandy, sojourning in remote forest hermitages where serious meditating monks retreat, and walking to ancient Buddhist sites all over the island. *Sacred Island*, his guide to Buddhist sites in Sri Lanka, accompanied me on most of my road trips.

In *The Broken Buddha*, Ven Dhammika excoriates Theravada's corruption of original Buddhism. The rot set in early. Theravada became literal, conservative, and fundamentalist. In a rather Brahminical way, it elevated the sangha to a pedestal; they became the sole, unquestioned guardians and purveyors of the dhamma, the Buddha's teaching. For the laity, generosity to the sangha, more than anything else, became the benchmark for accumulating merit for a good rebirth.

These beliefs were entrenched in Theravada's most revered doctrinal text, the *Visuddhimagga* (Path of Purification), written by the Indian monk Buddhaghosa in the fifth century CE while he sojourned at the Aluvihare rock temple in Matale. Buddhaghosa went into exhaustive detail on the dos and don'ts of the vinaya, the monastic code, and the duties of the laity towards the sangha. But he had precious little to say on the virtues of inward spiritual cultivation, compassion, and doing active good for one's fellow human beings.

Ven Dhammika says Westerners delude themselves with their image of temples full of other-worldly monks. Perhaps 5–10 per cent of monks meditate seriously and lead the austere, solitary, contemplative life the Buddha intended for them. He quotes a leading Sri Lankan Buddhist layman, writing under the pseudonym Parakrama, who accuses senior bhikkus of incessantly hunting for the patronage of rich businessmen and politicians. Often, *samaneras* (novice monks, usually village boys inducted from the age of ten) turn into hairy, unkempt, ignorant youths who go on political marches, yell and waive raised fists; they preach virulent communalism and utter racial slurs in the name of 'saving Buddhism'. Senior bhikkus and a passive, deferential laity turn a blind eye: rarely, if ever, are errant monks disciplined. Parakrama concludes, 'The Buddha's exhortation to show kindness to all living beings does not seem to extend to the non-Sinhalese peoples of Sri Lanka.'

The upshot is that the sangha are ethnocentric nationalists who take a dim view of ethnic and religious minorities – indeed of Buddhists in other countries, who do not count as 'real Buddhists'. Finally, they sometimes encourage warmongering 'to bring glory to the religion' – the *Mahavamsa*'s justification for Dutugemunu's defeat of the Tamil king Elara in the second century BCE.

A detractor might ask why I pick on Theravada when Sri Lanka's other religious traditions – Hinduism, Christianity and Islam – have their intrinsic defects. But Theravada's defects matter more in Sri Lanka precisely because it is the dominant religion, with overweening influence in politics and society.

~

Another historical legacy is Sri Lanka's combination of abundance and complacency. Robert Knox's eulogy to the coconut tree – how a single tree provides meat, drink, cloth, mats, rope, honey, oil and more besides – is an apt metaphor for the wet zone's natural bounty. It also breeds a fatal complacency.

Horace wrote in one of his *Odes*, 'Blessed is he to whom Nature has given with a sparing hand.' But Sri Lanka is the opposite of Switzerland, Singapore and Hong Kong. Their resource poverty meant their populations could not afford to be complacent; they had to be industrious and trade with the rest of the world to become prosperous. Too many Sri Lankans, and certainly their governing elite, expect coconuts to keep falling into their laps. A culture of hard work, thrift and enterprise has taken root among the minorities – hardy Tamils used to eking out a living in the barren north and east, Muslim traders, Colombo's tiny Bohra, Memon, Parsi and Sindhi trading castes, even Christians. But much less so among Sinhala Buddhists.

An accursed complacency made Sri Lanka miss so many proverbial buses, and take so many wrong turns at main junctions. After independence, the first disastrous wrong turn was the 1956 election and the 'Sinhala Only' policy. The second was Mrs Bandaranaike's government in the 1970s, which careened to the extreme left, crashed into public institutions and ethnic relations, and wrecked the economy to boot. The liberalization of the economy from 1977 opened a new road for economic take-off. But that was blocked by Black July 1983 and ensuing civil war. The war's end in 2009 opened another road, with a glimpse of political stability, economic progress and ethnic reconciliation. But that was never attainable with a Rajapaksa package of authoritarianism, economic nationalism and Sinhala Buddhist chauvinism.

Complacency continued unabated after President Rajapaksa's election defeat in January 2015. That presented a golden opportunity for change and renewal. But President Sirisena and Prime Minister Wickremesinghe, and the two parties they led in a fractious coalition, messed up royally.

High-level complacency includes ignoring the lessons of history. One example: The excesses of the Polonnaruwa kings – centralization of power, a crushing burden of taxation and labour duties to build their masterpieces, lavishing money on monasteries – so weakened the state that it collapsed astonishingly quickly. That reminds me of economic policy today, spending and borrowing profligately as if tomorrow will never come. Singapore's Lee Kuan Yew once quipped that Sri Lankan elections are auctions of non-existent resources. But tomorrow comes – always.

Another example: Polonnaruwa's Galpotha, the long 'stone book' in its Sacred Quadrangle, is full of over-the-top praise for Nissankamalla, that most egotistical of Sinhala kings. To me this echoes the inscriptions glorifying Mahinda Rajapaksa on triumphal post-war victory memorials at Elephant Pass and Kilinochchi. And Hambantota's vanity projects that bear his name. But, as ancient Greek mythology teaches us, nemesis invariably follows hubris.

Complacency is also pervasive, not restricted to the governing elite. My friend Chandra Jayaratne calls Sri Lanka a 'broken windowpane society'. If a windowpane breaks, say, in a school or hospital or other public building, chances are it is left unrepaired. I saw that metaphor for Sri Lankan apathy come alive on every visit. Roads, schools, hospitals and government offices were newly built or renovated. For a year or so they looked spanking new. But they were badly maintained. Soon they degenerated: paint peeled off walls, lawn grass remained unmown and grew tall, weeds spread, gates and doors came off their hinges, toilets got dirtier – and broken windowpanes were left unrepaired. This was not just a public sector problem: I saw it in the private sector too.

A final historical observation. Sri Lanka has had a disastrous political elite of all party colours – blue (SLFP), green (UNP) and red (the Communist parties) – since independence. Ivor Jennings's *Road to Peradeniya* rang prescient warnings of 'schoolboy politicians' and 'Bloomsbury Boys of Cinnamon Gardens' who would ruin the country. Now Bloomsbury Boys are near extinct: the coarse Sinhala Big Man sets the tone.

Sri Lanka's political culture plumbed new depths under the Rajapaksas. Intolerance of dissent, censorship, destruction of public institutions, extortion, ethno-religious chauvinism, institutionalized violence – thuggery, abduction, murder – all reached shocking extremes. President Rajapaksa's Big Man politics exploited war and subsequent military victory. But he also exploited deep traits in Sinhala culture – its 'habits of the heart'. Sinhala society is traditionally strongly hierarchical. It has a culture of knowing one's place and of deference to superiors, especially to a father figure, at every level – in the family, at school, at work, in religious practice, and in politics. It yearns for a king-like figure, a charismatic guardian and saviour, like the Sinhala kings of yore.

Political and civic life improved after the government changed in 2015. There was much more freedom of expression. The government did not sanction institutionalized violence against political opponents and ethnic minorities. Public institutions and civil society groups were a little stronger. But, in essence, political culture did not change. The players remained the same; many were dynastic veterans of the game. Their hallmarks were incompetence, knee-jerk populism, extensive patronage and pervasive corruption. They maintained a high barrier of entry to a younger generation who would like politics to be cleaner and deliver better governance.

～

And now to the present. My journeys left me a decade's worth of impressions, rich and kaleidoscopic, reflecting the land I criss-crossed. They gave me, I hope, glimpses of the Sri Lankan condition, a feel for its temper, as it came out of civil war and returned to a surface expression of peacetime normality.

I take the changing face of Colombo as a metaphor for my own changes, from a sheltered boy growing up 'half-half' in a Muslim family to a fifty-something who has spent the last decade rediscovering his roots. How Home Town has changed. Once smallish, quiet and green, later busier, noisier, with more people, buildings and traffic. For more than two decades its face and soul scarred by barbed wire and security checkpoints and bomb explosions. And now back to peacetime bustle, its face beautified. New condos, five-star hotels and shopping malls of shimmering glass rise high in what was a low-rise skyline, while a Chinese-built Port City emerges from the sea. Manners have coarsened. People have become more opportunistic and elbowing, aping their elites' deterioration. The races and religions mix less.

And yet. For all its development, Home Town still has a small-town vibe. It looks and feels spacious compared with other Third World cities. People still promenade down Galle Face Green during an Indian Ocean sunset. Timekeeping is as casual as it always was: punctuality passes by default. My Colombo characters from childhood have aged, of course, and some have passed away. But many remain voluble and gregarious – non-stop talkers and born storytellers.

Colombo's vigour is still its multi-ethnic mix. It showed its worst face in July 1983. It showed a better face on 8 January 2015, when Sri Lankans voted Mahinda Rajapaksa out of office, and, the day after, congregated at Independence Square to celebrate what they hoped would be a new beginning. It showed an ugly face again on Easter Sunday 2019, when Islamist suicide bombers murdered churchgoers, tourists and hotel staff. How wonderful it would be if that easygoing ethnic mixing of my parents' Ceylon were to return. But I know how everything in Sri Lanka is complicated, and how many things fall apart.

Then there is the juxtaposition of modernity and tradition. The first stop on my first road trip down south was Kalutara. The town is big by Sri Lankan standards, and bustling. Sinhala Buddhists, Sinhala Christians and Muslims live side by side; temples, churches and mosques flank Galle Road. But a few minutes' drive down a side road takes one into a Sinhala Buddhist village with its age-old traditions that Martin Wickramasinghe celebrated in his *Gam Peraliya*. Everything is embowered in greenery; paddy fields are tilled collectively; small houses have home gardens abundant with fruits, vegetables and herbs. Village life revolves around the temple with its dove-white stupa and saffron-robed monks.

The paradoxes thrown up by Sri Lanka's history, ancient and more recent, were ever present on my travels. These days I pass Weligama Bay once or twice a year. Today the scene is peaceful: the wide arc of the bay with Taprobane island at its centre, fishing boats, the rest house, and new hotels and guest houses, manifestations of the post-war tourist boom. But during the JVP rebellion in the late 1980s, there was an orgy of tit-for-tat killing here; mutilated corpses lined the beach road. Farther down the coast, in Tangalle, I stepped on to the town's small beach along with holidaying parents and their children one Sunday afternoon, even as my mind went back to a photo, on this spot, of the burning corpse of an alleged JVP activist.

On my road trips in the north and east, I saw a gradual return to peacetime normality. The densely packed Muslim towns on the coastal strip south of Batticaloa heaved with commerce. The main roads were new and smooth, as they were elsewhere in the island. Railway connections had been restored. Jaffna, Trinco and Batti were spruced up, though patchily. War refugees were resettled in donor-built housing, and electrification had reached remote villages. In Mullaitivu and Kilinochchi, rapid reconstruction made it difficult to imagine these were mass killing fields only a decade ago. Not least, the army's presence was much less obtrusive.

But I also saw the appalling poverty that still existed in the rural interior of the north and east, and plagued thin, ragged people, some still living in huts without running water or electricity. My mind goes back to that visit to a school near Kilinochchi and its scrawny, barefoot children with sores on their limbs. And, not far from there, to Father Dominic's shelter for war widows and their children. There, I recall as if it were yesterday, the figure of a one-eyed mother, and the deep well of sadness in her remaining good eye, grieving for a son who went missing during the fighting and never returned.

These psychological scars of war will take long years to heal, if they ever do. Will Jaffna society, now seemingly broken, with a lost, hedonistic younger generation, ever recover? And what about the spectre of Islamic fundamentalism, which I caught glimpses of in Colombo, and even more so in Muslim towns on the east coast? Will it lead to a new ethnic conflict, this time pitting Sinhalese and Tamils against Muslims?

On my journeys I was bowled over by Sinhala charm countless times. Never more so than on a night-time ascent up Adam's Peak, befriended by smiling pilgrims from small-town and rural Sri Lanka, offering me home-cooked sweets in the manner of their pilgrim forefathers. How many times, in outstation hotels, rest houses and roadside stalls, a face lit up with a flashing smile when I spoke in my broken Sinhala. That established a connection, and in quick time people went out of their way to be friendly and helpful. And how many times, coming back to the car from some remote temple or monastery, did I find my mother happily conversing with middle-aged and elderly Sinhala village ladies – she in English with Sinhala words thrown in, they in Sinhala with a smattering of broken English.

I think of Sinhala village guides who took me on day-long treks in back-of-beyond Sri Lanka: in the hill country and national parks and virgin rainforest; and through ancient, long-abandoned monasteries deep in the jungle, clambering over rocky outcrops, passing lonely forest pools, stopping to admire cracked, weather-beaten Buddha statues and stupas, and lingering in caves carved out of rock faces by monks who inhabited them 1000 to 2000 or more years ago.

I think of Kumar the war veteran, who led me expertly to a score or more caves where monks lived and meditated in Rajagala, a sprawling monastic complex in Eastern Province, abandoned to the jungle a thousand years ago. Of Dayarathne, who guided me through Ritigala, a long-abandoned monastery in Rajarata. After our trek he took me home for plain tea and Sinhalese sweets with his wife and two small children, which we had in the afternoon shade of a tamarind tree. Of Ishan, short and slight, in his mid-twenties but looking much younger, who took me deep into Sinharaja, Sri Lanka's last enclave of primary tropical rainforest. He was a walking encyclopaedia of birds and trees and plants and flowers, which he named for me in English, Sinhala and Latin. Of Chamara, who walked me through steep-sided paddy terraces, fruit orchards, isolated hamlets and then, higher up, through tea estates and a pine forest in Knuckles, in the hill country a couple of hours' drive from Kandy.

All these village guides spoke little English, which allowed me to practise my Sinhala all day long, uninterrupted. All were soft-spoken, even shy, with gentle manners and smiles. All came from poor village families. They showed me their love of Sri Lanka's cornucopia of flora and fauna, and village life in its midst. They

shunned the noise, crowds and pollution of the city. They went out of
their way to please, not so much for a generous tip at the end of the
trek, but because it came to them naturally, from the heart. When
I think of my most serendipitous moments in the land once called
Serendib, I think of these back-of-beyond treks, and the gentle,
soft-spoken village guides who kept me company.

Yet this same Sinhala culture is prone to eruptions of extreme
violence, not when left to its own devices, but when whipped up by
base politicians, sometimes colluding with militant monks. How this
Sinhala charm clashes with the ugly chauvinism and triumphalism
that came with war victory. How it jars with the kitsch victory
memorials in the north, and with the appropriation of religious sites
in Tamil areas to give them a dubious Sinhala Buddhist makeover
– as I saw with the ancient Lilliputian stupas at Kanthorodai in the
Jaffna peninsula.

Many Sri Lankans I got to know, or know better, through long
conversations in English. Some I disliked. But I also met the best of
Sri Lankans. I think of fine Colombo professionals with a strong civic
sense. They are fed up with quasi-feudal, dynastic politics, corruption
and ethnic strife. Some come from the upper middle class with wide
international exposure; some, like my friend Ranjini, are rooted
in simple small-town traditions. They come from different ethnic
communities and religious faiths. All yearn for a better-governed,
ethnically harmonious, prosperous Sri Lanka. My friend Chandra,
retired from the life of a corporate captain, makes this his full-time
civic occupation. And I think of Hanif, the super-successful Memon
entrepreneur married to a Burgher, who puts time and money into
interfaith dialogues – his way of 'putting Sri Lanka first'.

I came across individuals, embedded in the religious traditions
of their communities, who still treasured long-standing friendships
with those of other faiths, as was common in the old Sri Lanka.
They did their bit to build bridges across bigger ethnic and religious

divides. And how often I met resilient women who shouldered the burden of useless menfolk in the family and workplace; they are Sri Lanka's true unsung heroes. I think of my childhood ayah Fareeda in Hali-Ela, now looking much older than her years, bowed and shrivelled by family squabbles and worries. Like so many poor Sri Lankan women, she slaved for years as a housemaid in the Middle East to support an expanding family. Her daughter followed in her footsteps.

There were exceptional people who stood up and spoke truth to power when others conformed slavishly or stayed silent. They were conspicuous during the Rajapaksa years, when standing up and speaking out came at great personal risk. And even more so during the LTTE's reign of terror. I think of Vasantha the Colombo journalist and the soft-spoken yet grittily determined presence of Rajan Hoole in Jaffna.

Finally, I think of my humanitarian friends, mostly successful professionals, who do practical good for disadvantaged Sri Lankans. There is loquacious Renton and his Power of One in Hungama in the deep south. And Elmo, bursting with energy, and Dil, ever the perfectionist and steeped in her faith, in their river house in Moratuwa. And the happy band of brothers and sisters at Candle Aid who work with them.

These are some of my Sri Lankan impressions – some negative, even at times monstrous, but also many that are good and heart-warming that I had not noticed or appreciated before these journeys.

~

And what of Sri Lanka's future?

In December 2016 I gave a lecture in Colombo entitled 'Sri Lanka: Three Scenarios for the Future'. Scenario One I called 'Drift', Scenario Two 'Take-Off', and Scenario Three 'Relapse'.

Scenario One extrapolates Sri Lanka's present to the future. Sri Lanka drifts, performing well below its potential, having squandered the golden opportunity that came with regime change in 2015. The government is dysfunctional. Nepotism and corruption remain rife. No serious reforms have materialized to repair ethnic relations. And now Islamic fundamentalism, and the backlash it triggers, opens up a new divide between Muslims and other Sri Lankans.

The economy grows at under 4 per cent a year. The government is buried under a debt mountain and a bloated public sector. A coterie of businessmen dominates most sectors, protected by the politicians they bankroll; foreign investment and new entrepreneurs are deterred and consumers screwed. Foreign policy has drifted back to China's warm embrace; Chinese state-backed projects are the only big foreign investment game in town.

If this continues, Sri Lanka will drift into the future with an ossified political and business elite, highly politicized, third-rate institutions, corruption and nepotism, an underperforming economy always verging on crisis, simmering ethnic tensions, and overdependence on China. The Colombo chattering class will continue to predict stellar future achievements, which will always remain unachieved. Brazil, so the saying goes, is the land of the future: it always was and always will be. The same can be said of Sri Lanka.

The Colombo elite will continue to party regardless, enjoying the fruits of power and influence-peddling at home, educating their offspring at pukka schools and universities abroad, and indulging in shopping sprees in London, Paris, Dubai and Singapore. But most Sri Lankans will continue to be undereducated, underskilled, underemployed and underpaid, leading underdeveloped lives they will pass on to their children and grandchildren.

This is the lot of the swollen male army of three-wheeler drivers, hanging around street corners waiting for scraps of work; it is the lot of the swollen female army of housemaids in the Middle East, often subject to discrimination and abuse, leading lonely lives cut off from their families, condemning their children to a motherless childhood. That still leaves a desperate minority, perhaps 10 per cent or more of the population, who live hand to mouth, either in or on the borderline of abject poverty.

Scenario Two is 'Take-Off' – what aspirational Sri Lankans hoped for with regime change in January 2015. It envisions a Sri Lanka that achieves its long-heralded potential.

This starts with the economy. Growth will be much higher, driven by a productive private sector, international trade and foreign investment, not by more debt and the public sector. Real wages and living standards will rise sustainably. People will have better housing, education and health care. There will be more competition and entrepreneurship. Multinational firms will establish Sri Lankan hubs in their global supply chains. Sri Lanka will have much closer links with South India and its 300 million consumers.

None of this will happen without substantial policy reforms: fiscal and monetary stabilization, domestic deregulation, trade and foreign investment liberalization, downsizing of the public sector, deregulation of the land and labour markets, upgrading of education and skills, and liberalization of agriculture. It will also require reforms to the state itself: limits on the discretionary power of politicians and bureaucrats, overhauling the civil service, and decentralizing power from Colombo to cities and regions.

Economic take-off is also a prerequisite for ethnic reconciliation. A stagnant economy exacerbates ethnic tensions that erupt into mass violence – as happened in the 1960s and 1970s when unemployed and underemployed youth swelled the ranks of both the JVP and Tamil militant groups. A more productive, expanding economy, with more investment and jobs, will reduce ethnic tensions, and provide the resources – for education, housing, health care and infrastructure – to reforge inter-ethnic and inter-religious bonds.

Foreign relations will be balanced. There will be large-scale foreign investment from the West, India and elsewhere alongside Chinese investment. Sri Lanka will have stronger political, commercial and cultural links with its civilizational friends – the world's liberal democracies and open societies.

This vision is of a peaceful Sri Lankan Sri Lanka, not a strife-torn Sinhala Buddhist Sri Lanka. People will be freer, less dependent on the whims and favours of politicians and bureaucrats. A younger generation will break through and transform politics, public institutions, business and society. But this is a long way off. The odds are it will not happen.

Scenario Three is 'Relapse'. This means reverting to something like the Rajapaksa years, with echoes of previous UNP and SLFP governments led by Premadasa, J.R. Jayewardene, and Mr and Mrs Bandaranaike.

The few liberal gains since January 2015 will be reversed. A Big Man will return to power. This could be a Rajapaksa, or a combination of Rajapaksas. He will promise to cleanse politics and institutions and 'get things done'. He will co-opt opponents into his big tent, as Mahinda did so successfully. He will neuter remaining opponents and institutions he does not fully control, including the police, judiciary, armed forces and NGOs. He will centralize patronage politics and make it more comprehensive and systematic. There will be no rule of law. Sri Lanka will slide back to illiberal democracy, becoming again a tropical analogue to Vladimir Putin's Russia. The economy will be state-led again. The public sector will expand, crowding out the productive parts of the private sector. Trade will shrink further and non-Chinese foreign investment will stay away.

The new Big Man will pander to the worst instincts of Sinhala Buddhists. He will spur extremist groups like the Boddhu Bala

Sena to action. Ethnic tensions will be kept on the boil; Muslims in particular will be at risk. They and other minorities will retreat further into their shells. More than ever, Sri Lanka's ethnic communities will live in separate solitudes.

Sri Lanka will again distance itself from India and the West, and become even more dependent on Chinese projects and loans. The Chinese state and its proxies will buy up its political and business elites. It will be a Chinese tributary state – rather like a brief interlude in the fifteenth century, when Admiral Zheng He abducted the king of the Kotte and took him back to Beijing to pay obeisance to the emperor, after which Kotte kings paid an annual tribute to China.

This scenario is entirely plausible, more so than the Take-Off scenario. Ordinary Sri Lankans are intensely frustrated by dysfunctional politics. They see no improvement in their lives; prices keep rising, but without new investment and jobs. This is fertile ground for a Big Man to appeal to Sinhala Buddhist 'habits of the heart'.

Is Sri Lanka's history of feral communal violence behind it? Abominations happened in recent history, perpetrated by Sinhalese and Tamils. Muslims perpetrated the latest abomination, the Easter Sunday 2019 bombings. Their wounds still bleed, without genuine ethnic reconciliation. When I imagine how communal bloodletting might recur, I think of the second verse of *From Greenland's Icy Mountains*, Bishop Reginald Heber's missionary hymn from the 1820s:

What though the spicy breezes
Blow soft o'er Ceylon's isle;
Though every prospect pleases,
And only man is vile.

Even if it comes to this, Sri Lanka will still have its achingly lovely landscapes and warm, welcoming people. It will still have individuals – journalists, professionals, businesspeople, citizen-activists and humanitarians – who will fight the good fight for the disadvantaged and suffering. But that will hardly diminish another Sri Lankan tragedy.

~

At the very end of this Sri Lankan journey, I will turn my looking glass inward. Has this really been a voyage of self-discovery? I have got to know Sri Lanka much better, however incompletely. But has Sri Lanka changed me, this time as a middle-aged adult, not as a child in the 1970s? That, for me, is the most difficult question.

Identity has always been slippery for me, never fixed, periodically shifting in reponse to changes within and in my external environment. Wherever I am, for however long, I feel at least a half-outsider, never an insider. I have always found it difficult to give a simple answer to the question: 'Where do you feel at home?'

Until the early 1980s, I felt much more Sri Lankan than British, but still detached, some distance apart, from other Sri Lankans. Daddy, my uncles and aunts, cousins and schoolmates seemed 'all' Sri Lankan to me, but I never thought I was. And I felt even more an outsider during our family interludes in the UK in the 1970s. My solitary streak – the loner in me – played a part, but so did my 'half–half' Sri Lankan-British background. In my decades of absence from Sri Lanka I felt more British, European and Western, though still an outsider. But the pendulum swung again soon after I started coming back to Sri Lanka. I felt more Sri Lankan again – how could it not be so after such prolonged, intense journeying and book writing? Lanka – the Resplendent Isle: its shores and landscapes and people drew me back and pulled me in, now more powerfully than in my childhood. I do not live in Sri Lanka, but life has almost completed its circle. For the first time since I was a teenager, Sri Lanka feels more like 'home' than anywhere else.

On my early visits back, refamiliarizing myself with Colombo and going on long road trips, I never imagined these would be spiritual journeys. 'Spirituality' is a big word, deployed most often as a cliché, an open sesame to bloviate, like flatulence wafting in no particular direction. So I should be careful. But, the more I recall the past decade, framed by my Sri Lankan journeys, I find I cannot avoid spirituality.

I was brought up a conventional Muslim, and even had a brief mid-teen religious phase. But I lost my faith when I was nineteen and never returned to it. I take care to respect the faith and conventions of my Sri Lankan relatives, but I have not shared their faith in thirty-five years. I lost my faith not only in Islam, but also in God (or gods), a Soul (in the sense of an essential, metaphysical self) and an Afterlife. Until my late forties, spirituality, in any sense, did not matter to me: I was a conventional Western sceptic, agnostic and borderline atheist. A casual, unreflective ethic of knowing the difference between right and wrong, and acting on it, seemed sufficient.

That began to change soon after I started coming back to Sri Lanka. A health problem led me to Ayurveda, the traditional herbal-based medicine of Sri Lanka and parts of South India. Ayurveda radically simplified my diet and paved the way to teetotal vegetarianism, a dietary world away from the alcohol, meat, fish, cheese and cigars I used to consume joyfully.

I took up basic meditation around the same time. An old family friend took me to see the family's meditation teacher, Pemasiri Thera, a gentle, constantly smiling, septuagenarian monk who ran a meditation centre just outside Colombo. He taught me basic breathing meditation, which I practised fitfully at first, and then more regularly, reinforced by short retreats at his centre.

I found I really took to the practice. It complemented Ayurveda: I liked its simplicity, even austerity. It appealed to the solitary side of my nature. I was drawn to its ability to make my mind more detached, less stressed, calmer, more focused – the qualities of 'mindfulness' now so popular in the West. It helped to relax my body. By this stage I realized my meditation practice was not just a technique to sort out a physical ailment, but something deeper. I had spent the previous decade pursuing a life addicted to the senses, and found it an emotional mug's game, a never-ending, constantly frustrating ego trip, lost in a thick fog of self-absorption. It took its toll on my body and mind. I lacked meaning in life – a purpose beyond self-gratification. Meditation became my remedy.

In Singapore, I got further meditation instruction from Ven Dhammika, the Australian monk who wrote *The Broken Buddha* and *Sacred Island*. Bhante Dhammika (*Bhante* being an honorific for Theravada monks) had an incredible knack for conveying complex thoughts simply and effectively, leavened with wry, often irreverent humour. We had long chats about Sri Lanka, especially about the history and state of Buddhism there, and the scores, probably hundreds, of Buddhist temples and forest hermitages he had visited all over the island. I also found his weekly dhamma talks captivating, opening my eyes to Buddhist teaching for the first time. I began to make the connection between my meditation practice and Buddhism, and, more generally, to spiritual questions I had ignored since losing my Muslim faith. For me, meditation now meant something more than Western-type mindfulness.

I came to find Buddhism's spiritual core increasingly compelling: the Buddha's notion of 'suffering', arising from the dizzying merry-go-round of attachment and desire; his Four Noble Truths, Five Precepts and Noble Eightfold Path; the rational, empirical nature of his inquiry; the simplicity and austerity of his example; and the deep, solitary introspection – meditation, in other words – of

Buddhist practice. Some aspects of Buddhism I still thought of as religious embellishment, including fantastical stories of the Buddha's past lives, and realms of gods and evil spirits; I remained deeply sceptical of reincarnation.

The religious trappings Buddhism acquired in the two and a half millennia since the Buddha, necessary for its transformation into a mass religion, I found culturally interesting but not spiritually attractive. But the spiritual core of original Buddhism, stripped of religious baggage, I found compatible, more or less, with my articles of non-belief: no God, no Soul and no Afterlife. And Vipassana, the 'insight' meditation that comes directly from the Buddha's teaching, gave it a daily practice and discipline. It became central to my life. The 'me' sitting in my Galle Face Hotel room in December 2006, were he to see me today, would shake his head in utter disbelief.

What has all this got to do with Sri Lanka? A lot, I think. To begin with, I cannot escape a personal paradox. I have covered many pages of this book criticizing organized Buddhism in Sri Lanka, sometimes scathingly: I still think it a prime culprit in what has gone wrong with modern Sri Lankan politics and society. Many of its rituals and conventions, so ingrained in Sinhala culture, strike me as colourful displays of superstition and idolatry. The dour, determined, Bible-reading Robert Knox thought much the same roaming around the Kandyan kingdom three and a half centuries ago. So did Colonel Olcott two centuries later. Yet, during the past decade, Vipassana, and its foundation of Buddhist spirituality, beckoned me closer.

Sri Lanka provided an essential context for this inward journey, running alongside my road trips all over the island. It was Nandanie, the youngest daughter of Daddy's old friend Gilbert Paranagama, who planted the seed of meditation in my mind. The Paranagamas are Kandyan aristocracy and steeped in Sinhala Buddhist culture. Bhante Dhammika's teaching and conversation made me make a personal connection between meditation and Buddhist spirituality.

He and other Western monks who have lived in Sri Lanka have contributed hugely, way out of proportion to their small number, to Buddhist scholarship and meditation practice. With these new lenses I saw Sri Lanka, especially its Sinhala Buddhist heart, differently to the way I saw it before.

On my road trips, I stopped occasionally at a roadside bend with a sweeping panorama of the surrounding countryside, or somewhere deep in a valley bowl, or at a remote rocky outcrop. And there I found a low white parapet wall; it enclosed a small dove-white stupa next to a simple Buddha statue and shrine, all reposing on a bed of clean, neatly swept sand. A circle of frangipani trees provided shade and scent. Sometimes a stray dog or two dozed in the shade. A Buddhist flag fluttered in the breeze. The stripped-down simplicity of this scene never failed to pierce my being, inducing a combined physical and mental sensation of calm, rest and peace. Before this scene would have been of mere cultural, aesthetic interest, but no longer.

I felt something similar when I visited a site like Thiriyaya, in the Vanni off the north-west coast, walking alone around its Vatadage and fallen, cracked Buddha statues on its rock summit, abandoned to the jungle a thousand years ago. Or when gazing at the stupendous standing and recumbent Buddhas in Polonnaruwa's Gal Vihara, their svelte robed bodies and restrained, softly smiling countenances radiating inner stillness, peace and harmony. And even more so at remote aranyas in the midst of rocky outcrops, surrounded by jungle. Clambering over rock faces, savouring the panorama from a rock summit, exploring caves where monks lived and meditated 1000–2000 years ago: all this gave me great physical pleasure, but also inner satisfaction, a sense of intense presence in the moment, of prolonged calm, of affinity with the surrounding natural environment, that was not there before.

~

Kudumbigala is one of Sri Lanka's oldest and most remote aranyas, going back to the days of King Kavan Tissa of Ruhunu in the first and second centuries BCE. It lies slightly inland from the south-east coast, about a half-hour drive from Kumana National Park. I first heard about it from Bhante Dhammika, who sojourned there while he lived in Sri Lanka in the 1970s and 1980s. During one of his talks he showed a photo of a small red-brick stupa on a rock summit, surrounded by dramatic rock formations and a sea of jungle. Ever since Kudumbigala was on my bucket list. I finally made it there in early January 2019, on my last road trip before finishing this book.

After an early breakfast Nihal drove me from the bungalow where I was staying, near the surfing hub of Arugam bay, to the village of Panama (pronounced Pānama, not Panamā), the last human settlement on the east coast before reaching the wildlife sanctuaries of Kumana and Yala. There I met Priyantha, my guide for the day, and got into his jeep. Priyantha was short, slight and dark, a Sinhala from the village with little English, which gave me the excuse to converse in Sinhala all day.

It took us ten minutes to drive out of the village, past a water tower, a Buddhist temple, a Hindu kovil, a Sinhala school and a Tamil school, and a small district hospital; on the village outskirts we passed a newly built police station, a village council building and a paddy storage depot. Paddy fields of radiant green surrounded the village. Here and there, camouflaged by shoots of paddy, I noticed smallish crocodiles snoozing undisturbed, their jaws open and rigid, displaying their threatening teeth. On the road to Kumana we passed another sea of paddy, bordered by electric wire fencing to keep elephants out. Then we turned off on the side road to Kudumbigala. The towering rock with the little red-brick stupa – the one I saw in Bhante Dhammika's photo – loomed in the distance.

This side road took us into the jungle. We arrived at a clearing with two buildings, used by laity when they came to Kudimbigala on poya days, so Priyantha told me. Grey langurs, slim and sinuous with long looping tails, seemed to have the run of the place. A narrow path and then a few steps took us to a lovely little gleaming white temple built into a rock. Carved on the cave's drip ledge, the overhanging upper edge of the rock face, just above the white concrete temple facade, were Brahmi (Old Sinhala) characters that documented the monastery's provenance. Inside was a simple, unadorned shrine room with a samadhi Buddha in its centre, smiling contemplatively. Outside lay a short track for walking meditation, the sand between its concrete borders swept immaculately clean.

Around the corner was Balumgala, a large, steeply sloping rock, emerging from the dense vegetation we walked through. Ancient small steps were cut into it, running sheer up one side. On the way up I noticed elephant dung. These giant, lumbering creatures made their way up here at night, so Priyantha told me. Then we reached the summit. First I saw a cairn, to which the pilgrim added his or her stone, as I did now. Nearby was a circle of red-brick stones, just two rows high, the remnants of an ancient stupa. And at the very top was the red-brick stupa, a solid cylinder modelled on the famous stupa at Sarnath in India; a Buddha statue, encased in glass, stood in front.

I had a 180-degree view of thick, deep-green jungle stretching far to the south, north and west, only interrupted by clumps of rock here and there. To the south-east was Panama; to the east the paddy fields we drove past, and beyond an estuary leading to a lagoon and the sea. On the rock slopes, directly below and around the summit where we stood, were lovely little rock pools filled with pale-black water with a greenish tinge, each a chiaroscuro under the mid-morning sun. And each a magnet for animals – elephants, sloth bears, deer, wild boar, leopards, snakes and crocodiles – once the sun came down.

Priyantha pointed to a much larger pool in the distance, surrounded by little rocky outcrops with caves for meditating monks. About four or five were distinguishable from solar panels atop the rocks, to generate electricity for monks in their cave dwellings. Priyantha told me there were about 600 such caves at Kudumbigala, scattered over a sprawling site, nearly all abandoned over the centuries. But Kudumbigala remained a functioning aranya. About ten monks lived there now.

We descended and made our way back to the cave temple. On the other side of it was a narrow sandy path bordered by rocks and lined with meandering tree roots, with the sun almost blocked out by an arboreal canopy. We passed three kutis (monks' cell caves) on rock sides, each with a drip ledge carved across the overhanging rock to allow rainwater to fall straight down rather than drip into the cave interior. Small, simple concrete structures jutted out of the caves, each with a wooden door and a couple of windows, enclosing a room and a bathroom – along with the solar panels, Kudumbigala's concession to twenty-first-century modernity. Priyantha pointed to little paw prints in the sand – of a leopard and its cub from the night before, so he said.

The tree cover gave way to a large, undulating rock face exposed to the sun. We saw a small garden with well-tended shrubs and flowers, and then a *dhana* hall where monks gathered for breakfast (at 6 a.m.), lunch (at 11 a.m.) and an evening discourse and tea (at 5 p.m.). They made sure to be back in their kutis by 6 p.m. to avoid jungle animals out for their evening promenades and subsequent nocturnal prowls.

Priyantha and I walked around a mid-sized stupa next to the dhana hall and then across the rock face, passing by a large pool and a clump of stone pillars standing aslant at different angles, the ruins of what must have been a small temple centuries, or perhaps a millennium or more ago. An orange-robed apparition walked towards us, with part of his robe covering his head from the sun. As he came close I noted he was very lean, with a smooth, glowing complexion and a perfect set of long, glittering-white teeth. He smiled and introduced himself in good English. Priyantha dropped to his knees and paid obeisance in the Sinhalese way; I bowed slightly and put my hands together in greeting.

The monk told me his name was Mettevasa ('the abode of loving kindness' in Pali), and that he had been a monk for twenty-four years; he was a *samanera*, a child novice monk, before he was fully ordained. He first came to Kudumbigala ten years ago for a three-month rains retreat, but had lived here since 2012. 'I think of it as home now,' he said. 'When it gets too hot I go to my temple' – elsewhere in Sri Lanka. 'But I always come back here after a short while – to get away from the noise and distractions of the temple.' He told me he was lazy compared with other monks here because he liked to get up late. But this was relative, since all monks pitched up at the dhana hall for breakfast at 6 a.m. 'We all carry firecrackers in our robes, even during the day,' he said – to ward off animals, particularly elephants, they might encounter.

Bhikku Mettevasa asked me, out of the blue, 'Do you want to become a monk?' That disarmed me totally. I could only think of mumbling 'I don't know, I haven't really thought about it.' Then we parted company. He said, 'Come back. You are always welcome.' And offered me the blessings of the Triple Gem (the Buddha, the Dhamma and the Sangha).

Priyantha drove me back to Panama, and, on the way, talked about the village and its history. I was curious. At my bungalow in Arugam Bay I was told that Panama was mixed, with Sinhalese and Tamil families living side by side, peacefully, for two centuries or more. This Priyantha confirmed. He said Sinhalese and Tamils in the village could understand each other's languages. They even worshipped in each other's temples and participated in each other's religious festivals. The local monk was very popular: even Tamil couples sought his advice to sort out their marital problems. During the war some twenty–thirty LTTE fighters were active in the jungles nearby. They tried to turn Tamil villagers against their Sinhalese neighbours. On 25 October 1990, they killed and mutilated twelve Sinhalese farmers from the village, chopping their heads off and gouging their eyes out. But the village remained united.

Panama was very poor and isolated until a decade ago, but not just because of the war. The road ended not far south of Arugam Bay; villagers had to wade across a lagoon, taking off all but the bare minimum of clothing and carrying provisions on their heads, to get to Arugam Bay. After the war, the Rajapaksa government built a bridge across the lagoon and extended the tarmac road all the way to the village. That transformed Panama. Tourists had to pass through it on the way to Kumana for safari tours; that brought business for guides from the village. The enterprising Priyantha was head of the local jeep drivers' association, which had thirty-seven members. Homestay tourism took off. Priyantha added two rooms to his family house to accommodate tourists.

I noticed signs of new prosperity as we drove through the village. Many houses looked newly built, renovated or expanded, with satellite TV dishes on their roofs; many had small cars or jeeps under the porch or in a garage. Most houses looked simple yet cosy and inviting, surrounded by colourful gardens of flowers, fruit trees and vegetable patches. At the end of the main road we reached a bank of tall sand dunes, which saved the village from the tsunami in 2004. Beyond the dunes was a pretty lagoon with fishing boats, and beyond that the sea.

We drove back on the main road and along a side road that ended at the local devale. It was about 1 p.m. that Friday – the weekly puja day for the devale, so I encountered lots of villagers in the compound, worshipping at two little temples side by side, separated by a lone tree. One temple was for the male god, Loku Bandara, and the other for his wife. Sinhalese and Tamils were here, worshipping and mingling. There were husbands and wives, young single adults and children; stray dogs from the village joined the gathering. Food was shared. A group of youngsters offered me fruit and sweet *kiribath*, or milk rice with jaggery, honey and sugar.

This mingling, peaceful and harmonious, this unity in wartime terror, and now in new-found peacetime prosperity: what a lovely, sweet metaphor for the best of Sri Lanka's past and present. It reminded me of Sir James Emerson Tennent's serendipitous pleasure to find pilgrims of different religions mixing amiably on his ascent up Adam's Peak in the 1840s, as I found too on my ascent a decade ago. I mulled over it as Nihal drove me back to Arugam Bay. I thought of it as a metaphor of hope for Sri Lanka's future.

Acknowledgements

Sri Lankans have large circles of relatives, friends and acquaintances. Many I inherited from childhood. But most of the characters I met on my journeys, and most of those I write about, were new acquaintances, and some became new friends. Many I met through Colombo friends. I would like to thank two in particular. Chandra Jayaratne opened doors to the Colombo business elite, and to politicians and journalists. Much of my Colombo network came from his introductions. Elmo Jayawardena introduced me to a galaxy of characters all over the island. I write about Chandra and Elmo in this book, and thank them and their wives, Rohana and Dil, for their friendship.

Elmo and Dil hosted, and continue to host me, several times a year at their river house, treating me like a member of the family. They got me involved in Candle Aid. And became my role models for a life of service, filling every day with purpose and meaning. I am grateful to them – beyond words.

Nihal and Joseph were my two drivers on road trips around the island. I enjoyed tens of thousands of miles in their company. Both were professional, considerate and caring, going out of their way to be helpful. I thank them both: Joseph for his irrepressible geniality and sense of fun; and Nihal for his quiet, gentlemanly solicitude.

I am grateful to Ven Shravasti Dhammika for guiding my meditation practice, opening my eyes to Buddhism, educating me on the state of Theravada in Sri Lanka, and giving me a ground-level appreciation of ancient Buddhist sites that dot the island. *Sacred Island*, his guidebook, became an inseparable road-trip companion.

Nandini Mehta commissioned this book for Juggernaut, and Parth Mehrotra shepherded it to publication. Shamanthi Rajasingham, a talented young Sri Lankan artist and illustrator, created maps of my journeys that adorn this book's travel chapters. I thank them all.

I reserve a last and very special thank you for my editor, Supriya Nair. This book would look very different if not for her discerning eye. She saw exactly what was wrong with the draft I sent her, and her critical but encouraging advice prompted a major, time-consuming rewrite. She forced me to think and write more like a writer and less like a professor. Her detailed final edits, line by line, taught me so much about good writing. She has the first-class editor's knack of getting into a writer's mind and figuring out ways to enhance his content and style. And she conveys her advice with great sympathy and enthusiasm. I could not wish for a better editor.

Select Bibliography

History

Bawa, Bevis, *Briefly by Bevis*, Sapumal Foundation, Colombo, 2011

Clifford Holt, John (ed.), *The Sri Lanka Reader: History, Culture, Politics*, Duke University Press, Durham, 2011

De Silva, K.M., *A History of Sri Lanka*, Penguin, New Delhi, 2005

Emerson Tennent, Sir James, *Ceylon: An Account of the Island, Physical, Historical and Topographical With Notices of its Natural History, Antiquities and Productions* (in two volumes), Asian Educational Services, New Delhi, 2011 (1859)

Fernando, Nihal, Tammita-Delgoda, Sinharaja *et al.*, *Eloquence in Stone: The Lithic Saga of Sri Lanka*, Studio Times, Colombo, 2008

Geiger, Wilhelm, *Mahavamsa: The Great Chronicle of Ceylon*, Buddhist Cultural Centre, Colombo, 2007 (1912)

Geiger, Wilhelm, *The Culavamsa: Being the More Recent Part of the Mahavamsa*, Asian Educational Services, New Delhi, 2000 (1929)

Hopkins, Harry, *New World Arising* (Ceylon chapter), Hamish Hamilton, London, 1952

Ivan, Victor, *Paradise in Tears*, Vijitha Yapa, Colombo, 2008

Knox, Robert, *An Historical Relation of the Island Ceylon*, Tisara Publishers, Colombo, 1989 (1681)

Kumarasingham, Harsh (ed.), *The Road to Temple Trees: Sir Ivor Jennings and the Constitutional Development of Ceylon – Selected Writings*, Centre for Policy Alternatives, Colombo, 2015

Ludowyk, E.F.C., *The Modern History of Ceylon*, Weidenfeld and Nicholson, London, 1966

MacGregor, Neil, *A History of the World in 100 Objects* ('Statue of Tara', pp. 345–350), British Museum/Allen Lane, London, 2010

Raven-Hart, Roland, *Ceylon: History in Stone*, Lake House Publishers, Colombo, 1964

Richardson, John, *Paradise Poisoned: Learning About Conflict, Terrorism and Development from Sri Lanka's Civil Wars*, International Centre for Ethnic Studies, Colombo/Kandy, 2005

Roberts, Nora, *Galle: As Quiet as Asleep*, Vijitha Yapa, Colombo, 2005

Vittachi, Tarzie, *The Brown Sahib*, Andre Deutsch, London, 1962

Vittachi, Tarzie, *Emergency '58: The Story of the Ceylon Race Riots*, Andre Deutsch, London, 1958

Williams, Harry, *Ceylon: Pearl of the East*, Hale, London, 1950

Biography and Memoirs

Boyagoda, Commodore Ajith (as told to Sunila Galappatti), *A Long Watch: War, Captivity and Return in Sri Lanka*, Hurst, London, 2016

Clarke, Arthur C., *The View from Serendip*, Pan Books, London, 1978

Friend, Donald, *Diaries*, vol. 3 ('Ceylon 1957–1962', pp. 359–540), National Library of Australia, Canberra, 2005

Gladstone, David, *A Sri Lankan Tempest: A Real-Life Drama in Five Acts*, Wotton House, UK, 2017

Jennings, Sir William Ivor, *The Road to Peradeniya: An Autobiography*, Lake House Investments, Colombo, 2005

Lee, Kuan Yew, *From Third World to First: The Singapore Story, 1965–2000* (ch. 25: 'South Asia's legends and leaders'), HarperCollins, New York, 2000

Ludowyk, E.F.C., *Those Long Afternoons: Childhood in Colonial Ceylon*, Lake House, Colombo, 1989

Neruda, Pablo, *Memoirs* ('Ceylon', pp. 89–101), Rupa, New Delhi, 2005 (1974)

Ondaatje, Christopher, *Woolf in Ceylon: An Imperial Journey in the Shadow of Leonard Woolf, 1904–1911*, HarperCollins, London, 2005

Ondaatje, Michael, *Running in the Family*, Bloomsbury, London, 2009 (1982)

Piyaratna, Vinita, *Go Slowly Lovely Moon*, Samayawardhana Printers, Colombo, 2010

Weerakoon, Bradman, *Rendering Unto Caesar: A Fascinating Story of One Man's Tenure Under Nine Prime Ministers and Presidents of Sri Lanka*, New Dawn Press, Colombo, 2004

Woolf, Leonard, *Growing: An Autobiography of the Years 1904–1911* (vol. 2 of his *Autobiography*), Harvest/HBJ, New York, 1975 (1961)

Travel

Bouvier, Nicolas, *Le Poisson-Scorpion*, Gallimard, Paris, 1996 (1955)

Bowles, Paul, *Travels: Collected Writings 1950–1993* ('How to live on a part-time island', 'Letter from Ceylon', and 'An island of my own'), HarperCollins, New York, 2010

Briggs, Cherry, *The Teardrop Island: Following Victorian Footsteps Across Sri Lanka*, Summersdale, UK, 2013

Byron, Robert, 'The Traveller's Confession', pp. 9–11, in *First Russia, Then Tibet*, Penguin, London, 1985 (1933)

Dhammika, Ven Shravasti, *Sacred Island: A Buddhist Pilgrim's Guide to Sri Lanka*, Buddhist Publication Society, Colombo/Kandy, 2008

Handbook for the Ceylon Traveller, Studio Times, Colombo, 1974

Hesse, Hermann, *A Singapore Dream and Other Adventures: Travel Writings from an Asian Journey* ('Kandy promenade', 'Kandy diary', 'Pidurutalagala' and 'Return journey'), Shambala, Boulder, 2018

Gimlette, John, *The Elephant Complex: Travels in Sri Lanka*, Quercus, London, 2015

Hulugalle, H.A.J., *Ceylon of the Early Travellers*, Arjuna Hulugalle Dictionaries, Colombo, 1980

Ibn Batuta, *Travels in Asia and Africa, 1325–1354*, Routledge and Kegan Paul, London, 1984

Kapuscinski, Ryszard, *The Shadow of the Sun: My African Life*, Penguin, London, 2002

Maugham, Robin, *Search for Nirvana*, W.H. Allen, London, 1975

McGowan, William, *Only Man is Vile: The Tragedy of Sri Lanka*, Farrer, Straus and Giroux, New York, 1992

Morris, Jan, *Among the Cities* (ch. 7: 'Serendib 1967'), Penguin, London, 1985

Polo, Marco, *The Travels of Marco Polo* (ch. 19: 'Of the island of Zeilan'), Everyman's Library, London, 2008

Theroux, Paul, *Ghost Train to the Eastern Star: On the Tracks of the Great Railway Bazaar* (ch. 15: 'The coastal line to Galle and Hambantota' and ch. 16: 'The slow train to Kandy'), Houghton Mifflin, New York, 2009

Theroux, Paul, *The Great Railway Bazaar: By Train Through Asia* (ch. 14: 'The Talaimannar Mail' and ch. 15: 'The 16.25 from Galle'), Penguin, London, 1975

Twain, Mark, *Following the Equator: A Journey Around the World* ('In Ceylon', pp. 336–344), Dover, Toronto, 1989 (1897)

Waugh, Alec, *Hot Countries* (ch. 6 on Ceylon), The Literary Guild, New York, 1930

Current Affairs

Athukorala, Prema-chandra, and Jayasuriya, Sisira, 'Economic policy shifts in Sri Lanka: The post-conflict development challenge', *Working Papers in Trade and Development* no. 15, September 2012. https://crawford.anu.edu.au/acde/publications/publish/papers/wp2012/wp_econ_2012_15.pdf

Government of Sri Lanka, *Mahinda Chintana Vision for the Future: The Development Policy Framework*, Ministry of Finance and Planning. http://www.treasury.gov.lk/publications/mahindaChintanaVision-2010full-eng.pdf

Harrison, Frances, *Still Counting the Dead: Survivors of Sri Lanka's Hidden War*, Portobello Books, London, 2012

Hoole, Rajan, *Palmyrah Fallen: From Rajani to War's End*, University Teachers for Human Rights, Jaffna, 2015

Hoole, Rajan *et al.*, *The Broken Palmyrah: The Tamil Crisis in Sri Lanka, An Inside Account*, Sri Lanka Studies Institute, Colombo, 1992

Institute of Policy Studies, *Sri Lanka State of the Economy 2018*, Colombo, 2018

Kelegama, Saman (ed.), *Economic Policy in Sri Lanka: Issues and Debates*, Sage, New Delhi, 2004

Rao Sundarji, Padma, *Sri Lanka: The New Country*, HarperCollins, New Delhi, 2015

Subramanian, Samanth, *This Divided Island: Stories from the Sri Lankan War*, Atlantic Books, London, 2014

Weiss, Gordon, *The Cage: The Fight for Sri Lanka and the Last Days of the Tamil Tigers*, Vintage, London, 2012

Society, Culture and the Arts

Aldrich, Robert, *Cultural Encounters and Homoeroticism in Sri Lanka: Sex and Serendipity*, Routledge, London, 2018

Dhammika, Ven Shravasti, *The Broken Buddha: Critical Reflections on Theravada and a Plea for a New Buddhism*, The Nimmala Group, Singapore, 2006

Jayawardena, Elmo, *Yana Maga*, Samayawardhana Books, Colombo, 2012

Lal, Brij V. (ed.), *The Encyclopedia of the Sri Lankan Diaspora*, NUS/ Editions Didier Millet, Singapore, 2013

Lewcock, Ronald, *Laki*, The Geoffrey Bawa Trust, Colombo, 2014

Robson, David, *Geoffrey Bawa: The Complete Works*, Thames Hudson, London, 2002

Sansoni, Barbara, *Viharas and Verandas of Ceylon*, Barefoot, Colombo, 2007 (1978)

Weerakoon, Bradman, *Kalutara: An Odyssey*, Stamford Lake Publications, Colombo, 2010

Fiction

Jayawardena, Elmo, *Sam's Story*, Times Editions, Singapore, 2004

Jayawardena, Elmo, *The Last Kingdom of Sinhalay*, M.D. Gunasena, Colombo, 2004

Karunatilleke, Shehan, *Chinaman: A Novel*, Vintage, London, 2012

Ondaatje, Michael, *Anil's Ghost*, Bloomsbury, London, 2000

Selvadurai, Shyam (ed.), *Many Roads Through Paradise: An Anthology of Sri Lankan Literature*, Penguin, New Delhi, 2015

Sivanandan, A., *When Memory Dies*, Arcadia Books, London, 1997

Wijenaike, Punyakante, *The Waiting Earth*, Samaranayake Publishers, Colombo, 2011 (1966)

Woolf, Leonard, *The Village in the Jungle*, Eland, London, 2005 (1913)

juggernaut

THE APP FOR INDIAN READERS

Fresh, original books tailored for mobile and for India. Starting at ₹10.

juggernaut.in

1

CRAFTED FOR MOBILE READING

Thought you would never read a book on mobile? Let us prove you wrong.

juggernaut.in

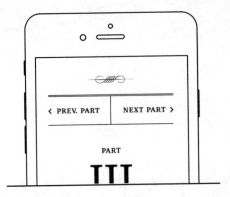

Beautiful Typography

The quality of print transferred
to your mobile. Forget ugly PDFs.

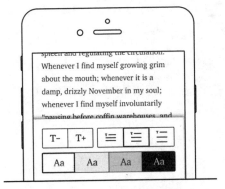

Customizable Reading

Read in the font size, spacing
and background of your liking.

AN EXTENSIVE LIBRARY

Including fresh, new, original Juggernaut books from the likes of Sunny Leone, Praveen Swami, Husain Haqqani, Umera Ahmed, Rujuta Diwekar and lots more. Plus, books from partner publishers and loads of free classics. Whichever genre you like, there's a book waiting for you.

juggernaut.in

3

DON'T JUST READ; INTERACT

We're changing the reading experience from passive to active.

Ask authors questions

Get all your answers from the horse's mouth.
Juggernaut authors actually reply to every
question they can.

Rate and review

Let everyone know of your favourite reads or
critique the finer points of a book – you will be
heard in a community of like-minded readers.

Gift books to friends

For a book-lover, there's no nicer gift than
a book personally picked. You can even
do it anonymously if you like.

Enjoy new book formats

Discover serials released in parts over
time, picture books including comics,
and story-bundles at discounted rates.
And coming soon, audiobooks.

juggernaut.in

4
LOWEST PRICES & ONE-TAP BUYING

Books start at ₹10 with regular discounts and free previews.

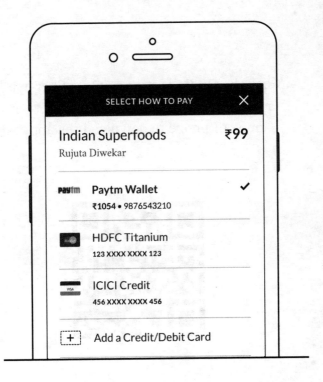

Paytm Wallet, Cards & Apple Payments

On Android, just add a Paytm Wallet once and buy any book with one tap. On iOS, pay with one tap with your iTunes-linked debit/credit card.

Click the QR Code with a QR scanner app
or type the link into the Internet browser
on your phone to download the app.

For our complete catalogue, visit www.juggernaut.in
To submit your book, send a synopsis and two
sample chapters to books@juggernaut.in
For all other queries, write to contact@juggernaut.in